Border-crossing in Education

Border-crossing in Education comprises a series of case studies covering a variety of cultural areas, in order to reveal the density of connections and exchanges that inform educational practices, policies, and systems. It attaches particular importance to individual and collective actors that govern these flows – initiating, promoting, or reconfiguring transfers of policy models.

The contributors explore various aspects of the circulatory mechanisms that have been deployed in the field of education during the modern and contemporary period. Varying the observation scales, from local to international, they demonstrate the multilateral character of the circulatory dynamics observed. The implementation of rich and varied approaches to these complex processes offers a perspective that complements and renews our knowledge of the genesis and evolution of educational policies and systems, most notably highlighting their foreign inspirations.

However, these studies do not merely evoke borrowings and hybridization, as if national borders proved porous or non-existent. Instead they show that the phenomena of resistance, reinterpretation, and rejection are also an integral part of transnational mechanisms of exchanges. The book thus demonstrates the relevance of a historical approach in addressing these transnational mechanisms in the field of education and childhood policy. This book was originally published as a special issue of *Paedagogica Historica*.

Joëlle Droux is a Senior Lecturer in the history of education, and co-leader of the Social History of Education Research Group (ERHISE), at the University of Geneva, Switzerland. She studies the history of international child welfare movements and humanitarian networks from a transnational perspective, with a focus on educational issues. She also develops research projects on the long-term evolution of Swiss policies for child and youth welfare.

Rita Hofstetter is a Professor in the Department of Educational Sciences, director of the Jean-Jacques Rousseau Institute's archives, and coordinator of the Social History of Education Research Group (ERHISE), at the University of Geneva, Switzerland. Her research focuses on the history of the educational sciences, the construction of the teaching state and the teaching profession, and international networks in education.

Border-crossing in Education

Historical perspectives on transnational connections and circulations

Edited by
Joëlle Droux and Rita Hofstetter

LONDON AND NEW YORK

First published 2017 by Routledge

2 Park Square, Milton Park, Abingdon, Oxfordshire OX14 4RN
711 Third Avenue, New York, NY 10017

Routledge is an imprint of the Taylor & Francis Group, an informa business

First issued in paperback 2018

Copyright © 2017 Stichting Paedagogica Historica

All rights reserved. No part of this book may be reprinted or reproduced or utilised in any form or by any electronic, mechanical, or other means, now known or hereafter invented, including photocopying and recording, or in any information storage or retrieval system, without permission in writing from the publishers.

Notice:
Product or corporate names may be trademarks or
registered trademarks, and are used only for identification and explanation without intent to infringe.

British Library Cataloguing in Publication Data
A catalogue record for this book is available from the British Library

ISBN 13: 978-1-138-67004-4 hbk
ISBN 13: 978-0-367-02822-0 pbk

Typeset in Times New Roman
by RefineCatch Limited, Bungay, Suffolk

Publisher's Note
The publisher accepts responsibility for any inconsistencies that may have arisen during the conversion of this book from journal articles to book chapters, namely the possible inclusion of journal terminology.

Disclaimer
Every effort has been made to contact copyright holders for their permission to reprint material in this book. The publishers would be grateful to hear from any copyright holder who is not here acknowledged and will undertake to rectify any errors or omissions in future editions of this book.

Contents

Citation Information vii
Notes on Contributors xi

Introduction – Going international: the history of education stepping beyond borders 1
Joëlle Droux and Rita Hofstetter

1. Within, between, above, and beyond: (Pre)positions for a history of the internationalisation of education practices and knowledge 10
Marcelo Caruso

2. The rivalry of the French and American educational missions during the Vietnam War 27
Thuy-Phuong Nguyen

3. New School of Mustafa Satı Bey in Istanbul (1915) 41
Filiz Meşeci Giorgetti

4. Condescension and critical sympathy: Historians of education on progressive education in the United States and England 58
William G. Wraga

5. Crossing borders in educational innovation: Framing foreign examples in discussing comprehensive education in the Netherlands, 1969–1979 75
Linda Greveling, Hilda T.A. Amsing and Jeroen J.H. Dekker

6. La réception des travaux scouts de Pierre Bovet en France (1912-décennie 1930) 92
Nicolas Palluau

7. Toiling together for social cohesion: International influences on the development of teacher education in the United States 107
Paul J. Ramsey

8. Fred Clarke and the internationalisation of studies and research in education 121
Gary McCulloch

9. "A miniature League of Nations": inquiry into the social origins of the International School, 1924–1930 136
Leonora Dugonjić

CONTENTS

10. Transnational treaties on children's rights: Norm building and circulation in the twentieth century — 149
    Zoe Moody

11. L'éducation sexuelle, entre médecine, morale et pédagogie: débats transnationaux et réalisations locales (Suisse romande 1890–1930) — 163
    Anne-Françoise Praz

12. Braille, amma and integration: the hybrid evolution of education for the blind in Taiwan, 1870s–1970s — 180
    Tasing Chiu

13. De Genève à Belo Horizonte, une histoire croisée: circulation, réception et réinterprétation d'un modèle européen des classes spéciales au Brésil des années 1930 — 193
    Regina Helena de Freitas Campos and Adriana Araújo Pereira Borges

14. Westward bound? Dutch education and cultural transfer in the mid-twentieth century — 211
    Nelleke Bakker

15. L'Association international des éducateurs de jeunes inadaptés (AIEJI) et la fabrique de l'éducateur spécialisé par delà les frontiérs (1951–1963) — 227
    Samuel Boussion

    Index — 243

Citation Information

The chapters in this book were originally published in *Paedagogica Historica*, volume 50, issues 1–2 (February-April 2014). When citing this material, please use the original page numbering for each article, as follows:

Introduction
Going international: the history of education stepping beyond borders
Joëlle Droux and Rita Hofstetter
Paedagogica Historica, volume 50, issues 1–2 (February-April 2014) pp. 1–9

Chapter 1
Within, between, above, and beyond: (Pre)positions for a history of the internationalisation of educational practices and knowledge
Marcelo Caruso
Paedagogica Historica, volume 50, issues 1–2 (February-April 2014) pp. 10–26

Chapter 2
The rivalry of the French and American educational missions during the Vietnam War
Thuy-Phuong Nguyen
Paedagogica Historica, volume 50, issues 1–2 (February-April 2014) pp. 27–41

Chapter 3
New School of Mustafa Satı Bey in Istanbul (1915)
Filiz Meşeci Giorgetti
Paedagogica Historica, volume 50, issues 1–2 (February-April 2014) pp. 42–58

Chapter 4
Condescension and critical sympathy: Historians of education on progressive education in the United States and England
William G. Wraga
Paedagogica Historica, volume 50, issues 1–2 (February-April 2014) pp. 59–75

Chapter 5
Crossing borders in educational innovation: Framing foreign examples in discussing comprehensive education in the Netherlands, 1969–1979
Linda Greveling, Hilda T.A. Amsing and Jeroen J.H. Dekker
Paedagogica Historica, volume 50, issues 1–2 (February-April 2014) pp. 76–92

Chapter 6
La réception des travaux scouts de Pierre Bovet en France (1912–décennie 1930)
Nicolas Palluau
Paedagogica Historica, volume 50, issues 1–2 (February-April 2014) pp. 93–108

Chapter 7
Toiling together for social cohesion: International influences on the development of teacher education in the United States
Paul J. Ramsey
Paedagogica Historica, volume 50, issues 1–2 (February-April 2014) pp. 109–122

Chapter 8
Fred Clarke and the internationalisation of studies and research in education
Gary McCulloch
Paedagogica Historica, volume 50, issues 1–2 (February-April 2014) pp. 123–137

Chapter 9
"A miniature League of Nations": inquiry into the social origins of the International School, 1924–1930
Leonora Dugonjić
Paedagogica Historica, volume 50, issues 1–2 (February-April 2014) pp. 138–150

Chapter 10
Transnational treaties on children's rights: Norm building and circulation in the twentieth century
Zoe Moody
Paedagogica Historica, volume 50, issues 1–2 (February-April 2014) pp. 151–164

Chapter 11
L'éducation sexuelle, entre medicine, morale et pédagogie: débats transnationaux et réalisations locales (Suisse romande 1890–1930)
Anne-Françoise Praz
Paedagogica Historica, volume 50, issues 1–2 (February-April 2014) pp. 165–181

Chapter 12
Braille, amma and integration: the hybrid evolution of education for the blind in Taiwan, 1870s–1970s
Tasing Chiu
Paedagogica Historica, volume 50, issues 1–2 (February-April 2014) pp. 182–194

Chapter 13
De Genève à Belo Horizonte, une histoire croisée: circulation, réception et réinterprétation d'un modèle européen des classes spéciales au Brésil des années 1930
Regina Helena de Freitas Campos and Adriana Araújo Pereira Borges
Paedagogica Historica, volume 50, issues 1–2 (February-April 2014) pp. 195–212

CITATION INFORMATION

Chapter 14
Westward bound? Dutch education and cultural transfer in the mid-twentieth century
Nelleke Bakker
Paedagogica Historica, volume 50, issues 1–2 (February-April 2014) pp. 213–228

Chapter 15
L'Association internationale des éducateurs de jeunes inadaptés (AIEJI) et la fabrique de l'éducateur spécialisé par delà les frontiérs (1951–1963)
Samuel Boussion
Paedagogica Historica, volume 50, issues 1–2 (February-April 2014) pp. 229–243

For any permission-related enquiries please visit:
http://www.tandfonline.com/page/help/permissions

Notes on Contributors

Hilda T.A. Amsing is an Associate Professor of Pedagogy and Educational Sciences at the University of Groningen, The Netherlands. Her work has appeared in journals including *European Educational Research Journal, Paedagogica Historica, History of Education, Journal of Social Science Education,* and *History of Education Review,* amongst others.

Nelleke Bakker is Associate Professor of the History of Education at the University of Groningen, The Netherlands. She has published books and articles on the history of childhood, education, parenting, schooling, gender and education, and education studies. In recent years her research has focused on children and health and on the reception of educational and psychological theories in The Netherlands.

Adriana Araújo Pereira Borges is a doctoral student in the Graduate Program on Education at the Universidade Federal de Minas Gerais, Brazil, where she is preparing a dissertation on the history of special education in Brazil and the practices dealing with exceptional children at Sociedade Pestalozzi de Minas Gerais. She is a member of the board of directors of the Center of Research and Documentation Helena Antipoff. Her publications deal with the history of special education in Brazil.

Samuel Boussion is maître de conférences in the Educational Sciences Department of the University of Paris-VIII (Saint-Denis), France, where he teaches history of education and of social work. He works in particular on the professional history of social educators in France, and in recent years his research has focused on the history of child welfare in France and in Europe.

Regina Helena de Freitas Campos is Professor of Educational Psychology and History of Psychology at Universidade Federal de Minas Gerais, Brazil. She has published on the history of psychology and educational science in both Brazilian and international journals, and organised a historical dictionary of biographies of Brazilian psychologists. She is the president of the Centre of Research and Documentation Helena Antipoff in Belo Horizonte, Brazil.

Marcelo Caruso is Chair of History of Education at the Institute of Education of Humboldt University, Berlin. His research focuses on cultural analysis of the international circulation and reception of educational programmes and technologies, including local developments in Germany, Spain, Argentina, and Colombia.

Tasing Chiu is an Associate Professor of Medical Sociology and Social Work at Kaohsiung Medical University, Kaohsiung, Taiwan. He is a sociologist of disability with subsidiary interests in blindness, and his specialist research has focused on blindness as well as disability. He is the associate editor of the *Taiwanese Journal for Studies of Science, Technology and Medicine*, and sits on the editorial board of the *Taiwanese Journal of Sociology*.

Jeroen J.H. Dekker is Professor of History and Theory of Education, and Head of the Department of Education, at the University of Groningen, The Netherlands. He is a former President of the International Association for the History of Education, and co-Editor-in-Chief of *Paedagogica Historica*. His publications deal with the social and cultural history of education, childhood, and parenting.

Joëlle Droux is a Senior Lecturer in the history of education, and co-leader of the Social History of Education Research Group (ERHISE), at the University of Geneva, Switzerland. She studies the history of international child welfare movements and humanitarian networks from a transnational perspective, with a focus on educational issues. She also develops research projects on the long-term evolution of Swiss policies for child and youth welfare.

Leonora Dugonjić is a researcher at the École des hautes études en sciences sociales (CESSP-CSE), Paris, France. She studies the sociology of education and culture, and the history of the social sciences. Her current research focuses on the history of the social sciences in the USA since 1945.

Filiz Meşeci Giorgetti is Associate Professor of the History of Education in the Education Sciences Department at Istanbul University, Turkey. Her teaching and research interests include the history of Turkish education in the nineteenth and twentieth century. Her historical research has focused on the roots of educational rituals and the educational politics of the early Turkish Republic period.

Linda Greveling is a Ph.D. candidate in the Faculty of Behavioural and Social Sciences at the University of Groningen, The Netherlands. Her research focuses on education in culture, and has been published in the *European Educational Research Journal, Paedagogica Historica,* and *History of Education.*

Rita Hofstetter is a Professor in the Department of Educational Sciences, director of the Jean-Jacques Rousseau Institute's archives, and coordinator of the Social History of Education Research Group (ERHISE), at the University of Geneva, Switzerland. Her research focuses on the history of the educational sciences, the construction of the teaching state and the teaching profession, and international networks in education.

Gary McCulloch is Professor of History of Education at the Institute of Education, University of London, UK. His works include *Secondary Education and the Raising of the School Leaving Age: Coming of Age?* (with Tom Woodin and Steven Cowan, 2013) and *The Struggle for the History of Education* (2011). He is currently working on a book on the historical development of educational studies. He is Joint Editor of the *British Journal of Educational Studies*.

Zoe Moody is Professor at the Swiss University of Teacher Education, Valais, Switzerland. Her interdisciplinary research and publications lie at the intersection between educational sciences and the field of children's rights, mobilizing alternatively historical and gender perspectives. Her work has appeared in *Paedagogica Historica,* the *Creativity Research Journal,* and *Recherches et éducations*.

NOTES ON CONTRIBUTORS

Thuy Phuong Nguyen is a research associate at the Université Paris Descartes, France, where she received her Ph.D. in Education Sciences in 2013. Her primary research interests are colonial and postcolonial education (with a focus on South-East Asia), French secondary education, educational policies, cultural diplomacy, and cultural decolonisation.

Nicolas Palluau is a research associate at the Centre Norbert Elias/Equipe HEMOC at the University of Avignon, France. He works mainly on the history of scouting and educational reform, and studies the relationship between the school system and extracurricular activities as part of social reform in the twentieth century.

Anne-Françoise Praz is Associate Professor of Contemporary History at the University of Fribourg, Switzerland. Her interests include historical demography, family history, gender, population politics, the history of sexuality, education and childhood. Her work has been published in journals including *Antipodes*, *History of the Family*, and *Gender & History*.

Paul J. Ramsey is an Associate Professor in the Department of Teacher Education at Eastern Michigan University, Ypsilanti, MI, USA. He is the author of *Bilingual Public Schooling in the United States: A History of America's "Polyglot Boardinghouse"* (2010) and *The Bilingual School in the United States: A Documentary History* (2012). His articles have appeared in an array of education and history journals, and he currently serves as the editor of the *American Educational History Journal*.

William G. Wraga is a Professor in the College of Education at the University of Georgia, Athens, GA, USA. His research on the history of curriculum reform has been published in journals including the *Journal of Curriculum Studies*, *The Classical Journal*, *History of Education* and *Historical Studies in Education/Review d'histoire de l'education*. He is the author of *Progressive Pioneer: Alexander James Inglis and American Secondary Education* (2007). He has served on the editorial board of the *History of Education Quarterly* and as president of the Society for the Study of Curriculum History.

INTRODUCTION

Going international: the history of education stepping beyond borders

Joëlle Droux and Rita Hofstetter

Faculty of Psychology and Educational Sciences, University of Geneva, Switzerland

Over the past two decades, historians have gradually tended to focus their attention on phenomena such as transfer, movement, dissemination, flows and exchanges between different spaces.[1]

The increase in studies, conferences and publications – including keynote books or published series – dedicated to the history of the mechanisms of internationalisation is undoubtedly due to the perceived pervasiveness, over the past decades, of phenomena linked to globalisation. Whether a matter of concern or an opportunity to rejoice in the creation of a global village, globalisation has inspired and prompted the renewal of research and input in the social sciences. As for historians, who are certainly more accustomed than their colleagues in the humanities to limiting their field to national territories and contexts, they took their time before getting excited about internationalisation.[2] Since the 1990s, however, they have definitely caught up, and their enthusiasm has resulted in an increase in approaches, perspectives and conceptions about processes that go beyond national boundaries. Whether labelled histoire croisée, connected or entangled history, world-global-transnational history or even, more recently, *histoire à parts égales*,[3] cross-border phenomena are a focus of attention for scholars. These simultaneous currents remain anchored in specific approaches and methodologies, resulting in quite compartmentalised issues and agendas. Many questions are thus raised about the rationale that inspires or resists these flows and

---

[1] Historians of education have already been particularly sensitive to approaches in terms of transfers and circulations. For example, an international conference dealing with worldwide aspects of internationalisation in education was held in Geneva, in June 2012, under the patronage of three societies: the International Standing Conference for the History of Education, the Society for the History of Children, and Youth and the Disability History Association.

[2] See, in particular, Akira Iriye's remarks in *Global and Transnational History: The Past, Present, and Future* (London: Palgrave Macmillan, 2013); Benedikt Stuchtey and Eckhardt Fuchs, eds., *Writing World History, 1800–2000* (Oxford: Oxford University Press, 2003); Pierre Grosser, "L'histoire mondiale/globale, une jeunesse exubérante, mais difficile", *Vingtième Siècle. Revue d'histoire* 110, no. 2 (2011): 3–18; and A. Caillé and S. Dufoix, eds., *Le tournant global des sciences sociales* (Paris: Bibliothèque du Mauss, La Découverte, 2013). More generally speaking, see Akira Iriye and Pierre-Yves Saunier, eds., *Palgrave Dictionary of Transnational History* (Basingstoke: Palgrave, 2009).

[3] Michael Werner and Bénédicte Zimmermann, eds., *De la comparaison à l'histoire croisée* (Paris: Seuil, 2004); Pierre-Yves Saunier, *Transnational History: Theory and History* (Basingstoke: Palgrave Macmillan, 2013); Romain Bertrand, *L'histoire à parts égales: récits d'une rencontre Orient-Occident: XVIe-XVIIe siècles* (Paris: Seuil, 2011); Dominic Sachsenmaier, *Global Perspectives on Global History: Theories and Approaches in a Connected World* (Cambridge: Cambridge University Press, 2011).

contacts, the impacts they trigger on both sides of connected spaces, or the territories and actors that kindle them (or, conversely, who suffer from them). Such overflowing enthusiasm does not go without occasionally fostering perfunctory studies or hasty conclusions, a risk clearly underlined by recent critical assessments.[4] All the same, the increasing interest in transnational dimensions of economic, social and cultural phenomena evidenced thanks to these new approaches has not only boosted the way history is studied, but has also affected our understanding of the phenomena they reveal.

In the past, historians of education have also been deeply concerned by the fascination for international and transnational phenomena.[5] It is precisely with the ambition of sharing these topics, beyond boundaries and schools of thought, that the international conference in Geneva (2012) was conceived in order to address issues, discuss concepts, identify sources and finally renew our current approaches to globalisation. The exceptional response to the call for proposals can actually be regarded as testimony to the centrality of transnational mechanisms for recent scholarship in the history of education. Because of editorial limitations, this book cannot claim to cover either the exceptionally wide range of contributions or the scope of insights and conclusions presented, shared and discussed during the conference. The articles collected here nevertheless aim to reflect the main trends of questioning related to the history of contemporary mechanisms of internationalisation in the field of education, to highlight the methodological views they inspire as well as the promising research avenues they open up.

If obviously lacking in ambitious synthesis – a gap largely remedied by Marcelo Caruso's wide-ranging and time-encompassing article – the present volume calls for a rise in empirical research and an alternation of different scales of historical analysis. To begin with, the present contributions share a common interest in modern and contemporary events and developments. Although they cover the full range of twentieth-century events, they nonetheless offer a place of choice to developments during the interwar years – a time period that undoubtedly saw the affirmation of a new regime of

---

[4] See, in particular, Heinz-Gerhard Haupt, "Une nouvelle sensibilité: la perspective transnationale", *Cahiers Jaurès* 200 (2011): 173–80.

[5] See four special issues: "'Empires Overseas' and 'Empires at Home': Postcolonial and Transnational Perspectives on Social Change in the History of Education", eds. Joyce Goodman, Gary McCulloch and William Richardson, special issue, *Paedagogica Historica* 45, no. 6 (2009); "Lost Empires, Regained Nations: Postcolonial Models, Cultural Transfers and Transnational Perspectives in Latin America (1870–1970)", eds. Gabriela Ossenbach and María del Mar del Pozo, special issue, *Paedagogica Historica* 47, no. 5 (2011); "Centre and Periphery – Networks, Space and Geography in the History of Education", eds. Gary McCulloch and Roy Lowe, special issue, *History of Education* 32, no. 5 (2003); "Setting education on the global agenda: a historical perspective", eds. Rita Hofstetter and Joëlle Droux, special issue Prospects 173, no. 1 (2015). See also Marcelo Caruso and Heinz-Elmar Tenorth, eds., *Internationalisierung/Internationalisation. Semantik und Bildungssystem in vergleichender Perspektive* (Frankfurt am Main: Peter Lang, 2002); Eckhardt Fuchs, ed., *Bildung International. Historische Perspektiven und aktuelle Entwicklungen* (Würzburg, Germany: Ergon, 2006); John W. Meyer, Francisco O. Ramirez and Yasemin Nuhoglu Soysal, "World Expansion of Mass Education, 1870–1980", *Sociology of Education* 65, no. 2 (1992): 128–49; Jürgen Schriewer, *Welt-System und Interrelations-Gefüge. Die Internationalisierung der Pädagogik als Problem Vergleichender Erziehungswissenschaft* (Berlin: Humboldt-Universität zu Berlin, 1994); "L'internationalisation des discours sur l'éducation: adoption d'une 'idéologie mondiale' ou persistance du style de 'réflexion systémique' spécifiquement nationale", *Revue française de pédagogie* 146 (2004): 7–26.

internationalisation, as already pointed out by various studies.[6] Yet the surrounding decades are not neglected and have yielded innovative outcomes. As a whole, this special issue specifically stands out from similar scholarly works in that it embraces the most recent decades, leading to a deeper understanding of the various temporalities inherent to internationalisation and globalisation processes in the field of education.

Knowledge related to the flows and tides of globalisation regarding education during this period has indeed become deeper and more complex. In particular, it reveals the emergence of specific spaces and historical contexts conducive to an acceleration of exchanges or, on the contrary, to their slowing down. For instance, both the declining Ottoman Empire depicted by Filiz Meşeci Giorgetti in its eager pursuit of European educational inspiration, and the United States, as described by Paul J. Ramsey, are striking examples of foreign-minded educational scenes, the latter unravelling a national context much more permeable to European influences than usually suspected or acknowledged among contemporary actors. Yet careful examination of cross-border phenomena also reveals perplexing cases of reluctance to accommodate foreign experiences. Thus the Netherlands, usually renowned for the permeability of their mental and cultural frontiers, is evoked by both Nelleke Bakker and Linda Greveling and Hilda T.A. Amsing and Jeroen J.H. Dekker as a more reluctant milieu, with educational actors prompt to select or even resist and back-pedal on transfer policy issues. Another example, on a different level, is William G. Wraga's contribution showing that the United States and anglophone historiographies are more partitioned than they appear to be, even regarding progressive educational movements whose audience is traditionally largely international. In any case, the studies collected here aim to modulate and deepen our knowledge of the timeline of globalisation. Indeed, they point to the fact that internationalising tropisms and trends did not go unchallenged and unresisted and did not proceed in any linear way, as is too commonly assumed among twenty-first-century, globally-connected citizens. Doubtless, future studies will provide further fine-tuning related to our knowledge of these processes and their historically-situated variations over times and spaces.

Another feature of the present issue concerns the breadth of spaces and geographical unities considered, in an effort to encompass both European and non-European countries and experiences. Still, most of the contributions remain closely tied to the western world, a characteristic they obviously share with recent similar collective publications dedicated to the mechanisms of internationalisation.[7] All the same, a focus on European or western case studies should not be disregarded, as it allows the fine mechanisms of shifts and transfers across national boundaries to be investigated. Nicolas Palluau's and Anne-Françoise Praz's articles on the complex connections played out at the heart of Europe give evidence of territories, milieus and collective actors favouring transfers and translations such as those observed, respectively, in Belgium and Switzerland. The specific role of frontier areas in these cross-cultural transfers and exchanges at the continental scale is

---

[6]Daniel Gorman, *The Emergence of International Society in the 1920s* (Cambridge: Cambridge University Press, 2012); Daniel Laqua, ed., *Internationalism Reconfigured: Transnational Ideas and Movements between the World Wars* (London: Tauris, 2011).
[7]Jasmien Van Daele, "Writing ILO Histories: A State of the Art", in *ILO Histories: Essays on the International Labour Organisation and its Impact on the World During the 20th Century*, eds. Jasmien Van Daele, Magaly Rodríguez García, Geert Van Goethem and Marcel van der Linden (Bern: Peter Lang, 2010): 13–39.

thus highlighted, a feature that other regions dealing with multicultural communities in Central and Eastern Europe would undoubtedly also have stressed.

Nonetheless, opening up to wider spaces produces valuable gains of knowledge and insightful perspectives to those who question the complex economy of transnational exchanges in the field of education. Such a widening of outcomes and de-centring of European-based approaches is precisely what the present issue intends to develop. Non-western continents are dealt with here through an inclusive range of case studies related to Asia, the Middle East and Latin America, all of them expanding our understanding of the processes of globalisation well beyond western frontiers. Circulatory flows are thus revealed, in which Europe is very much present, but all the same remains at the periphery of the kinetic movements examined. Such is the case of the European colonisers studied by Tasing Chiu, marginalised in Taiwan by a comparably aggressive Japanese imperialism. The full capacity of non-European initiatives in building up bridges and setting up circulatory draughts or influx is also uncovered. Thus, Filiz Meşeci Giorgetti describes how late-Ottoman educational missionaries were sent abroad in order to prospect Belgian, French and Swiss educational scenes in search of potential models of social and cultural reforms. Further studies, especially related to the diversity of experiences in Africa, will only add more detailed layers to this decentred perspective. They will probably reveal as many complex intra- or intercontinental exchange dynamics, comparable to the phenomena that Regina Helena de Freitas Campos and Adriana Araújo Pereira Borges unfold in the South American context. Their study highlights the transatlantic flows inspired by local proactive initiatives in search of importable models, drawing in their wake not only theoretical frameworks and underlying scientific discourses, but also individual experts invited to implement them (with women, already internationally connected through professional or gendered networks, playing a key role in the appropriation process). At the same time, alternatives to these straightforward transatlantic imports may occur regionally; we can thus observe how "intermediate" and hybridised models were being framed locally, which would serve both as a national testing ground of foreign experiences, and as a relay of innovation towards neighbouring countries. Indeed, there is no such thing as a linear and one-dimensional flux of circulatory phenomena, flowing seamlessly from "progressive" areas or countries to "backward" territories. Innovation seems to progress and circulate by leaps, jumping above and beyond frontiers, leaving in its wake a network of culturally mixed institutions. In any case, the contributions published here strive to integrate Europe into a complex web of circulatory transnational dynamics, as only one among many other major sources of these multidimensional jumps and transfers.

In spite of this decentring perspective, the power games behind the contemporary mechanisms of globalisation should not be euphemised, nor should cross-border circulations be naively depicted in terms of mutual agreements between equal partners in search of progressive tools to exchange. The studies focusing on circulatory phenomena in the field of education, when carried out in the colonies or in the aftermath of decolonisation, yield in fact a much starker image, that of an imposed globalisation and a series of enforced connections, as recently demonstrated by Rebecca Rogers.[8] Such is

---

[8] Rebecca Rogers *A Frenchwoman's Imperial Story: Madame Luce in Nineteenth-Century Algeria* (Stanford: Stanford University Press, 2013); Rebecca Rogers "Relations entre femmes dans l'Alger colonial: Henriette Benaben (1847–1915) et son école de broderies « indigènes »". *Genre & Colonization*, 1 (2013): 147–169.

the case for post-war Vietnam, as shown by Thuy-Phuong Nguyen: under the cover of a development policy, the local educational scene gave way to heavily funded confrontations between two imperialistic nations determined to defend their national prestige, oblivious to or incurious about the needs and interests of the local population. What we need here is to accumulate such thorough examinations of non-European responses to this enforced westernisation; whether in terms of resistance or selected acceptance, adaptation or alternative borrowings, they would help build narratives on decolonisation and the end of empires integrating a non-western perspective. This is a call that finally emphasises the status of educational issues in the access to modernity and independence – cultural and national – of non-European societies.

This national–international dichotomy is in many other respects at the centre of the scholarship gathered for this volume. As astutely observed by Marcelo Caruso, there is a need to think the nation in order to think the international, even if this very concept has varied considerably across time. The present contributions also address this issue, shifting their scope of analysis from the local to the supranational. In this regard, diving deep down into the mechanisms of internationalisation does not deny the validity of a national framework of analysis. Quite the contrary: it enhances its relevance by highlighting the ability of national actors, either civil servants or members from local civil society, to let go of their boundaries in order to initiate new policies, inspired by foreign experiences (or sometimes designed against their influence). These different degrees of transfers transcending and crossing national borders can be captured in a variety of metaphors: cross-fertilisation, translation, importation, appropriation, hybridisation. Whatever the label, the processes described emphasise the porosity of boundaries and the abilities of actors to play with this label, to use it or to contest it, consecutively or simultaneously. The concurrent practices of "framing" of foreign progressive education reforms by Dutch actors during the 1960s and 1970s described by Linda Greveling, Hilda T.A. Amsing and Jeroen J.H. Dekker offer a relevant example. Here, fabricated resémantisations (i.e. transformation by reinterpretation[9]) of foreign models are skilfully used by domestic groups in order to secure public support for controversial reform. Whether desired or endured, publicly advocated or insidiously carried out, exchange mechanisms and transfers have strongly contributed to elaborating policies and national educational systems. Moreover, transfers do not necessarily arise from ideological affinities, as the attraction of the Prussian model of secondary education for American reformers evoked by Paul J. Ramsey amply demonstrates. All in all, these transnationally constructed elective affinities, and the transfers which derive from them, inspire renewed insights into the nations' building process. It helps us consider the nation not only as a diachronic construction delving deep into domestic heritage, but also, even if seldom acknowledged by contemporary actors, as the product of complex horizontal influences.

It is also worth mentioning the emphasis placed by several scholars on individual or collective actors who were instrumental in keeping these flows alive by initiating, supporting or organising transfer of theories, discourses or models. Significant aspects of their influence are thus underlined. First of all, the wide range of institutions or networks that took part in exchange mechanisms should be mentioned, as they shaped the interventions of various intermediaries and smugglers. Well-known spaces and communities supporting transnational connections during the nineteenth century have

---

[9]Michel Espagne, *Les transferts culturels franco-allemands* (Paris: Presses universitaires de France, 1999).

thus been highlighted in several contributions: universities, congresses, militant associations, scientific networks, missionary organisations whose role in disseminating models and experiences have been studied according to several space and time spans (see the contributions of Marcelo Caruso, Tasing Chiu, Anne-Françoise Praz and Paul J. Ramsey). Women activists played a particularly prominent role in implementing and setting up their own networks, often mediating between various associations and cultures, as evident in the emblematic commitment of personalities such as Helena Antipoff (1892–1974), Joséphine Butler (1828–1906), Agnes Gutzlaff (1836–1869), Marie-Thérèse Maurette (1890–1989) and Emma Pieczynska (1854–1927).

Still, the rise of institutional actors mostly stands out as the most striking evolution of twentieth-century emerging globalisation, especially that of intergovernmental organisations (see for instance Leonora Dugonjić's article), American philanthropic foundations (Gary McCulloch) and non-governmental organisations (Samuel Boussion, Zoe Moody). According to several recent studies,[10] these organisations should be questioned, not so much from the point of view of their diplomatic activity as from that of their role as platforms organising and supporting exchanges, and as such instrumental in the production and diffusion of universal standards. Many contributions underline the involvement of these networks and organisations in internationalising educational policies, and their commitment to their circulation. They also reveal the new channels of connections that were set up over the century (scholarships, fellowships, student or academic exchanges, summer schools, international diplomas), leading to a deeper understanding of the resulting convergence phenomena. However dense these cross-border links and connections, there is no doubt that spaces dedicated to encouraging circulation between nations remain vulnerable to strong national, cultural, scientific and disciplinary competition. Concurrences and tensions are thus vividly evoked in Anne-Françoise Praz's study on international networks that discuss and produce knowledge related to social and moral hygiene. Another example is Zoe Moody's contribution on the sensitive negotiations, during the twentieth century, preliminary to establishing, advocating and supporting international treaties on children's rights.[11] This renewed interest in organisational and international actors will most certainly lead to other innovative studies on various circulatory platforms, particularly those functioning at a regional level. They will shed new light on the role of educational systems regarding the mechanisms of integration, particularly in Europe, which still remain largely under-researched.

The new attention given to the contemporary arborescence of organisations and networks might have hidden the forest of individuals who made them possible; fortunately, this is not the case. Several contributions address the ability of given people

---

[10] Sandrine Kott and Joëlle Droux, eds., *Globalizing Social Rights: The International Labour Organisation and Beyond* (Basingstoke: Palgrave Macmillan, 2013); Sunil Amrith and Glenda Sluga, "New Histories of the United Nations", *Journal of World History* 19, no. 3 (2008): 251–74; Akira Iriye, *Global Community: The Role of International Organisations in the Making of the Contemporary World* (Berkeley: University of California Press, 2002); Sluga, G., *Internationalism in the Age of Nationalism* (Philadelphia: University of Pennsylvania Press, 2013); Thomas Davies, *NGOs. A New History of Transnational Civil Society* (Oxford: Oxford University Press, 2013).

[11] See also Z. Moody(2014), "L'enfant sujet de droits. Processus transnational de genèse, d'institutionnalisation et de diffusion des droits de l'enfant (1924–1989)." Doctoral thesis, Université de Genève (FPSE).

(their agency) to contribute to building up international spaces for exchanges and multi-directional flows. Such individuals may have been destined to take on their smuggler's role and liaising function through a variety of causalities; a multicultural background or identity or a cosmopolitan education may play a crucial role, as shown in the case of Antipoff highlighted by Regina Helena de Freitas Campos and Adriana Araújo Pereira Borges. A professional commitment to the mechanism of internationalisation may also serve as a basis of cross-cultural ventures, as, for instance, in the case of the founders of the Geneva International Schoolan educational institution set up to cater to the offspring of international civil servants recruited in the wake of the creation of the League of Nations, as described by Leonora Dugonjić.[12] Whatever their motives or roots, the powerful actions carried out by these individuals in structuring the connections between nations appear to be just as crucial as the involvement of governments and political actors in building up a globalised society. The action of Fred Clarke (1880–1952), who relayed the wish of his government to open up to foreigners, is clear testimony to these individuals' agency and *marge de manoeuvre*, as made clear by Gary McCulloch. However, these women and men did not act alone, and behind their actions one can also get a glimpse of the mandate handed out by an epistemic community dedicated to internationalisation. Such is the case of the new profession, described by Samuel Boussion, of special educators, a handful of individuals who were trusted to build an international professional community. In this regard, transnational trade unions of teachers should also receive their share of historical research, as they already do regarding their role in the contemporary evolution of industrial relations on a global scale.[13] Other than these elites, transnational by vocation or by mandate, less audible mediators of internationalisation should also attract scholarly attention. Such is the case of diasporas or migrating communities, whose impact on structuring the educational supply and demand in their host country should receive more careful consideration.[14] No doubt in the future, an increase of *from below* or *microstoria* studies will offer a complementary view to the globalisation process as viewed *from above*, which would open up perspectives on globalisation as suffered or provoked by a wide range of actors coming to terms with the daily impact of internationalisation of educational phenomena (pupils, students, parents, teachers, administrators).

The intriguing issue of the impacts of globalisation, a somewhat blind angle of recent works on circulatory mechanisms, is also addressed from various standpoints. The wide range of analysis developed in the present contributions leads to multidimensional views regarding the effects of internationalisation on the local, regional and national educational scenes. One can observe how standards of universal scope progressively emerged through cooperation between networks and international

---

[12] See also L. Dugonjić (2014), "Les IB Schools, une internationale élitiste. Emergence d'un espace mondial d'enseignement secondaire au XXe siècle." Doctoral thesis, Ecole des hautes études en sciences sociales and Université de Genève (FPSE).
[13] For a recent review, see Thomas Fetzer, "Industrial Relations History in Transnational Perspective", *History Compass* 10, no. 1 (2012): 56–69.
[14] A point made clear in Pierre-Yves Saunier, "Learning by Doing: Notes About the Making of the Palgrave Dictionary of Transnational History", *Journal of Modern European History* 6, no. 2 (2008): 159–80; see also Pierre-Yves Saunier, "Going Transnational? News from Down Under", H-Soz-u-Kult, January 13, 2006, http://hsozkult.geschichte.hu-berlin.de/ forum/ id=877&type=diskussionen.

organisations, such as those related in asserting children's rights suggested by Zoe Moody. In lobbying the governments in favour of their ratification and the adoption of a new regime protecting human rights, these productions contributed to aligning contemporary public policies on a common normative base. Studies on other agencies producing international standards and on the unifying mechanisms generated during the second half of the twentieth century will undoubtedly promote appreciation of their impact on the evolution of national policies. However, internationalisation does not systematically materialise by establishing ambitious legal frameworks requiring meticulous consensuses or by promoting refined statistical models approved by self-proclaimed expert agencies.

Transfer of experiences can also occur as a result of a complex grid of indigenous borrowing and targeted appropriation, as described in several contributions (Anne-Françoise Praz and Nicolas Palluau, for instance): they report a step-by-step adjustment of models or theoretical inspirations depending on the highly volatile historical context in which these movements were set. Furthermore, transfers are not necessarily long-lasting or unstoppable processes. An environment that might be open (or resistant) to connections can be overthrown and thus shift an awaited course of events, as shown in Linda Greveling, Hilda T.A. Amsing and Jeroen J.H. Dekker's study about the Netherlands, which discusses foreign systems of comprehensive education. Examples given here show that transfers may depend on the activism of a handful of determined or powerful actors, backed up by efficient international *advocacy networks*. Such was the case with the institute of Belo Horizonte, which adopted and adapted a European model of special education in the 1930s, with the support of international networks playing a crucial part in the background (Regina Helena de Freitas Campos and Adriana Araújo Pereira Borges' article). One can also refer to the persistence of educators in favour of adapting the principles of the Geneva *Education nouvelle* movement in Ottoman and later Kemal's Turkey (in Filiz Meşeci Giorgetti's contribution). Finally, the role of missionaries, both Catholic and Protestant, acting on behalf of their respective spiritual authorities, figured in many examples of efficient smuggling of educational frameworks (as made clear in the case described by Tasing Chiu).

This particular case, as with several other articles in this issue, underlines the first-rate quality of historical scholarship carried out on various forms of special education that have been flourishing for a decade in the wake of the Disability Studies movement. In this regard, a focus on knowledge dissemination and transformation/appropriation related to transfer sheds new light on institutional practices in various national and local settings. A similar feature is also demonstrated in the contributions related to *Education nouvelle* (comprehensive or progressive education). Although a phenomenon immediately identified with an international audience, as mentioned by William G. Wraga, interpretations suggested by historians in the 1960s and 1970s remain deeply affected on the national level by academic and institutional contingencies. His contribution stands out as a request for historiographical reviews that deal with how historians interpret international phenomena and are able to step back to get a new view. There is hope that this will lead to critical reflexivity underlining how a scholar's interpretative context might overstretch his or her viewpoint and conclusions.

Exploring circulatory dynamics operating in the field of educational policies helps bring to light a wide range of events, phenomena and processes hitherto indistinguishable or unknown. Of course there is still a lot to be done to reveal, in all their intrinsic complexity, contemporary evolutions of educational policies relating to these transnational exchanges. A great many sources are to be explored in order to capture the multiple time spans of the phenomena so revealed, as well as the political, military or socio-cultural circumstances that determine them. The variety of approaches here implemented demonstrates how much the transnational perspective, focusing on exchanges and flows across borders but nonetheless paying attention to local and national contexts of reception, lead both to a renewal of our knowledge on educational phenomena and to further methodological refinements in order to perceive them. The studies collected here guide us towards this two-fold goal.

Acknowledgements

Our warmest thanks go to the numerous colleagues who helped us organise the ISCHE conference in Geneva (2012), and more specifically to the organising committee and the scientific committee of the conference who took part in reviewing the contributions of this volume. We thank Glen Regard for his editorial work and Nicole Rege Colet for translating the introduction.

Within, between, above, and beyond: (Pre)positions for a history of the internationalisation of educational practices and knowledge

Marcelo Caruso

Institute of Education, Humboldt University, Berlin, Germany

> Not only in education, but also in other social practices, the history of "internationalisation" is correlative to the history of "nationalisation". In this broad sense, this article outlines four main constellations of the links between education and nationalisation/internationalisation dynamics. After a brief description of the creation of "nations" *within* communities in the Church and universities from the Middle Ages onwards, the article focuses on a context in which the modern "nations", understood as a difference between distinct communities, emerged at the turn of the nineteenth century. This classical form of internationalisation *between* separate units eventually led to the emergence of a supranational level of communication *above* nations, basically in the form of international organisations and meetings. These experiences determined the nature of international communication regarding education for many decades. "Nations" certainly enacted this first wave of internationalisation. The breakthrough of new media and a world-market economy during the late twentieth century seems, however, to have favoured a second wave of supranational practices and discourses about education *beyond* any national frame. The article outlines these four main constellations and analyses the main features of scholarship dealing with them.

Introduction: Internationalisation and the nation

In the middle of the nineteenth century, the English journalist and author William Blanchard Jerrold (1826–1884) advanced a proposal for an "international" form of education. Given his biography and work, this was by no means unexpected. Blanchard Jerrold was a cosmopolitan journalist who had lived in Paris for many years, where he had been a correspondent for several London newspapers at the Paris international exhibition. It is this international background that led him to highlight the potential of internationality in education:

> The idea of a uniform international education appears to be at length on the point of being realized. It has been in the minds of many educational authorities for years. I remember that some ten years ago a prospectus was issued, describing an academy that was to move, under one principal, from one country to another; so that, under one general system of education throughout, the pupils might completely master the chief European languages.[1]

---

[1] William Blanchard Jerrold, "International Schools", in *On the Boulevards, or Memorable Men and Things Drawn on the Spot, 1853–1866* (Philadelphia: Lippincott, 1867), 94.

We know that such a utopian, all-encompassing international education system has never come into effect. Neither has the idea of itinerant educational institutions ever really been implemented. The internationalist drive in Blanchard Jerrold's belief in international education was clearly superseded by different waves of nationalist educational ideologies and policies. Moreover, the itinerant character of the schools proposed here represents a rather specific kind of internationality. In this view, the international can, merely by moving institutions around, displace the nation as the most important frame of reference for educational institutions. This is a generous, but elitist, view of the significance and role of the emerging international level in education that dreamt of an education free of national boundaries.

In the following, I will present a rather different view of the relationship between the national and the international levels in education. From this view, internationalisation cannot be analysed without simultaneously analysing the transformations of the "nation" and "nation-state"; that is, one cannot analyse it independently of the cultural or political units it consists of. Indeed, using the concept of the nation as a means of making sense of the world is a persistent pattern that, despite all the atrocities committed in its name, continues to be a strong form of identification.[2] It is on this basis that the "international" is seen to emerge – rather than the fact that people cross national borders.

I will argue that the internationalisation process has a relational nature in a double sense. First, it involves relations between these units called nations, producing links between them and rendering them more complex and intricate. Second, it always involves relations between the "national" and the "international", and changes in the substance of the former always impact on the dynamics of the latter.[3] In this view, there is no analysis of internationalisation without a simultaneous analysis of the nation. My point will be to differentiate "internationalisation" from other forms of crossing boundaries.[4] In my view, "internationalisation" is a particular form of national agency and, in turn, the emerging "international" sphere can be instrumental in constituting the "nation".[5]

---

[2]Elías José Palti, "The nation as a problem: Historians and the 'national question'", *History and Theory* 40 (2001); Gregory Jusdanis, *The Necessary Nation* (Princeton, NJ: Princeton University Press, 2001); Mattei Dogan and Ali Kazancigil, eds., *Comparing Nations: Concepts, Strategies, Substance* (Cambridge, MA: Blackwell, 1994); Walker Connor, *Ethnonationalism: The Quest for Understanding* (Princeton, NJ: Princeton University Press, 1994).
[3]I owe many of these insights to Jürgen Schriewer, *Welt-System und Interrelations-Gefüge. Die Internationalisierung der Pädagogik als Problem Vergleichender Erziehungswissenschaft* (Berlin: Humboldt-Universität zu Berlin, 1994). Heinz-Elmar Tenorth and I have also advanced some preliminary formulations in: Marcelo Caruso and Heinz-Elmar Tenorth, "'Internationalisierung' vs. 'Globalisierung': Ein Versuch der Historisierung", in Marcelo Caruso and Heinz-Elmar Tenorth, eds., *Internationalisierung/Internationalisation. Semantik und Bildungssystem in vergleichender Perspektive* (Frankfurt am Main: Peter Lang, 2002).
[4]Marcelo Caruso, "World systems, world society, world polity: Theoretical insights for a global history of education", *History of Education* 37, no. 6 (2008): 825–840.
[5]Here, I am following the analytical recommendation advanced by Caspar Hirschi, *The Origins of Nationalism: An Alternative History from Ancient Rome to Early Modern Germany* (Cambridge: Cambridge University Press, 2011), 13. It reads: "Definitions of a nation can be more instructive if they do not, as is the usual practice, focus on its *internal* construction as a political and cultural community, but instead highlight its *external* construction: that is to say, how the nation is perceived by and interrelates with foreign communities" (italics in original).

I will propose four different periods or stages in the changing relationships between the "national" and the "international" in Western education. For the characterisation of these historical periods of the international, I will take four prepositions – within, between, above and beyond – because these words indicate precisely the relations between entities and demonstrate the relational character of the international. Of course, the limits to this somewhat overambitious exercise are obvious: it is not possible to grasp the whole dynamics and the changing constellations of complex internationalisation processes by advancing a rather simple chronological scheme. Yet the very substance of "internationalisation" leads to the risky task of "thinking large" and, in doing so, of reducing culturally highly diverse – and conflicting – realities in education and society to a few significant constellations.

Two related purposes are part of my endeavour. First, I intend to expand the concept of internationalisation back to the Middle Ages.[6] In doing so, I am following recent research on the history of nations and nationalism that traces the issues of the national versus the international back to medieval and early modern times. Second, at the same time, I intend to differentiate "internationalisation" from other concepts dealing with the crossing of boundaries as well as from other trans-local developments, such as the ancient "world" systems of China, Mesopotamia and Egypt, that go even further back in time.[7] Be this as it may, in the view I am advancing here, "internationalisation" is not possible without the units and identities referred to as "nations". We now have to go back to the Western origins of collective "national" identities in order to grasp the early forms of the international.

Within: Education, educated classes and the invention of *nationes* in medieval times

Nation, derived from the Latin *nasci*, means "to be born". It used to be the usual category for describing people coming from a particular place or region. Yet, before the Middle Ages, it was rarely used to refer to a community sharing a common history and particular habits. This peculiar meaning of the term "nation" emerged only in a very specific context: in late medieval Europe, *nationes* designated groups of people having the same place of birth and sharing other characteristics such as language, customs and history in eminently *mixed* situations.[8] The "nation" as a way of classifying people was a reaction to the ever-increasing mobility of people. In the context of the Crusades, for example, but also as a result of the flourishing commercial life in the cities, lodgings for merchants, pilgrims, knights and students classified their guests according to their "nations". It was in situations like these that

---

[6] Excellent essays on the difficult topic of the "national" in the Middle Ages in the German countries are brought together in Joachim Ehlers, ed., *Ansätze und Diskontinuität deutscher Nationsbildung im Mittelalter* (Sigmaringen: Jan Thorbecke Verlag, 1989).
[7] Still a remarkable introduction: Christopher Chase-Dunn and Peter Grimes, "World-systems analysis", *Annual Review of Sociology* 21 (1995): 387–341. A more comprehensive proposal has been advanced by Stephen K. Sanderson, ed. *Civilizations and World Systems: Studying World-historical Change* (London: Sage, 1995).
[8] Aleksander Gieysztor, "Management and resources", in Hilde de Ridder-Symoens, ed., *A History of the University in Europe* (Cambridge: Cambridge University Press, 1992), 110–111. For an in-depth analysis of the *nationes* in three institutions, see Sabine Schumann, "Die 'nationes' an den Universitäten Prag, Leipzig und Wien. Ein Beitrag zur älteren Universitätsgeschichte" (PhD thesis, Freie Universität Berlin, 1974).

"nation" became a way of categorising otherwise amorphous masses of people and, in doing so, making them manageable.

In this context, the institutionalisation of nations at medieval universities developed a lasting legacy in the formation of nations as imagined communities. Examples can be found at universities such as Bologna, Padua and Paris.[9] Nations within universities were corporations of students and teachers who were organised according to their places of origin. They had institutionalised structures consisting of distinct rituals, common worship and also specific "services", e.g. in protecting their members in both legal and everyday matters. Elected officials led nations, and this fact gave "nation" a distinctive meaning pointing at a group of equals, a kind of "modern" meaning *avant la lettre*. In the limited but powerful context of the medieval university, the nation became a comprehensive principle for classifying individuals and forming group identities. As a result of its comprehensiveness, the principle of nationality became a model for organising identities, rivalling feudal relations and ecclesiastical organisations.

However, the nation as a classification scheme within the medieval universities could have many different meanings. Whereas at the University of Paris, "nations" included the French, the Normans, the Picards, the English and the Alemannians, other universities used different classifications. In Leipzig, for example, even the city of Meißen – which is located virtually around the corner – was also considered a distinct "nation".[10] Moreover, the numbers and the names of the nations within a particular university changed in the course of time, mirroring changes in the students' places of origin. The instability of these classifications clearly shows that these nations were an attribution of identity and not the description of a fact.[11] Whether these nations were instrumental in forging a common identity or not is not clear, yet the game of mutual attributions and the construction of stereotypes flourished in the university nations. The preacher Jacques de Vitry (1160/70–1240) in Paris, for example, believed that national characteristics were revealed in the different vices of students and teachers:

> The English are drunken cowards, the French proud, soft and effeminate; the Germans are quarrelsome and foul-mouthed, the Normans vain and haughty, the men of Poitou treacherous and miserly, the Burgundians stupid brutes, the Bretons frivolous and flighty, the Lombards miserly, spiteful and evil-minded, the Romans vicious and violent, the Sicilians tyrannical and cruel, the men of Brabant are thieves and the Flemings are debauched.[12]

Beyond national stereotypes and their performative potentials, the experience of belonging to a nation at the university was by no means marginal. Evidence suggests that it was in Italy that students coming from places as different as Hamburg, Munich, Cologne and Prague were perceived as speaking more or less the same language. What to Italian ears sounded like a "common language" later

---

[9] Jacques Verger, "Patterns", in Hilde de Ridder-Symoens, eds., *A History of the University in Europe* (Cambridge: Cambridge University Press, 1992), 35–76.
[10] Friedrich Zarncke, "Die urkundlichen Quellen zur Geschichte der Universität Leipzig in den ersten 150 Jahren ihres Bestehens", *Abhandlungen der Königlich Sächsischen Gesellschaft der Wissenschaften* 3 (1857): 647.
[11] Gieysztor, "Management and resources", 110.
[12] Quoted in Hilde de Ridder-Symoens, "Mobility", in de Ridder-Symoens, *A History of the University in Europe*, 282.

became a feature of the nation. The so-called "Germans" may have picked up this foreign attribution and brought it back home, although many of them were possibly unable to communicate in their respective mother tongues. On the whole, the performative force of, for instance, the *natio germanorum* at Bologna and other universities may have been a decisive factor in the early forging of later modern nations, at least at the level of the lettered elites. Together with the all-important practical aspects of belonging to a *natio* in a foreign city, the formative power of the *nationes* as an identity construct for these groups cannot be underestimated.[13]

Yet it was not at the universities but at the great Church Councils of this time that concrete groups emerging from face-to-face situations in defined institutions were organised as corporations and turned into "abstract communities", as if they were representing larger identities within the councils.[14] Again, in these somewhat confusing situations where an ordering principle was needed, the "nation" became a key instrument. In the Second Council of Lyon (1272–1274), *nationes* appeared as constituencies of the council for the first time. The decisive step, however, was taken at the Council of Constance (1414–1418). In the heated atmosphere of this Council – when the Council started, there were three "Popes" claiming to be the legitimate authority of Western Christendom – the organisation of formal proceedings and decision-making processes was a central question.[15] The solution was that, instead of voting as individuals, the bishops and other participants had to vote in national blocs, the *gallicana*, *italica*, *anglicana* and *germanica*. Most of the members of the council had received university training and, thus, were familiar with the organising principle of the *nationes*. Now they also had official functions at the highest meeting place in Western Christendom, and this led to a dispute over the defining features of the *nationes*. In these discussions, held in an eminently "international" setting for our present understanding, political, cultural and even linguistic criteria prevailed. *Nationes* were no longer merely concrete, organised groups of people; rather, they now denoted a much larger collective identity: "real" nations that were only "represented" by the dignitaries participating in the council. Against this background, it is only consequential to characterise early forms of nationalism as the invention of scholars, intellectuals or, more precisely, of scholars-cum-politicians. The principle of the *nationes*, having been practised within the most important institution for higher education since its inception, prevailed in other contexts as a principle of mutual attribution of collective identities in which educated dignitaries and scholars played the crucial role.

If nations are formed by their relations to other nations, the decisive context for the early stages of the gradual emergence of nations was undoubtedly certain types of "meeting places", such as universities, scholarly networks, church councils and so on, *within* which distinctions had to be made for both practical and political reasons. At these meetings, scholars played a crucial role in conceptualising nations,

---

[13]Ibid., 283. Also in some purportedly similar aspects of educational institutions, such as clerical education experiencing a process of slow differentiation; see Joachim Ehlers, "Was sind und wie bilden sich nationes im mittelalterlichen Europa (10.-15. Jahrhundert)?", in Almut Bues, ed. *Mittelalterliche nationes – neuzeitliche Nationen. Probleme der Nationenbildung in Europa* (Wiesbaden: Harrassowitz, 1995).
[14]This whole section draws heavily on the careful and illuminating analysis of Caspar Hirschi. See his results in Hirschi, *Origins of Nationalism*.
[15]Phillip H. Stump, *The Reforms of the Council of Constance (1414–1418)* (Leiden: Brill, 1993).

national characters and national languages.[16] This reveals the critical role of educational practices and institutions at the very beginning of the "national endeavour". Moreover, the writings of Petrarch, who condemned the "French" and celebrated the "Italian" spirit (*Epistolae rerum senilium*, ca. 1371–1372), and Erasmus' observations on the construction of national self-images (Praise of Folly, 1511) consolidated a certain way of thinking in individual sub-communities *within* the much greater imagined community of the humanists and, later, the republic of letters.[17] It may sound like a paradox, but it was precisely the cosmopolitan setting of these meetings and communicational networks that gave birth to the experience of belonging to a nation. At this first stage, nations as practical categories of structuring identities and loyalties became co-existent with "international" settings – they were two sides of the same coin, so to speak – and the preposition "within" – a nation *within* a larger entity – is the one most suitable for describing this early stage of the national–international relationship, a stage heavily marked by educated audiences.

Between: The reinforcement of the "national" on the eve of the nineteenth century

In the early modern period, constructions of national identity changed fundamentally. Mixed with the religious controversies of the time, "nation" acquired an exclusionary element that has remained a somewhat constitutive part of it ever since.[18] In the context of the emergence and consolidation of state authority, imagined collective identities and adoptions of foreign attributions gradually condensed into larger national identities. After cosmopolitan settings, as I have just described them, had formed the first notions and concepts of a nation in the Middle Ages, from early modern times onwards, the international was increasingly negotiated between the categories that were thus consolidated. Gregory Jusdanis has shown in his work on nationalism that old constructions of collective identities were politically and culturally activated in the second half of the eighteenth and the first half of the nineteenth centuries in the form of cultural nations that were defined in terms of a postulated "sameness".[19] This was the beginning of the classic period of internationalisation as a relationship marked by the tensions between two entities that had supposedly already been constituted. It is here that nations were established as larger identities in some Western countries, identities that were no longer limited to the educated classes or to scholarly audiences.

Particularly in the second half of the eighteenth century, education became one of the topics increasingly discussed by emerging public spheres communicating in "national" languages in different countries. Discussing educational institutions and practices at home, people increasingly referred to developments in other nations. It is also the time in which the idea of characteristic national "styles" that were either compatible or incompatible with specific educational proposals emerged. In this sense, there was a double movement: on the one hand, there was a movement

---

[16] As they also did in many other areas of administration and power; see the classic study by Jacques Le Goff, *Die Intellektuellen im Mittelalter* (Stuttgart: Klett-Cotta, 1986).
[17] Hirschi, *Origins of Nationalism*, 39 (for Erasmus) and 146 (for Petrarch).
[18] Anthony W. Marx, *Faith in Nation: Exclusionary Origins of Nationalism* (Oxford: Oxford University Press, 2003).
[19] Jusdanis, *Necessary Nation*.

towards a stronger "internationalisation" of educational knowledge and practices and, on the other hand, there was a widespread dynamic of national self-assertion in educational matters. I will show that an international negotiation of collective identities occurred in what I call a "between" mode; that is, a mode that largely supposed (and reinforced) the existence and educational relevance of the nation. For this purpose, I will briefly address two different developments: the discussion of Jean-Jacques Rousseau's (1712–1778) *Emile* in the last decades of the eighteenth century in the field of educational *knowledge*; and the national images activated by the circulation of the monitorial system of education in the first decades of the nineteenth century in the field of educational *practices*.

Discussing the national imagery activated by the wide circulation of Rousseau's *Emile* means addressing the main educational scandal of the time of the Enlightenment.[20] The process of reading, receiving and discussing Rousseau's political and educational works displayed an educational concern of not only international but even transatlantic dimensions. Many years later, *Emile* was still a crucial point of reference among educated circles on either side of the Atlantic Ocean. Francisco de Miranda (1750–1816), for example, one of the pioneer fighters for Latin American independence, who was in Newburyport, Massachusetts, in the 1780s, recorded in his travelogue: "We had a good American-style meal with something of Rousseau's doctrines in our conversation (Emile appeared at table)".[21]

Undoubtedly, when *Emile* was published in Paris in 1762, it was received so widely that the reactions against it revealed both general problems in the educational discussions of that time and the activation of "nations" as containers for dealing with the expansive drive of reformist discourses in education. The first commentaries on *Emile* in Germany were already evoking national frames or motives to deal with the storm unleashed by Rousseau's proposals. In 1763, not only did the leading medium of the educated elites in the northern German states – the *Göttingische Gelehrten Anzeigen* – consider the new book to be plainly "dangerous" but one reviewer also invoked a "German reader"; that is, a reader who was rational and critical and, thus, not fooled by the potent "spirit" of the French.[22] Yet, a truly "national reading" of *Emile* eventually emerged when the philosopher and educator Johann Gottfried Herder (1744–1803), one of the key German authors who defined national identity as based on a shared culture and language, activated a national interpretation of *Emile* in a travelogue written during his European journey in 1769. Needless to say, his confrontation with France during this journey – Herder came from the peripheral town of Riga, which was on the border between Prussia and Russia at that time – led him to put his national attachments to work. While travelling, Herder imagined his own contribution to a new era of education (*Bildung*), and he evoked Rousseau's

---

[20]For scholarly work on the wide circulation and reception of Rousseau's *Emile*, see Robert Thiéry, ed., *Rousseau, l'Emile et la Revolution* (Paris: Universitas, 1992). Some authors simply copied complete passages of *Emile* in other educational treatises, see Peter Jimack, "Some eighteenth-century imitations of Rousseau's *Emile*", in *Studies on Voltaire and the Eighteenth Century* (Oxford: Voltaire Foundation, 1991). See also Jacques Mounier, *La fortune des écrits de Jean-Jacques Rousseau dans les pays de langue allemande de 1782 à 1813* (Paris: Presses universitaires de France, 1980).
[21]Quoted in Jefferson Rea Spell, *Rousseau in the Spanish World before 1833: A Study in Franco–Spanish Literary Relations* (Austin. TX: University of Texas Press, 1938), 131.
[22]Peter-Eckhard Knabe, *Die Rezeption der französischen Aufklärung in den "Göttingischen Gelehrten Anzeigen" (1739–1779)* (Frankfurt am Main: Klostermann, 1978), 217.

"human wild Emil", whom he wanted to convert into "Livonia's national child".[23] In this founding document of a prospective national school – "get rid of Latin for the learning of Grammar, there is nothing better in the world than our mother tongue," he wrote – he characterised the French language as a barrier to a "philosophy of thinking". When asked whether French could be a philosophical language, Herder answered, "yes, it could be, only the French should not write it!" and continued to assert that "Helvétius and Rousseau confirm this...."[24] The lack of depth in French philosophy, which, for him, was a result of the French language, influenced his opinion that Rousseau's work was superficial and paradoxical.[25]

This kind of encounter clearly had two aspects. First, it activated preconceived national identities against the background of "foreign" challenges. Second, in dealing with these challenges, it further forged these identities. Reading Rousseau could lead to a reinforcement of national feelings and patterns because, internationally, it was circulated on an unprecedented scale. If Rousseau represented "French" identity, language and culture, the irruption of Napoleon onto the European scene often invoked concerns regarding a "national character" transported by educational ideas. One example is that central piece of German self-assertion, Fichte's *Addresses to the German Nation* (1808), a series of speeches delivered under French occupation. Here, Fichte – calling on the audience "to be German" – developed his concept of a national education in apparent tension – reference-cum-distance – to Rousseau's theories.[26]

The notions of what was "French", attributed to Rousseau's work in general and to *Emile* in particular, certainly underwent vast changes in the wake of the French Revolution and the Napoleonic Wars. In Gregory Jusdanis' view of the emergence of cultural nationalism, the expanding dynamic of universalistic principles and ideologies virtually brought about the formation and self-assertion of national cultures.[27] Not only was Fichte's *Addresses to the German Nation* a good example of this turn, but also the English reactions to the "scandal" of *Emile* and the proposals it contained. Edmund Burke (1729–1797), the well-known writer and politician, made use of the unprecedented diffusion of Rousseau's work in his condemnation of the French Revolution, *Reflections on the Revolution in France* (1790), a true best-seller. Burke presented the revolution in France not only as a political question, but also as a question of distinct national characters. Rousseau played a crucial role in his arguments:

> Thanks to our sullen resistance to innovation, thanks to the cold sluggishness of our national character, we still bear the stamp of our forefathers. ... We are not the converts of Rousseau; we are not the disciples of Voltaire; Helvetius has made no progress amongst us. Atheists are not our preachers; madmen are not our lawgivers.[28]

---

[23]Johann Gottfried Herder, *Journal meiner Reise im Jahr 1769* (Leipzig: Reclam, 1972), 31.
[24]Ibid., 90.
[25]Gilbert Py, *Rousseau et les éducateurs. Etude sur la fortune des idées pédagogiques de Jean-Jacques Rousseau en France et en Europe au XVIIIe siècle* (Oxford: Voltaire Foundation, 1997), 32–33.
[26]An extensive analysis of Fichte's references to Rousseau can be found in Py, *Rousseau et les éducateurs*, 214–220.
[27]Jusdanis, *Necessary Nation*, 17–43.
[28]Edmund Burke, *Reflexions on the Revolution in France* (Oxford: Oxford University Press, 2009), 86.

In Burke's negotiation between a national "we" and the national "other", Rousseau is the leading figure of the revolutionary process in France. In the National Assembly, "there is a great dispute amongst their leaders, which of them is the best resemblance to Rousseau". Moreover, "Rousseau is their canon of holy writ".[29] It is within this "we" and "they" that Burke delineated the opposition between the peoples of England and France. Moreover, education was a constitutive element in his argument: the English, Burke wrote, considered their church establishment "as the foundation of their whole constitution". Consequently, the education of the French – purportedly marked by Rousseau's thoughts – was not suitable for the English: "Our education is so formed as to confirm and fix this impression. Our education is in a manner wholly in the hands of ecclesiastics, and in all stages from infancy to manhood".[30] On the whole, in both rather benevolent readings such as Herder's and rather critical ones such as Burke's, *Emile* evoked intense national attributions.

Beyond the realm of educational *ideas*, similar patterns of constructing the international as a "between" of many distinct, self-contained nations were also effectual in the circulation of educational *technologies* and *practices*. This was particularly true in the case of the monitorial system of education. This was an organisational device for the elementary schooling of hundreds of children in one room that was based on the idea that the children could teach each other. As a result of its rationality and its promise of delivering school knowledge to the masses at relatively low cost, this system was extremely popular in certain educated circles across all continents during the first half of the nineteenth century. Its unprecedented diffusion from England motivated several evaluations and judgements that, among other things, also focused on national characteristics.[31]

In the German reception of the monitorial system, again, German "national honour" and identity played a crucial role. In German educational journals, for example, there were comparative views of the "German" and the "English Lancasterian" schools – as monitorial schools were labelled. Whereas German schools were idealised as places of "real", comprehensive education, English schools were portrayed as superficial and mechanical. Whereas German schools, the argument went, focused on the "inner being" of the students, English schools had very different foundations, foundations rooted in the English culture.[32] In England, "man needs only some skills in order to advance in the world; reading, writing and

---

[29]Ibid., 269.
[30]Ibid., 99.
[31]I have worked extensively on the subject of the early globalisation of this educational system. See Jürgen Schriewer and Marcelo Caruso, "Globale Diffusionsdynamik und kontextspezifische Aneignung. Konzepte und Ansätze historischer Internationalisierungsforschung", in Jürgen Schriewer and Marcelo Caruso, eds. *Nationalerziehung und Universalmethode. Frühe Formen schulorganisatorischer Globalisierung* (Leipzig: Leipziger Universitätsverlag, 2005); Marcelo Caruso, "Introduction: Independence, education, and the invention of new polities", *Paedagogica Historica* 46, no. 4 (2010): 85–98; Marcelo Caruso and Eugenia Roldán Vera, "Pluralizing meanings: The monitorial system of education in Latin America in the early nineteenth century", *Paedagogica Historica* 41, no. 6 (2005): 645–654.
[32]I have further developed this argument in Marcelo Caruso, "Wirksamkeit der Oberfläche. Anthropologien der Gewöhnung oder des Subjekts? Deutsche und spanische Deutungen des Bell-Lancaster-Systems im 19. Jahrhundert", in Heinz-Elmar Tenorth, Ulrike Mietzner and Nicole Welter, eds., *Pädagogische Anthropologie – Mechanismus einer Praxis* (Weinheim: Beltz, 2007).

ounting suffice; all the rest will be delivered by chance".[33] A negative image of a superficial commercial and industrial society based on profit-orientation emerged in these accounts and, interestingly, in marked contrast to German society and schools. One schoolteacher, who published an annihilating critique of the English system in 1827, ironically wrote that the use of this system would certainly yield a profit since "it is an English product".[34]

However, in dealing with the monitorial system, national character was an argument not only related to Germany. By means of the acceptance of monitorial schooling, some observers also believed they were able to "read" national characters. A German observer of the monitorial schools in the Swiss cantons of Geneva and Vaud explained the wide acceptance of the system he observed in terms of national preferences: "The French (!) think highly of external forms, of quick and bright results, of dressage for practical purposes of life; not the man, but the social man is for them everything... ."[35] Even the positive reception of this "English" type of school could lead to scenes of national assertion. At least in France, Italy, Portugal and Spain, some discussants considered the English system to be so rational, innovative and ingenious that they tried to convince their audiences that the idea of children teaching groups of children had local origins. For instance, a parliamentary commission in Madrid, taking up an argument advanced by local schoolteachers, advocated in 1822 the Spanish origin of the Lancasterian method and simply saw in the English techniques the "old Spanish system of pupil classification".[36]

The "between" displayed in these scenes of reception of educational knowledge (Rousseau) and practices (the monitorial system) reveals the binary character of the international. The international was explicitly embedded in a discourse of national honour that now included not only economic and cultural power, but also proper educational institutions. In these decades, educationalists travelled extensively to foreign countries in order to gather information on foreign educational realities in order to reform education "at home". This was a rather widespread early form of internationalisation in education and beyond. The international construed in these processes alludes not only to the classical, somewhat idealised motive of "learning from abroad", but also – particularly if we look at the intricate paths of reception that I have briefly outlined before – to a "self-assertion from abroad". It is also the time of the first wave of expansion of Western educational models beyond Europe and the Americas, preaching the allegedly beneficial effects of purportedly "English" and "French" models of educational progress. However, the missions sent from Egypt, the Ottoman Empire, the Madagascan kingdoms and many other places to the

---

[33]"Bell und Lancaster oder nähere Entwicklung des wechselseitigen Unterricht-Systems (Schluß)", *Allgemeine Zeitung für Deutschlands Volksschullehrer* 4, no. 21/22 (1820): 161–166.
[34]Justus Photophilus, *Briefe über die Lancaster-Methode im deutschen Sinne und Geiste, oder das Nachtheilige der deutschen Lancasterei* (Leipzig: Hartmann, 1827), 14.
[35]"Die Lancasterschulen in den Cantonen Wadt und Genf", *Allgemeine Schulzeitung* 10, no. 40 (1833): 321–326, here 321.
[36]See "Proyecto de un plan metódico de primera enseñanza presentado á la direccion general de estudios por la comision nombrada con este objeto", *Esposicion sobre el estado de la enseñanza pública hecha á las Cortes por la Direccion General de Estudios* (Madrid: Imprenta de Alban y Cía., 1822), 54–87, here 55. I have presented a comprehensive analysis of the German and Spanish reception of the monitorial system in Marcelo Caruso, *Geist oder Mechanik. Unterrichtsordnungen als kulturelle Konstruktionen in Preußen, Dänemark (Schleswig-Holstein) und Spanien, 1800–1870* (Frankfurt am Main: Peter Lang, 2010).

European "model countries" also showed the emerging unavoidable status of these practices of internationalisation in the "between" mode in the field of education.

Above: The emergence of a supranational level in education (1850–1980)

By the middle of the nineteenth century, a new form marked by governmental and nongovernmental organisations working on an international level had rapidly developed. In this process, international networks had crystallised in the framework of special institutions and recurrent "international" meetings. With the installation of the permanent commission of the River Rhine in 1816, the first intergovernmental international organisation came into being; the establishment of the YMCA (Young Men's Christian Association) in 1844 is credited as being the first nongovernmental international organisation. These two kinds of international organisation, despite all further differences, exhibit similar patterns of expansion and contraction over time.[37] Yet, it is only in the second half of the nineteenth century that they significantly helped to reshape the relationship between the national and the international. For scholars of the history of international organisations, the year 1864/1865 represents a kind of *annus mirabilis* in the development of this new kind of actor. In addition to the first organisations, the establishment of the International Telegraph Union in 1865 initiated a new type of international organisation: the international administrative union. With the establishment of the International Red Cross in Geneva and the International Working Men's Association – both in 1864 – new types of international organisation also emerged.[38] Together with the multiplication of international political and scientific meetings, they helped to contour a sense of the international as supranational; that is, as being somewhat "above" the existing national units. To be sure, this "above" was never entirely independent of national realities. Rather, it refers to two different dimensions of internationalisation. First, it was about the international level as a meeting place for individual nations. Second, it was about the emergence of a specific level of reality located somewhere "above" national frames, although this did not mean any linear subordination of individual nations to an emerging supranational level.

The new phenomenon of the international as something "above" the nations, or supranational, took on many different expressions. The first concerned the international dimension as a mere addition of many nations. This became particularly visible in international exhibitions and fairs. From 1851 onwards, these exhibitions had specific educational sections, and the first really international educational congress took place at the World's Fair in Philadelphia in 1876.[39] From 1851 to 2001, more than 300 such large international exhibitions took place, mostly in Europe, mostly before the Second World War, and mostly somewhat anticipating the modern slogan of the "global village". These monumental fairs, attended by millions of people, have attracted much scholarly attention in recent years. Critical analyses claim that precisely these international settings helped to constitute and to reinforce national

---

[37]John Boli and George M. Thomas, "INGOs and the organization of world culture", in John Boli and George M. Thomas, eds., *Constructing World Culture: International Nongovernmental Organizations since 1875* (Stanford, CA: Stanford University Press, 1999), 28.
[38]Madeleine Herren, *Internationale Organisationen seit 1865. Eine Globalgeschichte der internationalen Ordnung* (Darmstadt: Wissenschaftliche Buchgesellschaft, 2009), 18–19.
[39]Eckhardt Fuchs, "Educational sciences, morality and politics: International educational congresses in the early twentieth century", *Paedagogica Historica* 40, no. 5–6 (2012), 759.

identities and stereotypes.[40] Be this as it may, however, these exhibitions and fairs went far beyond the "within" mode of medieval times. By then, the modern nation states had already been constituted, as well as the purportedly distinct "national" cultures and histories to be displayed at the exhibitions. At the fairs, individual nations were arranged in the serial order of a "world as exhibition", as characterised by Timothy Mitchell in his famous essay on the Egyptian pavilions at the *Exposition universelle* in Paris in 1889.[41] Again, these exhibitions, which are paramount examples of modern forms of the international,[42] reveal the intricate relationship between the national and the international levels: they were both mutually exclusive terms and, at the same time, mutually reinforcing realities. Yet, even if the hypothesis is true that, in the context of these exhibitions, the international arena reinforced the attribution of national identities, it mostly rests on an investigation of what was displayed in the individual pavilions. However, little work has been done on whether and how visitors actually received the national stereotypes that were displayed.

A second thread of the emergence of the international level that exceeded the mere addition of nations was certainly the impressive expansion of a new type of international meeting: namely, international congresses, many of which were scientific congresses. Between 1860 and 1869, on average ten international congresses took place each year. In subsequent years, this number noticeably increased. Between 1910 and 1913, there was an average of 230 international congresses per year.[43] In the field of education, not only were there general educational congresses; rather, in the course of time, a thematic differentiation occurred. Congresses on art instruction, moral education, popular education, vocational and agricultural education, school hygiene, child protection and the meetings of the New Education Fellowship, among others, exhibit an unprecedented variety of educational topics. Moreover, not only scholars but also actors working in the education system, such as teachers' associations, began to organise international meetings.

The pervasive impact of internationalisation by means of meetings and organisations that brought together national identities, traditions, stereotypes and so on can hardly be underestimated. A case in point is the education of the deaf, for it clearly shows the strong thematic differentiation that even reached areas that hitherto had been rather marginal in terms of educational exchange. The education of the deaf had been attracting the attention of religious circles for a long time already.[44] The challenge of communicating the idea of God to persons incapable of verbal communication had fascinated certain Spanish friars, for instance, as early as the seventeenth century. Yet, the development of pioneering institutions for the

---

[40]An overview in Alexander C.T. Geppert, "Welttheater: Die Geschichte des europäischen Ausstellungswesens im 19. und 20. Jahrhundert. Ein Forschungsbericht", *Neue Politische Literatur* 47 (2002): 12.

[41]Timothy Mitchell, *Colonizing Egypt* (Berkeley and Los Angeles: California University Press, 1991), 1–28.

[42]Martin Lawn, ed. *Modelling the Future: Exhibitions and the Materiality of Education* (Oxford: Symposium Books, 2009). Also see Noah Sobe, "Attention and spectatorship: Educational exhibits at the Panama-Pacific International Exposition, San Francisco 1915", in Volker Barth, ed., *Innovation and Education at International Expositions* (Paris: International Bureau of Expositions, 2007).

[43]Fuchs, "Educational sciences", 759, Table 1.

[44]Susan Plann, *A Silent Minority: Deaf Education in Spain, 1550–1835* (Berkeley and Los Angeles: University of California Press, 1997).

instruction of the deaf did not occur until later: in the time of the "between" mode in internationalisation. A prominent example is Thomas Hopkins Gallaudet (1787–1851), an American educationalist, who travelled to Europe in order to visit leading institutions for the schooling of the deaf and, after his return, established the first American school of this kind in Hartford, Connecticut.[45] Although the internationality experienced by Gallaudet was still that of the "between" mode, his sons – who also worked in the education of the deaf – witnessed the emerging sphere of international meetings as a new reality "above" the national. At the second international congress for the education of the deaf in Milan (1880), Thomas Gallaudet (1822–1902) and Edward Miner Gallaudet (1837–1917) were members of the American delegation. The resolutions adopted at the congress – the preference of oralist methods over sign language – had far-reaching consequences in many nations. The two Gallaudets, who opposed the oralist frenzy displayed at the meeting, did not deal with particular experiences they had witnessed in foreign countries, as their father had done, but rather with a new "international opinion" articulated by the participants of the meeting.[46] This international opinion, which was condensed in a resolution, developed a force of its own and exercised real pressure on national decisions. Yet, even this new level "above" the national met with national realities and never fully superseded the existent "between" mode in internationalisation.

These were not the only forms and patterns of international cooperation: international exchanges of students and teachers, multilateral standardisation, the increasing integration of the world by means of telegraphs, railways and – later – radio and television generated and accompanied the emergence of the new supranational reality. Interrupted by two world wars, the international sphere increasingly became an additional reality to the national one. Undoubtedly, the meetings helped to forge a sensibility in tension with the nation as a unit for ordering the diversity of the world. The delegate from Russia at the World Congress of Education in Chicago in 1893 welcomed the participants with a passionate appeal to the prevalence of the international:

> And so the union of these two words, "international" and "educational" – may it be blessed; may it resound in the hearts of all who will be present here; may it inspire the words and acts of the congress with great ideas of universal impartiality; may it loudly proclaim that every one of us belongs, first, to humanity, and, secondly, to one or another nation; may it teach us that there is more honour for any one of us in being a man than in being an American, or a Russian, or a German, or an Italian, or a Greek, or a Japanese, or whatever else it may be.[47]

Yet national frames continued to be the main force shaping educational initiatives. Even for Léon Bourgeois (1851–1925), the first president of the League of Nations and an experienced voice in educational affairs, the centrality of the national frame remained uncontested. In his famous report to the League of Nations, "Organization of intellectual work" (1921), he affirmed "systems of education, scientific or philosophical research may lead to great international results, but they would never be

---

[45]Heman Humphrey, *The Life and Labors of the Rev. T. H. Gallaudet* (New York: Robert Carter & Brothers, 1857).
[46]Edward Miner Gaulladet, "The Milan Convention", *American Annals of the Deaf* XXVI, no. 1 (1881).
[47]Quoted in Robert Sylvester, "Mapping international education. A historical survey 1893–1944", *Journal of Research of International Education* 1 (2002), 98–99.

initiated or would never prosper if they were not bound up with deepest national sensibilities".[48]

In the first decades of the twentieth century, the educational movements related to pacifism and the reformist "new education" certainly provided novel impulses to a qualitatively new form of internationalism in which the nation was subsumed beneath supranational agencies and truly "universal" values. However, the persistence of the national principle was not only particularly noticeable between the two world wars; it also became the main principle in the liberation movements against colonial domination during the 1950s and 1960s. Against this background, it is not surprising that the concept of the international as something "above" individual nations still remained centred around these nations – as is obvious from the large number of governmental international organisations. There were, of course, also nongovernmental actors that, for example, helped to establish the International Bureau of Education (IBE) in Geneva in 1925. Yet, only four years later, the IBE became the first intergovernmental body focused on education. Without the support of national governments, this rather local Geneva initiative would have been unable to survive on a long-term basis. Likewise, international meetings such as the International Conferences of Public Education, which were organised by the IBE from 1934 onwards, would have been unable to take place without the support of national governments.[49]

In the context of the Cold War, the international scene focused strongly on the role of governmental international organisations in order to discuss and advance educational matters.[50] In particular, the emergence of the United Nations Educational, Scientific and Cultural Organization (UNESCO) highlighted the role of national governments – at the expense of international nongovernmental organisations. At the same time, other actors such as the Organisation for Economic Cooperation and Development (OECD), now a very visible actor in the international educational scene, emerged. Perhaps the only exception was adult education, for this was a field in which nongovernmental international actors were more active in comparison to other areas of education. On the whole, there is evidence that, although international nongovernmental actors continued to grow, they played a rather subordinate role between 1945 and 1980 in international educational matters. In this sense, the "above" level of the international in the field of education was – paradoxically – effectuated and accompanied by a consolidation of the nation state on a world scale.

Beyond?: New qualities of the international (*c.* 1980)

The international in the "above" sense that I have just described certainly still determines the contemporary international scene in education. However, some changes have occurred in the last decades that indicate the possible emergence of a new constellation of the international level. The end of the Cold War, the fall of the communist bloc and the subsequent unleashing of global market forces, the spread of

---

[48] Quoted in Daniel Laqua, "Transnational intellectual cooperation, the League of Nations, and the problem of order", *Journal of Global History* 6 (2011), 238–239.
[49] Pedro Rosselló, "Historical note", International Bureau of Education, http://www.ibe.unesco.org/fileadmin/user_upload/Publications/Institutional_Docs/Rossello_historical_note_en.pdf.
[50] Robert Sylvester, "Framing the map of international education (1969–1998)", *Journal of Research of International Education* 4 (2005): 123–151.

information technologies, the noticeable growth of worldwide interdependencies and connections now generally known as globalisation and – at least in Western countries – the contested legitimacy of the nation, have created a different context for the internationalisation of education. In recent decades, the international level in education has not merely been an addition of individual nations or a supranational level coexisting with the plurality of nations; rather, under these new "global" conditions, a differentiated international regime has emerged, a regime that is no longer state-centred.

In this sense, the international now also entails a "beyond" that exceeds national frames by means of, among other factors, new communicational practices and the emergence of a transnational civil society. For example, the passing of the Convention on the Rights of the Child in 1989 is part of this new configuration. Eckhardt Fuchs, who has researched this process in detail, has shown that the development and adoption of these new standards for the rights of children has largely been an achievement of NGOs. The history of the Rights of the Child reaches back to 1890 and the organisation of the first international congresses concerned with the protection of children. In the adoption of the First International Declaration for the Rights of Children in 1924, representatives of transnational nongovernmental organisations played a vital role. Yet, in Fuchs' account, the period after 1945 was dominated by UNESCO/UNICEF (United Nations Children's Fund) – that is, governmental organisations. It was at this time that children's rights became an issue beyond the Western core countries that had already embraced them in the 1920s. This culminated in the adoption of a non-binding Declaration of the Rights of the Child in 1959 by the General Assembly of the United Nations (UN), a declaration that also included certain social and cultural rights. This declaration is a classic case in relation to internationality in the sense of something "above" the national level.[51]

However, the further development of the declaration on children's rights was largely an outcome of nongovernmental activism. In 1977, a committee of nongovernmental organisations was established, which rapidly grew into a "dense" network of support for a binding and extended declaration. After more than ten years of close cooperation with UN agencies, in 1989 the UN General Assembly adopted the binding Convention on the Rights of the Child. Fuchs considers this an important step in UNICEF's transition to a "human rights agency specializing in children's rights".[52] The rather autonomous work of these nongovernmental agencies as advocates of universalistic norms and their – still – crucial role in monitoring the implementation of the convention show a new level of the international beyond the national frame. Fuchs is clear in his conclusions:

> It appears that NGOs and global networks have become the main bodies that create "cultural models" in the field of children's rights and that link them to regional, national and local educational changes. In addition to the traditional discursive level, they have also become enactors of these models into reality....[53]

---

[51] Eckhardt Fuchs, "Children's rights and global civil society", *Comparative Education* 43, no. 3 (2007): 393–412; Eckhardt Fuchs, "Internationale Nichtregierungsorganisationen als Global Players. Zur Herausbildung der transnationalen Zivilgesellschaft am Beispiel der Kinderrechtsbewegung", *Zeitschrift für Pädagogik* 53, no. 2 (2007): 149–165; John Eekelaar, "The emergence of children's rights", *Oxford Journal of Legal Studies* 6, no. 2 (1986): 161–182.
[52] Fuchs, "Children's rights and global civil society", 407.
[53] Ibid., 408; Fuchs, "Internationale Nichtregierungsorganisationen".

To be sure, this kind of international dynamic in a "beyond" mode still addresses individual national states, but, at the same time, it also organises advocacy coalitions on post-national levels – and it is not limited to children's rights. This is particularly obvious in the World Education Forums concerned with the Education for All initiative. In these, an unprecedented level of interaction between different actors, including many NGOs, has emerged. Karen Mundy and Lynn Murphy have found evidence that transnational advocacy supported by an emerging transnational civil society has given the international dynamic of the Education for All initiative a new point of reference. They have found clear signs "of a new and qualitatively different wave of transnational nongovernmental advocacy initiatives in education".[54] An additional aspect has to be considered in analysing the actors of this emerging transnational civil society: not only have the level and the intensity of international nongovernmental activities in education considerably expanded;[55] rather, these organisations are becoming increasingly autonomous from national frames because, in contrast to earlier decades, they are now obtaining their money mainly from nongovernmental sources.[56]

The emergence of novel international nongovernmental forces is certainly not the only phenomenon of this kind. In addition, many international governmental organisations are increasingly operating on universalistic principles that are no longer necessarily tied to the nation. The United Nations, for example, as well as regional organisations for development and economy, has developed more universalistic goals. International staff and the cosmopolitan social and cultural contexts in which they are often embedded increasingly provide organisational settings that no longer simply mirror national interests.

The international as a phenomenon "beyond" the national does not completely change the older modes of "between" and "above". Yet, the state-centredness of the classic modern internationality of the "above" mode is now being challenged and complemented by the new dynamics that I have just described. It is a central challenge for the historiography of internationalisation in the field of education to assess the extent, pace and pervasiveness of this shift in the construction of the international.

Historicising the international in the field of education

I have proposed an outline of a history of the internationalisation of educational knowledge and practices with reference to international and national frames. Following a rather nominalistic path (the use of the word nation as depicting identities and polities), I have tried to map the historical development of the international in education. The prepositions I have suggested intrinsically refer to dominant relationships and links at certain periods of time, and this relational nature corresponds to the international as a relational phenomenon itself. Following a period during which the international and the national, so to speak, "co-emerged" *within* groups of rather different people, for example at the medieval universities, the second constellation

---

[54]Karen Mundy and Lynn Murphy, "Transnational advocacy, global civil society? Emerging evidence from the field of education", *Comparative Education Review* 45, no. 1 (2001), 86.
[55]Lester M. Salamon et al., eds. *Global Civil Society: Dimensions of the Nonprofit Sector* (Baltimore, MD: Johns Hopkins Center for Civil Society Studies, 1999).
[56]Maggie Black, *Cause for Our Time: Oxfam, the First Fifty Years* (Oxford: Oxford University Press, 1992).

of internationalisation as a *between* emerged during the Enlightenment and the early nineteenth century. From then on, the international partially shifted to something constructed *above* the individual nations. In the middle of the nineteenth century, both international governmental and nongovernmental organisations began to virtually mushroom, and international congresses became central mechanisms of internationalisation. In the face of emerging information technologies and following the cultural and political context that was highly critical of the nation at the end of the twentieth century, there are now international educational agendas *beyond* the nation, challenging the inherited nature of the international as a state-centred reality.

This proposal for defining the characteristic periods of internationalisation in education is clearly based on fragmentary evidence and, moreover, focused on Western contexts. Furthermore, this approach does not fully fit with some aspects of the internationalisation of educational practices and ideas such as migrations. Examining the international as a level of reality that is always redefined in the context of national identity constructions, it has avoided the competing category of "globalisation". Thus, following the "national path", my proposal has consciously avoided other major concepts and theories of our times. Certainly, theoretical approaches to globalisation, to the "world systems", the "world polity" and the "world society" will remain necessary in order to organise the huge volume of data and scholarship already available. However, the "great" narratives resulting from these theoretical drafts may be too consistent and too narrow when dealing with the rather ambivalent and by no means consistent processes in the educational field.

As scholars in the history of education, we have dealt with issues related to the internationalisation of education in many ways. Valuable scholarship on virtually all world regions is now available. The focus has moved away from an exclusively Western orientation, and different practices of internationalisation – meetings, organisations, identity constructions, migration, transfer processes – have become the focus of a large number of studies. Beyond the admittedly rather sketchy and reductionist approach I have proposed in this piece, it is time to advance different narratives of the international in the field of education. It will be by discussing these comprehensive narratives, integrating specific scholarly work on single processes of internationalisation, that we will be able to make sense of the international condition of educational practices and knowledge in modern times and beyond.

The rivalry of the French and American educational missions during the Vietnam War

Thuy-Phuong Nguyen

Paris Descartes University, Paris, France

From 1955 to 1975, the French and the Americans were both active in the educational field in South Vietnam, but their objectives were different. The French were concerned with preserving their influence with the Vietnamese elites and relied on the Mission Culturelle – the heir of the colonial Direction of Education – and its prestigious high schools. The Americans wanted to improve the level of education of the population and strived to reform the Vietnamese administration in order to make South Vietnam a nation strong enough to bar the advance of communism. The main operator was USAID, which coordinated and funded the activities of expert teams, and particularly of academic missions. The French deeply resented the American intrusion into what they believed to be their historical area of cultural influence, and they perceived the United States as aggressive towards them. The Americans did not oppose the French cultural presence but they did try to eliminate those parts of the French legacy – particularly the teaching methods and the administrative structures – that they considered to be obsolete and an obstacle to their reforms. The battle between those two cultural traditions was waged by their Vietnamese supporters, with long-time Francophiles on one side and US-trained educators and administrators on the other. However, this competition was partly artificial, as the French and Americans actually needed each other. Their educational missions also had to deal with the circumstances of the war in Vietnam. In the early 1970s, the French resigned themselves to the dismantling of their educational network while American reform met with substantial resistance in South Vietnamese society, which resented the Americanisation of an educational system that mixed the Confucian and the French academic traditions, as symbolised by the enduring popularity of the Baccalaureate examination that still exists today in Vietnam.

Introduction

In 1954, France withdrew politically and militarily from Vietnam after eight years of war and a historical defeat by the Vietnamese People's Army at Điện Biên Phủ. The Geneva Agreements divided Vietnam into two separate states, the pro-communist Democratic Republic of Vietnam in the North and the pro-Western State of Vietnam (later Republic of Vietnam) in the South. France passed the baton of the fight against communism in Southeast Asia to the Americans. The United States, which had largely underwritten the French war in Indochina, now provided military assistance to South Vietnam, and proceeded to transform the fledgling country into a strong state able to oppose North Vietnamese ambitions. A key element of this nation-building effort was the reform of the educational system in South Vietnam. The French, who had ruled Vietnamese education for 80 years, and were particularly attached to the "civilising" dimension of their colonial past, deeply resented the intrusion of the US into what they considered to be their private domain. Without directly confronting each other, the French and American educational missions competed for the favour of the Vietnamese throughout the Vietnam War.

A French cultural policy targeted at elites

In the late 1910s, the traditional educational system had been replaced by the "Franco-indigenous" system. Contrary to popular belief, native children in French colonies were not taught "Our ancestors the Gauls". The keyword was *adaptation*: in Indochina, particularly, the Franco-indigenous curriculum was tailored to the needs of the colonial economy. The goal was not to create assimilated natives, but to train proficient employees and subordinates. Until 1945, the Franco-indigenous system operated in parallel with the French educational system, which served the French children and selected children of Indochinese elites (about 20% of enrolment[1]). In 1943, almost 1 million pupils[2] attended Franco-indigenous and French schools. While this number made the French proud of their "civilising mission", it only represented 8% of school-age children. The vast majority of Vietnamese people could neither read nor write, and Vietnamese nationalists could claim that 90% of the population was illiterate,[3] a figure that nobody could dispute since the literacy problem had never been addressed or even quantified by colonial authorities. However, despite such failings, the colonial educational system in Vietnam resulted in the emergence of a French-speaking or even Francophile elite – journalists, lawyers, doctors, scientists, businessmen, landowners – many of whom became figures of the independence movement, in the name of the ideals of the French Republic they had been taught in school.

After the end of the Second World War, the French hoped to reclaim their former colony but found that they could no longer rule Vietnam as they had done before, since Vietnamese independence had been proclaimed by the Japanese in March 1945, and then by Hồ Chí Minh in September. The Franco-indigenous school system and the University of Indochina were transferred to new Vietnamese authorities favourable to the French while France retained the most prestigious *lycées* (high schools). With most of the French population gone, those *lycées* opened their doors wide to native students, and Vietnamese enrolment rose to 60% in 1954 and then to more than 80% in 1956.[4] Still, during the Indochina War, the French believed that they could continue

---

[1]Direction de la documentation, Service des statistiques, "Renseignements statistiques sur l'Indochine, avril 1946", 1946, Agence économique de la France d'outre-mer, Carton 163, Dossier 1, Archives nationales d'outre-mer.
[2]Albert Charton, "Tableau statistique de l'enseignement en Indochine (1930, 1938, 1944)", 1946, Fonds ministériel, Nouveau fonds, Indochine 4, Carton X 2, Dossier 1323, Archives nationales d'outre-mer.
[3]Phạm Văn Đồng, "Les rapports culturels entre la France et le Viet-Nam, Discours prononcé le 6 mai 1946 à la Cité universitaire à Paris", *La Pensée* 8 (September 1946).
[4]Mission d'enseignement français et de coopération culturelle, "Bulletin annuel de la Mission d'enseignement français et de coopération culturelle 1954–1956", 1956, Fonds Ho Chi Minh-ville, Service de coopération culturelle et technique, Carton 331, Centre des archives diplomatiques de Nantes.

to assert their cultural domination over the Vietnamese by means of the French language, which Inspector General Albert Charton, a prominent figure of French colonial and postcolonial education in Vietnam, considered the "natural tool" of Vietnamese culture.[5] But French hopes collapsed after 1954. The new communist regime in North Vietnam expelled or nationalised all French economic and cultural assets except one, the Lycée Albert-Sarraut. South Vietnam, now ruled by the uncompromising nationalist president Ngô Đình Diệm, was overtly hostile to France but let the French stay in the country. Indeed, even though France no longer played a pivotal role in the Vietnamese economy, part of the economic structure inherited from the colonial era was still in place. The French owned the majority of rubber plantations as well as many major companies – breweries, banks, trading and shipping firms.[6] France also maintained a strong cultural presence. In addition to hospitals and research institutions, it operated three major *lycées* and a number of lesser schools. The French operator was the Mission culturelle, which was the direct heir of the colonial Direction Générale de l'Instruction Publique and had about 1000 employees on its payroll. In addition to the public schools run by the Mission culturelle, dozens of private schools of all sizes followed the French curriculum. In 1956, about 24,000 students were enrolled in French schools in South Vietnam, a third of them in public schools.[7]

Why did the French maintain such an expensive school system in Vietnam? This distant country was now inimical to French interests, and, after the humiliation of 1954, many people in France would rather forget that Indochina had ever existed. Furthermore, the French government was more preoccupied with the Algerian War and sub-Saharan Africa than with Asia. Still, the diplomats and cultural attachés in Saigon advocated firm cultural and educational action. They claimed that it was of utmost importance that France kept on supporting its schools in Vietnam; Vietnamese elites, they said, were being seduced by the Anglophone sphere of influence, and France had to court them back if it wanted to maintain its position in Asia. They pointed to the decline of French speaking in Vietnam, which had begun in the mid-1950s. They were particularly worried that the US were asserting its supremacy over that quintessentially French realm, culture.

French discourse was now completely focused on keeping within France's orbit the elites that had been attracted by the social status associated with French culture. The French Ambassador of France in South Vietnam, Roger Lalouette, expressed this view in 1963:

> Today, [our schools] educate the children of the Vietnamese elite, and these children will become the elite of tomorrow. This alone should compel us to increase our efforts in this area, because our lycées guarantee us essential political (and therefore economic) positions in Vietnam. The current government is composed of alumni of our schools. It will necessarily be the same in the future.[8]

---

[5]Commissariat général du Plan, "Rapport général de la Section enseignement et éducation" (1946), 4–5, Fond du Haut Commissariat, Conspol, Carton 23, Archives nationales d'outre-mer.
[6]Pierre Brocheux, *Une histoire économique du Viet Nam, 1850–2007. La palanche et le camion* (Paris: Les Indes Savantes, 2009), 175.
[7]Mission d'enseignement français et de coopération culturelle, "Bulletin annuel de la Mission d'enseignement français et de coopération culturelle 1954–1956".
[8]Roger Lalouette, "Note N°3238/CC" (Ambassade de France au Vietnam, May 1963), 3, Série Asie-Océanie, Sous-série République du Vietnam 1956–1964, vol. 49, Centre des archives diplomatiques de La Courneuve.

As in the colonial period, the *lycées* and the Baccalaureate examination continued to play a central role in this policy, strengthened by the true enthusiasm of Vietnamese families who rushed to send their children to the French schools that were tuition-free until 1958. French officials spoke derisively of those nationalist Vietnamese ministers who adopted a public anti-French discourse while sending their children to the schools of the Mission culturelle. Pleased and worried at the same time, French diplomats attended as spectators the pro- and anti-French language debate in relation to the "vietnamisation" of the university.

In the late 1950s, the responsibility for the Mission culturelle was transferred from the former Ministry of the Overseas France to the Ministry of Foreign affairs, which already operated many French schools outside France, thus severing the link between the Mission and its colonial past. The Ministry of Foreign affairs considered the existence and operation of the Mission as an "anomaly". It transformed the Mission into a service of the French Embassy in Saigon and significantly downsized it.[9] The reduced budget – which still paid the salaries of about 400 teachers throughout the 1960s – did not allow for the expanded cultural activities that were recommended by the diplomats and Mission chiefs in Saigon. As a consequence, French educational activities in South Vietnam increased very slowly after 1955 before levelling off in the late 1960s. The prestigious French *lycées* were still favoured by wealthy Vietnamese families, but they could not accommodate more students. To the very end, cultural advisors complained bitterly that the *lycées* were unable to meet demand due to lack of funds. It was only in the mid-1960s that French authorities started developing other tools of "soft power", such as cooperative activities and cultural centres. The colonial "civilising mission" had finally morphed into a modern cultural diplomacy.

The American "enemy"

In the reports of Saigon-based French officials, the cultural enemies of the French were not the Vietnamese Communists, but the Americans. The former were respected foes: the French grudgingly admired those Vietnamese intellectuals who were educated in French schools and universities, spoke fluent and refined French, and claimed to be heirs to the French Revolution. The Americans, on the other hand, were viewed with suspicion. The ambiguous attitude of the US towards the French presence in Indochina in 1945, demonstrated for instance by Roosevelt's outspoken anti-colonialism, the sidelining of France at the Potsdam conference and the friendship of certain OSS officers towards Hồ Chí Minh had made the French wary of American intentions in Vietnam, and even the fact that the US had paid for the Indochina War did not appease some resentful French officials. According to the historian Pierre Journoud, there is a "myth according to which the French have been chased off South Vietnam by an American plot to replace the political, military, economic and cultural influence of the former colonial power",[10] and this myth was

---

[9] Michel Fourré-Cormeray, "Rapport sur les services de l'Ambassade de France au Sud-Vietnam" (Ministère des Affaires étrangères, 1957), Série Asie-Océanie, Sous-série République du Vietnam 1956–1964, vol. 1, Centre des archives diplomatiques de La Courneuve.
[10] Pierre Journoud, "Les relations franco-américaines à l'épreuve du Vietnam entre 1954 et 1975, de la défiance dans la guerre à la coopération pour la paix" (Thèse de Doctorat, Université Paris I Panthéon Sorbonne, 2007), 395.

relayed at the time in the French media. When US missions and agencies started to arrive in Saigon in the early 1950s, the French soon became exasperated with the "civilising" activities of the Americans, and suspected them of trying to "defrenchify" Vietnam[11]. They were also openly disdainful of American culture, which a French cultural advisor jokingly called an "un-culture" in a report.[12] An American teacher of political science working in Saigon in 1958 stated that the French were actively belittling Americans in the eyes of the Vietnamese:

> Vietnamese ignorance of things American is overwhelming. General lack of knowledge has been made even worse by the persistent efforts of the French to convince all who will listen that Americans are mass-produced, uncultured, unrefined, uncouth, unlettered and unimaginative.[13]

In 1957, the chargé d'affaires Arnaud d'Andurain explained to the Vietnamese Minister of Foreign Affairs, Vũ Văn Mẫu, how nefarious would be the consequences of an Americanised Vietnamese education:

> The day when they stop looking up to France for their intellectual training, and turn to America instead, the Vietnamese will no longer be the subject of flattering comparisons; from that day on, nothing would make them intellectually different from the Siamese, for instance.[14]

The French would condemn the importance of money for "some of our allies who tend to think that wealth can replace culture",[15] and would rejoice that "Americans, despite all their dollars, do not know, alas!, how to win the hearts of those sentimental Asians".[16] We can surmise that "Alas!" actually means "fortunately" in that context.

The early months of the American presence in Vietnam after the Geneva Agreements were indeed a difficult period for the French. In December 1954, General Paul Ély and his American counterpart signed an agreement in which the US stated that they had no intention of replacing France in the cultural domain.[17] A few months

---

[11]Kathryn C. Statler, *Replacing France: The Origins of American Intervention in Vietnam* (Lexington, KT: University Press of Kentucky, 2007), 41–43.
[12]Conseiller culturel, "Les activités américaines au Vietnam sur le plan culturel, N° 70/ECF/S, Confidentiel", 1956, 8, Série Asie-Océanie, Sous-série République du Vietnam 1956–1964, vol. 51, Centre des archives diplomatiques de La Courneuve.
[13]Bernard E. Brown, "Excerpts from report by Dr Bernard E. Brown, Smith-Mundt Visiting Professor of Political Science, University of Saigon, Vietnam, February–July 1958" (Conference Board of Associated Research Council, July 1958), 4, Série Asie-Océanie, Sous-série République du Vietnam 1956–1964, vol. 51, Centre des archives diplomatiques de La Courneuve.
[14]Arnaud D'Andurain, "Le Vietnam se ferme aux ouvrages français" (Ambassade de France au Viet-Nam, May 1957), 5, Série Asie-Océanie, Sous-série République du Vietnam 1956–1964, vol. 48, Centre des archives diplomatiques de La Courneuve.
[15]Jean Michelin, "Proposition de résolution tendant à inviter le Gouvernement à rétablir la gratuité dans les établissements français d'enseignement au Viet-Nam" (Conseil de la République, N°138, Session ordinaire de 1957–1958, December 1957), 2, Série Asie-Océanie, Sous-série République du Vietnam 1956–1964, vol. 48, Centre des archives diplomatiques de La Courneuve.
[16]Robert Guillain, "Le Vietnam et nous. I. Premier bilan d'une décolonisation", *Le Monde*, 25 December 1957.
[17]Statler, *Replacing France*, 210.

later, French authorities were shocked to learn that the National Institute of Administration (NIA), which they had created in 1953, was placed under the supervision of the Michigan State University Vietnam Advisory Group, which immediately started to Americanise both the curriculum and management.[18] From then on, French officials in Saigon never failed to denounce to their superiors the "war" that Washington was waging against France. Jean-Pierre Dannaud, head of the Mission culturelle in 1956, wrote for instance:

> Our allies from across the Atlantic wage a "war to the knife" that will ensure that the French presence suffers the same fate as the Sioux and the Seminoles. Such unanimity in the smiling refusal of any sort of cooperation or even contact with the French cannot be forever explained by God knows what insubordination of American missions towards the American Embassy. This can only be decided in Washington.[19]

The intense energy and impressive budget of the American missions sent the French into a panic, as they were stunned both by the efficiency of the American "steam-roller"[20] and by the support of the South Vietnamese authorities. They saw themselves as "the old artisan who is forced to close shop by the large factory whose walls are rising".[21] Roger Lalouette reported his pressing concerns to his superiors:

> If our actions were limited to the narrow scope of our traditional education, not only our relative importance in the university system would decrease due to the swelling of enrolment coming from the Vietnamese secondary education system, but we would be quickly overwhelmed, both in the educational sector and outside of it, by American activities, which are largely present everywhere, and which aim at replacing the French language by the English one within 5 or 6 years. American efforts are ever increasing, and the results will (soon) be obvious. Time is running out, and I would be thankful if you would make arrangements ... to mount an immediate and efficient counter-offensive in that domain.[22]

Later, when the Americans experienced their first setbacks in the cultural field – in the diffusion of the English language and in the management of the NIA – French officials reported these failures in private communications with undisguised satisfaction. They saved their harshest words for the Vietnamese suspected of being friendly to Americans, and particularly when those "traitors" had personal ties with France. For instance, when the Rector of the University of Saigon implemented the utilisation of Vietnamese as a teaching language in 1961, the French cultural advisor explained to

---

[18] Jean Payart, "Activités culturelles américaines au Vietnam" (Ambassade de France au Viet-Nam, 12 October 1957), 8–9, Série Asie"Océanie, Sous"série République du Vietnam 1956–1964, vol. 51, Centre des archives diplomatiques de La Courneuve.

[19] Jean-Pierre Dannaud, "Rapport sur le fonctionnement de la Mission française d'enseignement et de coopération culturelle au Vietnam pendant les années 1955–1956, N°393/ECF/JPD" (Haut Commissariat de la République française au Viet-Nam, 4 September 1956), 13, Série Asie-Océanie, Cotation provisoire, vol. E124, Centre des archives diplomatiques de La Courneuve.

[20] Conseiller culturel, "Les activités américaines au Vietnam sur le plan culturel, N° 70/ECF/S, Confidentiel", 7.

[21] Ibid., 9.

[22] Roger Lalouette, "Télégramme à l'arrivée, N°986/88" (Ambassade de France au Vietnam, 8 September 1959), 1–2, Série Asie-Océanie, Sous-série République du Vietnam 1956–1964, vol. 48, Centre des archives diplomatiques de La Courneuve.

his superiors that the rector "was forced to appease ultra-nationalists so that they would forgive him his French wife".[23]

But admiration and envy also played a part in French attitudes towards Americans. Some officials, such as Ambassador Jean Payart, noted that American cultural efforts had always been "more spectacular than ours ever were".[24] The ambition, efficiency, relentlessness and missionary-like devotion of Americans in their reform, propaganda and cultural activities made the French painfully aware of their own deficiencies:

> For the impartial observer, what is most striking about the efforts carried out by Americans to spread their language is the crusading zeal they bring to their task. The teachers who are sent to give lectures in suburban public halls on Sundays and the wives of civil servants who work in Vietnamese orphanages all do their job with the sort of passion that is not just patriotic, but also mystical. This particular aspect [is] totally absent from our own traditional methods of cultural policy.[25]

The French also perceived how ineluctable was the decline of France and of the French language in this part of the world:

> We should harbour no illusions about this: the number of applicants to our schools may never have been so high as it is today, but we have never seen so many Vietnamese eager to learn the English language either.[26]

France was by now largely uninterested in its former colony, and provided means that were insufficient to redress the situation and only allowed for limited activities. Indeed, French criticism towards the Americans ceased in the mid-1960s when the Vietnam War entered its main phase. The French, who were more than ever threatened by South Vietnamese nationalists enraged by the "neutralist" policy of President De Gaulle, now kept a low profile. It was only after 1972, when the US had disengaged from the Vietnam War, that the French, "threatened to be overwhelmed by the onslaught of Anglo-Saxon culture",[27] hoped to regain a foothold in South Vietnam "without attempting to compete with the sensational means of the United States".[28] This was, of course, too late.

The legacy of French education as seen by the Americans

While French officials were obsessed with the American "invaders", this obsession was not reciprocated. The Americans were bothered neither by the existence of

---

[23]Jean Martinelli et Jean-Félix Charvet, "Note N°185/IG" (Ambassade de France au Viet-Nam, August 1961), 4, Série Asie-Océanie, Sous-série République du Vietnam 1956–1964, vol. 49, Centre des archives diplomatiques de La Courneuve.
[24]Jean Payart, "L'aide économique américaine au Vietnam" (Ambassade de France au Viet-Nam, June 1957), 6, Série Asie-Océanie, Sous-série République du Vietnam 1956–1964, vol. 63, Centre des archives diplomatiques de La Courneuve.
[25]Payart, "Activités culturelles américaines au Vietnam", 12–13.
[26]Ibid., 9.
[27]Philippe Bréant, "Note a/s de notre politique de coopération culturelle et technique au Sud-Vietnam" (Ministère des affaires étrangères, Direction générale des relations culturelles, scientifiques et techniques, June 1973), 14, Série Asie-Océanie, Sous-série Sud-Vietnam 1965–1976, vol. 290, Centre des archives diplomatiques de La Courneuve.
[28]"Notes d'instructions générales à l'intention de notre Ambassadeur au Sud-Vietnam" (Ministère des affaires étrangères, DGRCST, 22 November 1973), 1, Série Asie-Océanie, Sous-série Sud-Vietnam 1965–1976, vol. 290, Centre des archives diplomatiques de La Courneuve.

French schools and institutions nor by the residual French-speaking of Vietnamese elites. Indeed, they put up with the French presence, and used the French language themselves when necessary, as was the case in the early years when Americans and Vietnamese had to speak French to understand each other. Americans occasionally sent their children to the French *lycées* and kindergartens.

However, the Americans in Vietnam were highly critical of the French educational legacy, which pervaded the Vietnamese system they were trying to reform. In 1959, the University of Kentucky published *A Historical Survey of Educational Developments in Vietnam*, written by Vu Tam Ich, a Vietnamese teacher now residing in the US.[29] In this book, which is often cited in later American documents about Vietnamese education, the author drew a merciless picture of the French-Vietnamese school system:

> Like its French counterpart, it was overintellectualized and overcentralized. French-Vietnamese schools were institutions where bookish training prevailed to the detriment of worthwhile social and cultural activities. It is true that those students who successfully passed the rigorous examinations achieved a relatively high academic standard, but it is questionable whether they had sufficient opportunity in school to develop their social behavior as well as to explore their leadership qualities. Furthermore, the emphasis put on classical subjects tended to create an educational elite with a literary bias, which regarded itself as the cream of the Vietnamese society. As a result, technical and vocational education was neglected, whereas the study of law and humanities was favored in a nation which needed a great deal of engineers and technicians to keep up with the modern world.[30]

Vu Tam Ich's assessment of the teaching methods used in those schools was equally negative:

> So far as class procedure was concerned, teacher-controlled discipline tended to discourage initiative and individual responsibility for one's success. Preconceived learning activities did not offer much challenge to the creative power and native energy of the student, who did his studies in a rather routine way. Despite the overintellectualized spirit of French-Vietnamese schools, there were no adequate library facilities in the lycées, much less in the primary and elementary schools. This deficiency tended to make the Vietnamese student depend much on his notes and handbooks, and left him unprepared to use original documents and source materials. With the exception of maps and globes, audio-visual aids were practically non-existent in the classroom. In addition, teaching methods were pedantic and verbal, based as they were mainly on lectures and recitations. Generally speaking, the teacher did not encourage original thinking on the part of his students, who were thus inclined to memorize and repeat what was taught.[31]

Vu Tam Ich contrasted the traditional aims of the French-Vietnamese schools with the educational goals of the Diệm regime, which were "quite modernistic and possibly influenced by the concepts adopted in the United States".[32]

---

[29] Vu Tam Ich, a former high school teacher in Hanoi, had come to the US in 1950 with a Smith-Mundt (Fullbright) scholarship and was possibly one of the first Vietnamese to study in the US. Ray Johnson, "Goodbye: Two longtime DLI employees say adio, chào, so long", *Globe*, 30 January 1991.
[30] Vu Tam Ich, "A historical survey of educational developments in Vietnam", *Bureau of School Service, University of Kentucky, College of Education* XXXIII, no. 2 (1959): 96.
[31] Ibid., 96–97.
[32] Ibid., 120–121.

American criticisms of French education were therefore numerous: administrative centralisation, excessive emphasis on humanities and literature rather than on science and technology, disdain for the development of social behaviour (such as leadership qualities), disregard for technical and vocational education, barren elitism, outdated teaching methods based on rote learning and forbidding student participation.[33]

American educators found Vietnamese students polite in the extreme, but inhibited in the classroom by the traditional reverence for teachers. Libraries was highly symbolic of the difference between French and American education: French-style libraries hid their books in locked cupboards or in the back of the stacks, "safe from the insulting attention of students",[34] while American-style libraries, scientifically organised according to the Dewey Decimal Classification system, welcomed the students with their generous open shelves.[35] As a Vietnamese educator once told his American counterpart: "The trouble is not just that we have a French system ... but we have the French system of 1890...."[36]

The other French legacy that Americans were trying to fight was the prominence of examinations, and particularly of the Baccalaureate. Edgar N. Pike, the head of the Asia Foundation in Vietnam, remarked in 1961 that, "one of the most serious problems confronting educators in Vietnam is the high status value of the diploma":[37]

> Through the efforts of dedicated educators [the colonial education system in Vietnam] had, however, begun to evolve into a potentially excellent and well-balanced system. Its most unfortunate legacy was its exaggerated emphasis on the diploma, whose symbolic and status value became more important to the students than the education it was intended to symbolize.[38]

The South Vietnamese system at the time, which featured cycles with no American equivalent, school years numbered in reverse order to those in the American system and French-named and French-patterned examinations and curricula, was something of a mystery to educational advisors from the US:

> The emphasis placed upon competitive examinations and upon certificates in contrast to American practices has led to misinterpretation here and in the United States of the academic value of the final secondary certificate, namely the Baccalaurat II.[39]

Orin Hascall, a consultant for USAID on the Baccalaureate examination in Vietnam, wrote in 1972:

> One who is deeply oriented in the United States' system of secondary education will wonder if this elaborate and complicated examination program is really necessary.

---

[33]Ibid., 96.
[34]Brown, "Excerpts from report by Dr Bernard E. Brown", 2.
[35]Wesley R. Fishel, "Third report of the Michigan State University Vietnam Advisory Group in Public Administration to the Government of Vietnam" (Saigon: Michigan State University Vietnam Technical Assistance Project, 30 June 1956), 12.
[36]Ralph D. Purdy, "Evaluation and planning for secondary education in South Vietnam" (Athens, OH: Ohio University, and Saigon: USAID, Education Division, 28 August 1971), 19.
[37]Edgar N. Pike, "Problems of education in Vietnam", in Wesley R. Fishel, ed. *Problems of Freedom: South Vietnam Since Independence* (New York: Free Press of Glencoe, 1961), 78.
[38]Ibid., 76.
[39]"Student records from Vietnam: Their evaluation for placement of students in American educational institutions" (USOM–United States Operations Mission to Vietnam, April 1962), 3.

Why can't the student's high school simply issue him a graduation certificate when he satisfactorily completes the twelfth grade?[40]

Throughout the 1960s, the Americans strived to reform the curricula in order to decrease the weight of examinations and to curb the "the Baccalaureate fixation"[41] of Vietnamese society. This was not merely an educational issue: like other American efforts at reforming the South Vietnamese state, it was directly related to the war. A USAID employee told the *New York Times* in 1966 that the inability of the underprivileged Vietnamese youth to obtain the desirable Baccalaureate degree led them to join the communist ranks:

> In South Vietnam, the second baccalaureate degree is a virtual necessity to become an officer in the army or a civil servant. Yet it can be obtained in almost all cases only by the children of the privileged classes, which already control Vietnamese society and like it that way. "It is still virtually impossible for a child born in a poor rural family to obtain a baccalaureate degree, without which he is permanently relegated to an inferior social position," Mr. Burnham said. "Primary education by itself only increases the frustration by encouraging the appetite," he said. "To these children the Vietcong offers the only real outlet for their energy."[42]

The Americans sought to undermine the influence of the "French elitists",[43] that is, those Vietnamese who owed their privileges to their French education and who stubbornly opposed the changes proposed by the US, such as the massification of education or the new emphasis on technology in the curricula. Ralph Purdy, a consultant in secondary education for USAID, was particularly frustrated by those "elitists":

> The direction was established for a transition from the French secondary elitism for the few to comprehensive programs for the masses. These proposed transitions in educational direction and motivation were immediately challenged by the traditionally oriented segment of society, especially those with convictions committed to the 1906–1954 French points of view. Again, the ultimate solution to this ideological conflict is not readily identifiable. While the political leadership continues to move forward with the directions established in 1959, each such move brings with it reserved opposition and antagonism... Reliance on the inherent fear of foreign domination tends to become the verbalized stock-in-trade for the French elitists and traditionally oriented Vietnamese in order to maintain the status quo.[44]

Until the 1970s, American advisors kept on blaming "the elite system, the old French elite class" and its alleged hold on the national education system.[45]

---

[40]Orin W. Hascall, "The Baccalaureate examination in the Republic of Vietnam" (Stevens Point, WI: University of Wisconsin-Stevens Point, July 1972), 16.
[41]Stanley A. Barnett, Erroll D. Michener and C. Walter Stone, "Developmental Book activities and needs in the Republic of Vietnam" (New York: Wolf Management Services/Contract No. AID/csd-1162, October 1966), 103.
[42]Charles Mohr, "Saigon social ills worry U.S. aides", *New York Times*, 21 February 1966.
[43]Purdy, "Evaluation and planning", 28.
[44]Ibid., 25.
[45]Lee Sherman Dreyfus, President of Wisconsin State University-Stevens Point, cited by Thomas C. Reich, "Reforming higher education in a society at war: Wisconsin State University-Stevens Point's Advisory Mission in South Vietnam, 1967–1974", *Journal for the Study of Peace and Conflict* 2008–2009 annual edition (2009): 17.

The French, of course, formed the opposite impression, that South Vietnamese education was ruled by pro-US Vietnamese. There is some irony in the fact that the francophile Vietnamese elites, which the French considered to be their greatest achievement, were perceived by the Americans as a major obstacle to their plans to reform education. The American consultants saw these elites as archaic, holding to outdated modes of thinking, teaching methods, curricula and competitive examinations patterned on nineteenth-century French education. Far from being obsessed with the French presence, the Americans' concern was the current war: the residual French influence on the current Vietnamese educational system contributed to maintaining the social status quo, and, by hampering the "great and fortunate mobility of class"[46] so dear to Americans, was driving the Vietnamese poor into the arms of Communists.

True or false rivalry?

The French and the Americans rarely confronted each other in educational matters in South Vietnam. When French diplomats voiced their discontent after the incident concerning the National Institute of Administration in 1956, the Americans averted the conflict by putting the blame on Ngô Đình Diệm.[47] The endless and sometimes violent debate on the Vietnamisation of the university, which worried French officials for at least a decade, pitted the new generation of US-trained Vietnamese administrators and educators against their older Francophile counterparts. In fact, as has been shown by Pierre Journoud, the US administration chose to protect certain French interests, including in education. During the 1960s, even when de Gaulle's "neutralism" was infuriating Washington, the US knew that it was unable to fully replace the French: large sectors of the South Vietnamese economy, medicine, culture and education still depended on French companies and employees, and US officials made clear to the Vietnamese authorities that they would oppose significant anti-French actions.[48] The activities of the French and American cultural missions were actually complementary, and they sometimes worked together.[49] French professors taught, for instance, at the Phú Thọ College of Technology, an American creation. According to a British observer, the French had even one clear advantage over the Americans: French teachers could easily stay in Vietnam for long periods of time, since their public status ensured that they would be able to go back to their former position once they returned to France. Private American contractors, on the other hand, enjoyed no similar safety net and stayed in Vietnam only for the duration of their mission.[50]

It should be noted that French officials were critical of their own schools for reasons similar to those of the Americans. The French recognised that the needs

---

[46]Brown, "Excerpts from Report by Dr Bernard E. Brown", 7.
[47]Payart, "Activités culturelles américaines au Vietnam", 8–9.
[48]Journoud, "Les relations franco–américaines", 395–396.
[49]Pierre Journoud, "Face-à-face culturel au Sud-Vietnam 1954–1965", in Publications de la Sorbonne, ed. *Entre rayonnement et réciprocité, Contributions à l'histoire de la diplomatie culturelle* (Paris: Université Paris I Panthéon-Sorbonne, 2002), 161.
[50]P.H.M. Jones, "Vietnam at school", *Far Eastern Economic Review* 36, no. 3 (1962): 556.

of contemporary Vietnam, notably in the field of technology, were not well met by the French educational system.[51] During the colonial period, this criticism had been directed at the Vietnamese themselves, who were accused of preferring intellectual and administrative careers to technical ones: colonial authorities were at the time less concerned with the economic development of Indochina than with the potential danger of "unemployed intellectuals".[52] The Americans experienced similar difficulties with Vietnamese civil servants who had been sent to the US for training between 1958 and 1960 (the "Scholarship for Leadership" programme) and had found themselves unemployable after their return to Vietnam: the American scholarship programme had to be changed to target more technology-orientated careers.[53]

The French were also aware that the perceived elitism of their schools was a sensitive issue in a country at war, where a diploma could prevent or delay mandatory drafting. In order to deflect those accusations, the Mission culturelle gave scholarships to good students from underprivileged families and created special classes for children who did not speak French fluently enough.[54]

French and American educators shared an interest in modern teaching methods and progressive education: they opposed obsolete methods based on rote learning and promoted instead the active pedagogy proposed by UNESCO or by the "École Nouvelle" movement in France. The Americans funded a "comprehensive school"[55] for testing new pedagogical approaches and sent Vietnamese educators to the US to learn these methods. The newsletter of the French Mission culturelle praised some innovative teachers of French schools in Vietnam, such as Jean Faure, the energetic principal of the École Française de Nha Trang, who had been using such methods since 1948.[56] Finally, while French officials in the 1950s and 1960s were still fond of the French Baccalaureate, colonial administrators used to condemn, just like the Americans a few decades later, the excessive weight of these diplomas in Vietnamese society. The French and the Americans, while still believing in their respective educational models, were in agreement more often than not.

The course of the French and American educational missions ended abruptly on 30 April 1975, when Saigon fell to the People's Army of Vietnam. In retro-

---

[51] Camille Bergeaud, "Allocution au Club de Rotary de M. Camille Bergeaud, Inspecteur général, Conseiller culturel de l'Ambassade de France", 8 January 1959, 2, Série Asie-Océanie, Sous-série République du Vietnam 1956–1964, vol. 48, Centre des archives diplomatiques de La Courneuve.

[52] Justin Godart, *Rapport de mission en Indochine, 1er janvier–14 mars 1937* (Paris: Editions L'Harmattan, 1994), 152–153.

[53] "General Scholarship Program: Project agreement between the Department of State, Agency for International Development, and the Directorate General for Budget and Foreign Aid" (USAID, 26 May 1970), 2.

[54] Mission d'enseignement français et de coopération culturelle, "Bulletin annuel de la Mission d'enseignement français et de coopération culturelle 1954–1956", 42.

[55] Dương Thiệu Tống, "A proposal for the comprehensive secondary school curriculum in Vietnam" (New York: Teachers College, Columbia University, 1968), 110.

[56] Jean Faure, the director of the École française de Nha Trang, had been using such methods since 1948. Mission d'enseignement français et de coopération culturelle, "Bulletin annuel de la Mission d'enseignement français et de coopération culturelle 1952–1953", 1953, 92–93, Fonds Ho Chi Minh-ville, Service de coopération culturelle et technique, Carton 331, Centre des archives diplomatiques de Nantes.

spect, the French could take comfort in the fact that the Vietnamese elites had been loyal to them, at least from a cultural perspective: up to the last days, these elites had been sending their children to French schools, despite anti-French demonstrations and the dismantling efforts of the Vietnamese government. Indeed, those elites had supported the French school system when it was under attack and had opposed the Americanisation of the national school system. For instance, the abolition of the national Baccalaureate examination, planned for the mid-1960s, had been delayed several times. The Vietnamese educator Dương Thiệu Tống, who participated in the negotiations about the Baccalaureate, explained this rejection as follows:

> Examination practices have such deep role and prestige that any educational innovation which goes against them is hardly welcomed by many educators or students or parents. ... The entire training of teachers and a major part of the school activities are, therefore, geared to helping students pass examinations. The present examination system in Vietnam has thus been a great challenge to any attempt at educational reform and to the idea of educational equality so necessary for educational modernization.[57]

The French language itself had unexpectedly resisted the advance of English in secondary education – in 1967, half of Vietnamese high school students were still choosing French as their first foreign language[58] – and at the university. The Americans too had met with some success. A large number of Vietnamese could more or less speak English at the end of the 1950s. American aid had made mass education a reality: school enrolment in South Vietnam stood at 4 million in 1973,[59] tenfold the enrolment of 1954, and illiteracy had been virtually eliminated. Finally, the Americans had trained an entire generation of Vietnamese educators in modern pedagogy.

The failures were no less glaring. The French had been unable to prevent the disappearance of the French language from the daily lives of the Vietnamese, the Vietnamisation of their cultural and scientific institutions and, by the end of the 1960s, the dismantling of their educational system by Vietnamese governments eager to make a scapegoat of "neutralist" France (thereby sending a clear political message to their American allies). In 1967, the seven-year lease on the buildings of the *lycées* was not renewed and classes were progressively transferred to the national education system. Vietnamese students were forbidden to go to France to complete their studies. The end of the French school system was scheduled for the late 1970s.

American efforts at reforming South Vietnamese education had met with substantial resistance, at all levels, from students' parents to the top administration. Indeed, Vietnamese and American expectations in relation to education were not aligned. The adoption by the Vietnamese of the French educational model had

---

[57]Dương Thiệu Tống, "A Proposal", 131.
[58]Jacques de Folin, "Avenir de la langue et de la culture française au Sud-Viêtnam (1ère partie)" (Consulat général de France à Saigon, Feburary 1973), Annexe no 1, Série Asie-Océanie, Sous-série Sud-Vietnam 1965–1976, vol. 290, Centre des archives diplomatiques de La Courneuve.
[59]USAID, *United States Economic Assistance to South Vietnam, Volume II* (Washington, DC: USAID, 1975), 177.

been facilitated by its similarities with the traditional Confucian model. Like its Sino-Vietnamese counterpart, French education emphasised literary aesthetics and intellectual pursuits over practical knowledge. Teaching methods made ample use of passive and rote learning. Both systems were meritocratic, theoretically at least. The teacher and the scholar were highly respected and even revered figures. The Baccalaureate in the French system, and the civil service degrees in the Confucian system were both coveted as much for their symbolic and status value as for their actual academic value. Those convergences may partly explain the American difficulties in trying to eradicate the Baccalaureate and other French idiosyncrasies from the national Vietnamese educational system. Joseph Dodd, an American educator from the University of Tennessee who was a consultant for USAID, noted in 1972 that the US had been trying to impose changes that were much too drastic for a Vietnamese educational system still steeped in the Franco-Confucian tradition:

> The United States, in attempting to stimulate changes with respect to both curricula and method, has been introducing change items which are diametrically opposed to both pre-French and French items. Immediately one thinks of agricultural and home economics education, engineering, the social sciences, and learning by participation, all of which are essentially alien to Vietnamese cultural traditions. A comparison of the American and French experiences certainly seems to support the generalization that the greater the change attempted, the less likely it is to succeed.[60]

A symbolic example of the futility of such changes was the attempt, in 1974, to rationalise the Baccalaureate examination by replacing some of its essay tests with multiple choice tests, unknown in France and Vietnam but widespread in the US. This major change required the import in Saigon of two expensive IBM computers. According to a Vietnamese observer, this well-intentioned innovation was mostly used to facilitate large-scale fraud.[61]

What is left, 40 years later, of the Franco-American competition for the "hearts and minds" of the South Vietnamese students and their families? Vietnam is now a member of the Francophone organisation, but use of the French language has all but disappeared, while French remains a vehicular language in numerous countries of Maghreb and sub-Saharan Africa. Vietnamese bookshops have entire sections filled with books for learning English, Japanese or Chinese, more rarely French. There are about 300 French companies operating in Vietnam – the same number as in 1960! – but more than 1000 American organisations. In a way, some of the fears of the French diplomats in the 1950s and 1960s have materialised. There is, however, one enduring legacy of the French influence on the Vietnamese educational system: every June, almost 1 million students sit the Vietnamese Baccalaureate (*Tốt nghiệp trung học*), the national examination that crowns the 12 years of primary and secondary schooling and opens the doors of the university.

---

[60]Joseph W. Dodd, "Aspects of recent educational change in South Vietnam", *Journal of Developing Areas* 6, no. 4 (1972): 569.
[61]Lê Phuong, *La corruption au Vietnam* (Montreal, QC: Editions Québec/Amérique, 1978), 83.

New School of Mustafa Satı Bey in Istanbul (1915)

Filiz Meşeci Giorgetti

Education Sciences, Istanbul University, Istanbul, Turkey

This study has two purposes: the first is to present the general condition of public education in the late nineteenth and early twentieth centuries by showing the reformation process in educational institutes and teacher training, and the relationship between this process and the New Education movement in the Ottoman Empire; the second is to determine to what extent Mustafa Satı Bey, often referred to as the Pestalozzi of the Ottoman Empire, contributed to the New Education movement through the analysis of his opinions on education, and his attempts to open a New School. As a result of Mustafa Satı Bey's analysis, New Education practices in the Ottoman Empire were stated to be practising a unilateral receiving-and-adapting procedure and the Ottoman Empire was positioned at the periphery in terms of the circulation of the movement. In his New School and in the Teacher Training School, Satı Bey was concerned with the New Education movement both on an administrative and operative level. However, his practices were not sufficient to create his own theory and examine any other theory. Thus, when evaluated in terms of his contributions to the New Education movement, Satı Bey is positioned somewhere between *practical reformer* and *practitioner*.

Introduction[1]

In the nineteenth century, governments in the west experienced social, political and economic revolutions and believed schooling could be the solution to many of these problems. Thus, education and schooling became a matter for the state. However, a reformist movement (the New Education) was initiated by people who thought public school systems and their actual practices were unable to meet the special needs of children. In education, a 'Copernican Revolution' came about through support of the idea that education should be defined by students and be framed according to their desires and needs. These developments were also in a close relationship with the development of educational sciences and the institutionalising of teacher training. In time, concepts and expressions from the New Education appeared in

---

[1] Two calendars were used in the Ottoman Empire: Hicrî and Rumî. In 1926 the Turkish Republic started to use the Gregorian calendar, like the Europeans. In the article, all references before 1926 give the original date first, followed by the Gregorian date (for example, 1335/1917).

educational systems and became a part of the discourse of governmental educational systems, though not a part of its practices.²

Concepts and expressions from the New Education were introduced to the Ottoman Empire in the early twentieth century by several of the Empire's most renowned and respected teachers, such as Mustafa Satı Bey, Nafi Atuf Kansu, İsmail Hakkı Baltacıoğlu, Tevfik Fikret, Selim Sırrı Tarcan and İbrahim Alaaddin Gövsa. The translations, writings and practices of these pioneers, as well as their attempts to open a new school, had a major effect on the dissemination of New Education thought and the institutionalising of educational sciences.

New Education is a large concept. The meaning of the name "New Education" originates from its opposition to the old education and therefore, its general meaning is directly related to the current conjecture.³ The concept of New Education in this study is taken to exist within a framework that contains teaching methods and reformation movements that locate the student at the centre. Thus, the term is also related to the French *Education Nouvelle* and *Ecole Active*, English *Progressive Education* and *New Education*, German *Reformpädagogik* and, in Ottoman, *Yeni Mekteb*.

The present study has two purposes. The first is to present the general condition of public education in the late nineteenth and early twentieth centuries by showing the reformation process in educational institutes and teacher training, and the relationships between this process and the New Education; the second is to determine to what extent Mustafa Satı Bey (Satı-El-Husri) (1879–1968), often called the "Pestalozzi of the Ottoman Empire", contributed to the New Education through the analysis of his opinions on education and his attempts to open a New School.

While analysing the interaction between the New Education and the Ottoman Empire, the *centres* and *peripheries* distinctions of Hofstetter and Schneuwly were considered. Analysing the circulation of the New Education among countries, Hofstetter and Schneuwly defined institutions in countries that operate in relative autonomy, mutually enrich and echo the knowledge branching out from other centres and have propositional force as the *centres* of the New Education. Examples of these countries included Germany, Belgium, the United States, the UK and Switzerland. They classified the countries that receive references and suggestions from these centres and which have more of a unilateral relationship with these centres as the *peripheries*.⁴ The present study shows that the interaction between the Ottoman Empire and Europe in terms of the circulation of the New Education movement was unilateral and that the Ottoman Empire was positioned as the periphery.

The second objective of the study is to determine the levels of Mustafa Satı Bey's contributions to the New Education. In order to position Satı Bey appropriately within the New Education, we refer to Hofstetter and Schneuwly's distinctions of *practical reformers, practitioners* and *theorists*. They defined the protagonists who affected the formation, transfer and transformation of the knowledge related to

---

²Rita Hofstetter and Bernard Schneuwly, "Introduction: Progressive Education and Educational Sciences," in *Passion, Fusion, Tension: New Education and Educational Sciences*, ed. Rita Hofstetter and Bernard Schneuwly (Bern: Peter Lang, 2006), 1–15.
³Kevin J. Brehony, "From the Particular to the General, the Continuous to the Discontinuous: Progressive Education Revisited," *History of Education* 30, no. 5 (2001): 413–32.
⁴Rita Hofstetter and Bernard Schneuwly, "Introduction: Contrasted Views of New Education on Knowledge and its Transformation. Anticipation of a New Mode or Ambivalence?," *Paedagogica Historica* 45, no. 4–5 (2009): 453–67.

the New Education, separating them into three groups in terms of their social and professional backgrounds. *Practical reformers* act as practitioners and endeavour to reform educational practices, discourses and concepts. These people are well known in their fields. Far from simply reporting an experience, their contributions to the field are related to the theorisation of the movement. *Practitioners* are related to the movement on an administrative level. They focus their attention on the school system itself, bringing their reformist preoccupation to bear on its efficiency. They act as intermediaries between reformers and theorists as well as between the New Education and the current educational system. *Theorists* mainly help through their writings, condensing the constructed knowledge and principles of the reformist movements. The reformist movements in education and the circulation and transformation of knowledge are products of these collective practices.[5] To determine to which of these three areas Satı Bey belonged, I will discuss his life, professional experiences, social and political position and corporate relationships. I will then review his works and analyse his readings of the New Education and the opinions he reached as a result of his observations in Europe. Finally, I will examine the educational approach he put into practice, especially in the new school he opened in Istanbul.

Context

In the Ottoman Empire of the early nineteenth century, educational institutions could be gathered under three topics: Ottoman primary schools (*sıbyan mektebleri*) and madrasahs which provide religious education; Ottoman palace schools (*enderun*); and military schools which the Ottoman Empire, after its defeats in the eighteenth century, copied from the French and English models. In the nineteenth century, modern schools that were structured on western models, embracing religious as well as secular education, were opened. At the level of primary school, *iptidaiye* schools – the equivalent of Ottoman primary schools – were opened in 1869; secondary schools – *rüşdiye* (1839), *idadiye* (1845) and *sultaniye* – were created in 1868; a higher education school – *Darülfünun* – was founded in 1863; a teacher training school for male students – *Darülmuallimîn* – was established in 1848; and a teacher training school for female students – *Darülmuallimat* – was formed in 1870. With a regulation brought into effect in 1869, all these schools were positioned in a single system and were entrusted to the Ministry of Education (*Maarif-i Umumiye Nezareti*). In Ottoman primary schools and madrasahs no serious educational reforms were made, and these schools vanished with the founding of the Turkish Republic.[6]

In the second half of the nineteenth century, innovative movements in education under the concept of *usûl-i cedîd* ("new method") were widespread in primary and *rüşdiye* schools. The new method opposed the old method of rote learning in Ottoman primary schools, where students were taught in the same classes, in the same schools and without materials. The new method, however, included religious knowledge as well as secular knowledge; it referred to a collective education that used desks, blackboards and platforms in classes, as well as concrete materials like maps and globes. In time, schools that were shaped according to the characteristics

---
[5] Ibid., 463–4.
[6] Osman Ergin, *Türkiye Maarif Tarihi*, vol. 1–2 (Istanbul: Eser Matbaası, 1977).

of the new method came to be called *usul-i cedid* schools or primary schools (*iptidai*).[7]

After 1908, Ottoman institutions, teacher training schools and the education system entered a new process. With the independence movements led by students sent to Europe in the nineteenth century, sovereignty came under criticism, and in 1908 *Meşrutiyet* (Constitutional Monarchy) was declared again. The Ottoman Empire lost part of its territories in the Balkan War (1912–1913) and the First World War. Under war conditions, primary education became compulsory and free in 1913.[8]

Satı Bey, Ziya Gökalp and İsmail Hakkı Baltacıoğlu, three of the most famous educators of the time, discussed educational issues of the period through educational journals. These issues included: structuring the relationship between the individual and society through education; the weight of private enterprise in education and other fields; the weight of religion in education; and new educational methods. Different questions were discussed, such as: should education be centralised or decentralised; on which level should the reforms in education start; should education be personalised or nationalised?[9] Satı Bey and Ziya Gökalp especially discussed the views of Spenser and Durkheim. Ziya Gökalp's opinions were favoured as he had the support of the ruling political party of the period, *İttihat ve Terakki*.[10] These discussions are important since they form the theoretical infrastructure of the national centralised educational system of the Turkish Republic.

Taking schools in France as examples, a number of modern schools were opened in the Ottoman Empire. These schools lacked qualified teachers. In the early twentieth century, when compared to missionary schools or foreign and minority schools in the Ottoman Empire, the insufficient quality and quantity of Muslim Turkish schools was becoming increasingly apparent. In 1914, there were 49 Muslim primary schools (*ibtidai* and *rüşdi*), 46 non-Muslim primary schools and 24 foreign primary schools in Istanbul.[11] Archive documents make it clear that Muslim schools were not only too few, but also mostly in poor condition.[12] The Ministry of Education was considering a separate budget for opening new schools to prevent Muslim students from going to foreign schools and was encouraging qualified schools to open more classes.[13]

Investigations into ways of increasing the quality of education and teacher training started in teacher training schools. Personnel were renewed, especially after Satı

---

[7]Yahya Akyüz, *Türk Eğitim Tarihi*, 6th ed. (Ankara: PegemA, 1997): 180–3.
[8]Akyüz, *Türk Eğitim Tarihi*, 231–2. Legal obligation for primary schools was brought about with the constitutional law of 1876. With the provisional law of the primary school in 1913, compulsory and free primary education came into force for the first time.
[9]See also Satı, "Terbiye ve Milliyet," *Muallim* 1, no. 4 (1332/1916): 102–7; "Ferdi Şuur ve İçtimâî Vicdan," *Muallim* 1, no. 5 (1332/1916): 129–35; "Ma'şeri vicdan etrafında I," *Muallim* 1, no. 8 (1333/1917): 231–41; "Ma'şeri vicdan etrafında II," *Muallim* 1, no. 9 (1333/1917) 272–81; "Ma'şeri vicdan etrafında III," *Muallim* 1, no. 11 (1333/1917): 328–35; "Mekteblerde efkar-ı hissiyat-ı amme," *Muallim* 2, no. 22 (1334/1918): 767–71.
[10]Muhsin Hesapçıoğlu, "Türkiye'de Cumhuriyet Dönemi Eğitim İdeolojisi," *Liberal Düşünce* 13, no. 49 (2008): 87–100.
[11]*1330 senesi Istanbul Belediyesi İhsâiyât Mecmuası* [Year 1914, Istanbul Municipality Journal of Statistics] (Dersaadet [Istanbul]: Arşak Garviyan Matbaası, 1331/1915): 124–5.
[12]Dahiliye, İdare-i Ummiye Ekleri, file 39/54, date 18 Zilhicce 1335/1917; Maarif Nezareti Mektubi Kalemi, file 187/126, date 14 Cemaziyelevvel 1311/1893, Başbakanlık Osmanlı Arşivi (BOA) [Prime Ministry Ottoman Archives].
[13]Yıldız, Başkitabet Dairesi Maruzatı, file 60/24, date 04 Rebiülahir 1317/1899, BOA; Yıldız, Mütenevvi Maruzat Evrakı, file 260/200, date 30 Rebiülevvel, 1322/1904, BOA.

Bey was appointed as principal of the Istanbul Teacher Training School in 1909. Important educators such as Hamdullah Suphi, Ruşen Eşref, Tevfik Fikret, Muallim Cevdet, İsmail Hakkı Baltacıoğlu, Sabri Cemil and Nafi Atuf were appointed. A Practice School under the supervision of the Teacher Training School was opened. Courses studied in the Practice School, developments regarding educational theories and conference proceedings were published in journals of teacher training schools such as *Tedrisat-ı İbtidaiye Mecmuası* (*Journal of Elementary School Instruction*) and *Yeni Mekteb* (*New School*).[14]

In this period, many educators were sent to Europe by the Ministry of Education to make observations. For example, Kazım Nami Duru went to the Austro-Hungarian Empire in 1909; when he returned he opened the Ottoman Empire's first kindergarten, where he practised the Fröbel method. In 1911, he also prepared a kindergarten programme based on the Fröbel method.[15] Between 1910 and 1916, Satı Bey travelled to Italy, Germany, Switzerland, France, Belgium, England and Romania to make educational observations. In these countries he visited open-air schools, child sanatoria and – especially – schools that followed the Montessori method. He was deeply influenced by the thoughts and practices of western New Education. These travels were crucial to the shaping of the Practice School, and later to the shaping of his own New School.

İsmail Hakkı Baltacıoğlu, who was another teacher of the Teacher Training School, was sent to Europe in 1910 to observe pedagogy and manual works courses. He made his observations in Paris over six months at the École normale. He visited Abbotsholme School in England and met Dr. Reddie. Baltacıoğlu built up an important stage in his pedagogical approach with two facts. One of them was Bedale's words, "the New School does not prepare you for life, it makes you live life" and the second one was the real life-based activities that Baltacıoğlu saw in Clayesmore School. Baltacıoğlu's visit to England took away his trust in an intellectualist pedagogical culture and he began to believe in the creative power of a socially active environment in education. Later, Baltacıoğlu met Dr. Decroly and visited his two schools, where he was especially influenced by the agricultural work and methods used to teach history. İsmail Hakkı Baltacıoğlu says he used this part-to-whole method while he was creating the principles of his pedagogy. In Germany, he visited Wald Schule, the school supervised by Herr Seining; while he was creating his own pedagogy principles, he found the arts education provided in the book *Die Redende Hand* considerably useful. When he returned, he gave a detailed report to the Ministry of Education about his observations. While writing his book *Talim ve Terbiyede Inkılâp* (*Reform in Education and Training*) after his visits, he compared Ottoman schools with the schools in Europe and criticised the former. In his *İçtimai Mektep* (*Social School*), he formed a pedagogy that had very comprehensive and original principles. Affected by the observations he made in Europe, he diversified the manual work practices in the Istanbul Teacher Training School. Releasing manual work education from the limits of teacher training, he provided primary schools with manual works and arts lessons. He opened an open-air school in Istanbul based on the ones he saw in France, and he practised his own pedagogical principles in this

---

[14]Cemil Öztürk, *Atatürk Devri Öğretmen Yetiştirme Politikası* (Ankara: Türk Tarih Kurumu, 1996).
[15]İbrahim C. Türk, "Osmanlı Devleti'nde Okul Öncesi Eğitim," *Millî Eğitim* 192 (2011): 160–73.

short-lived school. He based his pedagogy not on educational psychology but on social psychology.[16]

Trips, articles and translations had great importance for the introduction of the New Education to the Ottoman Empire. European educational movements, new schools, pioneer educators and photographs were published in the educational journals of the era.[17] In 1912, Nafi Atuf Kansu summarised and translated Edmond Demolins' *L'Éducation nouvelle: L'École des Roches* into Turkish. Kazım Nami Duru translated *The Kindergarten Guide* and *L'éducation des petits enfants par la méthode frœbélienne*.[18] In 1914, *Practice and Training Lessons with Froebel and Pestalozzi methods* was translated by a member of the Translation Commission of the Ministry of Education, Sami Bey. Translations actually increased during the Republican period.[19] In 1928, the head of the International Bureau of Education in Geneva, Prof. A. Ferrière, came to Turkey to give lectures, opened a branch of the Bureau and, upon the request of the Ministry of Education, wrote a report about the Turkish educational system.[20]

New educational principles were reflected on the curricula of kindergartens, primary schools and teacher training schools in the Second Constitutional Period (1908–1918) and the first years of the Turkish Republic. For example, the 1913 primary school curriculum and the 1914 kindergarten curriculum aimed at providing the feeling of freedom for students as well as the possibility for students to express themselves independently, create their own imaginary world, and adopt an operative approach based on creativity, especially in the practice of language, gym, natural history and living and movement courses.[21]

Through the New Education, the Ottoman Empire had access to a scientific approach to education. A scientific transformation of education in Turkey gained speed as the university students sent to Europe by the Ministry of Education returned to their countries. These educators included Halil Fikret Kanad, the first

---

[16] Ismail H. Baltacıoğlu, *Hayatım* (Ankara: Dünya, 1998).
[17] Examples of these publications include *Terbiye Mecmuası* 1, no. 1 (1330/1914): 40–1; *Terbiye Mecmuası* 1, no. 3 (1330/1914): 118, 129. *Terbiye Mecmuası* 1, no. 4 (1330/1914): 152–3, 160–1, 174–5; Mustafa Rahmi, "İstiklâl Terbiyesi," *Terbiye* 1, no. 1 (1334/1918): 29–32; Necmi, "Çiçekçiğim, Fröbel'den," *Terbiye* 1, no. 2 (1334/1918): 66–8.
[18] Maarif Nezareti Mektubi Kalemi, file 1197/41, date 07 Cemaziyelahir 1332/ 1914, BOA.
[19] Between 1929 and 1938, 247 educational books were published in Turkey. Of these books, 63 were about the New Education and of these, 24 were translations of the pioneers of the New Education movement (11 Decroly, eight A. Ferrière, four Kershensteiner and one Montessori books were translated). For the complete list and content summaries of books published between 1928 and 1938, see Fuat Gündüzalp, *Öğretmen Meslek Kitapları Kılavuzu 1928–1938*, vol. 1 (Ankara: MEB, 1951).
[20] Adolphe Ferrière, *Faal Usuller ve Yeni Türkiye Mektepleri*, trans. M. Baha (Istanbul: Sinan Matbaası, 1932).
[21] For 1914 kindergarten curricula in which New School methods were in the foreground, see Yahya Akyüz, "Anaokullarının Osmanlı'da İlk Programları ve Ders Uygulamaları ile Yaratıcı Dramanın İzleri," *Aklın ve Bilimin Aydınlığında Eğitim Dergisi* 51(2004): 19–24. For detailed primary school programmes between 1913–1926, see Erhan Kanpolat, "Hazırlanışı ve Uygulaması Açısından Osmanlı'dan Cumhuriyet'e İlköğretim Programları (1919–1968)" (master's thesis, Istanbul University, 2005). For detailed information on the conditions, problems and programmes of iptidai schools opened in the Second Constitutional Period, see Betül Batır, *Geleneksel Eğitimden Çağdaş Eğitime Türkiye'de İlköğretim (1908-1924)* (Istanbul: Elif Kitabevi, 2010). For detailed information on the problems of practising and associating the principles of the New School with 1913 and 1914 primary school curriculums, see Şehbâl Deryâ Acar, *Yeni Dünyaya Mukaddime Yeni Okullar* (Istanbul: Akademik Kitaplar, 2012).

educator to receive the title 'doctor of pedagogy', with his thesis on Pestalozzi completed at the University of Leipzig in 1910; Sadrettin Celal Antel, who studied at the École normale between 1911 and 1913; and İbrahim Alaaddin Gövsa, who studied pedagogy and philosophy at the Rousseau Institute, in 1913. After they returned, these students established pedagogy platforms at Istanbul University and at the Ankara Gazi Education Institute. They promoted the adaptation of intelligence tests, teaching of child psychology at university level and the pursuit of large-scale educational research.

As we can see, in the Ottoman Empire, an innovation process in education was being experienced that started with trips to Europe, continued with translations and was put into practice through curricula. Those who started and continued the New Education in the Ottoman Empire were the teachers at the teacher training schools, as was the case in many European countries. These teachers were supported largely by the Ministry of Education of the period in order to support and initiate innovations. The New Education became the medium for the modernisation of education and the sole criterion for the development of the educational system in the Ottoman Empire, and later in the Turkish Republic. The Ministry of Education financed trips to Europe and later made changes in the educational curricula in compliance with reports and suggestions. However, whether or not these renewed curricula were actually implemented is unclear. Moreover, these practices did not reach every part of the country equally.

When we look at the observation trips and translated books, it can be said that Germany, Belgium, the UK and Switzerland acted as the centres in terms of relations with the New Education during the Second Constitutional Period. The United States may also be included in the list, since J. Dewey was invited to Turkey in 1924. For the Ottoman Empire, which was looking for a new identity, a European identity for itself, and which believed in the necessity of educational reformation, practices in these countries and their educational pioneers and books became a roadmap to be studied attentively and eagerly.

The relationship of the Ottoman Empire with the centres of the New Education is a unilateral one, similar to the cases of Brazil, Hungary and Greece.[22] Observation trips and translations always followed a path from the Ottoman Empire to Europe. Ottoman educationalists made great efforts with regard to New Education practices. However, they did not try to transfer their experiences and opinions to the centres, nor did they provide original support to the New Education. Although educators such as Ferrière and Dewey were invited to write reports on the Turkish educational system during the Republican period, the purpose here was to enhance education on a local level.

---

[22]Martin Stauffer, "Reformpädagogik als Umgestaltung Öffentlicher Bildungsinstitutionen: Perspektiven der Brasilianischen Escola Nova," *Paedagogica Historica* 45, no. 4–5 (2009): 535–59; András Németh, "A Chapter in the History of an Ambivalent Relationship. Connection Between the 'New Education Movement' Outside of the Universities and Academic Pedagogy in Hungary," in *Passion, Fusion, Tension: New Education and Educational Sciences*, ed. Rita Hofstetter and Bernard Schneuwly (Bern: Peter Lang, 2006), 169–89; Despina Karakatsani and Vassiliki Théodorou, "Processus d'introduction des principes de l'éducation nouvelle en Grèce au début du 20e siècle: enjeux idéologiques et enjeux de savoir," *Paedagogica Historica* 45, no. 4–5 (2009): 515–33.

A life dedicated to education: Mustafa Satı Bey

Mustafa Satı Bey is one of the most important figures in the strengthening of the relationship between the centres of the New Education movement and the Ottoman educational system. Mustafa Satı Bey was born in 1879 in Yemen. The son of a high-ranking official, he studied political sciences and spoke Arabic, Turkish, French, Greek, Armenian and Persian. He worked as a district governor and taught science and geometry in several Ottoman provinces. He came to Istanbul after the Second Constitutional Period was declared. There, he taught in different educational institutions such as madrasahs and universities and published a number of articles on various areas of social sciences. In 1909, he became the principal of the Istanbul Teacher School (*Darülmuallim*). As the principal of the Teacher School, he opened a Practice School for the teacher candidates to study in a professional and practical environment (1910). He edited the first academic education journal of the Ottoman Empire, *Tedrisat-ı İbtidaiye Mecmuası* (*Journal of Elementary School Instruction*), with other teachers of the Teacher School (1910). At this stage in his career, Satı Bey's ideas on education were reaching large amounts of people through conferences and publications, and he became an authority on education. However, he retired from office in 1912 due to a disagreement with the Minister of Education. He worked as the Principal of Dârüşşafaka, one of the most prestigious high schools of the Ottoman Empire, between 1912 and 1914. Satı Bey edited other important education journals, such as *Terbiye Mecmuası* (*Journal of Education*) from 1914 and *Terbiye* (*Education*) in 1918.

During this complex period, in which discussions on education continued and the First World War increased complications, Satı Bey founded his own school (*the New School*) in 1915. Here he continued to practise his innovative ideas. However, as a result of the First World War, Beirut, Syria and Iraq were separated from the Ottoman Empire as of 1918. As Satı Bey was of Arabic origin, he thought he needed to work in Arabic countries. He left the New School in 1919, refused the position of undersecretary of education for Turkey, and went to Syria. There, he obtained high-ranking positions: he eventually went on to become the Syrian Minister of Education and worked as a professor in universities in Syria, Iraq and Beirut, and continued to publish extensively. He contributed to the formation of the national educational systems in several Arabic countries but his ideas about the adoption of a modern and secular education, independent of religious education, were rejected in Arab countries. He died in Baghdad in 1968.[23]

Satı Bey is the writer of the book *Fenn-i Terbiye* (*Education Science*) (1909), which is acknowledged as the first Ottoman Empire educational book to have been written from a contemporary and positivist point of view. In fact, in the Ottoman Empire, pedagogical books were written to be studied in teacher training schools only from the last quarter of the nineteenth century. Herbert Spencer's *Education; Intellectual, Moral and Physical* (1861) was translated into Turkish in 1897. Spencer's trilogy of intellectual, moral and physical education came to form the

---

[23] For detailed information on Satı Bey's life and ideas on education, see Mustafa Ergün, *İkinci Meşrûtiyet Devrinde Eğitim Hareketleri (1908-1914)* (Ankara: Ocak, 1996); Hilmi Ziya Ülken, *Türkiye'de Çağdaş Düşünce Tarihi* (Istanbul: Ülken Yayınları, 1979); Osman Kafadar and Faruk Öztürk, *Eğitim ve Toplumsal Sorunlar Üzerine Konferanslar: M. Satı Bey* (Ankara: Kültür Bakanlığı, 2002); Şehbal D. Acar, *Eğitimde bir Üstad: Satı Bey'i Tanımak* (Istanbul: Ak, 2009).

topic titles of most of the pedagogy books written in the Ottoman Empire.[24] At the same time, similar to Spencer's opinions, these books emphasised the importance of complete living in which knowledge prepares for life, as well as the centrality of experience over rote learning. The general discourse and the content of the books involve the importance of education and teaching as a profession and the necessity to consider the child's developmental characteristics in education and teaching methods. The knowledge transferred in these books, which were written in the Ottoman Empire at the beginning of the twentieth century, mostly involves philosophical and deductive implications, and they mainly use normative language. Satı Bey also used H. Spencer's trilogy of intellectual, moral and physical education in his book *Fenn-i Terbiye* but, unlike other books, this one has a relatively positivist point of view.

Satı Bey's *Fenn-i Terbiye* does not include a bibliography. However, it can be seen that he reflected the thoughts of both Ottoman and Western thinkers. His book shows that he tried to formulate the traditional moral mentality of the Ottoman in a European manner, similar to other intellectuals of the period. It points to patterns, rules and causalities regarding the development and training of the child. According to *Fenn-i Terbiye*, the purpose of education is to prepare the child for the realities of life, so school should be a reflection of life. Children should have the will to solve their problems on their own.[25]

According to Satı Bey, the root of a qualified education system is a qualified teacher. He believed that the educational reform that could change society should start from primary school, not from university. He pioneered the use of gym, music, manual work, children's literature and observation trips to museums in the education of children.[26] In their courses, Satı Bey and İsmail Hakkı Baltacıoğlu applied the intuitive method, which developed children's questioning and thinking abilities and which they observed during their visits to France. They also published their course samples in education journals. İsmail Hakkı Baltacıoğlu states that this method represented a major revolution for the pedagogy of the Constitutional Period as it demolished the rote learning tradition.[27] Through conferences and publications, Satı Bey announced his innovative educational opinions which opposed the traditional educational approach of the Ottoman Empire, and was confirmed as an authority in shaping the education of the Second Constitutional Period.

Travels to Europe and the ripening of the New School idea

Satı Bey's travels to Europe for educational research were influential in the opening of the New School (1915). Satı Bey travelled extensively to Europe in 1910, 1914 and 1916. He went to Europe for the first time in early 1910, for two months, while principal of the Teacher School. The Ministry of Education assigned him the task of analysing the educational methods and programmes of the elementary schools and teacher schools in Europe and writing a series of reports. He travelled to about 60 schools in Italy, Germany, Switzerland, France, Belgium, England and Romania and

---

[24]Examples of these books include Ayşe Sıdıka Hanım, *Usûl-i Tâlim ve Terbiye Dersleri* (Dersaadet: Alem Matbaası, 1313/1897); Aristokli Efendi, *İlm-i Terbiye-i Etfâl* (Dersaadet: 1907); Fazıl Ahmet, *Terbiyeye Dair* (Dersaadet: Tanin Matbaası, 1326/1910).
[25]Mustafa Gündüz, *Mustafa Satı Bey ve Eğitim Bilimi: Fenn-i Terbiye*, vol. 1–2 (Ankara: Otorite, 2012).
[26]Ibid., 17–20.
[27]Baltacıoğlu, *Hayatım*, 115.

participated in two or three courses in each school. When he returned to Turkey, he talked at conferences and defined the schools in Switzerland as "excellent". However, he decided that methods practised in Belgium could be beneficial in shaping the system of education with a small budget.[28] In his articles, he described his observations of lessons in European schools, as well as the relationship between the student and the teacher.[29] He thought that Europeans had the skills to enjoy activities, whereas in the Ottoman Empire this tendency was restrained due to the pressure applied in Ottoman schools and the "silence and laziness" that subjugated children.[30] He came to the conclusion that European civilization was "developed" not because of a difference in intelligence but because the European environment, atmosphere, social structure, understanding and character were different.[31]

After Satı Bey's resignation from office as the principal of the Teacher School, he made a four-month trip to Europe, in July 1914, to observe educational institutions. According to information he gave to a newspaper, he visited child sanatoria, open-air schools and vacation colonies in Germany and Austria. He wanted to improve his knowledge by specifically analysing the schools practising the Montessori method, and by observing the effects of this method on children. Thus, after observing different institutions practising the method, he went to visit Rome to see the original institution.[32] Afer this trip, Satı Bey went to Europe once again in 1916 to study schools in Switzerland.[33] Satı Bey's travels to Europe, especially the visit in 1914, were influential in the choice of educational methods for his New School, which he would open the following year.

Establishment of the New School

While the New School in Istanbul was being established and after it was founded, major journals and newspapers dedicated papers and reports to it, and a notice about the opening of the school appeared in *İçtihad*.[34] After the opening, news about the school appeared in *Servet-i Fünun*. These were the positivist and western magazines that represented the new ideological movements in the Ottoman Empire.[35] *Servet-i Fünun* in particular gave considerable praise to the New School and introduced information and photographs of the school's educational methods in an advertisement-like style. Pointing out Satı Bey's expertise in educational sciences and his grasp of educational methods, the magazine stated that the New School was the long and heartily awaited scientific institution that the country needed and which the innovation and improvement period deserved.[36] Undoubtedly, Satı Bey's New School was strongly supported by the intelligentsia who adopted the western point of view.

---

[28]Satı Bey, *Sabah*, May 17, 1910; "Mektepler ve Ahval-i İçtimaiye," *Tedrisat-ı İbtidaiye Mecmuası* 7 (1326/1910): 1–10.
[29]Satı, "İsviçre'de Bir Ders," *Tedrisat-ı İbtidaiye Mecmuası* 7 (1326/1910): 26–9.
[30]Satı, "Faaliyet Zevki," *Terbiye Mecmuası* 1 (1330/ 1914): 2–6.
[31]Satı, "Çocuklarımızın Zekası," *Yeni Mekteb* (1327/1912). Quoted in Kafadar and Öztürk, *Eğitim ve Toplumsal Sorunlar*, 33–43.
[32]Satı, "Talim ve Terbiye Hakkında bir Fenn-i Terbiye Mütahassısı ile Hasbıhal," *Sabah*, June 18, 1330/ 1914.
[33]Maarif Nezareti Mektubi Kalemi, file 1216/28, date 21 Recep 1334/ 1916, BOA.
[34]"Yeni Mektep," *İctihad* 127, Kânûn-i sâni 30, 1330/1915, 477–8.
[35]Ülken, *Türkiye'de Çağdaş Düşünce Tarihi*, 135; Ergün, *İkinci Meşrûtiyet*, 50.
[36]"Yeni Mekteb," *Servet-i Fünun* 317, June 30, 1331/1915, daily edition.

Indeed, Satı Bey got the best support from one of the most renowned educators and poets of the time, Tevfik Fikret (1867–1915), who also supported the idea of western, personalized and enterprising education, just like Satı Bey himself. Tevfik Fikret also made an attempt to open a New School but failed due to financial problems, although he had determined the principles of the school.[37] Satı Bey's foundation of the New School can thus be defined as Tevfik Fikret's dream come true. Satı Bey confessed, after the death of Tevfik Fikret in 1915, that they had both adopted similar educational principles and had long conversations during the establishment of the New School.[38] Tevfik Fikret published *Şermin,* one of the first and most important works in Turkish child literature, in which he included a footnote dedicating a poem to children of the kindergarten of Satı Bey's New School.[39]

Another supporter of Satı Bey was Tevfik Efendi, who opened the private Feyziye Elementary School in Salonika in 1885; this school rapidly became an important institution known for the quality of its education. However, when the population migrating from Salonika to Istanbul increased, the Committee of Feyziye School decided to open a school in Istanbul similar to the one in Salonika. The committee, presided over by Tevfik Efendi, had heard that Satı Bey was considering opening a school that would practise new methods of education, and it was decided that they would establish the school together.[40] Agreements were made and duties were set: the principal of the New School was Satı Bey, while the founder of Salonika Feyziye School, Tevfik Efendi, was the head of the administrative committee.[41] Nakkiye Hanım, who would later be one of the first members of parliament in the early years of the Turkish Republic, was the second principal.[42]

Characteristics of the New School

Satı Bey doubtlessly established the New School with influence from the New School movement in Europe. Adolphe Ferrière explained the characteristics of the New School through 30 items; one stated that the New School should be established in the country, in the child's natural environment.[43] Satı Bey's New School was situated in the large and airy garden of Bekir Efendi Konağı in the centre of Beyazıt, a district of Istanbul, for two years.[44] Satı Bey left Feyziye in 1917 and transferred the New School to Hacı Said Bey's mansion in Nişantaşi Teşvikiye, which made female attendance particularly easy.[45] Photographs of these two mansions show the gardens were considerably sized and that children conducted some of their activities in the open air (see Figures 1 and 2).

---

[37] Cahit Kavcar, "Tevfik Fikret'in Eğitimciliği ve Yeni Mekteb," *Ankara Üniversitesi Eğitim Fakültesi Dergisi* 5, no. 3–4 (1972): 111–36.
[38] Satı, "Fikret ve Terbiye," *Muallim* 2, no. 14 (1333/1917): 427–9.
[39] Tevfik Fikret, *Şermin* (Istanbul: Kanâ'at Matba'a ve Kitâphânesi, 1330/1914). Verse from the poem dedicated to the kindergarten students includes: "Come on, go to your school little kid/It is the house of skills/It is the house virtue/Your thoughts will wake up there/Your wings will open there/You will fly high".
[40] Mert Sandalcı, *Feyz-i Sıbyan'dan Işık'a Feyziye Mektepleri* (Istanbul: Feyziye Mektebleri Vakfı, 2005), 112.
[41] "Yeni Mekteb," *Servet-i Fünun* 317.
[42] Sandalcı, *Feyz-i Sıbyan'dan,* 112.
[43] Ahmet Hikmet, *Yeni Mektep Nedir* (Istanbul: Devlet Matbaası, 1932).
[44] "Yeni Mekteb," *Servet-i Fünun* 317; "Yeni Mekteb," *İctihad* 127.
[45] "Yeni Mekteb," *Muallim* 2, no. 14 (1333/1917): 415.

Figure 1 "Yeni Mekteb." Source: *Servet-i Fünûn* 1257, July 02, 1331/1915: 156–7, weekly edition.

When the school opened, it consisted of a kindergarten for children under the age of seven, an elementary school and a nursery teacher school. On September 1918, the school added a girls' high school to its body.[46] The New School was primarily a girls' school but boys under the age of eight were also accepted.[47] As

---

[46]"Yeni Mekteb," *Servet-i Fünun* 317; "Yeni Mekteb Tevsigen Açılıyor," *Muallim* 2, no. 24 (1334 /1918): 843.
[47]Sandalcı, *Feyz-i Sıbyan'dan*, 113.

Figure 2 "Yeni Mekteb." Source: *Servet-i Fünun* 317, June 30, 1331/1915, daily edition.

attempts regarding the education of girls were considerably limited, the school occupied an important position given its services to the schooling of female pupils.

The New School was a private institution charging a tuition fee. Educators of the time criticised the school on the grounds that it only provided education for children of high-income families.[48] The annual fee for kindergarten students was 12 Lira and the fee for elementary school and the special class was 18 Lira, including lunch. The fee for the boarding school was determined to be 40 Lira.[49] However, Satı Bey considered this school a laboratory of practical pedagogy, and not a house for commerce. He shared Ferrière's view that the New School should be a laboratory of applied pedagogy.

According to Satı Bey, private schools might not be a remedy for the Ottoman Empire's lack of schools, but they could be beneficial to solve many of the problems related to schools and education. He thought that the official education organism was a tremendous machine; making elaborate regulations in one of the wheels of this machine would be difficult and making big changes would be dangerous. Private schools, however, did not trigger these difficulties and disadvantages.[50] As a matter of fact, Satı Bey used the school as a pedagogical laboratory, and in his articles he mentioned his practices and experiments. For instance, in one of his articles he gave examples from C. G. Jung's experiments and mentioned experimental studies regarding the suggestion method in classes of 14 students, as well as describing the importance of inspiration in education.[51]

Practices in the New School

Many established methods were taken as examples in the New School's kindergarten, particularly the Fröbel and Montessori methods, which Satı Bey considered primarily in the education of children under the age of seven. As he put it, the New School's kindergarten was not an imitation of the French *École maternelle*, the German *Kindergarten* or the Italian *Casa dei Bambini*. Research on the psychology of children and the latest studies were all taken into account and the theoretical principles as well as materials from the Fröbel and Montessori methods were combined in the school's method. Here, Satı Bey mentioned that the school formed a synthesis by integrating the methods with the eastern culture and its morals, needs and psychology.[52]

Before Satı Bey travelled to Europe in 1914, he gave an interview to a newspaper about the principles of the Montessori method. He stated that in order to improve the intelligence and understanding of the children, this method avoided any kind of limitation; its development was unchained, and the point of the method was

---

[48]İbrahim Alaaddin, "Ana Mektepleri – Çocuk Bahçeleri," *Tedrisat Mecmuası* 10, no. 51 (1919–1920): 444.
[49]"Yeni Mektep," *İctihad* 127. In order to understand the level of school fees, official pensions of the period can be used as a measure. For example, in 1915 the principal of the Makriköy Numune Mektebi took 150 liras, whereas the pensions for teachers varied between 40 and 100 liras (Maarif Nezareti Istanbul Maarif Kalemi Evrakı, file 53/47 date Safer 25, 1333/1915, BOA). Pensions of principals and teachers of Feriköy Numune mektebi varied between 20 and 100 liras (Maarif Nezareti Istanbul Maarif Kalemi Evrakı, file 53/77, date Safer 29, 1333/1915, BOA).
[50]"Mektebsizlik," *Terbiye* 1, no. 3 (1334/1918): 118–20. There is no information about the author of this article published in the *Terbiye* journal. However, as Satı Bey was the founder and the editor of this journal, it most probably was him.
[51]Satı, "Telkin ve Terbiye I," *Muallim* 1, no. 3 (1332/1916): 71–4; "Terbiye ve Telkin II," *Muallim* 1, no. 6 (1332/1916): 161–5.
[52]"Yeni Mekteb," *Servet-i Fünûn* 1257, July 2, 1331/1915: 156–7, weekly edition; "Yeni Mektep," *İctihad* 127.

to improve children's abilities by using the necessary materials. Montessori developed materials to improve the intelligence and comprehension of children. In keeping children busy with these materials, their growth is supported mentally and morally through their own determination, through stimulated curiosity and enthusiasm and according to their own interests and desires. Satı Bey had some concerns about the practice of the Montessori Method in the Ottoman Empire. He evaluated this method starting from the environmental effects on the student, the needs of the children and the habits transferred to the child through social heritage. He noted that, materials of this method that have been considerably beneficial in other countries or environments, would be taken as toys by the students rather than helpful instruments for mental activities when used within the existing environmental conditions of Ottoman schools. This would capture the child's attention in the completely opposite way, restricting her/him to playing merely with toys and resulting in handicapped development.[53] He argued that copying Europe in educational matters would be damaging, and that the system of every country should be analysed; in the selection of a model, priority must be given to one that is compatible with Ottoman society, precisely because education is tightly related to society.[54]

Satı Bey's travels, especially those to the Montessori schools in 1914, did not resolve his doubts about the practice of the method in the Ottoman Empire. He made a comparison between the Montessori and the Fröbel methods: he stated that in Fröbel's time, since psychology was not regarded as a science and since children's psychology was not understood, there were major deficiencies in the initial and older forms of Fröbel's method. He stated further that the unfavourable items in the Fröbel method should be eliminated and the form called "the mature Fröbel method" by the Belgians should be taken into account. According to Satı Bey, there were deficiencies and superiorities in each of the methods.[55]

Satı Bey stated that he did not regard any of the methods as completely superior to the others in terms of their principles. In terms of materials, the Montessori method is successful in basic educative principles and more scientific and effective with respect to sensory education. Nevertheless, it is unlikely to meet children's need to imitate and create. He said the activities of Fröbel would be beneficial in terms of imitating and creating, if practiced within the confines of the principles recommended by Montessori.[56] For Satı Bey, the Fröbel method was stronger for strengthening the social abilities, whereas the Montessori method seemed to be more efficient in increasing entrepreneurial skills. According to Satı Bey, being content with providing the necessary environment for the children to improve themselves would not be effective within the environment of the Ottoman Empire. He justified his idea by emphasising that the educational system of the Empire was stereotyping and altering children's natural tendencies on such a scale that leaving the children to their own devices would not be sufficient. Thus, the Ottoman children needed to be stimulated and directed by instruments to get rid of the drowsiness and laziness originating from the educational system. However, these instruments had to be chosen and organised in such a way to avoid paralysing the children's characters and

---

[53] Satı, "Talim ve Terbiye Hakkında."
[54] Satı, *Layihalarım* (Istanbul: Matbaa-i Hayriye, 1326/1910): 57; quoted in Ergün, *İkinci Meşrûtiyet*, 182.
[55] "Yeni Mekteb," *Servet-i Fünûn* 1257.
[56] Ibid.

entrepreneurial skills. Here, Satı Bey argues, the principles of Montessori should be taken into account.[57] As we can see, he tried to create a synthesis of the practices of Fröbel and Montessori in the kindergarten, paying attention to the characteristics of the Ottoman educational system.

With the expression "mature Fröbel method", Satı Bey is presumably referencing the revolutionary Froebelianism movement that started in the twentieth century. Based on rational knowledge, the Fröbel method was dominant for a long time, especially in the education of younger children. However, positivist and empiricist child studies led by Hall and Montessori in the twentieth century transformed the educational understanding and materials of the Fröbel method. The emphasis was on less schooling, less adult supervision and more opportunities for individual and creative activities. Here, Montessori's positivist opinions, which set out a belief in the perfection of humankind through external observation, evaluation and experiments, were prioritized. Thus, the new Fröbel method and the practices of Montessori represent an epistemological turn from rationalism to empiricism in terms of child-oriented knowledge.[58] Although Satı Bey analysed the differences of the Fröbel and Montessori methods, his writings do not make very apparent the extent to which he was aware of the epistemological break behind these differences. He was rather focused on the practice of this knowledge.

In light of the information given above, according to Hofstetter and Schneuwly's distinction of *practical reformers*, *practitioners* and *theorists*, Satı Bey can be positioned somewhere between the *practical reformers* and the *practitioners*. Indeed, in his New School and Teacher Training School, Satı Bey was concerned with the New Education both on an administrative and operative level. He was the leader of the reformation movement conducted in the Ottoman educational discourse and system via teacher training. His baseline for the educational activities in his own school was based on the principles of the New Education. Satı Bey usually took a positivist approach and we know that he used observations in his lessons. However, his observations were not on a sufficient level to create a systematic theory. Instead they remained an Ottoman adaptation of what had been brought from Europe.

Conclusion

In the Ottoman Empire, especially during the Second Constitutional Period (1908–1918), there was a great interest in educational matters that undeniably focused on creating a new type of individual at a key period in Turkish history. On the one hand, educational developments that focused on the western child were followed with great enthusiasm; on the other, there was an effort to protect traditional values. As in other peripheries, the New Education movement in the Ottoman Empire found its first supporters in the teacher training institutions. The concepts and discourse of the New Education movement reached large masses of teachers through seminars, conferences and publications on teacher training. New Education practices in peripheries started mainly by translating the books and articles produced in centres and by following and observing the pioneers of the movement. Practices and concepts of

---

[57]Ibid.
[58]Kevin J. Brehony, "Transforming Theories of Childhood and Early Childhood Education: Child Study and the Empirical Assault on Froebelian Rationalism," *Paedagogica Historica* 45, no. 4–5 (2009): 585–604.

the New Education from centres were adapted to the peripheries; however, experiences and opinions of the peripheries were usually not shared with the centres. Thus, the peripheries' contributions to the New Education were limited to their own geography. In this respect, the practices of representatives of the New Education in the Ottoman Empire are regarded as similar to those of Lourenço Filho and Azevedo, two prominent figures in reformation pedagogy. But their contributions to the centres of the New Education could not reach the level of Obara Koniyoshi's contributions to the New Education in Europe.[59]

Satı Bey's extraordinary attempts to circulate the ideas of the New Education within Ottoman teacher training institutions and schools suggests that he stands somewhere between *practical reformer* and *practitioner*. Satı Bey's New Education practices were not aimed at testing or developing a specific theory; they were applied in an eclectic manner, by taking the best qualities of different practices. Satı Bey shared his observations and practices on the New Education through his articles and conferences with all students and teachers of the teaching schools in the large Ottoman Empire. His mediating role between Europe and the New Education movement on the one hand, and the Ottoman Empire on the other, came to an end when he went to Syria in 1919. He not only worked for the formation of the national educational system in several Arabic countries; he also spread new and modern educational ideas through his publications. Thus, his role as mediator in the Ottoman Empire continued in Syria, Iraq and Beirut after 1919, but in a smaller geographical area.

Acknowledgement

This work was supported by the Scientific Research Projects Coordination Unit of Istanbul University [Project number UDP-24028].

---

[59] The schools of Obara, who was regarded as the founder of Japanese reform pedagogy and the Pestalozzi of Japan, were visited by German pedagogues and had an effect on physical training in Europe as part of training the willpower. For detailed information, see: Toshiko Ito, "Reformpädagogik aus dem Osten? Körperauffassung und Körpererziehung" *Paedagogica Historica* 42, no. 1–2 (2006): 93–107; Margaret Mehl, "Lessons from History? Obara Kuniyoshi (1877–1987), New Education and the Role of Japan's Educational Traditions," *History of Education* 38, no. 4 (2009): 525–43.

Condescension and critical sympathy: Historians of education on progressive education in the United States and England

William G. Wraga

College of Education, University of Georgia, Athens, USA

> Although progressive education was an international phenomenon, historical interpretations of it may be affected on the national level by academic and institutional contingencies. An analysis of how US and English historians of education interpret progressive education reforms in their respective countries identified a strain of condescension toward progressive education in history of education scholarship in the US, which often resulted in misrepresentations of the historical record. English historians of education tend to regard progressive education with critical sympathy. These findings are possibly explained by different institutional and academic circumstances of historians of education in England and the US.

Progressive education is widely understood as an international phenomenon. While histories of the origins, exchange, dissemination and adaptation of "new education" ideas and practices are readily available, historiographical comparisons of academic interpretations of progressive education are rare but potentially useful for understanding progressivism.[1] This article reports the findings of an analysis of interpretations of progressive education advanced by US and English education historians, and then speculates as to why differences of interpretation exist. The findings are summarised by describing how historians of education in each country represent major progressive education reform reports, significant progressive education practices and criticisms of progressive education.

Such a comparative analysis of course has its limitations. Progressive education in England and the US, while sharing some characteristics, clearly occurred under significantly different sociopolitical circumstances in the midst of different historical conditions and in the context of different traditions of educational priorities and practices, and assumed unique forms. Additionally, history of education scholarship in the two countries occurred in different contexts. The summary analysis that

---

[1] For example, Hermann Rohrs and Volker Lenhart, eds. *Progressive Education Across the Continents: A Handbook* (Frankfurt am Main: Peter Lang, 1995); Maria del Mar del Pozo Andres, "The transnational and national dimensions of pedagogical ideas: The case of the project method, 1918–1939", *Paedagogica Historica* 45 (2009): 561–84.

follows, which is limited to major books published in each country, is not exhaustive but, hopefully, is representative.

This analysis identified a strain of condescension toward progressive education in history of education scholarship in the US, which often resulted in misrepresentations of the historical record. English historians of education seem relatively sympathetic, though not uncritical, of progressive education. This difference in interpretation of progressivism in education may be explained by the different professional and academic circumstances of historians of education in England and the US. Transfer of historical interpretations of progressive education between historians of education in the US and England appears to have been minimal, if it occurred at all. More nuanced and accurate interpretations of progressive education perhaps may be achieved by facilitating exchange between historians of education in the US and England.

Progressive education in histories of education

This discussion focuses on scholarship conducted after 1960 in the US and mostly after 1970 in England, when the field of history of education in each country was considered to be coming into its own. Space limitations prevent presentation of a detailed discussion of each book that was analysed for this study. To illustrate the strain of condescension toward progressive education in history of education scholarship in the US, and to juxtapose it with the critical sympathy with which historians of education in England treat progressive education in that country, this section presents notable examples of how historians in each country represent education reform reports, progressive practices and criticisms of progressive education.[2]

Education reform reports

A tendency exists in history of education research in the US to present noted reform reports that advocated progressive practices negatively and to present those that advocated traditional academic curriculum reforms positively. Krug depicted the recommendations of the Commission on the Reorganization of Secondary Education negatively as advocating fitting students into society, rather than as a vision of educating all students for democratic living, and defended the traditionalist report of the Committee of Ten.[3] Powell et al., using scare quotes, reduced the recommendations in the *Cardinal Principles* report to an effort to make "the curriculum of secondary

---

[2]The analysis excludes consideration of the so-called "revisionist" historians in the US because their work was inherently critical.

[3]Edward A. Krug, *The Shaping of the American High School, 1880–1920* (Madison, WI: University of Wisconsin Press, 1964), 379, 381, 387, 400–402, 392–393. Also see Theodore R. Sizer, *Secondary Schools at the Turn of the Century* (Westport, CT: Greenwood Press, 1964), 132, 197, 201. Cf. Commission on the Reorganization of Secondary Education, *Cardinal Principles of Secondary Education,* Bulletin 1918, No. 35, Department of the Interior, Bureau of Education (Washington, DC: US Government Printing Office, 1918), 9; William G. Wraga, "A progressive legacy squandered: The *Cardinal Principles* report reconsidered", *History of Education Quarterly* 41 (2001): 494–519. See *Report of the Committee on Secondary School Studies* (Washington, DC: US Government Printing Office, 1893).

schools easier and more practical", as they provided a favourable treatment of the recommendations of the Committee of Ten.[4]

Kliebard presented a favourable representation of the recommendations of the Committee of Ten, neglecting to indicate the committee's condonation of an exclusive secondary school. He maintained that Clarence Kingsley "was to engineer, almost single-handedly" the *Cardinal Principles* report, noted that the report endorsed the comprehensive high school and highlighted the seven aims of education articulated by the commission. He suggested that the *Cardinal Principles* report reflected a "growing belligerence toward academic subjects through the ascendance of social efficiency", acknowledging also that the *Cardinal Principles* report represented a "moderate" statement of such.[5]

Herbst endorsed the traditional academic curriculum proposals of the Yale Report and the Committee of Ten, and embraced them as the curriculum of his ideal "people's college", an institution that offered a single academic curriculum to all students and that enjoyed its hey day around the middle of the nineteenth century in the US. Herbst regarded the urban "people's college" as "the American counterpart to the German *gymnasium*, the French *lycee*, and the English endowed grammar school".[6] Herbst identified Clarence Kingsley as the sole author of the *Cardinal Principles* report and, though acknowledging its democratic rhetoric, identified the report with a commitment to social efficiency. He concluded his analysis of the commission's recommendations by depicting the "ambitious vision" of the unifying function of the comprehensive high school – the feature that set it apart from the exclusive nineteenth-century US high school as well as from forms of secondary education in Europe – as "to serve as catch basin for all youth of high school age" and "to thrive as a compulsory educational monopoly in the hands of the public schoolmen". Herbst even seemed to attempt to discredit the commission by indicating that it included only a single woman and no representatives of racial or ethnic minorities in its membership, though he made no such observation of the Committee of Ten, nor of the Yale Report.[7]

Angus and Mirel favourably represented recommendations of the Committee of Ten, characterising its four-track college-preparatory curriculum as a "vision of equal

---

[4]Arthur G. Powell, Eleanor Farrar and David K. Cohen, *The Shopping Mall High School: Winners and Losers in the Educational Marketplace* (Boston, MA: Houghton Mifflin, 1985), 256, 347, note 91; also see Robert L. Hampel, *The Last Little Citadel: American High Schools Since 1940* (Boston, MA: Houghton Mifflin, 1986), x.

[5]Herbert M. Kliebard, *The Struggle for the American Curriculum, 1893–1958* (Boston, MA: Routledge and Kegan Paul, 1986), 112, 114. Kliebard later reinforced this interpretation; see Herbert M. Kliebard, *Schooled to Work: Vocationalism and the American Curriculum, 1876–1946* (New York: Teachers College Press, 1999), 143, 147, 154–155. Cf. *Report of the Committee on Secondary School Studies*, 51; Commission on the Reorganization, *Cardinal Principles*, 27–28; Wraga, "A progressive legacy squandered"; Thomas D. Snyder and Charlene M. Hoffman, *Digest of Education Statistics 2002*, National Center for Education Statistics (Washington, DC: US Government Printing Office, 2003), 69; Susan B. Carter et al., eds. *Historical Statistics of the United States: Earliest Times to the Present*, Millennial Edition, vol. 2, part B, Work and Welfare (Cambridge: Cambridge University Press, 2006), 2-421.

[6]Jurgen Herbst, *The Once and Future School: Three Hundred and Fifty Years of American Secondary Education* (New York: Routledge, 1996), 51; Committee of the Corporation and Academical Faculty, *Reports on the Course of Instruction in Yale College* (New Haven, CT: Hezekiah Howe, 1828).

[7]Herbst, *The Once and Future School*, 156, 142.

educational opportunity", though they neglected to note, even by editing a passage quoted from the 1893 report, that the committee condoned the high school serving a very small proportion of the adolescent population. They viewed the *Cardinal Principles* report as an early volley in the attack on academic subject matter, claiming erroneously that the report "made no reference to subjects or their arrangement into curricula". They suggested that the main contribution of the *Cardinal Principles* report was to promote "the ideas and ultimately the interests of professional educators even further".[8]

Ravitch also considered the recommendations of the Committee of Ten to be more egalitarian and educative than the recommendations of the Commission on the Reorganization of Secondary Education. She accomplished this, however, by claiming that the Ten recommended "[t]hat all children should receive an academic education", when in fact the recommendation was for all *students* to receive an academic education; at the time, high school enrolments in the US represented about 7% of the adolescent population. Ravitch claimed that for the commission "the academic component of schooling had been an afterthought" and characterised the report as "social efficiency with a vengeance".[9]

Reese recapitulated the false claim that Clarence Kingsley was the main author of the *Cardinal Principles* report, criticised the report for being "suffused with anti-academic rhetoric", suggested that Kingsley "skillfully blended themes of social efficiency and democracy" neglecting to elaborate on the latter, and characterised the principles of secondary education advanced by the commission merely as "comforting ideals".[10] Urban and Wagoner devoted more attention to describing the recommendations of the Committee of Ten than to the recommendations of the *Cardinal Principles* report, also neglecting to note the small proportion of adolescents who attended secondary school in the US. They identified the comprehensive high school exclusively with social efficiency, which they characterised as seeing the "high school's role as preparing its students for their adult lives" by "identifying the strengths and weaknesses of students and then fitting the students into appropriate social and vocational roles", though the commission advocated no such role for the school.[11]

In comparison, English historians of education are critical of yet sympathetic toward major reform reports that advocated progressive education principles and practices in England, particularly the Plowden report. Beginning with the Hadow

---

[8]David L. Angus and Jeffrey E. Mirel, *The Failed Promise of the American High School, 1890–1995* (New York: Teachers College Press, 1999), 15, 10, 15, 16. See quote on 10; cf. *Report of the Committee on Secondary School Studies*, 51. For mention of academic subjects in the *Cardinal Principles* report, see Commission on the Reorganization, *Cardinal Principles*, 12, 14, 15, 20, 22, 23, and esp. 27–28 and the footnote on 18.
[9]Diane Ravitch, *Left Back: A Century of Failed School Reforms* (New York: Simon & Schuster, 2000), 42, 125; *Report of the Committee on Secondary School Studies*, 51; Snyder and Hoffman, *Digest of Education Statistics 2002*, 69.
[10]William J. Reese, *America's Public Schools: From the Common School to 'No Child Left Behind'* (Baltimore, MD: Johns Hopkins University Press, 2005), 192, 191, 290. Cf. Commission on the Reorganization, *Cardinal Principles*, 9, 14, 27–28, 21.
[11]Wayne Urban and Jennings Wagoner, *American Education: A History*, 4th edn. (New York: Routledge, 2009), 235–237, 272. Cf. Commission on the Reorganization, *Cardinal Principles*, 9, 10.

report, Armytage characterised it as a "major breakthrough" in expanding the reach of secondary school attendance.[12] Selleck characterised acceptance of education as social control in the Hadow reports not as an educational tragedy but as a sociopolitical reality. He explained *The Education of the Adolescent* in the context of growing post-First World War concerns about the failure of the existing provision for secondary education to harness and foster talent in service of society. Selleck recognised that this represented a "view of the education system as a means of social control, especially as a means of conserving and directing the resources of the nation". Selleck presented this view as reflective of the era without disparaging it.[13]

Dearden's analysis of the Plowden report described shortcomings and criticism of progressive education, but without condemning it. Dearden clarified that the Plowden report "saw what was happening in the 1960s as the fulfillment of Hadow rather than something totally novel" and noted also that middle schools were not a novel recommendation of Plowden but an endorsement of Circular 10/65 recommendations. Yet Dearden also summarised Bennett's findings to the effect that the Plowden philosophy of fostering the development of children's interests through teacher guided, integrated activities was neither widely practised nor demonstrably effective. Dearden criticised a passage quoted from the Plowden report on fitting students into society not as a manifestation of social efficiency-social control, but for its inconsistency in relation to other goals of child-centred education. Dearden concluded "that both theoretical and practical objections to Plowden would account for much of the reluctance to adopt its prescriptions in anything like their pure form". Dearden's analysis sought to correct misrepresentations of the report, but also to represent its shortcomings in an academically critical fashion.[14]

Cunningham considered what amounted to propagandistic aspects of Plowden as an established policy strategy rather than as an indictment of progressive educators. He recognised the report's "wide-ranging significance as a policy study and a work of empirical research". He reported thoroughly dissatisfaction with, dissent from and criticism of Plowden without misrepresenting the report. He seemed favourably disposed toward the Plowden initiative.[15]

Jones accurately summarised the central proposals of the Plowden report, as well as of similar reports about primary education issued in Wales and Scotland, and reviewed academic criticisms of them. Jones concluded that these "three reports took the ideas developed by progressive educators over the previous century to the height of their influence". Yet he also observed that these reports manifested the "influence" that professional educators enjoyed in a still decentralised system of education. Jones attributed Plowden's subsequent disfavour to its de-emphasis of consideration of the role of schooling in social and economic development. Like

---

[12]W.H.G. Armytage, *Four Hundred Years of English Education* (Cambridge: Cambridge University Press, 1970), 208. See Board of Education (Great Britain) Consultative Committee, *The Education of the Adolescent* (London: His Majesty's Stationary Office, 1926).
[13]R.J.W. Selleck, *English Primary Education and the Progressives, 1914–1939* (London: Routledge, 1972), 135.
[14]R.F. Dearden, "The Plowden philosophy in retrospect", in R. Lowe, ed. *The Changing Primary School* (London: Falmer Press, 1987), 69, 70, 76, 84; Central Advisory Council for Education (England), *Children and their Primary Schools*, vol. 1: The Report (London: Her Majesty's Stationary Office, 1967), 185, par. 494.
[15]Peter Cunningham, *Curriculum Change in the Primary School Since 1945: Dissemination of the Progressive Ideal* (London: Falmer Press, 1988), 155–160, 173; quote from 155.

other English historians of education, Jones treated Plowden accurately and sympathetically.[16]

Progressive education practices

A tendency exists in history of education research in the US to depict progressive education practices negatively by characterising many of them under the banner of social efficiency-social control ideology, notwithstanding their stated goals of personal and civic development. For Krug, the emergence in early twentieth-century US of the doctrine of social efficiency-social control represented the most influential force to shape the American high school. Although he offered the caveat that not all educators accepted this doctrine, Krug detected it in nearly every aspect of school reform, including in the origins of the social studies as a progressive alternative to traditional history instruction, and in efforts to promote teacher participation in curriculum development. He claimed that the latter was not an attempt to democratise expanding school bureaucracies and to professionalise the teaching corps, but rather a cynical effort to compel teachers to accept social efficiency-social control doctrine.[17]

Tyack viewed the practices of so-called administrative progressives as calculated attempts to exploit social efficiency ideology to systematically seize control of the public schools in an act of self-aggrandising careerism that had little if anything to do with any genuine effort to manage the burgeoning system of public education.[18] Tyack and Hansot elaborated this investigation of the professional networking and coalition-building of the administrative progressives in a study of educational leadership. By employing scare quotes around terms such as "science of education", "research" and "scientific" by criticising vocational educators, for example, for exposing poor work conditions and then seeking to improve vocational education instead of work conditions and management–employee relations in the economy at large, to suggesting, "Whatever one actually learned substantively in a graduate program in educational administration, to pay tuition was often to gain the sponsorship of a member of the educational trust, which was as sound an investment as buying a commission in the Czarist army", Tyack and Hansot insinuated into their narrative a discernable condescension toward and even condemnation of administrative progressives.[19]

---

[16]Ken Jones, *Education in Britain, 1944 to the Present* (Cambridge: Polity Press, 2003), 83, 84.

[17]Krug, *Shaping of the American High School*, xi, 354, 325. Also see Kliebard, *Struggle for the American Curriculum*, 89ff. Several recent studies have problematised the evidentiary grounds of the social efficiency-social control interpretation of early twentieth-century school reform in the US. See J. Wesley Null, "Social efficiency splintered: Multiple meanings instead of a hegemony of one", *Journal of Curriculum and Supervision* 19 (2004): 99–124; Michael Knoll, "From Kidd to Dewey: The origin and meaning of social efficiency", *Journal of Curriculum Studies* 41 (2009): 361–391; Thomas D. Fallace, "John Dewey's influence on the origins of the social studies: An analysis of the historiography and new interpretation", *Review of Educational Research* 79 (2009): 601–624; and Thomas Fallace and Victoria Fantozzi, "Was there really a social efficiency doctrine? The uses and abuses of and idea in educational history", *Educational Researcher* 42, no. 3 (April 2013): 142–150.

[18]David Tyack, *The One Best System* (Cambridge, MA: Harvard University Press, 1974), 126–127, 196–197.

[19]David Tyack and Elisabeth Hansot, *Managers of Virtue: Public School Leadership in America, 1820–1980* (New York: Basic Books, 1982), 6–7, 113, 130, 141.

Historians of education in the US also frequently treat the Eight-Year Study and life adjustment education, two progressive initiatives in the US, dismissively. Powell et al. devoted much of their historical analysis of secondary school reform to suggesting that progressive practices were essentially about lowering academic standards. Omitting the Eight-Year Study from their account, they focused on the proposals for life adjustment education Charles Prosser proffered in his 1939 Inglis lecture, implying inaccurately that the life adjustment initiative had begun by that time. Similarly, Hampel suggested that the principal effect and even the intent of progressive education were simply to make school easier. Hampel exaggerated the significance of life adjustment education and used labelling to denigrate it, though he did not cite its principal reports. In these representations, life adjustment education and progressive education served as straw men against which to advocate for more academic-focused reforms.[20]

Kliebard's discussion of the Eight-Year Study associated the core curriculum developed in some participating schools with social efficiency, suggested that curriculum development in the participating schools followed a production metaphor and soft pedalled the success that the graduates enjoyed in college. Kliebard devoted extensive attention to life adjustment education disproportionate to its actual impact in schools, presented it pejoratively as one of numerous "curriculum concoctions" brewing at the time and depicted it as a rejection of subject matter and as another in a line of manifestations of social efficiency in curriculum reform.[21]

Herbst understated findings of the Eight-Year Study by discussing the circumstances at only one of the participating schools and by citing not from the original published reports but from excerpts edited for an anthology. Herbst dismissed life adjustment education, implying that it was a widespread movement, claiming that in life adjustment education, "[a]cademic subject matter became a scorned concept" and suggesting that it represented "the schoolmen's appetite for self-aggrandizement".[22] Angus and Mirel's account ignored the Eight-Year Study, and

---

[20]Powell and others, *Shopping Mall High School*, 274–277; Hampel, *The Last Little Citadel*, 105, 43, 44, 47; also Ravitch, *Left Back*, 331. Charles Allen Prosser, *Secondary Education and Life* (Cambridge, MA: Harvard University Press, 1939). US Office of Education, *Life Adjustment Education for Every Youth*, Bulletin 1951, no. 22, Office of Education, Federal Security Agency (Washington, DC: US Government Printing Office, 1951); US Office of Education, *A Look Ahead in Secondary Education,* Bulletin 1954, no. 4, Office of Education, Federal Security Agency (Washington, DC: US Government Printing Office, 1954). For a comprehensive history of life adjustment education in the US, see Dorothy E. Broder, "Life adjustment education: An historical study of a program of the United States Office of Education, 1945–1954" (PhD thesis, Teachers College, Columbia University, 1977); also see William G. Wraga, "From slogan to anathema: Historical representations of life adjustment education", *American Journal of Education* 116 (2010): 185–209.
[21]Kliebard, *Struggle for the American Curriculum*, 219, 221, 221–222, 242. For curriculum development in the Eight-Year Study, see H.H. Giles, S.P. McCutchen and A.N. Zechiel, *Exploring the Curriculum* (New York: Harper, 1942); *Thirty Schools Tell Their Story* (New York: Harper, 1942). For the follow-up study, see Dean Chamberlin, Enid Straw Chamberlin, Neal E. Drought and William E. Scott, *Did They Succeed in College?* (New York: Harper, 1942). For a comprehensive history of the Eight-Year Study, see Craig Kridel and Robert V. Bullough, Jr., *Stories of the Eight-Year Study: Reexamining Secondary Education in America* (Albany, NY: State University of New York Press, 2007); Broder, "Life adjustment education"; US Office of Education, *Life Adjustment Education*, 12. Also see Kliebard, *Schooled to Work*, 205.
[22]Herbst, *The Once and Future School*, 241 note 12, 178, 177; cf. US Office of Education, *Life Adjustment Education*, 12.

saw in life adjustment education not only a widespread anti-subject matter movement, but also "a dramatic shift in the perceived function of the high school, from an institution commonly associated with increasing social mobility to one deliberately trying to get young people to limit their aspirations and accept menial roles in society".[23]

Reese mentioned the Eight-Year Study only in passing and parenthetically in a single sentence: "Professional journals cited the study approvingly and said it proved that the traditional curriculum, like the concept of mental discipline, lacked any scientific basis." His representation of the life adjustment education initiative was presented through the lens of Arthur Bestor's critique of it, rather than through the language of its advocates.[24] Urban and Wagoner's representation of the Eight-Year Study was characterised by understatement. They suggested that only "several noted colleges and universities" waived normal entrance requirements for the graduates of the participating schools, claimed that the results of the study "showed no measurable difference in college success between graduates of experimental high schools and traditional high schools" and reduced the core curriculum to a focus on "'functional' objectives" and "any attempt to combine studies in two or more academic subjects". They characterised life adjustment education as "another version of the functional curriculum movement [that] can be viewed as another assault in the recurring war on the traditional academic curriculum".[25]

In comparison, English historians of education seem to take pains to present balanced accounts of progressive education practices in England. Armytage's history presented a descriptive, almost matter-of-fact recounting of educational developments in England that included early twentieth-century progressive efforts at the primary level and, during the 1950s and 1960s, comprehensivisation. In each case, he summarised the claims of supporters and the objections of critics.[26] Similarly, Barnard described shortcomings of the tripartite system of secondary education that emerged from the Hadow report and others, presented arguments addressing those shortcomings through comprehensivisation and summarised criticisms of comprehensivisation. He concluded, "It is obvious therefore that the whole situation bristles with difficulties, and equally that determined attempts have been made to deal with them." He nevertheless suggested that it was "undoubtedly advisable" to pursue comprehensivisation, albeit "tentatively".[27]

Selleck explained the impact of war and depression on a movement, "a loosely united band" of education reformers, whose advocacy of mainly child-centred forms of educational experiences during the interwar years earned them the label "progressives". Selleck described early progressive ideas, their educator advocates, schools, methods and associations in a narrative that was at once sympathetic and analytical.

---

[23]Angus and Mirel, *Failed Promise*, 82. Also see Ravitch, *Left Back*, 327ff.
[24]Reese, *America's Public Schools*, 2, 308, 224–225; Arthur E. Bestor, *Educational Wastelands: The Retreat from Learning in Our Public Schools* (Urbana, IL: University of Illinois Press, 1953).
[25]Urban and Wagoner, *American Education*, 307, 307–308, 332. According to Aikin, "Practically all accredited colleges and universities" in the US participated. *Story of the Eight-Year Study*, 12; see Wilford Aikin, *The Story of the Eight-Year Study* (New York: Harper, 1942) 12, 111–112, 113–114, 115.
[26]Armytage, *Four Hundred Years*, 228–2230, 242–243, 260–261.
[27]H.C. Barnard, *A History of English Education, From 1760* (London: University of London Press, 1963), 330. Barnard endorsed the contribution of experimental "progressive" schools, as well (p. 248).

Selleck's candid analysis of the rhetorical tactics of these progressives was critical but neither dismissive nor defensive. Even Selleck's choice of a metaphor for these progressives, "missionaries", could easily be employed pejoratively as a caricature of this group of purported professionals, but Selleck engaged in no such rhetorical flourish. Selleck recognised how the popularisation of progressive ideas resulted in their dilution, and acknowledged the failure of advocates to fulfil these ideals in practice in English primary schools, without pronouncing the movement a failure.[28]

Contributors to Lowes' edited volume on *The Changing Primary School* presented a nuanced and critical but largely sympathetic analysis of progressive practices in English primary schools since 1945. From accounts of efforts to implement progressive practices in Leicestershire to a description of attempts at open-plan schooling, contributors presented shortcomings and criticism of progressive education, but without condemning them. No criticism of progressive education as anti-intellectual or as anti-subject matter appeared.[29]

Although Cunningham criticised the hagiography typical of mid-century progressive advocates in England, referring to it as "a tendency of the progressive movement to make saints", his portraits of "promoters of progressivism" such as Christian Schiller and John Blackie were not uncritical of contradictions in their work but also avoided the extreme of negative biography. In his documentation of the ways in which professional associations, school architecture and even propaganda techniques were employed to promote progressive education, Cunningham identified contradictions in, but nevertheless maintained a relatively sympathetic stance toward, the movement. Cunningham explained that the shifting sociopolitical context of the late 1960s and early 1970s made progressive ideas and practices increasingly inconsistent with and ultimately irrelevant to policy trends. Progressive advocates, though not without faults, were victims, in effect, of cultural forces beyond their control.[30]

To suggest that Simon's representation of progressive education was sympathetic to its ideals would amount to an understatement. Simon recognised that during the post-war period progressive "successes" in primary schools were local and uneven and not as pervasive as the authors of the critical Black Papers later claimed. Yet his account of progressive Tyndale primary school during the 1970s was celebratory. Its teachers "took the bit between their teeth and set out progressively to operate what some interpret as an extreme version of the Plowden Committee's philosophy of 'child-centred' education".[31]

Simon's representation of comprehensivisation was similarly enthusiastic, if not more so. He presented the comprehensive school as a response to growing dissatisfaction with the highly selective system of education in England. He reported a "veritable explosion of grass-roots activity" during the early 1960s to convert existing

---

[28]Selleck, *English Primary Education*, 61, 64ff, 127.
[29]Roy Lowe, ed. *The Changing Primary School* (London: Falmer Press, 1987), 32ff, 50ff.
[30]Cunningham, *Curriculum Change*, 48, 213.
[31]Brian Simon, *Education and the Social Order, 1940–1991* (New York: St Martin's Press, 1991), 380, 444–445, 445; C.B. Cox and A.E. Dyson, *Fight for Education* (London: Critical Quarterly Society, 1969), 6. On the impact of Simon's politics on his scholarship, see Gary McCulloch, "A people's history of education: Brian Simon, the British Communist Party and *Studies in the History of Education, 1780–1870*", *History of Education* 39 (July 2010): 437–457; Gary McCulloch and Tom Woodin, "Learning and liberal education: The case of the Simon Family, 1912–1939", *Oxford Review of Education* 36 (April 2010): 187–201.

secondary schools to comprehensives, noting that grammar school heads were among those most resistant to comprehensivisation. For Simon, the comprehensive high school was not a mechanism of social control, but a means of social levelling that would mitigate class divisions through a non-selective education system. Simon's principal criticism of comprehensivisation was that too often it did not go far enough, that the internal organisation of schools did not reflect its egalitarian ideal or that comprehensives existed alongside grammar schools, which "creamed" the top academic performers from the comprehensives.[32]

Gordon et al. provided straightforward descriptions of progressive practices in primary schools and of the origins and development of comprehensive schools. They offered a sobering analysis of comprehensivisation efforts. Their apparent sympathetic take on the comprehensive school was perhaps indicated when, for example, after summarising divisions between supporters of comprehensivisation who embraced a meritocratic view that sought to capture talent and those who took an egalitarian view that sought to dismantle the class system, they suggested, "Divisions of this kind have not always made it easy to withstand the criticisms of the Right". While Gordon et al. offered a factual description of the deprofessionalisation of teaching in England during the 1980s, which they saw stemming from increased accountability and the rolling back of teacher training requirements, they gave the sense that these developments were problematic.[33]

Jones reported that the enthusiasm of progressive educators between the wars was rediscovered mainly by primary teachers after the Second World War. He noted a "disparity" between the progressive emphasis on the growth of the child through collaborations with classmates and the teacher and government priorities of using education policy to serve shifting economic conditions, but passed no judgement either way. With respect to the comprehensive school, Jones explained the nuances of its reception in Wales, Scotland, England, Ireland and Northern Ireland and provided a candid account of the successes, limitations and subsequent retreat from comprehensivisation, judging it largely against the goals of comprehensive schooling and in the political context of the time.[34]

Lowe analysed the changing nature of teachers' work in England since the Second World War, particularly the ways in which it has been impacted by the imposition of a vast accountability scheme in the form of a national curriculum and "the establishment of testing at ages seven, eleven and fourteen and in the publication of league tables of school performance as well as of the reports on school inspections". Lowe asked, "To what extent has this meant the marginalization, or even ending, of so-called 'progressive' approaches to teaching?" To answer this question, Lowe drew from extant research to reveal the complexities of education reform. His discussion of comprehensive schools included recognition of the limits of their implementation, such as in the fact that early comprehensives were restricted in their comprehensiveness by the reality that they were streamed. Lowe demonstrated a sympathy for progressive reforms that did not soften his analysis of their implementation or effectiveness.[35]

---

[32]Simon, *Education and the Social Order*, 272, 280, 301–302, 348.
[33]Peter Gordon, Richard Aldrich and Dennis Dean, *Education and Policy in England in the Twentieth Century* (London: Woburn Press, 1991), 186, 198, 260–261.
[34]Jones, *Education in Britain*, 54–55, 103.
[35]Roy Lowe, *The Death of Progressive Education: How Teachers Lost Control of the Classroom* (London: Routledge, 2007), 3, 47–48, 59–60.

For Lowe, the accountability regime that both Conservative and Labour governments imposed on teachers and schools has not been a favourable development for progressive education. He closed his analysis with a not so sanguine assessment of the current educational scene and the policies that drive it: "There is a far better experience of childhood, and of schooling, which we might offer to our children. ... I see little prospect of the major redirection of our education system which I believe is needed."[36]

Criticisms of progressive education

A tendency exists in history of education research in the US to accept uncritically popular criticism of public schools and progressive education and even to interpret progressive practices through these criticisms. Sizer, after using scare quotes to question the very existence of "'professional' educators", closed his study with a favourable reference to a resurgence of interest in the Committee of Ten report by advocates of traditional academic curricula from the 1950s, citing progressive education critic John Latimer and the traditionalist Council for Basic Education.[37] Sizer presented an interpretation of the report that resembled the views of conservative school critics of the previous decade. In an effort to reject any reform that did not fit his ideal of the mid-nineteenth century "people's college", Herbst accepted at face value and uncritically every criticism of secondary education in the US that appeared from the end of the Second World War through the 1990s.[38] As noted above, Reese represented life adjustment education through the lens of Arthur Bestor's critique of it, rather than through the language of its advocates.[39] And although Urban and Wagoner concluded that life adjustment education probably had little impact in schools, they nevertheless devoted significant attention to a discussion of Bestor's attacks on the initiative.[40]

In comparison, English historians of education presented critical analyses of the anti-progressive Black Papers and never interpreted progressive practices, such as comprehensivisation and the recommendations of Plowden, through the Black Papers. Gordon et al. summarised the view espoused in the Black Papers that a "climate of permissiveness" spawned in English society during the 1960s was the outcome of progressive practices in primary schools, which had eroded "habits of work and discipline" among children. They then presented the progressive response to the Black Papers, which included evidence that a widespread progressive "revolution" in primary schools had never materialised. Gordon et al. did not seem sympathetic to the conservative critics of progressive education; they seemed impatient with the tactics of conservative critics of the Plowden report and of comprehensives.[41]

---

[36]Ibid., 161.
[37]Sizer, *Secondary Schools*, 201, 206–207; Bestor, *Educational Wastelands*, 105–106; John Latimer, *What's Happened to Our High Schools?* (Washington, DC: Public Affairs Press, 1958); James Koerner, ed. *The Case for Basic Education* (Boston, MA: Little, Brown, 1959).
[38]Herbst, *The Once and Future School*, 179, 198–200, 208.
[39]Reese, *America's Public Schools*, 224. Bestor, *Educational Wastelands*, 81ff.
[40]Urban and Wagoner, *American Education*, 332–335; Bestor, *Educational Wastelands*, 81ff.
[41]Gordon et al., *Education and Policy*, 88–89; Central Advisory Council, *Children*; Cox and Dyson, *Fight for Education*; C.B. Cox and A.E. Dyson, eds. *Black Paper Two* (London: The Critical Quarterly Society, 1970); C.B. Cox and A.E. Dyson, eds. *Goodbye Mr Short* (London: Davis-Poynter, 1971); C.B. Cox and Rhodes Boyson, eds. *Black Paper 1975* (London: Dent & Sons, 1975); C.B. Cox and Rhodes Boyson, eds. *Black Paper 1977* (London: Temple Smith, 1977).

Simon summarised the criticisms of progressive education in the Black Papers, quoting from the first a contention that progressive education was misguided in its abandonment of education for fitting students into society in favour of education for self-development, and then attacked that conservative argument on historical grounds. He demonstrated that the student revolutionaries of the late 1960s who were influenced by progressive education experiences, according to the Black Paper authors, were in fact largely products of unreformed, hierarchical, traditional primary schools. Simon suggested that the first Black Paper, the appearance of which he characterised as having "exploded like a bomb", "is perhaps best seen (and most sympathetically) as a somewhat hysterical response by university teachers to the student upsurge of 1968".[42]

The reader senses in Jones' discussion of the Black Papers an effort to report accurately but also to characterise the source of the vision behind their proposals with just a hint of incredulity, as in: Brian "Cox, likewise, found his reference points in a vanished past, but for him the values created there were recuperable, in a state system purged of progressive influence – to which end his energies for the next ten years were devoted".[43]

Musgrove's chapter analysing the Black Papers in Lowes' edited volume was the most critical contribution to the collection. Musgrove demonstrated that available evidence of student performance in English schools flatly contradicted claims in the Black Papers that educational standards had slipped in recent years, and instead attributed to the Black Papers a certain "moral rectitude". As he bluntly put it, "Black Paper One was a lightweight affair by men who felt no need to produce evidence for the decline they alleged". Musgrove cast the Black Papers as part of a conservative tradition of resisting progressive tendencies, which he characterised as "one of the most powerful and disastrous demodernizing impulses of our age", and which he claimed "keeps us anchored in a past which is now a gigantic irrelevance".[44]

Contexts of history of education scholarship in the US and England

A tendency exists among some historians of education in the US to depict traditional academic curricula positively and progressive education negatively, to misrepresent progressive education by overstating its faults or understating its accomplishments, to accept uncritically criticisms of progressive education, to interpret progressive education through its critics, and even to employ scare quotes and pejorative language when describing progressive education. Together these tendencies comprise a strain of condescension toward progressive education in history of education scholarship in the US. In comparison, English historians of education tend to provide a balanced account of the successes and failures of progressive education, implicitly and explicitly endorse progressive education and provide sharp criticism of conservative critics of progressivism. English historians of education tend to treat

---

[42] Simon, *Education and the Social Order*, 379, 319, 396; Cox and Dyson, *Fight for Education*, 6.
[43] Jones, *Education in Britain*, 103.
[44] Frank Musgrove, "The Black Paper movement", in Roy Lowe, ed. *The Changing Primary School* (London: Falmer Press, 1987), 106, 108, 106, 123; Cox and Dyson, *Fight for Education*.

progressive education with critical sympathy. It is almost as if English historians of education write about progressivism in the style of a White Paper, while some US historians of education tend to write about progressive education more in the style of a Black Paper. A compelling explanation for these dissimilarities in interpretation can be found in the differences in the institutional contexts and the status of the field of history of education in the US and England. Let us first turn to the US scene.

The strain of condescension toward progressive education in history of education scholarship in the US appeared during a definitive period in the life of that field. Cohen reported that the emphasis on serving professional educators established during the early twentieth century by Ellwood Cubberley and Paul Monroe was reinforced during the 1930s by social reconstructionist educators who sought to put the school in the service of resolving social problems. From this context emerged "social foundations of education" as a concerted effort to integrate and apply foundational disciplines, including philosophy, psychology, sociology and history, to prepare professional educators to view the school as a vehicle of social change. By the 1950s this functional role of foundations of education was firmly entrenched in colleges of education in the US. History of education scholarship aimed at contributing to the practical and professional mission of the foundations of education.

From the late 1950s to the late 1960s, however, a series of events effectively revisioned history of education scholarship in the US from serving professional educators to identifying with the academic discipline of history, a change Cohen characterised as the field's "rise to respectability".[45] Lawrence Cremin's scholarship, James Bryant Conant's criticisms of educational foundations courses, the work of the Committee on the Role of Education in American history, which included Bernard Bailyn's interpretation of colonial era education in the US, the reorganisation of the History of Education Society and its journal, and the establishment of Division F of the American Educational Research Association, together turned the focus of the field of history of education in the US away from the professional preparation of educators and toward the academic discipline of history. These developments provided historians of education "an opportunity to reconnect with the rigorous canons of historical scholarship" and enabled them "to renounce the requirement that ... [their] work be immediately relevant" to present-day school practice.[46]

In his analysis of Bailyn's famous interpretation Gaither found not only that Bailyn's claims about progressive era history of education scholarship in the US were unsubstantiated, but also that subsequent research in the history of education in the US failed to act on Bailyn's recommendations. As Gaither summarised, "Just as Bailyn's synthetic ideal and the specific recommendations for achieving it have proved illusory, so his goal of liberating educational historiography from its service to public education has failed." Gaither concluded that, despite the attention it garnered, Bailyn's noted interpretation has in fact enjoyed "a surprisingly limited legacy".[47]

---

[45]Sol Cohen, "The history of American education, 1900–1976: The uses of the past", *Harvard Educational Review* 46 (1976): 324.
[46]Ibid., 325.
[47]Milton Gaither, *American Educational History Revisited: A Critique of Progress* (New York: Teachers College Press, 2003), 163, 161; Bernard Bailyn, *Education in the Forming of American Society: Needs and Opportunities for Study* (New York: Norton, 1960).

Gaither also noted, however, that:

> Bailyn's style in *Education in the Forming of American Society*, to the chagrin of many established professional educators and to the delight of many of his younger readers, was thick with the smirk and sneer of satire. It was this attitude, this pose, that did so much to make his book both engaging reading and the fodder for heated discussion.[48]

Gaither found that Bailyn inherited this style from a certain anti-professional -educator milieu that had been fostered at Harvard by his mentors, academic historians Samuel Eliot Morison and Perry Miller. Moreover, the conference in Williamsburg, Virginia, for which Bailyn prepared his historiographical interpretation, was part of an agenda to shift educator preparation in the US from colleges of education to colleges of arts and sciences. In the anti-professional educator spirit of the times, Bailyn referred, for example, to "a whole generation of passionate crusaders for professionalism in education", who were "not otherwise historians" and who "lacked ... the historian's instinct", but who nevertheless wrote educational history. On their brand of educational history, Bailyn wrote, "the more parochial the subject became, the less capable it was of attracting the kinds of scholars who could give it broad relevance and bring it back into the public domain". Gaither concluded, "Bailyn's immensely influential historiographical critique, then, turns out to be simply a commonplace of Sputnik-era educationist bashing".[49]

Although Bailyn's characterisation of the professional progressive era educational historians as exhibiting "a condescension toward the past that exaggerated the quaintness and unreality of the objects they described" applied also to Bailyn's own interpretation, it also may have validated for educational historians the traditional academic attacks on US progressive education of the 1950s.[50] It may be that Bailyn's essay served as a turning point in history of education scholarship by establishing a precedent for condescension toward progressive education. And it was a prestigious precedent, the recapitulation of which enabled historians of education to distance themselves from their professional educationist predecessors by identifying with academic historians through an emulation of what Gaither referred to as Bailyn's "pose". Not all educational historians in the US joined in this refrain – exceptions included the work of Cremin, Cohen, Tanner and Tanner, Zilversmit and Rury.[51] But its reappearance, usually despite available evidence, makes it a documentable and so far resistant strain of interpretation. Historians of education in the US may not have turned their scholarship completely away from serving professional educators, as Gaither noted, but some turned it against progressive education.

---

[48]Gaither, *American Educational History Revisited*, 143.
[49]Bailyn, *Education in the Forming of American Society*, 8, 10, 9; Gaither, *American Educational History Revisited*, 159.
[50]Bailyn, *Education in the Forming of American Society*, 11–12.
[51]Lawrence A. Cremin, *The Transformation of the School* (New York: Knopf, 1961); Sol Cohen, *Progressive and Urban School Reform: The Public Education Association of New York City, 1895–1954* (New York: Bureau of Publications, Teachers College, Columbia University, 1963); Daniel Tanner and Laurel Tanner, *History of the School Curriculum* (New York: Macmillan, 1990); Arthur Zilversmit, *Changing Schools: Progressive Education Theory and Practice, 1930–1960* (Chicago, IL: University of Chicago Press, 1993); John L. Rury, *Education and Social Change: Themes in the History of American Schooling* (Mahwah, NJ: Lawrence Erlbaum, 2005).

It seems reasonable also to consider whether the bias against progressive education evident in this interpretive strain was influenced by revisionist scholarship in the US. This may be, at least in the case of work conducted after the appearance of revisionist interpretations. Indeed, some non-revisionist historians concede an influence of revisionist work on attention paid to power relations.[52] But sharp criticism of progressives emerged prior to revisionist work and subsequent to Bailyn's. And misrepresentations of the historical record in revisionist interpretations have been corrected.[53] Yet condescension toward progressivism persists, despite the publication of corrective work.

Richardson's discussion of the field of history of education in England since the Second World War may help explain the relatively sympathetic treatment of progressive education by historians of education in England. Richardson documented that history of education first emerged in England not in the so-called ancient universities, but "in younger universities more open to the influence of other emerging disciplines of which psychology was the most important". As a result, during the late nineteenth and early twentieth centuries, history of education research in England was "written by educationists for trainee teachers drawing on philosophy with the purpose of directly linking interest in the educational past with its operation in the present". Like educational psychology, history of education manifested "a liberal, improving intention which promoted and celebrated the spread of state-sponsored education since the mid-nineteenth century and the accompanying rise in the teaching profession". During the interwar years in England institutional confusion and financial retrenchment put a damper on history of education research, while professional historians in academic departments looked down upon departments of education and upon the history of education research conducted there, resulting in a "continuing absence of engagement between educationists and academic historians".[54]

During the late 1950s and 1960s a number of forces created circumstances in both history and education departments in English universities that fostered innovation in historical research methodology. Yet while history departments, especially those at Oxford, Cambridge and London, enjoyed professional autonomy, "colleges and departments of education ... were subject to the judgement of their outcomes by external government Inspectors, had little control over the student numbers allocated to them by government ... and were plagued with uncertainty over standards".[55] Moreover, historians of education were largely ignored by academic historians, leaving them isolated in their academic units. During the late 1960s, academic historians in England reproduced the attacks on history of education that had occurred a decade earlier in the US. Partly as a result of these attacks, but also in spite of them, history of education research in England became more robust both in history departments and education departments. By the early 1970s it seemed possible that some kind of collaboration could emerge between academic and educational historians. However, "the chasm which lay between the historians and the educationists remained as wide as ever in terms of professional lifestyle and academic status", and

---

[52]Tyack, *The One Best System*.
[53]William J. Reese and John L. Rury, eds. *Rethinking the History of American Education* (New York: Palgrave Macmillan, 2008).
[54]William Richardson, "Historians and educationists: The history of education as a field of study in post-war England. Part I: 1945–72", *History of Education* 28 (1999): 2, 5, 3.
[55]Ibid., 8.

such collaboration was not to materialise.[56] Richardson reported that condescension toward educationist historians of education continued through the 1980s and 1990s.[57]

It seems, then, that historians of education in the US had more interest and even success in identifying with academic historians than did historians of education in education departments in England. In response to criticisms of their work from academic historians, historians of education in the US were more inclined to emulate critics of progressive education, such as Bestor and Bailyn, than were historians of education in education departments in England. Although the affiliations of historians of education in the US continued largely to be in colleges of education, their aspiration was to be identified with academic historians in arts and science departments, or at least with their work. English historians of education seem to have experienced more disdain and distance from academic historians and, with it seems little if any chance of impressing academic historians, remained both institutionally affiliated with and professionally orientated toward educator preparation. Thus they seem to have harboured little if any interest in and made no real effort to emulate progressive education critics, and instead remained aligned with progressive policies and practices that found support in education departments. Moreover, some English historians of education, such as Simon and Lowe, had participated in the progressive reforms of the 1950s and 1960s. These circumstances may be a source of the critical sympathy that English historians of education maintain toward progressive education, compared to the strain of condescension toward progressivism manifest in history of education research in the US.

Conclusion

Critical sympathy seems a more constructive historical perspective on progressive education than condescension, especially to the extent that the latter results in misrepresentation of the historical record. This also may be a practically important matter given, for example, Green and Wiborg's finding that, with respect to comparative levels of equal educational opportunity across countries, "what the more equal countries have in common, which is absent in the less equal countries, are the structures and processes typically associated with radical versions of comprehensive education: non-selective schools, mixed ability classes, late subject specialization and measures to equalize resources between schools".[58] Such findings make accurate representation of progressive education practices and policies more than just an academic matter.

The history of progressive education internationally is replete with examples of exchange and transfer; in the case of England and the US, examples of such transfer include the influence of John Dewey and of the comprehensive high school model on progressive education in England, and, negatively, the influence perhaps of

---

[56] Ibid., 14.
[57] William Richardson, "Historians and educationists: The history of education as a field of study in post-war England. Part II: 1972–96", *History of Education* 28 (1999): 109–141.
[58] Andy Green and Susanne Wiborg, "Comprehensive schooling and educational inequality: An international perspective", in Melissa Benn and Clyde Chitty, eds. *A Tribute to Caroline Benn: Education and Democracy* (London: Continuum, 2004), 239–240; Susanne Wiborg, *Education and Social Integration: Comprehensive Schooling in Europe* (New York: Palgrave Macmillan, 2009).

Bailyn's critique of history of education in the US on English academic historians' criticisms of history of education scholarship in England. Perhaps further exchange between US and English historians of education on interpretations of progressive education can foster more nuanced and robust interpretations of progressivism in historical scholarship in England and especially in the US.

Acknowledgements

Earlier versions of this article were presented at the 2012 meeting of the Society for the Study of Curriculum History, Vancouver, Canada, and at the 2012 International Standing Conference for the History of Education, University of Geneva, Switzerland.

Crossing borders in educational innovation: Framing foreign examples in discussing comprehensive education in the Netherlands, 1969–1979

Linda Greveling, Hilda T.A. Amsing and Jeroen J.H. Dekker

University of Groningen, Groningen, The Netherlands

In the Netherlands, crossing borders to study comprehensive schools was an important strategy in the 1970s, a decisive period for the start and the end of the innovation. According to policy-borrowing theory, actors that engage in debating educational issues are framing foreign examples of comprehensive schooling to convince their audiences. Framing therefore became the leading concept behind our study of the intellectual debate, examined through the leading Dutch scientific journal *Pedagogische Studiën* (Educational Studies), and the public debate, examined through recordings of television programmes. Assuming that those debates were influential in the political middle school process, our analyses show that foreign examples indeed functioned as a framing device in the form of legitimisation, glorification, sensationalisation and caution. However, the impact of framing differed. In the phase of cross-national attraction, the reform-minded perspective in the scholarly debate had a stimulating effect on the development of the plans, but little influence on the governmental decision-making process. This contrasts with the frames that were brought forward by television programmes. Although the negative frames, such as "a factory-made sausage", were rejected by the programmes, such frames could linger in people's minds as a means to interpret ideas about middle schools. At the end of the 1970s, the middle school was reduced to a minor feature of educational policy and, eventually, the middle school experiments were brought to a close. As a result, the foreign solution of introducing comprehensive education was never transferred to the Netherlands.

Introduction

In the 1970s, a broad debate took place in the Netherlands regarding unifying the first phase of secondary education into one single comprehensive school. The main argument in favour was that education should give equal opportunities to all children by postponing the moment of school choice.[1] Within this debate, actors regularly referred to foreign examples of comprehensive schooling, this being an international

---

[1]Bregt Henkens, "The rise and decline of comprehensive education: Key factors in the history of reformed secondary education in Belgium, 1969–1989", *Paedagogica Historica* 40 (2004): 194–195; Susanne Wiborg, *Education and Social Integration: Comprehensive Schooling in Europe* (New York: Palgrave Macmillan, 2009), 8.

phenomenon. The process of "going comprehensive" started in the period after the Second World War in Western Europe with, among others, the Education Act in Great Britain (1944), the Swedish School Commission (1946), the Langevin–Wallon report in France (1947) and the publications of "educational advisor" Marion Coulon in Belgium. As in other countries, this ideal of comprehensive education was also a burning issue in the Netherlands. However, eventually Dutch comprehensive schools were not established, apart from some experimental ones called *Middenscholen* (middle schools).

The different actors that engage in educational innovation debates, such as political parties, pressure groups, teachers' unions, the media and academics, make use of references to educational systems in other countries to build their case for reform or resistance.[2] This strategy of looking abroad fits the theoretical framework of "policy borrowing and lending in education".[3] The policy-borrowing cycle starts with one country's interest in foreign educational practices, called cross-national attraction. The second stage is the governmental decision-making process. The third and fourth stages focus on the implementation and the internalisation of the borrowed educational innovation into the existing educational system.[4] Therefore, the Dutch middle school process only covered the first two phases of the policy-borrowing cycle. Driven by ideological and political agendas, actors in these two phases consciously create opportunities to "get their message out". Their "references to elsewhere" can give contested reforms legitimacy and assist policy actors in making their case.[5] This phenomenon, in communication and media studies known as "framing", can influence how the public perceives an issue.[6] The study of educational borrowing shows that framing by actors in educational innovation debates could function as a means to legitimate, caution, sensationalise or glorify educational systems at home or "elsewhere".[7]

In the Dutch debate, the strategy of looking abroad to build a case for resistance was used by the teachers' union, the *Nederlands Genootschap van Leraren* (Dutch Association of Teachers). This association, which was "the only association that regularly and consistently made a stand against the middle school policy", used foreign examples to build a case for resistance to this innovation. In 1981, Tromp studied their position in the period 1973–1977 by analysing their periodical, *Het Weekblad voor Leraren* (*Het Weekblad* (Teachers' Weekly)). A comparison of the

---

[2] Jeremy Rappleye, "Reimagining attraction and 'borrowing' in education: Introducing a political production model", in Gita Steiner-Khamsi and Florian Waldow, eds., *Policy Borrowing and Lending in Education* (London: Routledge, 2012), 125, 137.
[3] David Phillips and Kimberley Ochs, eds., *Educational Policy Borrowing: Historical Perspectives* (Oxford: Symposium Books, 2004); Steiner-Khamsi and Waldow, *Policy Borrowing and Lending*.
[4] Jeremy Rappleye, "Theorizing educational transfer: Toward a conceptual map in the context of cross-national attraction", *Research in Comparative and International Education* 1 (2006): 236; Kimberley Ochs and David Phillips, "Processes of educational borrowing in historical context", in *Educational Policy Borrowing*, 10–11.
[5] Gita Steiner-Khamsi, "Understanding policy borrowing and lending: Building comparative policy studies", in *Policy Borrowing and Lending*, 11; Rappleye, "Reimagining attraction and 'borrowing' in education", 125, 137.
[6] Raymond Kuhn, *Media and Politics in Britain* (Basingstoke: Palgrave Macmillan, 2007); James W. Dearing and Everett M. Rogers, *Agenda-setting* (London: Sage, 1996).
[7] Rappleye, "Reimagining attraction and 'borrowing' in education", 125; Rappleye, "Theorizing educational transfer", 229, 233.

portrayal of the foreign models of England, West Germany and Sweden in *Het Weekblad* with the main source used by its authors, the British educational magazine, the *Times Educational Supplement*, led Tromp to the conclusion that the information provided matched the negative expectations of the *Nederlands Genootschap van Leraren* about the potential of Dutch middle schools and was used to stimulate unity among its members, who were mainly teachers in higher general secondary and pre-university education. According to Tromp, the use of foreign examples operated as a deterring myth that, "legitimises the resistance offered to an educational policy that seriously considers introducing comprehensive education in the Netherlands".[8]

In this article, both the intellectual and the public debate on comprehensive education in the Netherlands in the 1970s are studied and related to the political debate. The central question asked is how examples of foreign comprehensives were framed in these debates to strengthen arguments for or against comprehensive schools in terms of caution, legitimisation, glorification or sensationalisation. With framing as our leading concept, we analysed the leading scholarly journal, *Pedagogische Studiën* (Educational Studies), to gain an insight into the intellectual debate in the phases of cross-national attraction and of governmental decision making. *Pedagogische Studiën* was the leading journal on educational studies in the 1970s, and therefore it became our source for the analysis of the scholarly debate.[9] The journal was also important in the constitution of the discipline of educational science in the Netherlands and functioned as an "intermediary of educational science".[10]

Our source for the study of both the phase of cross-national attraction and the decision-making process in the public debate are television programmes about the middle school. From the 1950s onwards, television started to play an increasingly important role in debating social and political issues and thus constructing and offering a particular reading of them to the public. The impact of this process was related to the increasing number of television sets: in 1957 approximately 25% of Dutch households owned a television, but in 1973 96% of all Dutch households had at least one set.[11] Television's capacity to show people visual images, enhancing a particular reading of an issue, means it can influence people using a combination of text and images. In our analyses, we take into account the framing power of both text and images.

In studying those television programmes, we need to take into account that Dutch society was "pillarised". From the 1930s, this "pillarisation", or compartmentalisation of society along socio-political lines, was reflected in the public broadcasting system too, which was divided in ideologically different companies that fitted the historically established pillars of Dutch society.[12] Alongside the ideologically

---

[8]Henk Tromp, *Het Nederlands Genootschap van Leraren en de strijd om de middenschool* (Leiden: Centrum voor Onderzoek van Maatschappelijke Tegenstellingen, 1981), 244.
[9]Nelleke Bakker and Hilda T.A. Amsing, "Discovering social inequality: Dutch educational research in the post-war era", *Paedagogica Historica* 48 (2012): 315–333.
[10]Ivo van Hilvoorde, *Grenswachters van de pedagogiek. Demarcatie en disciplinevorming in de ontwikkeling van de Nederlandse academische pedagogiek* (Amsterdam: HB uitgevers, 2002), 99.
[11]Kees Schuyt and Ed Taverne, *1950: Prosperity and Welfare* (Assen, Netherlands: Van Gorcum, 2004), 254–255.
[12]Sonja de Leeuw et al., "TV nations or global medium? Television between national institution and window on the world", in Jonathan Bignell and Andres Fickers, eds., *A European Television History* (Malden and Oxford: Blackwell, 2008), 139, 141.

neutral *NOS* (*Nederlandse Omroep Stichting*), more or less comparable to the British BBC, the system also contains several public broadcasting corporations with, respectively, a Protestant, Catholic, liberal and socialist background. To be allowed into the broadcasting system, those corporations need a minimal number of members. In comparison to other countries, broadcasting time was "laughably scarce" in the 1970s.[13] In those years, only two national channels were available, and even then only the evening between 6 and 11pm. The available broadcasting time on these channels was divided between the broadcasting corporations according to the size of their membership.

In the "pillarised" Dutch society, with pillars having their own political parties, trade unions, schools, youth organisations, newspapers, broadcasting agencies and, from the 1950s, television corporations, television was special in creating the opportunity for the public to consume all of the scarce programmes that were televised, regardless of the pillar that produced the programmes. The effect was that views from different pillars were now brought into people's homes.[14] Although the impact of compartmentalisation as such decreased from the late 1960s onwards, television corporations remained "pillarised" and closely related to their historically developed ideological bonds in the 1970s. It is therefore to be expected that broadcasting agencies framed foreign examples in television programmes to strengthen an opinion that fitted their religious or political background. But what about educational scholars in the 1970s: did they also use framing in their strategy to influence the debate, or did they only produce neutral findings when engaging in the debate?[15]

The political debate on comprehensive education

Crossing borders was an important strategy for the political leaders who wanted to introduce comprehensive education into the Dutch educational system. Although the scholarly debate about comprehensive education began in the 1950s,[16] it was not until 1969 that comprehensive education was placed on the educational policy agenda.[17] From that moment, regarded as the start of the policy-borrowing cycle, successive centre-right politicians started to develop the middle school plans and related their ideas to foreign systems of comprehensive schooling. Moreover, these politicians promised to start experimenting with middle schools. The press and television media noticed the interest in this subject and started to report on the issue.[18]

The ideal of comprehensive education received a huge boost between 1973 and 1977, when the ambitious centre-left Den Uyl government was in office. The social democrat Minister of Education, J.A. van Kemenade, started experimenting and pub-

---

[13] Schuyt and Taverne, *1950: Prosperity and Welfare*, 254.
[14] Friso Wielenga, *Die Niederlande. Politik und politische Kultur im 20. Jahrhundert* (Münster, Germany: Waxmann Verlag, 2008), 328–329.
[15] Rappleye, "Theorizing educational transfer", 237.
[16] Bakker and Amsing, "Discovering social inequality".
[17] P.N. Karstanje, *Beleidsevaluatie bij controversiële onderwijsvernieuwing* (Amsterdam: SCO Stichting Kohnstamm Fonds voor Onderwijsresearch, 1988), PhD thesis, University of Utrecht, 78–118.
[18] For an elaborate description of the political situation, see Hilda T.A. Amsing, Linda Greveling and Jeroen J.H. Dekker, "The struggle for comprehensive education in the Netherlands: The representation of secondary school innovation in Dutch newspaper articles in the 1970s", *History of Education* 42, no. 4 (2013): 460–485.

lished his plans for the middle school system. However, van Kemenade's plans led to tension between proponents and opponents. The Minister encountered massive resistance from the *Nederlands Genootschap van Leraren* and the right-wing opposition liberal party (*Volkspartij voor Vrijheid en Democratie, VVD*). In fact, in an interview with the right-wing newspaper *De Telegraaf* in September 1973, the *VVD* spokeswoman on educational issues, N. Smit-Kroes, blamed the Minister for adding a socialist tone to the middle school idea. The interview led to a vehement discussion in Parliament, which was well-documented in Dutch newspapers.[19]

Nonetheless, van Kemenade laid down his ideas about a new educational system in a memorandum entitled *Contourennota*, published in June 1975 and marking the start of the decision-making process.[20] Van Kemenade was already familiar with international literature about comprehensive systems because he was a former professor of sociology of education and president of the scientific board of the social democrat party (*Partij van de Arbeid, PvdA*), which published a report about the structure of the education system.[21] Therefore, he could easily incorporate these ideas into his memorandum. Being academically trained, he warned against an unaltered adoption of foreign systems within the Dutch educational system because of cultural differences between countries.[22] Van Kemenade was especially inspired by the Swedish model, with a non-selective school for all children of compulsory school age.[23] The educational systems of England and some German *Länder* were perceived less positively in the *Contourennota* by van Kemenade because in these systems the comprehensive schools existed alongside grammar schools.

The English comprehensive schools, introduced in the 1950s, were portrayed as schools for children with less academic capacity. This led to an increasing "creaming off" of the brightest children and, as a result, increasing differences between the existing school types. Despite the ideal of equal opportunity, English secondary education therefore still fulfilled the function of social selection.[24] In West Germany, similar problems arose in their comprehensive school, the so-called *Gesamtschule*, which was introduced in experimental form in 1969 by social democratically governed German *Länder*, for example North-Rhine-Westphalia, Hessia and Lower Saxony.[25] As in England, the *Gesamtschule* did not function as a common school for all children, but as an option alongside the already existing secondary school

---

[19] Amsing et al., "Struggle for comprehensive education".
[20] P.N. Karstanje, "Voortgezet onderwijs", in J.A. van Kemenade et al., eds., *Onderwijs: Bestel en beleid 3* (Groningen, Netherlands: Wolters-Noordhoff, 1987), 285–366.
[21] Wiardi Beckman Stichting, *Uitgangspunten voor onderwijsbeleid* (Deventer, Netherlands: Kluwer, 1973); Ed Schüssler, *Weg van de middenschool. Dertig jaar na de start van het middenschoolexperiment* (Antwerp, Belgium: Garant, 2006), 24.
[22] J.A. van Kemenade, G. Klein and A. Veerman, *Contouren van een toekomstig onderwijsbestel* ('s Gravenhage, Netherlands: Staatsuitgeverij, 1975), 53.
[23] Susanne Wiborg, "Education and social integration: A comparative study of the comprehensive school system in Scandinavia", *London Review of Education* 2 (2004): 84.
[24] Alan C. Kerckhoff et al., *Going Comprehensive in England and Wales* (London: Woburn Press, 1996), 242.
[25] Achim Leschinsky and Karl Ulrich Mayer, "Comprehensive schools and inequality of opportunity in the Federal Republic of Germany", in Achim Leschinsky and Karl Ulrich Mayer, eds., *The Comprehensive School Experiment Revisited: Evidence from Western Europe* (New York: Peter Lang, 1999), 17, 20.

types, *Hauptschule, Realschule* and *Gymnasium*,[26] with the result that less than 4% of pupils attended the Gesamtschule.[27] According to van Kemenade, the English and German systems could not solve the problems of social inequality because within those systems children were also differentiated.[28]

Van Kemenade presented his memorandum as a working paper to launch a broad debate in society.[29] This new approach in educational policy worked: alongside an unprecedented number of 338 responses from a variety of organisations, boards, committees, schools and individuals, four legal advisory bodies gave their advice. In March 1977, van Kemenade published a revised memorandum that incorporated these responses.[30] The political significance of this memorandum was limited because just a week before its publication the Den Uyl government fell as the result of frictions within the coalition on other issues.

In Parliament, opinions on the plans for a middle school system differed. The main objection of the right-wing opposition liberal party was that, in its opinion, these schools would lead to the levelling of learning results. The social democrat party supported their minister, but the position of the Christian democrat coalition parties was complex: while supporting the general elements of the middle school ideas, they feared for the position of Christian schools in the educational system.[31] Nonetheless, in 1973 a Parliamentary majority supported van Kemenade's decision to start experimenting in schools. These experiments, which officially started in September 1976, soon lost political support because van Kemenade's successor, the liberal Arie Pais, a member of the right-wing coalition government, Van Agt-Wiegel, was not in favour of comprehensive education. In 1979 he proposed plans to postpone school choice without changing the streamed school structure. This educational policy marked the beginning of the end of the Dutch middle school.[32]

In the following sections, we concentrate on forms of framing in reference to foreign comprehensive schools in both the intellectual and the public debate on comprehensive schooling considered as discourses that have been influential in the governmental decision-making process.

Scholarly debate on foreign comprehensive schools

Between 1969 and 1979, *Pedagogische Studiën* published 17 articles about comprehensive education, 13 of them discussing foreign comprehensives in Sweden, West Germany, England, Belgium and Italy, and comprehensive education in Western Europe in general. Thus, *Pedagogische Studiën* shows an international perspective in discussing comprehensive schooling. The authors, among them educational scholars, university-trained teachers and one physical engineer, came from the academic

---

[26]Susanne Wiborg, "Why is there no comprehensive education in Germany? A historical explanation", *History of Education* 39 (2010): 541.
[27]Leschinsky and Mayer, "Comprehensive schools and inequality of opportunity in the Federal Republic of Germany", 16.
[28]Van Kemenade et al., *Contouren van een toekomstig onderwijsbestel*, 54.
[29]Wiardi Beckman Stichting, *Uitgangspunten voor onderwijsbeleid*, 54–55.
[30]J.A. van Kemenade, G. Klein and K. de Jong Ozn., *Contouren van een toekomstig onderwijsbestel 2* ('s Gravenhage, Netherlands: Staatsuitgeverij, 1977), 5, 99–106.
[31]Karstanje, *Beleidsevaluatie*.
[32]Petra Boezerooy and Jeroen Huisman, "From secondary to tertiary education in the Netherlands", *Journal of Institutional Research in Australasia* 9, no. 1 (2000), http://www.aair.org.au/journal/volume-9-no-1.

milieu in the Netherlands and Belgium. They discussed the ways in which foreign educational systems were organised and implemented, and examined didactical solutions from abroad as means of informing educational practice in dealing with diversity issues in the heterogeneous classes of Dutch middle schools.

Evaluating foreign education systems

In *Pedagogische Studiën*, scholars discussed the advantages as well as the shortcomings of several foreign educational systems, while being in favour of introducing middle schools into the Dutch school system. In the 1970s, several scholars writing in *Pedagogische Studiën* referred to Sweden as a model country. Among them was E. Velema, a professor in educational sciences at the Catholic University of Nijmegen and a member of the editorial staff of *Pedagogische Studiën*, who praised the Swedish comprehensive school and the way Sweden had organised the innovation process:

> The Swedish first designed a plan, then they built a house. After that they took care of the interior and later on they also reconsidered this interior.

L. van Gelder, a professor of educational sciences at the University of Groningen and a key advocate of Dutch middle schools,[33] and his colleague, J.F. Vos, framed the Swedish system as a shining example in which "children have the opportunity to make up arrears" and "no mediocrity" exists. With the latter argument, the authors tried to refute the oft-heard counter-argument that middle schools lead to levelled learning results.[34]

Other scholars writing in *Pedagogische Studiën* cautioned against the unaltered borrowing that was suggested by Van Gelder, and Vos. D. Jansz, a teacher at the national teachers' training college in The Hague, argued that "the differences in schooling between countries could be caused by other factors than the way the education system was organised".[35] To find out whether a horizontal structure could work in the Netherlands, he proposed starting experimenting with comprehensive schools. This fitted the state of affairs within the political debate of 1972, in which the centre-right coalition government, Biesheuvel II, promised to start such school experiments.[36] Several other countries had already started experimenting: Germany starting with *Gesamtschulen* in 1969[37] and English comprehensive schools having an experimental status until 1965.[38]

---

[33] Hilda T.A. Amsing, "De Middenschool: over een ideaal van een icoon. Van Gelders ideeën over de organisatie en inrichting van de onderbouw van het voortgezet onderwijs", in Doret J. de Ruyter, Gerdien D. Bertram-Troost and Stijn M.A. Sieckelinck, eds., *Idealen, idolen en iconen van de pedagogiek: bijdragen aan de Twaalfde Landelijke Pedagogendag* (Amsterdam: SWP, 2005), 74–85.
[34] Leon Van Gelder and Jaap F. Vos, "Misverstanden rondom de middenschool", *Pedago-gische Studiën* 48 (1971): 311–327.
[35] D. Jansz, "De problematiek van de middenschool", *Pedagogische Studiën* 49 (1972): 215–218.
[36] Ch. Van Veen, *Nota over het onderwijsbeleid*. 12 000. Bijlage IV, Memorie van Toelichting, no. 6, Rijksbegroting voor het dienstjaar 1973 (September, 1972), 10–12.
[37] Henkens, "Rise and decline of comprehensive education", 195.
[38] Anthony Heath and Sheila Jacobs, "Comprehensive reform in Britain", in *Comprehensive School Experiment Revisited*, 102.

As well as the Swedish system, the reform-minded scholars of *Pedagogische Studiën* studied the educational systems of Italy, Belgium and England. The Italian *scuola media unica* existed in a horizontal structure – just as in Sweden – and, therefore, the Dutch scholars also applauded it. It was described as "an instrument for the effective and the active participation of all people that live in the Italian nation", and considered a milestone in the history of education in Italy.[39] Although aware of the fact that in Italy the counter-argument of levelling learning results was also debated, scholars writing in *Pedagogische Studiën* did not consider this a consequence of the Italian school system, but the result of the quality of education provided by its teachers. F.J. Wielemans, an educational scholar from the University of Leuven in Belgium who specialised in the Italian school system, concluded that it was necessary to reform Italian secondary teacher training, because until now "not all teachers are capable of giving full and continuous attention to the same class and of teaching various subjects to that class".[40]

The reform-minded scholars writing in *Pedagogische Studiën* also referred to the Belgian *Vernieuwd Secundair Onderwijs* (*VSO*, Reformed Secondary Education), stating that "secondary education has once and for all taken the path of innovation" and "basically no one who started with the *VSO* wants to go back to the old system".[41] In *Pedagogische Studiën*, it was pointed out that the broad two-year observation period in the *VSO* in which children's interests, capabilities and talents were stimulated and studied, led to a more conscious school choice and that the *VSO* diminished the influence of children's social background.[42] However, critical remarks about this system were also made, because comprehensive schools existed alongside traditional secondary education in a so-called "double system", which was also the case in Germany and England. G.K.J. van Horebeek, a scholar at the Catholic University of Leuven and an author on the topic of Belgian comprehensive education in *Pedagogische Studiën*, cautioned against the "double system" and argued that the abolishment of the traditional schools "would be a point scored for the *VSO* in the evolution of Belgian secondary education".[43]

The English case was examined by J. de Reus – an internationally orientated scholar who worked at the development institute of the Wolters Noordhoff publishing house. According to de Reus, the English double system led to the "creaming off" of gifted children, resulting in numerous comprehensive schools not being truly "comprehensive". Also, some comprehensive schools were not so comprehensive themselves, as they had a heterogeneous, eleven-plus phase followed by strict tests and early selection into streams to prove that they were at least as good as the "un-comprehensive" grammar schools. This abandonment of early selection was precisely the core issue that comprehensive schools were established to address.[44] By

---

[39] F.J. Willy Wielemans, "Italiaanse middenschool van 11 tot 14 jaar", *Pedagogische Studiën* 48 (1971): 176.
[40] Ibid., 182-183.
[41] G. van Horebeek, "Het Vernieuwd Secundair Onderwijs in België", *Pedagogische Studiën* 52 (1975): 458.
[42] L. Lycke, "Het vernieuwd secundair onderwijs in België", *Pedagogische Studiën* 49 (1972): 85.
[43] Van Horebeek, "Het Vernieuwd Secundair Onderwijs in België", 461.
[44] J. de Reus, "De comprehensive school en de toets der kritiek", *Pedagogische Studiën* 51 (1974): 435-41.

revealing these shortcomings, de Reus pressed for an accurate comprehensive school idea in educational policy and cautioned against a "double system".

Our analysis of *Pedagogische Studiën* in the first half of the 1970s shows that, in the phase of cross-national attraction, these educational scholars took a clear position: they were reform-minded and supported the introduction of middle schools in a horizontal structure by glorifying the Swedish and Italian examples. Furthermore, they used the Belgian and English examples to caution against "a double system", in which comprehensive schools existed alongside traditional schools. Moreover, they brushed aside the doubts about comprehensive schooling leading to levelled learning results by pointing at factors outside the school system.

Didactical solutions to heterogeneous classes in foreign comprehensives

While the scholarly debate in *Pedagogische Studiën* until 1975 focused on the evaluation of foreign educational systems and on the position of comprehensive schooling in these systems, from 1975 onwards, when the governmental decision-making process started, the debate shifted to discussing lessons that could be learned from foreign comprehensive school practices, such as didactical methods. In fact, in 1972, some attention was already directed at implementation issues but was not explicitly related to the Dutch situation. In that year, *Pedagogische Studiën* published a translation of an article written by the German teacher G. Brinkmann, who had a doctorate in education and worked at the *Pädagogische Hochschule Ruhr* in Dortmund. Brinkmann articulated an enormous faith in the didactical approaches adopted in German comprehensive schools, the so-called *Integrierte Gesamtschulen*.[45] The shift in the debate towards practical solutions shows that the scholars writing in *Pedagogische Studiën* were already discussing the implementation of middle schools – the third stage of the policy-borrowing cycle[46] – while the government had just started the decision-making phase.

From 1975, when van Kemenade's *Contourennota I* placed the introduction of middle schools at the heart of his educational policy,[47] scholars writing in *Pedagogische Studiën* started to discuss foreign practical solutions. One of these scholars, M.J.W. Stuart, explicitly noticed that the debate needed this change of focus. Stuart, a member of the *Innovatie Commissie Middenschool* (ICM, Innovation Committee Middle School) installed by van Kemenade to provide plans for the innovation process and the school experiments, stated: "In the national debate, it gradually becomes clear what is intended *with* a middle school. Now, information is needed about what is desirable and possible *in* the middle school". Therefore, "information regarding examples on 'goals and methods in comprehensive schooling' becomes very relevant, considering the current state of affairs on the middle school in the Netherlands".[48]

Scholars stressed the importance of scientific support for a sound implementation of the Dutch middle schools. Two aspects were discussed: the educational goals of the Dutch middle school and academic supervision of the announced school

---

[45] Günter Brinkmann, "Differentiatie in 'integrierte Gesamtschulen'", *Pedagogische Studiën* 49 (1972): 485–499.
[46] Rappleye, "Theorizing educational transfer", 236.
[47] Van Kemenade et al., *Contouren van een toekomstig onderwijsbestel*.
[48] M.J.W. Stuart, "Achtergronden van de Bielefeldse schoolexperimenten. Middenschool – Nieuw onderwijs?", *Pedagogische Studiën* 52 (1975): 433 (italics in original).

experiments. In both cases, scholars referred to Germany. Stuart argued that the German *Gesamtschule* was established without developing an educational philosophy beforehand. He emphasised that the Dutch government should make decisions on the goals of education before introducing middle schools into the school system. Stuart also emphasised that Minister van Kemenade should pay attention to academic supervision of the experiment in his announced memorandum.[49] And indeed, in his memorandum, van Kemenade dedicated a key role to academic supervision.[50]

Scholars discussed technical aids that could be helpful in differentiation in the classroom. The physical engineer at the *Philips' Natuurkundig Laboratorium* (the Physics Laboratory of Philips), N. Hazewindus, embedded the development towards middle schools within an international perspective to show the necessity of "developing new didactical methods that meet the existing differences between children". In these new didactical methods for instruction, the computer could be used in two different ways, both developed in the United States. Computer-assisted instruction (CAI), the successor of the so-called Teaching Machine and based on the didactical principle of programmed instruction, could be helpful.[51] With CAI, children used a computer with didactical software to test their knowledge and skills and received individualised feedback on the computer accordingly.[52] According to Hazewindus, this application of the computer was too complex to put into practice, because for a proper use of CAI, it was necessary to store all sorts of didactical material onto the computer, and the costs involving the development of didactical software were very high.[53] Therefore, Hazewindus suggested studying the application of computer-managed instruction (CMI). CMI allowed teachers to administer and guide the instructional process using the major features of CMI, which are diagnosis, testing, analysis, record keeping and prescription.[54] Hazewindus pled for the initiation of experiments to find out what CMI could offer to address the issue of differentiation in experimental middle schools classes, so that the gained insight could be brought into practice.[55]

Furthermore, scholars discussed reported problems in the highest phase of the Swedish *Grundskola*. These problems, such as "skipping school, lack of motivation and problems with discipline and aggression", influenced the work atmosphere at school negatively and led to overworked teachers. According to de Reus, these problems were not caused by the educational system, but were consequences of teachers' inadequacies.[56] Again, teachers were blamed for the existing problems in comprehensive schools, not the system.

Finally, educationists writing in the *Pedagogische Studiën* discussed how children could formally finish at a future Dutch middle school. P. de Koning, who worked at the University of Amsterdam, claimed that this issue "is of major

---

[49] Ibid.
[50] Van Kemenade et al., *Contouren van een toekomstig onderwijsbestel*.
[51] N. Hazewindus, "Toepasbaarheid van een computer-managed instructiesysteem in geïntegreerde vormen van voortgezet onderwijs", *Pedagogische Studiën* 53 (1976): 57–59.
[52] Paul Saettler, *The Evolution of American Educational Technology* (Greenwich, CT: Information Age Publishing, 2004), 296297, 306.
[53] Hazewindus, "Toepasbaarheid computer-managed instructiesysteem", 57–59.
[54] Frank B. Baker. *Computer Managed Instruction: Theory and Practice* (Englewood Cliffs, NJ: Educational Technology Publications, 1978), 231
[55] Hazewindus, "Toepasbaarheid computer-managed instructiesysteem", 59–60.
[56] J. de Reus, "Het Zweedse onderwijs-anno 1977", *Pedagogische Studiën* 54 (1977): 450.

importance for a future middle school"[57] and that "it is necessary to have clear agreements about the content and form of how children can finish the middle school, to avoid endless experimenting and to pursue whether the final attainment levels are in agreement with the principles of the middle school".[58] De Koning illustrated his case by referring to solutions in England, West Germany and the US. He referred to the German *Gesamtschule* in cautioning against the proposed plans of van Kemenade to give children a so-called *dossioma*, a contraction of "diploma" and "dossier" describing the child's capabilities and interests. De Koning stated that such a *dossioma* decreased communication with parents, other schools and society, and also diminished the value of the qualification, as, according to him, was the case in the *Gesamtschule*.[59] By using foreign examples, he cautioned for a sound implementation of the middle school in which the goals and the way children finish it should be attuned.

In sum, scholars writing in *Pedagogische Studiën* were clearly reform-minded, pleading for the introduction of a Dutch middle school in a horizontal structure by using the shining examples of Sweden and Italy. Moreover, they brushed aside criticism that such a horizontal system did not work by blaming teachers' lack of capability. In the period 1969–1979, the study of foreign examples of good practices in comprehensive schooling was an important strategy for scholars, with the focus of attention in 1975 changing from evaluating foreign systems to practical solutions regarding the implementation of comprehensive schooling. This shift reflects the publication of the *Contourennota I*, in which van Kemenade presented his ideas about the middle school together with an innovation strategy. So, educational scholars were already discussing the implementation of the middle school while, on the governmental level, the decision-making process was just starting. The shift also reflects the mission of educational sciences at that time; namely, to be subservient to educational practice. As a result, research was mainly practically orientated.[60]

The reform-minded scholars writing in *Pedagogische Studiën* therefore framed the foreign examples studied to strengthen their own arguments. By glorifying the horizontal systems of Sweden and Italy and by cautioning against "double systems" with middle schools alongside traditional schools in England and Germany, they legitimated their opinion that Dutch middle schools should be introduced.[61] In the next section, we examine the public debate by looking at the use of the foreign example in television programmes.

---

[57]P. de Koning, "Functies van afsluitingen: een opsomming", *Pedagogische Studiën* 55 (1978): 438.
[58]Ibid., 433.
[59]Ibid., 438, 445, 448.
[60]Leon van Gelder, *Deelname en distantie* (Groningen, Netherlands: J.B. Wolters, 1964), 6; van Gelder and Jaap F. Vos, *Wetenschapsbeleid, Onderwijsbeleid en Onderwijskunde. Interne Nota Instituut voor Onderwijskunde der Rijksuniversiteit te Groningen* (Groningen, Netherlands: Rijksuniversiteit Groningen, 1971), 2.
[61]The scholarly debate on middle schools did not end here. A few years after the decisive period (1969–1979), *Pedagogische Studiën* started to evaluate the experiments. See *Pedagogische Studiën* 58 (1981): 357–405.

Foreign examples in public debate on Dutch middle schools

Twenty-one television accounts of the middle school in the 1970s have been archived. These differ significantly in length, consisting of short news reports, episodes of current affairs programmes and documentaries.[62] From those 21 programmes, three accounts treated comprehensive schooling from an international perspective, by reflecting on specific foreign models of schooling: *Observing Children* (*Kijken naar kinderen*), *Taking a Closer Look* (*Nader bekeken*) and *Middle School – factory-made sausage?* (*Middenschool - eenheidsworst?*). These two episodes of current affairs programmes and one documentary were televised in 1975, when the decision-making process was initiated by the publication of the *Contourennota I*. The explicit announcement of these broadcasts in newspaper articles reflects the importance of the issue in the public debate.[63] A fourth documentary did refer in general to learning from "experiences with middle schools in foreign countries" for decision making on the Dutch comprehensive schools. This programme did not make explicit references to specific models and is therefore excluded from the analysis below.[64]

Observing Children

Several months before the publication of van Kemenade's memorandum, the ideologically neutral broadcasting company *NOS* focused on a Danish middle school in an episode of the programme *Observing Children*.[65] This episode was broadcast on 2 April and focused on the daily school life of children in a middle school in Copenhagen. This is seen in the many visuals that show children working and playing in this school: we see images of children working, reading, laughing and enjoying their school day, in various classrooms, during the lunch break and walking from one classroom to another. To a lesser extent, teachers were displayed when giving instructions to children or reading a story. In these visuals, we see teachers and pupils interacting seemingly naturally, without visible hierarchy between them.

The images were explained by a voice-over. The main idea brought forward was that this Danish middle school succeeded in innovating on both pedagogical and didactical levels, which was one of the goals of the Dutch innovation plans.[66] The voice-over emphasised the benefits of the different atmosphere in this comprehensive school in comparison to other school types, by mentioning that this school has "a relaxed atmosphere" and "relaxed relations between children and teachers". The attitude of the children was praised; although children have "a lot of freedom", and although there are "just a few rules", the children "work very hard". The epi-

---

[62] Twenty were found in the central Dutch archive for television programmes and one in the personal archive of Hans Knot (University of Groningen, media historian).

[63] "'Kijken naar kinderen' over middenschool", *Leeuwarder Courant*, 19 February 1975, 2; "Meindert Leerling gaat in 'Nader bekeken' vragen stellen over de middenschool", *Leidsche Courant*, 9 October 1975, 2; "De Middenschool, eenheidsworst?", *Nieuwsblad van het Noorden*, 17 November 1975, 8.

[64] "Schooling – sense or nonsense?" (*Onderwijs, wijs of onwijs?*), broadcast by the right-wing, conservative broadcasting agency *AVRO*, on channel *Nederland 1*, 20.40–21.30pm, 5 March 1979.

[65] Broadcasting context: duration 24 minutes; the last minute of the film is missing. Broadcast by the general broadcasting company *NOS*, on channel *Nederland 1*, 22.05–22.30pm, 2 April 1975.

[66] Van Kemenade et al., *Contouren van een toekomstig onderwijsbestel*.

sode also stressed the joint responsibility of teachers and children as a positive difference between this school and other schools, for instance in describing the new architecture of the school. This "open school structure", in which "all classrooms are connected to each other, and when needed ... can be divided ... makes children and teachers jointly responsible for the daily school life". These pedagogical and didactical changes were presented as advantages of this new school type, with no mention of critics. So, just before van Kemenade was about to unfold his plans on comprehensive education, this programme glorified the foreign example as a shining example and a model for the Dutch case.

Taking a Closer Look

On 9 October 1975, several weeks before the discussion of the *Contourennota I* in Parliament took place, the Christian Evangelical *EO*, which was the smallest and youngest broadcasting agency of the 1970s, presented the opinions of orthodox Protestant secondary schools in the current affairs programme *Taking a Closer Look*.[67] This episode showed that teachers and school leaders from these schools applauded the proposed new educational structure and the educational goals of the middle school, but – in line with the view of the Christian democrat coalition parties[68] – were also concerned that breaking through the existing streamed system could influence the position of orthodox Protestant schools negatively. This issue was related to the constitutional freedom of education. The position of orthodox Protestant schools was established after a fierce political struggle in the Netherlands in the period 1857–1920, as a result of which denominational schools received full subvention without state intervention in educational matters, if they followed a number of guidelines on good quality. Now, however, the Minister expressed clear ideas on the curriculum: middle schools should have a broad range of subjects and should develop children's social awareness. Afraid of losing their identity within a prescribed curriculum, these orthodox Protestants were hesitant. This position was also reflected in newspaper articles on the subject.[69]

We found two references to foreign comprehensives. In the introduction, the voice-over related the development of middle schools to the international process of "going comprehensive" by mentioning that the educational field wanted to test new methods of delivering secondary education, one example of which, the comprehensive school, had already been introduced in several foreign countries. Subsequently, the episode showed interviews with various Dutch orthodox Protestant teachers and school leaders who were proponents of the middle school. The interviewed teachers reacted positively, one of them saying:

> Yes, indeed, we believe that the middle school educates children better to obtain a fully-fledged position in society and therefore to better function in that society, because

---

[67]Broadcasting context: duration 20 minutes; in some parts the screen turns black. Broadcast by the Evangelical broadcasting company *EO*, on channel *Nederland 1*, 21.50–22.15pm, 9 October 1975.
[68]Karstanje, *Beleidsevaluatie,* 100; Eerste Kamer, Zitting 1973–1974, 5de vergadering, 20 November 1973, 78; Tweede Kamer, Zitting 19731974, 52ste vergadering, 26 February 1974, 2712.
[69]Amsing et al., "Struggle for comprehensive education".

in this new educational system the child will be much more educated than before on many more subject areas.

After this positive introduction, the episode focused on a conversation between *EO*'s anchorman, Meindert Leerling, and the editorial chair of the already mentioned *Nederlands Genootschap van Leraren*, Ko Traas, who was a well-known opponent of the middle school. After Traas' presentation of his main objections to the middle school concept, Leerling responded: "In particular, England, West Germany, and Sweden already have experiences with middle schools". In his answer, Traas chose the example of Sweden to strengthen his argument, sensationalising the usually highly-praised Swedish model in two ways. First, he criticised Swedish comprehensive schools by arguing that the "in-one-go" introduction of the Swedish system, meaning that it was established all in one go without an initial experimental phase or resistance or debate, "does not necessarily mean that this system is flawless". In contrast to the educational scholars writing in *Pedagogische Studiën*, Traas blamed the new system for the major problems with unmotivated children and incapable teachers experienced by the Swedish:

> If you look at it honestly, I don't believe that the goals people did have are truly realised. There are many difficulties with unmotivated pupils. There are difficulties with children who don't want to go to school. There are difficulties with teachers who cannot live up to the expectations, etcetera.

Then, while looking straight into the camera several times, so speaking directly to the people at home, Traas also characterised the middle school concept as an invention of the socialists, claiming that the Swedish comprehensive school was able to be established as the result of succeeding Swedish socialist governments. With this remark, Traas was referring to the political debate of 1973 in which van Kemenade was blamed by the right-wing liberal party for adding the goal of developing children's social awareness to the middle school idea of his predecessors, which gave the plans a clear socialist tone.[70] For the rest, the Dutch middle school was no socialist invention, since the first plans for starting comprehensive school experiments were developed by conservative centre-right politicians.

In using the Swedish example, Traas consciously or unconsciously misinterprets the history of the Swedish comprehensive school. For the Swedish comprehensive school was not established "in one go" and introduced by socialists; rather, it was established in two separate phases by ideologically different governments, the nine-year comprehensive *Grundskola* being the result. Moreover, this school type was implemented nationally after an experimental phase of more than 10 years. So, the Swedish comprehensive school was the result of a historical process lasting more than 50 years.[71]

In sum, in a seemingly predominantly positive story presenting the favourable attitude of orthodox Protestant secondary schools to the middle school plans, at the end of the programme the *EO* created the opportunity for a non-orthodox Protestant opponent to state his criticism of middle schools. In line with the results of Tromp,[72] this analysis shows that this opponent, Traas of the *Nederlands Genootschap van*

---
[70] Ibid.
[71] Wiborg, "Education and social integration", 8.
[72] Tromp, *Nederlands Genootschap van Leraren*.

Leraren, invited by a remark of *EO*'s anchorman Leerling, sensationalised the foreign example to frame the middle school development explicitly as a deterrent. Through this remarkable shift, the programme seems to put forward the message that, although there is support for the plans, even within orthodox Protestant schools, the middle school should not be implemented because it leads to many problems.

Middle School – Factory-made Sausage?

About one month later, on 17 November 1975, the conservative broadcasting agency *AVRO*, one of the largest broadcasting companies of the 1970s, broadcast the television documentary *Middle School – Factory-made Sausage?*[73] This documentary followed the middle school debate from both the societal and the political perspective, and gave the floor not only to adherents of the middle school concept but also to one opponent, again the *Nederlands Genootschap van Leraren*. The main objection of this association was that middle schools would lead to the levelling of learning results and a corresponding "boring uniformity". This argument was strengthened by applying the Dutch metaphor of a factory-made sausage, *eenheidsworst* in Dutch or *Einheitswurst* in German, which became an important frame in the debate.[74] Because produced by the conservative *AVRO*, we expected that the programme would, at the very least, be critical of the innovation. On the contrary, the programme perceived the arguments made by the *Nederlands Genootschap van Leraren* as a misconception of the middle school concept and described the middle school plans positively, with the voice-over stating that "misconceptions about this innovation are hopefully eliminated" and "it is clear that basically there is no relationship between the middle school and *eenheidsworst*".

Two references were made to foreign comprehensive schooling, in this case in England. After introducing the subject, the voice-over stated that the middle school was not just a socialist ideal, as argued by van Kemenade's opponents, and emphasised that the plans of van Kemenade were not new but built on the work of his predecessors. Furthermore, comprehensive education was portrayed as an international phenomenon, stating that "in about 50 other countries comprehensive education is developed".

The Minister himself appeared in the programme to explain his point of view. Van Kemenade first explained that the goals of the middle school could not be arranged within the existing types of school because "if we want to experiment with a new school type then we need to do something completely new and break through the existing system, because the experience can only be gained in a totally new school type". Next, the voice-over introduced the opinion of opponents who stated that the existing school system should be maintained alongside the implementation of a new comprehensive school system. In his response, Minister van Kemenade reasoned that in a period of transition between the old and the new educational system such a "double system" could work, but after a certain period of time "the new system should be laid down in law". To emphasise his rejection of such double systems, van Kemenade referred to England:

---

[73]Broadcasting context: duration 53 minutes; broadcastd by *AVRO*, on channel *Nederland 1*, 21.50–22.40pm, 17 November 1975.
[74]Jos van Kemenade, "Karikaturen van de Middenschool" in *Weg van de Middenschool*, 55–66.

> In the long term, as I see it now, I do not think that it [a double system] is a good way of arranging the educational system. We can see that, for example, in England, where as a matter of fact some kind of social selection occurs. I think that it is essentially inconsistent with the idea pursued in a middle school: teaching children, pupils, to go to school together, and teaching them to socialise with each other. I believe that it [a double system] is not good, because the middle school then becomes a kind of appendix. It becomes the appendix of education.

So, van Kemenade emphasised the societal selection of a double system in which middle schools would only be attended by children from lower social classes because parents from higher social classes would send their children to other types of school.

In sum, van Kemenade sensationalised the example of England, using it explicitly as a "deterrent" to strengthen his argument that the English model was not appropriate for the Netherlands.

Conclusion

This article discussed how examples of foreign comprehensive schools were framed in scholarly and public debates on comprehensive education during the 1970s to strengthen arguments for or against it in terms of caution, legitimisation, glorification or sensationalisation. The period studied covers the cross-national attraction phase, which began in 1969, and the governmental decision-making phase, which began in 1975. The scholarly and public debates are considered to have been influential in terms of the decision-making process. With framing as the main concept of this article, attention is given to possible differences between these debates, focusing on the process of educational borrowing. Sources were the leading educational journal *Pedagogische Studiën* for analysis of the scholarly debate, and television programmes for analysis of the public debate. The scholarly journal reached a small audience consisting of educational scholars, whereas the television programmes reached a broad audience from various backgrounds. Thus, the impact of framing differed substantially between these sources.

Analysis of *Pedagogische Studiën* shows that only reform-minded scholars wrote about comprehensive education. They shifted from discussing foreign systems to discussing foreign solutions in the educational practices of comprehensive schools from 1975 onwards. They did not produce neutral findings and indeed framed foreign examples to legitimate the introduction of middle schools by glorifying foreign models and cautioning against certain foreign solutions.

In the television programmes, with a much larger audience, both proponents and opponents, driven by their ideological and political agendas, framed foreign examples to strengthen their arguments for reform or resistance by sensationalising or glorifying them. Proponents used only two models, Sweden as a shining example and England as a deterrent. The opponent, the *Nederlands Genootschap van Leraren* (Dutch Association of Teachers), who provided its members with distorted, negative images of foreign comprehensives through its periodical to build resistance against the middle school, was also given free rein in television programmes to disseminate its negative view. In doing so, the association consciously criticised the example of Sweden so embraced by van Kemenade.

In relating the two debates to the policy-borrowing cycle, our analyses also suggest that, in the cross-national attraction phase, the reform-minded perspective in the scholarly debate initially had a stimulating effect on the development of the plans. Eventually, however, it had little influence on the governmental decision-making process, which is in contrast to the frames being promoted by television programmes. The image of the middle school was seriously dented in the 1970s; it was portrayed as an idealistic, socialist and impractical idea, and also as a factory-made sausage. Those frames all appeared in the television programmes and were partly demonstrated as proven flaws by using foreign examples. Some frames were consciously used by opponents, others, such as the frame of a "factory-made sausage", were definitely rejected by the television programmes. However, such frames could still linger in people's minds and could thus be used to interpret ideas about middle schools. Thus, it seems that the middle school opponents succeeded in delivering their message. As a result, van Kemenade's successor, from the right-wing liberal party, was able to reduce the middle school to a minor feature of educational policy. Eventually, the experimental middle schools were officially closed. As a result, foreign examples of comprehensive education, although playing an important role in the associated debates, were never applied to Dutch comprehensive school practice.

La réception des travaux scouts de Pierre Bovet en France (1912–décennie 1930)

Nicolas Palluau

Equipe HEMOC, Université d'Avignon, Avignon, France

Le scoutisme français n'a pas toujours vu Baden-Powell comme un modèle. A leur fondation en 1911, les Eclaireurs de France refusent de traduire Scouting for boys. Mais, le philosophe genevois Pierre Bovet le traduit dès 1912 pour l'éditeur neuchâtelois Delachaux et Niestlé. Le texte anglais arrive en France malgré le nationalisme des Eclaireurs qui le maintient dans un purgatoire sévère. La traduction est saluée par un réformateur social comme Georges Bertier, directeur de l'Ecole des Roches. Dès 1921, celui-ci préside les Eclaireurs et les ancre dans l'Education nouvelle. En 1919, l'éditeur Delachaux et Niestlé a ouvert une succursale dans la capitale française. L'essor des traductions scoutes est contemporain, notamment par des cadres suisses, tels Ketty Jentzer, commissaire genevoise ou Jean Carrard, chef à Lausanne. Mais, alors qu'en 1920, Bovet écrit son livre-maître Le Génie de Baden-Powell où il analyse cette pédagogie au prisme de l'Education nouvelle, d'autres frontières émergent. Les Français qui possèdent leurs propres travaux, ont moins besoin des traductions suisses. La frontière se recompose selon une autre ligne, l'étude savante. Les Français travaillent avec des philosophes comme Edmond Goblot et Pierre Mendousse autour de la question sociale, objet absent chez Bovet. Les Français défendent le merveilleux pédagogique au détriment de l'analyse savante pouvant le mettre en cause. Bovet demeure un simple passeur. Le scoutisme ouvre et ferme les frontières, recombinées selon les modalités propres à chaque époque.

French scouting has never seen an authentic model in Robert Baden-Powell. When they were founded in 1911, the *Eclaireurs de France* (Boy-Scouts of France) did not want to translate *Scouting for Boys*. Because of their nationalism, they published their own manual. The translation came from Switzerland thanks to the work of the philosopher Pierre Bovet. French-speaking Switzerland was the crossroads of British pedagogical texts translated into French that French scouts rejected. *Scouting for Boys* was translated by Bovet and published by Delachaux et Niestlé. This was possible because of the former camping practices of the Young Men's Christian Association, of which Bovet was a member. However, Bovet's scout translation arrived in France thanks to pedagogues such as Georges Bertier and Georges Gallienne, fighters for New Education and social reformers. The situation changed in the 1920s because of the *Eclaireurs*' engagement in the world scout organisation, which was under the leadership of the scouts' founder Baden-Powell. Publishers Delachaux et Niestlé opened a branch in Paris in 1919. The publishers engaged several other translators, all Swiss scout chiefs, such as Ketty Jentzer or Jean Carrard. They translated Baden-Powell and Lady Baden-Powell's books on games, knots, wolf cubs, rover scouts and girl scouts. These books were in each French scoutmaster's library. In 1920, Bovet wrote his scouting master-book, *Le Génie de Baden-Powell* (Baden-Powell's Genius), which analysed scouting education according to New Education. But other borders appeared. French scout associations did not need Swiss translations because they published their own works in the 1930s. The border was any scholarly analysis of their project. French scouts worked with philosophers (Edmond Goblot and Pierre Mendousse), principally on social questions that Bovet's books did not mention. French scouts wanted to distance their marvellous pedagogic universe from scientific works. For the French scoutmasters, Bovet's work became commonplace. Linguistic borders were opened or closed according to the actors and were recombined within different boundaries.

Introduction

Dès sa fondation en 1911, le scoutisme en France reçoit de façon complexe l'oeuvre du Britannique Robert Baden-Powell (1857-1941). Les Eclaireurs de France (EDF) refusent de traduire l'ouvrage *Scouting for boys*. Ils mobilisent ce programme d'éducation civique en plein air au service d'un farouche nationalisme pédagogique. Les Français ferment la frontière. Or, l'impossible dialogue international est contemporain des traductions de Baden-Powell par le pédagogue suisse Pierre Bovet (1878–1965). En 1912, il traduit *Scouting for boys* sous le titre *Eclaireurs* pour Delachaux et Niestlé. Durant la première moitié du XXe siècle, le catalogue de l'éditeur neuchâtelois compte jusqu'à onze ouvrages de Baden-Powell. La Suisse demeure le premier atelier francophone de traduction de ses ouvrages. Il émerge au moment où Bovet dirige l'Institut Jean-Jacques Rousseau à Genève. La traduction scoute française et l'institutionnalisation de l'Education nouvelle sont donc contemporaines. Quels enjeux révèle la diffusion francophone du programme scout anglais quand les Français prétendent eux-mêmes la contrôler?

Pendant l'entre-deux-guerres, le scoutisme fait l'objet d'une étude savante par Bovet qui l'analyse au prisme de la psychologie de l'adolescence dans *Le Génie de Baden-Powell* (1921). Son ouvrage prolonge *L'Instinct combatif* (1917), centré sur la construction de l'adolescence par l'affrontement ludique entre pairs. Puis, les traductions françaises de Baden-Powell portent le sceau de l'Institut Rousseau. Plusieurs dirigeants scouts suisses assurent ces traductions pour Delachaux et Niestlé. Cette complémentarité légitime le programme scout dans l'Education nouvelle, d'autant qu'au même moment, l'internationale scoute s'organise sous le magistère de Baden-Powell.

En France, les Eclaireurs élisent en 1921 leur nouveau président, Georges Bertier, directeur de l'Ecole des Roches. Ils sont actifs dans la fondation de l'internationale scoute au congrès de Paris en 1922. Mais, bien que Bertier participe au Bureau International de l'Education nouvelle, les Eclaireurs demeurent indifférents aux travaux de Bovet.

Les Eclaireurs défendent toujours une frontière. Ils sont ouverts à la pédagogie scoute anglo-saxonne mais dressent un barrage aussi discret que solide devant l'analyse savante. En défendant le merveilleux scout, ils témoignent du refus d'interroger la fiction et l'univers symbolique dans lequel baignent les scouts. Ceci est d'autant plus vrai que les Eclaireurs se rapprochent de l'école publique. Fort de ce rayonnement dans le champ éducatif français, les Eclaireurs surveillent toujours une frontière. Il s'agit de maîtriser l'espace de l'enchantement du monde. La méthode scoute peut-elle coexister avec son analyse savante? Entre le merveilleux scout d'un côté et la construction savante de Bovet de l'autre, les Eclaireurs mettent à distance la seconde pour mieux garantir la première. La faible réception française des travaux suisses tend-elle à montrer que l'espace pédagogique reste avant tout national?

Les échanges franco-britanniques passent par la Suisse. Mais cette relation triangulaire se recompose selon les intérêts des Eclaireurs. La frontière linguistique du début du siècle évolue vers la frontière intellectuelle après le conflit mondial. L'étude des relations entre les Eclaireurs de France et la production pédagogique suisse repose sur le dépouillement de publications françaises, spécialement la revue *Le Chef* (1922–1940). Ont été étudiées les traductions publiées par Delachaux et Niestlé. Nous déployons cette question en trois parties chrono-thématiques. La première interroge les raisons du maintien ferme de la frontière linguistique par les Français (1912–1921). La deuxième s'efforce d'explorer l'assise intellectuelle du scoutisme en Suisse francophone (1921–1941). La troisième discute la réception indifférente des travaux de Bovet en France.[1]

1. Tenir la frontière nationale 1912–1921

Eclaireurs et "génie national"

Fondés par la campagne de presse du *Journal des Voyages* en 1911, les EDF achètent les droits de traduction et d'adaptation de Baden-Powell. Dès 1912, l'escamotage de *Scouting for boys* est justifié en note en bas de page du *Livre de l'Eclaireur*. Ce dernier remplace l'ouvrage anglais. Il n'est pas question de *"traduction littérale"* ni *"d'adaptation étroite"* de *Scouting for boys*. Les Français ne sauraient imiter sans risque une initiative anglaise:[2]

> Chaque peuple a son génie particulier. C'est ainsi que Français et Anglais ne peuvent se trouver dans des conditions semblables, quant à la compréhension de diverses choses: ils n'ont ni les mêmes institutions, ni les mêmes mœurs, ni les mêmes habitudes, ni les mêmes traditions. En plus, de profondes différences séparent les méthodes éducatives de l'enfance employées chez les deux peuples. Avant tout, nous avons donc tenté de faire un livre POUR LES PETITS FRANÇAIS [*sic*], un livre qui corresponde à leur tempérament propre et ne contienne rien de nature à les surprendre ou à les désorienter. Le "Scouting for boys" comporte une suite de conversations familières autour du feu de camp, au cours desquelles sont introduites, sans ordre naturel, comme elles se présentent, toutes les matières constituant le Scoutisme. Il nous a paru que cette façon de traiter les sujets "au hasard de la fourchette" dérouterait nos enfants habitués à l'ordre et à la clarté d'exposition qui forment le fond de nos méthodes pédagogiques et sont le bien propre de notre génie national.

---

[1] Nous remercions la professeure Anne-Françoise Praz (Université de Fribourg) pour son encouragement à étudier les travaux scouts de Bovet.[n]typesetter: please remove the '1' before 'Nous' as I cannot do this. Copyeditor[/n].

[2] Avertissement à *Le Livre de l'Eclaireur*, by Maximin-Léonce Royet (Paris: Eclaireurs de France, 1912), 39-40.

L'ordre contre le désordre, la netteté contre le flou, *Le Livre de l'Eclaireur* revendique la surveillance frontalière. Il soumet la pédagogie britannique au "*génie national*". L'antagonisme franco-britannique est un facteur de mobilisation nationale reposant sur la rationalité attribuée au continent. Il faut proscrire les règlements cabalistiques. On n'élève pas les Français par des méthodes "qui eussent prêté à rire" ni avec "les saluts spéciaux". Un choix raisonnable masque toujours un jugement de valeur: "Il a paru utile de proscrire tout ce qui pouvait évoquer l'idée d'un compagnonnage secret, d'une initiation rituelle, en un mot d'une secte fermée".[3] Le *scouting* s'intègre dans un clivage qui l'englobe et le dépasse. Le mot anglais désignant un soldat en reconnaissance prend un sens plus large. Quand l'impérialisme européen couvre le monde, le *scout* évoque l'explorateur. Il possèderait une étymologie latine venant des "*escoutes*" du chroniqueur médiéval Froissart.[4] Il retrouverait ainsi sa véritable origine, "une idée gréco-latine, qui tout naturellement refleurit dans notre civilisation française. Rien de nouveau sous le soleil!"[5] Sans influence latine et méditerranéenne, l'initiative britannique est disqualifiée. Les parrains furent donc les Normands du XIe siècle![6] L'identité nationale se cristallise dans des stéréotypes. Le comité EDF interdit les contacts outre-Manche, au point que des lecteurs s'interrogent sur la réalité des échanges avec un Baden-Powell peu cité dans le périodique.[7] Le "*génie national*" tient fermement la frontière pédagogique. Mais cette ignorance cordiale s'arrête là où débute la politique. Au printemps 1914, l'agenda diplomatique franco-britannique consolide l'Entente cordiale. Pour le dixième anniversaire, George V est l'invité de la République pour les célébrations parisiennes (22–24 avril 1914). Les Eclaireurs relatent discrètement la visite car leur nationalisme ne saurait désavouer le gouvernement.[8]

Plein air protestant

La Suisse est la porte d'entrée de Baden-Powell en francophonie. Trois éléments la conditionnent: l'expérience d'un pédagogue, sa direction d'un institut de pédagogie et une politique éditoriale. Pierre Bovet (1878–1965) est au centre de cette rencontre.[9] En 1902, il a soutenu sa thèse de philosophie à Genève. Elevé dans le solide protestantisme paternel à Grandchamp, Bovet est un cadre actif des Jeunesses protestantes, les Unions chrétiennes de Jeunes Gens (UCJG; *Young Men's Christian Association*, YMCA). Il préside la section neuchâteloise et suit en 1900 la conférence mondiale à Chicago où les jeunes chrétiens apprennent le réveil de la foi par le camp de toile. Les YMCA européens l'intègrent dans leurs activités. En Suisse romande, on campe sur les bords du lac Léman dès 1902. En France dès 1906, les

---

[3] Maximin-Léonce Royet, "L'adaptation française au scoutisme anglais," in *Les Eclaireurs de France et le rôle social du scoutisme français* (Paris: Larousse, 1913), 39–40.
[4] Jean Froissart (v. 1337–v. 1410), auteur de récits de la vie aristocratique pendant la guerre de Cent Ans.
[5] Capitaine Royet, "Comment le mot scout est d'origine française. L'Escoute," *L'Eclaireur de France* 4 (10 January 1914): 103.
[6] Royet, "L'œuvre du général Baden-Powell," in *Les Eclaireurs de France*, 18–19.
[7] "Le Courrier des Eclaireurs," *L'Eclaireur de France* 10 (15 July 1914): 319.
[8] "Le jour des boy-scouts," *L'Eclaireur de France* 8 (15 May 1914): 251. Sur les conditions de fondation des Eclaireurs, cf. Daniel Denis, "Une pédagogie du simulacre: l'invention du scoutisme (1900–1912)," *Agora débats/jeunesse* 11 (1er trim. 1998): 7–18.
[9] Jean-Michel Martin, *Pierre Bovet, l'homme du seuil: sa position par rapport à la pédagogie, à la psychanalyse et à la psychologie religieuse* (Cousset, Switzerland: Delval, 1986).

camps de la Fédération des étudiants chrétiens rassemblent en Charente-inférieure 350 campeurs.[10] Parmi les Unions suisses, Bovet est un campeur assidu quand sort *Scouting for boys* à Londres en 1908.[11]

En 1912 le pédagogue Edouard Claparède fonde à Genève l'Ecole des sciences de l'Education, institut privé d'enseignement supérieur, de recherche pédagogique et psychologique sous le patronage de Jean-Jacques Rousseau. Si, en France, cet enseignement est universitaire, l'initiative privée revendique sa filiation d'avec l'auteur d'*Emile*.[12] Bovet dirige l'établissement et répond aux attentes d'une galaxie d'acteurs genevois, officiels et privés souhaitant l'essor d'une science de l'enfance tout en mettant à distance l'intégration universitaire. La traduction de Baden-Powell intervient dans un contexte de défense de l'autonomie scientifique face à la pression de l'enseignement public réclamant une expertise synonyme de tutelle.[13] L'événement académique répond à l'actualité éditoriale. La vie d'aventure de Baden-Powell narrant l'art de se débrouiller aux colonies est offerte aux jeunes Occidentaux là où Rousseau proscrivait les livres pour édifier Emile, à l'exception d'un seul, *Robinson Crusoé*. Une heureuse coïncidence psychopédagogique préside la rencontre entre la littérature de l'officier colonial et l'institutionnalisation de l'Education nouvelle. 1912 est aussi l'année où l'éditeur neuchâtelois Paul Delachaux cède à son fils Arthur sa maison. *Eclaireurs un programme d'éducation civique* est le premier titre de la nouvelle collection des actualités pédagogiques.[14]

Contrebande

En France de rares personnalités reçoivent *Eclaireurs*, deux pédagogues à la tête des premières troupes scoutes. Georges Bertier (1877–1962) dirige l'Ecole des Roches. Georges Gallienne (1871–1953) est pasteur à la Mission populaire évangélique.

L'Ecole des Roches est un établissement secondaire privé pour héritiers richement dotés. Il se présente comme l'avant-poste de l'Education nouvelle, notamment par la "vie de famille" animée par les professeurs.[15] Bertier y ouvre une troupe scoute dès mars 1911 en important l'équipement de Grande-Bretagne. Il enrôle le chef Bateman, "ancien sous-officier de Baden-Powell". En septembre 1911, la revue de Bertier, *L'Education*, s'ouvre à un adepte enthousiaste, Paul Vuibert, fils de l'éditeur Henry Vuibert.[16] En décembre, Bertier adhère au comité fondateur des Eclaireurs de France mais reste en retrait. Son nom n'apparaît pas dans les diatribes anglophobes. Homme de la circulation des idées, Bertier observe le mouvement en Angleterre et aux Etats-Unis. *L'Education* contredit le dogmatisme des EDF et

---

[10]Arnaud Baubérot, "De l'éducation populaire à l'éducation nouvelle: les protestants français et la naissance du scoutisme (1910–1914)," *Revue du Nord* 28 Hors-Série (2012): 197–209.

[11]*Scouting for Boys: A Handbook for Instruction in Good Citizenship*, sort chez Horace Cox (397 pp.) et chez Arthur Pearson (288 pp.).

[12]Daniel Hameline, "L'Institut Jean-Jacques Rousseau et l'Education nouvelle," in *L'Education nouvelle, histoire, présence et devenir*, ed. Annick Ohayon, Dominique Ottavi et Antoine Savoye (Bern: Peter Lang, 2004), 145–62.

[13]Rita Hofstetter, *Genève: creuset des sciences de l'éducation (fin du XIXe siècle–première moitié du XXe siècle)* (Genève: Droz, 2010).

[14]Robert Baden-Powell, *Eclaireurs un programme d'éducation civique*, trans. Pierre Bovet (Neuchâtel: Delachaux et Niestlé, 1912). Collection "Actualités pédagogiques."

[15]Nathalie Duval, *L'école des Roches* (Paris: Belin, 2009).

[16]Paul Vuibert, "Les 'Boy-Scouts,'" *L'Education* 3 (September 1911): 321–40.

recense les articles anglo-saxons pour un lectorat cultivé et savant.[17] *L'Education* compte Baden-Powell parmi les pédagogues, comme Georges, Dewey ou James dont Bertier fait aussi connaître l'œuvre.[18]

L'autre pasteur, Georges Gallienne, anime à Paris la Mission populaire évangélique où il lance une troupe dès l'automne 1910. Les garçons construisent une pompe à bras pour imiter les pompiers. Ces activités physiques complètent la moralisation des classes populaires par l'aide maternelle ou la tempérance antialcoolique dont Gallienne est un prosélyte fervent. Depuis son installation après la Commune, la Mission populaire évangélique cherche la solution pédagogique à la question sociale. Au début du XXe siècle, la Mission de Gallienne rue de l'Avre voisine l'usine d'optique de l'ingénieur genevois Louis Sautter (1825–1912). Son fils, Emmanuel (1862–1933), est secrétaire du comité national des UCJG puis secrétaire du comité universel des YMCA à Genève.[19] La convergence entre réformisme social et pédagogie du camp de toile fonctionne déjà bien au sein des jeunes protestants. Ceci conditionne la circulation entre Paris et Genève à l'opposé de l'anglophobie des EDF. Gallienne préfère les rejoindre au détriment des sections cadettes des UCJG organisées en Eclaireurs unionistes. Mais Gallienne lit *Eclaireurs* traduit par Bovet. Il en rédige une critique élogieuse dans le journal protestant *Le Christianisme* où il remercie Bovet, l'interprète "si consciencieux":[20]

> Sous sa vêture française il a conservé jusqu'à l'exagération son allure britannique, mais nous l'aimons mieux ainsi. Il n'a pas essayé, en effet, de s'adapter à notre intellectualisme raffiné parfois plus soucieux de la forme que du fond; il nous apporte en de simples causeries autour du feu de bivouac, la pensée et surtout le cœur d'un homme qui connaît et qui aime l'âme de l'enfant. Vous ne trouverez chez lui aucune arrière pensée intéressée, il ne cherche pas à gagner des élèves, à grossir les rangs de son club, à attirer dans son groupement de nouveaux adeptes. Ce qu'il veut ardemment c'est de former le caractère et ennoblir les vies de ceux qui demain auront à porter leurs lourdes responsabilités d'hommes et de citoyens. Pour cela il ne craint pas de les faire sortir de la cité, il les conduit aux champs, leur fait dresser la tente au bord du ruisseau, puis quand le frugal repas du soir est terminé et que joyeuses montent les clartés. Entrons dans le cercle lumineux magister, pédagogues, graves catéchistes et, accroupis sur les talons – saine gymnastique pour nos genoux ankylosés, écoutons le conteur.

L'expérience des campeurs protestants confirme le scoutisme comme pédagogie aboutie du plein air, non plus à des fins missionnaires mais plus largement éducatives. La souplesse de pensée des protestants dépasse le nationalisme des EDF. Ces derniers sont alors le double inversé de l'internationale des jeunes protestants. Les EDF, plus jeune, connaissent une fascination mêlée de répulsion à l'égard du

---

[17]Lucien Cellerier, "Les Boy Scouts aux Etats-Unis," *L'Education* 3 (September 1912): 439–40; id., "Les Boy Scouts en Grande-Bretagne," ibid.: 442–43.

[18]William James, *Précis de psychologie traduit par E. Baudin professeur de philosophie au Collège Stanislas et G. Bertier directeur de l'Ecole des Roches* (Paris: Marcel Rivière, 1909).

[19]Georges Gallienne, *Les éclaireurs de Grenelle, les débuts du scoutisme en France* (1946, notes dactylographiées inédites, archives Eclaireuses Eclaireurs de France, document non côté): 35; Hélène Trocmé, "Un modèle américain transposé: les foyers du soldat de l'Union Franco-Américaine (1914–1922)," in *Les Américains et la France (1917–1947). Engagements et représentations*, ed. Marie-Claude Genet-Delacroix, Hélène Trocmé and François Cochet (Paris: Maisonneuve et Larose, 1999), 5–23.

[20]Georges Gallienne, "*Eclaireurs* par Baden-Powell, traduit par P.B.," *Le Christianisme* (27 March 1913), coupure de presse, Archives municipals de Toulouse, 9Z–1.

pédagogue britannique. Entre les deux postures inconciliables, Bertier et Gallienne se frayent une place discrètement autonome.

Littérature populaire

Lorsque Gallienne suit le "*conteur*" Baden-Powell, il le relie au merveilleux du roman populaire. Les auteurs étudiés lisent Baden-Powell grâce aux romanciers pour la jeunesse. L'auteur du *Livre de l'Eclaireur* l'a découvert grâce à Paul Zimmermann, romancier d'aventures. Zimmermann, auteur de *Jack l'Eclaireur*, a apporté la "compréhension judicieuse de la psychologie enfantine".[21] Cette découverte par le roman populaire n'est pas seulement française. Bovet la connaît aussi. Il lit *Scouting for boys* grâce au secrétaire des UCJG de Neuchâtel, Gaston Clerc "le premier qui ait fait des démarches pour le mettre en français".[22] En 1912 Gaston Clerc écrit *Le Secret de la porte de fer* paru dans le bulletin des UCJG. Dans un château, trois jeunes suisses démasquent des faux-monnayeurs. Les garçons sont dirigés par leur cousin français, chef de l'équipe.[23] Bovet doit à Gaston Clerc le "beau chapitre sur la Chevalerie" d'*Eclaireurs*. De part et d'autre de la frontière franco-suisse, on demeure sous l'influence du roman d'aventure. Les EDF liés à la presse d'aventure du *Journal des Voyages* ont leur siège dans la rédaction dont le directeur est aussi leur secrétaire. On sait combien la littérature coloniale est à la genèse des Eclaireurs de France.[24] En Suisse francophone, les jeunes protestants jouent aussi avec la porosité entre pédagogie et roman d'aventure.

2. Foyer intellectuel romand 1921–1941

Étude savante

Depuis 1912 Bovet à la tête de l'Institut Rousseau met en objet savant la pédagogie scoute. Il traduit le *Wolf cubs handbook* en 1916 dans lequel Baden-Powell puise son imaginaire chez Rudyard Kipling, *Kim* et le *Livre de la Jungle*. *Le Livre des louveteaux* sort en 1919. Baden-Powell est intronisé à la tête de l'internationale scoute au jamboree de Londres (1920) puis à la conférence de Paris (1922). Dans l'organisation du monde après le conflit, le mouvement scout s'affirme autour de la Société des nations. En 1921, Bovet revoit la traduction de *Aids to scoutmastership* (le *Guide du chef Eclaireur*) destiné aux cadres. Enfin et surtout, il analyse *Le Génie de Baden-Powell*. Il relie le mouvement, ses rituels et sa symbolique à la psychologie de l'adolescent dont l'essor est contemporain. *Le Génie* est éditée à Genève chez

---

[21] Royet, "Note de l'auteur," in *Les Eclaireurs de France*, 8. Royet signe des romans xénophobes, cf. Pierre Versins, *Encyclopédie de l'utopie, des voyages extraordinaires et de la science fiction* (Paris: L'Age d'Homme, 1972).

[22] Pierre Bovet, "Avant-propos du traducteur à la deuxième édition," in *Eclaireurs. Un programme d'éducation civique*, 8th ed., Robert Baden-Powell (Neuchâtel: Delachaux et Niestlé, 1936), 6.

[23] Gaston Clerc, *Le Secret de la porte de fer* (Genève: Société générale d'imprimerie, 1913; Lausanne: L'Aire, 1981). Henri Reber, "Un précurseur du roman scout," in *Le roman scout (1927–1962): un genre littéraire?*, ed. Janus Bifrons, *Revue universitaire de l'adolescence* 4 (Nancy: PUN, 1992): 180–82.

[24] Daniel Denis, "'L'école de la vie sauvage': un bain de jouvence du Parti colonial?," in *A l'école de l'aventure. Pratiques sportives de plein air et idéologie de la conquête du monde 1890–1940*, ed. Daniel Denis and Christian Pociello (Voiron, France: PUS, 2000), 21–35.

Forum. Nous ignorons pourquoi, en 1921, l'ouvrage ne sort pas chez Delachaux et Niestlé, comme pour l'édition suivante (1934).[25]

D'où vient ce génie? Etre éclaireur réalise pleinement la vie de l'adolescent. En se battant par jeu, le garçon prépare par l'affrontement ludique entre pairs sa future condition d'adulte. L'art du chef éclaireur consiste à canaliser ces manifestations naturelles selon les normes socialement admises. Encourageant l'activité spontanée dans un sens social, le chef demeure, aux yeux des garçons, celui capable de guider cette vie intense "il y a là une invention pédagogique géniale". On donne aux jeunes comme supérieurs "des 'types' pourvus des qualités qui s'imposent à son admiration".[26] Le chef de jeunes est un homme d'exemple dont le caractère et la "grandeur morale" subliment cet "instinct de combat". Au comportement combatif des jeunes, répond celui, moral, du chef tirant ses éclaireurs, comme une humanité tirée du chaos: "Seuls les hommes qui savent goûter les âpres joies de la lutte nous en imposent par leur caractère".[27] Comme le précise Jean-Michel Martin, l'éducation scoute agit par la consigne donnée aux enfants. Elle provoque un double mouvement de pensée, montant à la recherche d'une formule générale et descendant en même temps vers des exemples concrets.[28] Sa portée éducative repose aussi sur le passage symbolique des étapes de la civilisation. Bovet reprend les travaux du psychologue Granville Stanley Hall sur la construction individuelle par étapes symboliques.[29]

Bovet avait déjà développé la question dans *L'Instinct combatif* (1917). Se battre offre de revivre les temps archaïques de l'affrontement entre mâles pour contrôler l'espèce.[30] Les activités physiques conditionnent la moralisation de l'adolescent. *Le Génie de Baden-Powell* fait suite à *L'Instinct combatif*. Le scoutisme veut transformer cette violence archaïque en fins admissibles, à l'image du tournoi judiciaire englobé dans le monopole de la guerre par l'Etat. Après le conflit mondial, l'adhésion de l'internationale scoute à la Société des nations, stade supérieur de civilisation, répond à l'argumentaire psychologique.[31]

Mais Bovet n'est plus un praticien. Ce fin psychologue aime peu l'éducation physique, allergie héritée de son père.[32] Il reproche à la tenue scoute son évocation trop militaire. L'ancien campeur protestant tient à bonne distance le plein air. *Le Génie de Baden-Powell* demeure un exercice littéraire. Bovet cite des réformateurs du christianisme médiéval (François d'Assise), des XVIIe et XVIIIe siècles (Georges Fox, William Penn, John Woolman) et des contemporains (Charles Wagner). Les

---

[25]Pierre Bovet, *Le Génie de Baden-Powell. Ce qu'il faut voir dans le scoutisme. Ses bases psychologiques. Sa valeur éducative. L'instinct combatif et l'idéal des jeunes* (Genève: Forum, 1921).
[26]Bovet, "Berton," in *Le Génie de Baden-Powell*, 19.
[27]Id., "Valeurs morales," in *Le Génie de Baden-Powell*, 25.
[28]Martin, *Pierre Bovet, l'homme du seuil*, 34-35.
[29]Chaque être humain récapitule l'histoire de l'humanité qui doit son essor à l'accumulation d'expériences. Florian Houssier, "S. G. Hall (1844–1924): un pionnier dans la découverte de l'adolescence. Ses liens avec les premiers psychanalystes de l'adolescent," *La psychiatrie de l'enfant* 462, no. 2 (2003): 655-68.
[30]Pierre Bovet, *L'Instinct combatif. Psychologie, éducation* (Neuchâtel: Delachaux et Niestlé, 1917). Collection "Actualités pédagogiques."
[31]Bovet, "Les altérations de l'instinct combatif," in *Le Génie de Baden-Powell*, 24. Cf. Mario Sica, "Le rendez-vous manqué de Baden-Powell avec la Société des Nations (1919–1933)," in *Le scoutisme entre guerre et paix au XXe siècle*, ed. Arnaud Baubérot and Nathalie Duval (Paris: L'Harmattan, 2006), 53–65.
[32]Martin, *Pierre Bovet, l'homme du seuil*, 65.

philosophes (Socrate, Bergson, Boutroux, Bréal, Payot) et les pédagogues (Froebel, Rouma, Varendonck, Ferrières) cités sont ceux dont il fréquente le plus les textes. Les romanciers semblent relever de son panthéon personnel. Outre Kipling, ce sont des romanciers suisses de l'enfance. Philippe Monnier (1864–1911), auteur du *Livre de Blaise* (1904) est largement cité comme modèle de chef éclaireur dans l'espace urbain, et Johanna Spyri (1827–1901), auteure de *Heidi* (1881) pareillement dans le monde rural. Tout indique combien *Le Génie de Baden-Powell* est analysé au miroir de la littérature suisse de l'enfance. Cette connaissance demeure liée à la culture livresque de l'auteur.

Traducteurs

Baden-Powell compte comme auteur au catalogue de Delachaux et Niestlé. Neuf éditions d'*Eclaireurs* paraissent de 1912 à 1939, une tous les trois ans en moyenne. De 1918 à 1937, l'éditeur édite cinq fois *Le Livre des Louveteaux*, autant que *Le Livre des Eclaireuses*. La traduction par Bovet garantie le sérieux de la maison. Pour autant, il n'est pas seul. *L'homme du seuil* préfère rester l'homme d'une intuition, celle de la traduction de Baden-Powell dès 1912. Il ne semble pas souhaiter prolonger ce travail. A la suite du maître, les traductions mobilisent une dizaine d'hommes et de femmes. Plus jeunes que lui, ils ont grandi avec le mouvement scout et ont goûté le sel de ses équipées. Ils connaissent le mouvement suisse comme cadres.[33] Ce compagnonnage est sans équivalent dans l'hexagone. Nous tirons ici quatre figures notables. Celui qui traduit *Aids to scoutmastership* sous le titre du *Guide du Chef Eclaireur* est Jean Carrard.[34] Il dirige la Brigade de Sauvabelin à Lausanne (1920–1922), doyenne des troupes du canton de Vaud. Carrard s'entoure d'autres chefs scouts et d'enseignants anglais. Il est reconnaissant à Bovet pour la "*grande sécurité*" ressentie par sa relecture.[35] La traduction scoute concerne aussi des ouvrages américains avec Marcel North (1909–1990). Cet illustrateur neuchâtelois formé aux Arts décoratifs de Strasbourg, traduit Hillcourt et Baden-Powell.[36]

La traduction est aussi féminine. Tout indique le lien d'Estelle West-Jullien avec l'éditeur genevois Alexandre Jullien chez qui elle traduit dès 1923 l'anglais Hargrave. Pour Delachaux et Niestlé, ses traductions concernent les jeux. Sa traduction de

---

[33] Pour les cantons suisses, cf. la thèse de Dominik Stroppel, *Der Schweizerische Pfadfinderbund 1918 bis 1945* (PhD diss., University of Zurich, 1996). Signalons l'exposition aux Archives d'Etat de Genève pour le centenaire du mouvement, cf. http://www.scout.ch/de/3/za-m/, consulté le 2 octobre 2013.

[34] Robert Baden-Powell, *Le Guide du chef éclaireur, traduit de l'anglais par Jean Carrard instructeur en chef de la brigade Sauvabelin, à Lausanne* (Neuchâtel: Delachaux et Niestlé, 1921).

[35] Jean Carrard, "Avant-propos du traducteur," in *Le Guide du chef éclaireur*, 3rd ed., by Robert Baden-Powell (Neuchâtel: Delachaux et Niestlé, 1931), 6. Sur la brigade de Sauvabelin, http://2012.sauvabelin.ch/index.php?page=historique, consulté le 3 octobre 2013.

[36] William Hillcourt, *Le Manuel du Chef de Patrouille. Traduit d'après l'édition des Boys Scouts d'Amérique par Marcel North* (Neuchâtel: Delachaux et Niestlé, 1936). Robert Baden-Powell, *Pour devenir un homme*, trans. Marcel North (Neuchâtel: Delachaux et Niestlé, 1938). Michel Schlup, *Marcel North, dessinateur, aquarelliste, graveur, illustrateur, scénographe, écrivain et chroniqueur* (Neuchâtel: BPU, 2009), 180.

Scouting games en 1930 vient après huit éditions anglaises.[37] Le travail le plus significatif vient de la gymnaste Ketty Jentzer (1881–1965). A l'Institut Rousseau, elle enseigne de 1913 à 1939 les danses populaires et les jeux sportifs. En 1919, Delachaux et Niestlé édite son ouvrage *Jeux de plein air et d'intérieur*, succès avec 10 rééditions jusqu'en 1964. Ketty Jentzer, commissaire cantonale des Eclaireuses genevoises, traduit le manuel des éclaireuses.[38] Notons que Ketty Jentzer, formée à l'Institut de gymnastique de Stockholm, enseigne à l'Institut Rousseau la gymnastique suédoise. Contrairement à la France, le scoutisme à Genève voisine paisiblement avec la gymnastique analytique et segmentée venant de Suède. Ketty Jentzer traduit aussi le manuel de gymnastique suédoise féminine.[39] La traduction reste fidèle à l'oeuvre de Baden-Powell mais rares sont celles qui, telle Ketty Jentzer, laissent une oeuvre propre. Un second cercle de traducteurs gravite autour de l'éditeur et de l'Institut.[40]

3. Réception française
Discrète bienveillance

La Grande Guerre modifie le statut de l'Angleterre aux yeux du scoutisme français en atténuant l'anglophobie des EDF. Toutefois, les traductions leurs sont extérieures. 1916 voit sortir l'édition française du *système des patrouilles* de Roland Phillips.[41] En 1921, *Le Génie de Baden-Powell* est diffusé à Paris par la Maison des Scouts, enseigne tenue par le chef Jean Loiseau. Celui-ci est promoteur du "*vrai scoutisme*", contre la préparation militaire. Dès 1917, Loiseau a initié les Eclaireurs méthode Baden-Powell (EMBP), adeptes de "*l'application intégrale*" du modèle anglais. Point de frontière linguistique pour le *scoutmaster* et les *patrol leaders*. L'emploi du vocabulaire anglais montre un intérêt inédit pour le *scouting*. En 1921, les Eclaireurs de Loiseau rejoignent les EDF. La même année, celui-ci entre aussi au comité directeur quand Georges Bertier est élu président. Les libéraux et les familiaux leplaysiens de l'Ecole des Roches évincent la formation prémilitaire de la jeunesse. En 1922, le congrès international de Paris intronise Baden-Powell chef scout du monde. L'organisation de jeunesse des pays vainqueurs de la guerre est une internationale subtilement dominée par les anglo-saxons.

---

[37]Estelle Wuest-Jullien traduit: John Hargrave, *Le Livre du Wigwam* (Genève: Jullien, 1923). Robert Baden-Powell, *Les mille et une activités de l'Eclaireur: propos du chef scout* (Neuchâtel: Delachaux et Niestlé, 1929). Id., *Jeux d'éclaireurs* (Neuchâtel: Delachaux et Niestlé, 1930). D. W. Pinkey, *Le jeu de la corde et du lasso* (Neuchâtel: Delachaux et Niestlé, 1935).
[38]Ketty Jentzer, *Jeux de plein air et d'intérieur: cent descriptions illustrées de diagrammes* (Neuchâtel: Delachaux et Niestlé, 1919). Robert Baden-Powell, *Le Livre des Éclaireuses. Manuel pour les lutins, les éclaireuses, les guides et leurs chefs*, trans. Ketty Jentzer (Neuchâtel: Delachaux et Niestlé, 1923).
[39]Elli Björksten, *Gymnastique féminine: 1ère partie. Psychologie et physiologie* (Neuchâtel: Delachaux et Niestlé, 1926). Nous remercions Véronique Czáka, doctorante à l'Université de Genève.
[40]W. Breithaupt, A. C. Demole, Jean-Jacques Dessoulavy, Pierre Imhof et Eugène Porret. Un étudiant de l'Institut, Camillo Bariffi (1893–1982), fonde une école à Lugano, anime les scouts du Tessin puis devient vice président de la Fédération des Eclaireurs suisses. Cf. http://aicos-italia.org/Doc/Storia%20di%20SpR.pdf, consulté le 3 octobre 2013.
[41]Roland Philipps, *The Patrol System* (London: Boy Scouts Association, 1914). Il est tué en 1916 sur la Somme. *L'éducation nationale par le scoutisme, le système des patrouilles par Capt. The Hon. Roland E. Philipps*, trans. Jules Dangay (Paris: Grande Maison, 1916), 59.

Or, ce moment correspond à un accueil très modeste des travaux suisses. Les Eclaireurs de France reçoivent avec sympathie mais discrètement *Le Génie de Baden-Powell*.[42] *Le Guide du chef Eclaireur* est pourtant salué – en une page – dans l'organe des cadres.[43] Ces articles étudient l'émulation et les marques distinctives des éclaireurs obtenues hors de tout concours. Pour réussir, le garçon doit se montrer non pas à la hauteur de ses concurrents mais à hauteur de la situation. Les EDF cernent parfaitement le plaisir naturel existant à se mesurer aux autres sans donner lieu à des récompenses. Ceci nourrit leur réflexion sur la réforme de la compétition scolaire par l'acquisition des brevets.[44] A l'initiative du président Bertier, les Eclaireurs de France et l'enseignement primaire se rapprochent. Dès 1927, des liens avec les écoles normales prolongent la formation d'instituteurs en plein air. Les chefs et cheftaines formés au camp école de Cappy doivent lire les classiques *Eclaireurs*, *Le Guide du chef Eclaireur* ainsi que *Le système des patrouilles*. Les impétrants rédigent leur analyse du projet scout, ceci constituant l'épreuve théorique du brevet de chef.[45] Mais, à part ces articles, les EDF ne reviennent pas sur Bovet et ses émules. La lecture obligatoire de Baden-Powell rend le traducteur transparent, effacé devant l'auteur.

Nous y voyons la réussite de la transcription d'un auteur reçu naturellement hors de sa langue natale. Le dessein accompli de Baden-Powell se paye de l'oubli des traducteurs. Mais d'autres raisons permettent d'expliquer cette mise à l'écart. Nous en voyons trois. La première est liée à l'organisation concurrentielle de l'édition scoute en France, la deuxième tient à la présence de philosophes parmi les EDF. Enfin, la troisième est la défense de l'enchantement du monde devant l'objectivation savante.

Frontière recomposée

Concurrence éditoriale

L'édition scoute reflète la concurrence entre associations. Le scoutisme catholique est en plein essor. Les Scouts de France créés en 1920 traduisent avec des éditeurs comme Redier ou SPES, puis deviennent autonomes.[46] Ceci affaiblit le carrefour éditorial romand dans le champ francophone, bien que Delachaux et Niestlé, souhaitant se rapprocher de Paris, possède depuis 1919 sa succursale dans la capitale. Les EDF éditent leurs propres publications, en moyenne cinq par an. Les publications des Eclaireurs unionistes sortent de la maison protestante La Flamme.

La concurrence concerne les Routiers (16–20 ans) et les Louveteaux (8–11 ans). En 1923, l'EDF Marty appelle à traduire *Rovering to Success* écrit par Baden-Powell pour les plus de 16 ans, la "vie sportive pour jeunes gens".[47] Cet appel sans effet n'est entendu que dix ans plus tard par les Scouts de France. Entre temps, ils ont fondé en 1929 leur maison, les Presses d'Ile de France. En 1932, ils participent à la traduction de *Rovering to Success* chez l'éditeur de droite Redier. L'ouvrage

---

[42]"Pierre Bovet, Le génie de Baden-Powell," *L'Eclaireur de France* 73 (December 1921): 13–14.
[43]Emile Guillen, "Le guide du chef éclaireur," *Le Chef* 2 (20 April 1922): 16.
[44]La progression personnelle par les brevets se généralise. *Le livre des brevets – Carnet de badges* (Paris: Eclaireurs de France, 1921), 80.
[45]"Les Camps. Camp-école de chefs," *Le Chef* 15–16 (May–June 1923): 80.
[46]La jeune maison Alsatia lance la collection "Signe de piste" en 1937. Le Seuil édite les équipées de Guy de Larigaudie dès 1939. Cf. Christian Guérin, "La collection Signe de piste, pour une histoire culturelle du scoutisme," *Vingtième siècle, revue d'histoire* 40 (October–December 1993): 45–61.
[47]Henri Marty, "Revue des livres," *L'Education* (January 1923): 221.

préfacé par Lyautey donne le ton de mystique virile et nationale. La conversion du maréchal avant sa mort en 1934 rejaillit sur l'association.[48] Tous les scouts français vénèrent le *chief scout*, mais l'édition catholique conquérante contredit l'éditeur neuchâtelois demeuré religieusement neutre.

Pour former leurs cadres Louveteaux, les Scouts de France embauchent dans leur camp école de Chamarande la catholique britannique Véra Barclay (1893–1985) et traduisent ses livres.[49] La traduction du *Wolf Cub's Handbook* par Bovet est donc peu reçue en France.[50] Il est vrai aussi qu'hors du scoutisme, Bovet travaille peu l'animalité en philosophie. La traduction du *Jungle book* de Kipling est déjà ancienne.[51] En 1929, son traducteur Louis Fabulet visite une meute de louveteaux EDF en forêt de Meudon. Il sort enchanté de l'imitation par les enfants des démarches animales. Sa perception de la "libre noblesse des animaux de Kipling – libre noblesse dont à ma joie [les garçons] semblent conscients et pénétrés" dit le modèle moral tiré des animaux. La frontière entre humanité et animalité est toutefois contrôlée. Les enfants sont assis en grand cercle "dont la cheftaine simule la fermeture". Le patronyme scout des adultes, le "totem" tiré d'un animal éponyme, capte l'attention de la petite société enfantine, la cheftaine *Bagheera* "rentrée d'un camp d'entraînement anglais", un *Akela* ou d'une cheftaine *Phaona* "dont les genoux disparaissaient sous un groupe de louveteaux".[52] Le traducteur paraît porter le salut du maître Kipling à la joyeuse mise en scène de ses textes. Dans cet enchantement, Bovet est un intermédiaire lointain et austère et, au même moment, la politique éditoriale de Delachaux et Niestlé dans les sciences du vivant est encore dominée par les oiseaux et les insectes. Les mammifères n'ont qu'une petite place au catalogue animalier.[53]

Point de vue franco-français

Les Eclaireurs de France comptent deux philosophes dans leurs rangs. Ils assurent, bien que cela ne soit pas intentionnel, une autonomie vis-à-vis du maître de Genève. Edmond Goblot (1858–1935) enseigne à l'université de Lyon et Pierre Mendousse (1870–1933) au lycée d'Auch.

Goblot est ancien élève de l'Ecole normale supérieure où il eut Boutroux comme professeur, Jaurès et Bergson comme camarades. Franc-maçon et dreyfusard, il

---

[48] Robert Baden-Powell, *La Route du succès. Dessins de l'auteur. Préface du maréchal Lyautey* (Paris: Scouts de France-Redier, 1932).
[49] Véra Barclay, *Le Louvetisme. Comment conduire une meute. Traduit de l'anglais, par Louis Doliveux, commissaire des Scouts de France* (Paris: Editions Spes, 1926). Id., *Le Louvetisme et la formation du caractère. Traduit de l'anglais par Jacques Sevin* (Paris: Editions Spes, 1927). Id., *Le Louvetisme. Comment conduire une meute. Traduit de l'anglais par Louis Doliveux* (Paris: Editions Spes, 1928). Id., *Jeux pour Mowgli. Traduit de l'anglais par Renée Magon de Saint-Elier, cheftaine brevetée de Chamarande* (Paris: Scouts de France-Redier, 1931). Pierre Peroni, "Aux origines du mouvement scout. Visite à Vera Barclay," *Kim, revue du réseau Baden-Powell* 15 (3e trimestre 1983): 5–8.
[50] Robert Baden-Powell of Gilwell, *The Wolf Cub's Handbook* (London: C. A. Pearson, 1916). Traduit sous le titre *Le livre des Louveteaux: Aux Éclaireurs de demain*, trans. Pierre Bovet (Neuchâtel: Delachaux et Niestlé, 1919).
[51] Rudyard Kipling, *Le Livre de la jungle*, trans. Louis Fabulet and Robert d'Humières (Paris: Mercure de France, 1899).
[52] Louis Fabulet, "Les Livres de la jungle et le scoutisme," *Mercure de France* (1 February 1929): 747–49.
[53] Jusqu'à Robert Hainard, *Mammifères sauvages d'Europe* (Neuchâtel: Delachaux et Niestlé, 1948), 258.

défend des idées pédagogiques libérales et laïques dans la revue primaire *Le Volume* et dans l'association l'Art à l'Ecole. Goblot est un esprit non conformiste, à l'image de vêtements de couleurs vives diversement appréciés dans la société provinciale. Président le comité EDF lyonnais, le scoutisme est la grande joie de sa vie d'adulte. Elu vice président en 1925, il le demeure jusqu'à son décès en 1935.[54]

Auprès des Eclaireurs, Goblot est davantage sociologue. Son objet est la distinction sociale, développée en 1925 dans *La Barrière et le Niveau*. Il interroge la consommation grandissante de loisirs. Son essai reflète le réformisme social des Eclaireurs de France. La véritable élite n'est pas une classe mais des comportements individuels.[55] La bourgeoisie est condamnée à céder la place à une élite véritable, sans confusion avec les frontières de classe. Faire éclore une élite du comportement probe et honnête est possible, quelle que soit l'origine sociale des enfants. L'émergence des individualités est la version éducative de l'individualisme démocratique contemporaine car, dit-il, "ce qu'on apprend surtout aux Eclaireurs, c'est la *Justice*, qui égalise et nivelle, et la *Fraternité*, qui rapproche et qui unit".[56] Or, à Genève, Bovet ne travaille pas la question sociale. La mise à distance de la question sociale par le perfectionnement individuel des garçons est surtout reçue par un collègue de Goblot, le doyen de la philosophie à Lyon Charles Chabot qui souhaite diffuser ces principes dans l'école républicaine lorsque l'enseignement primaire est dirigé par le philosophe Paul Lapie.[57]

Le philosophe Pierre Mendousse, professeur à Auch et président du comité Eclaireur, est aussi un réformateur social.[58] Mendousse applique localement le postulat socioéducatif des Eclaireurs. Ce collaborateur de *L'Education* intègre le scoutisme à son oeuvre de psychologue. Son livre *l'âme de l'adolescent* (1910) fondait la psychologie française de l'adolescence. La quatrième édition (1930) évoque le rôle du scoutisme dans l'encouragement à l'initiative et aux responsabilités.[59] Pourtant, curieusement, la bibliographie dans le livre ne cite pas *L'Instinct combatif*.

Défense du merveilleux

Le silence des EDF sur Bovet masque une défiance devant la rationalisation scientifique. D'autant que l'Institut Rousseau devient en 1929 un institut universitaire. L'objectivation est perçue comme une menace mettant en danger le merveilleux, condition de la réussite éducative. L'analyse savante met à distance l'enchantement du monde. C'est pourquoi le camp école de Cappy n'est pas un centre intellectuel d'étude pédagogique. C'est aussi pourquoi de tous les travaux de Bovet pendant la

---

[54]Jean Kergomard, Pierre Salzi and François Goblot, *Edmond Goblot 1858–1935, la vie, l'œuvre* (Paris: Alcan, 1937), 211.
[55]Edmond Goblot, *La Barrière et le niveau. Etude sociologique sur la bourgeoisie française moderne* (Paris: Alcan, 1925), 160.
[56]Id., "Les Eclaireurs de France et leurs chefs. Conférence faite aux étudiants de l'Université de Lyon, 20 mars 1929," *Revue de l'Université de Lyon* (1929): 8.
[57]"Discours du président Georges Bertier," *Le Chef* 35–36 (January–February 1925): 8–9. Cf. Hervé Terral, *Paul Lapie. Ecole et société* (Paris: L'Harmattan, 2003).
[58]*Pierre Mendousse pédagogue et photographe. Un gersois dans son siècle*, Abbaye de Flaran Centre patrimonial départemental exposition temporaire 28 mai–27 juin 2004 (Valence-sur-Baïse, France: CDP, 2004), 36.
[59]Préface de la 4e édition (janvier 1930): I. Pierre Mendousse, *L'âme de l'adolescent* (Paris: Alcan, 1938), 315. 5e édition. Sur la "dédramatisation de l'adolescence" par Mendousse, cf. Agnès Thiercé, *Histoire de l'adolescence 1850–1914* (Paris: Belin, 1999), 230–43.

Tableau 1. Réception de trois livres de Bovet.[63]

Période	Titre	Articles
1917–1929	*L'instinct combatif*	14
1922	*Le génie de Baden-Powell*	2
1925–1926	*Le sentiment religieux...*	8

décennie 1920, *le Génie de Baden-Powell* est le moins commenté. Alors que de nombreux commentaires élogieux fleurissent dès la sortie de *L'Instinct combatif*, le *Génie* en connaît très peu, comme le montre le tableau 1. La formation des chefs demande de lire Baden-Powell et non son exégèse savante, fut-elle accessible à tous. Les chefs doivent maîtriser l'essentiel de la psychologie de l'adolescence davantage que l'analyser. Mais, comme le note un chef, un manque de sens critique menace l'appropriation de la méthode: "Avons-nous jamais songé à discuter, à raisonner le pour et le contre d'un programme, à l'exécuter ensuite sans hésitation, et à le critiquer ensuite, lui et son exécution, entre chefs?"[60] Le chef ne se préoccupe pas d'analyser le scoutisme. Cette connaissance heurte le modèle scout dans son merveilleux, notamment l'univers romantique de la chevalerie, des Indiens ou le bestiaire de Kipling. Il est vrai que Bovet reste réservé à l'égard de la "*ferblanterie*" et de l'indianisme scout prêté à la puérilité anglo-saxonne, concluant à des pratiques de "*grands enfants*".[61] Bovet décrit aussi la menace accrue par la bureaucratisation du mouvement.[62]

La filiation de Bovet est ailleurs, dans la production savante. En 1933, le philosophe et chef scout Henri Bouchet (1896–1972) soutient sa thèse *le scoutisme et l'individualité*, la première consacrée intégralement au mouvement. L'auteur poursuit la réflexion entamée dans sa première thèse, *l'individualisation de l'enseignement*, considérée comme audacieuse. La préface d'Edmond Goblot au *scoutisme et l'individualité* répond à celle d'Adolphe Ferrière pour la première. Bovet est à l'honneur dans la "rationalisation de l'instinct combatif". La thèse se nourrit des travaux précédents dans l'enceinte savante vouée au débat. Henri Bouchet demeure lié au réseau français de l'Education nouvelle et entre en 1937 au comité de *L'Information pédagogique* créé la même année par Albert Châtelet, directeur du second degré au ministère de l'Education nationale et président des Eclaireurs de France.

Conclusion

Au début du XXe siècle, la traduction française de Baden-Powell échappe largement aux Français pour des raisons historiques liées à la construction nationaliste des Eclaireurs de France. En achetant en 1912 les droits de traduction, ils prétendent empêcher la diffusion d'idées qu'ils désirent appliquer. Ceci exprime une crainte

---

[60] B., "Ce qui nous manque – le sens critique," *Le Chef* 44 (December 1925): 192.
[61] Bovet, "Ingonyâma," in *Le Génie de Baden-Powell*, 39.
[62] Bovet, "Les dangers du succès," in *Le Génie de Baden-Powell*, 5–6.
[63] Source: Martin, *Pierre Bovet, l'homme du seuil*, 387–98. La recension du *Génie* est du à Chessex (*L'Educateur* 5, 1922): 192 et à un éloge de Claparède (*Archives de psychologie* 18, 1922): 226. Martin, *Pierre Bovet, l'homme du seuil*, 393.

devant la circulation internationale de la pensée éducative. En leur sein, les minoritaires qui font transiter les premières traductions suisses accèdent au pouvoir dans le contexte du règlement du premier conflit mondial.

Pierre Bovet écrit *Le Génie de Baden-Powell* dans cet arrière plan. Il est au centre d'une entreprise de traduction du pédagogue britannique, activité qui repose économiquement sur l'éditeur Delachaux et Niestlé et scientifiquement sur l'Institut Rousseau. Ces travaux se diffusent dans l'espace francophone et sont considérés comme les traductions de Baden-Powell les plus fidèles. Mais *Le Génie de Baden-Powell* doit plus sa diffusion en France à l'écho dans d'autres travaux savants qu'aux mouvements scouts eux-mêmes. Ils ne veulent pas d'analyse savante de leur projet. De linguistique, la frontière est devenue sémantique, évolution que l'éditeur neuchâtelois reproduit dans son catalogue. Les écrits du *chief scout* restent d'actualités mais ils ne sont plus seuls à la fin de la décennie 1930. Baden-Powell écrit plus rarement, ses manuels ne nourrissent plus un marché, par ailleurs concurrentiel comme en France. Le catalogue de Delachaux et Niestlé se réorganise avec l'essor du genre biographique par Baden-Powell ou ses hagiographes dans la collection de la Bibliothèque de l'éclaireur. En 1912, *Eclaireurs* sortait dans la collection Actualités pédagogiques ouvertes au champ intellectuel. Vingt ans plus tard, la Bibliothèque de l'éclaireur est plus proche du roman pour la jeunesse. Ainsi la frontière entre pédagogie savante d'un côté et littérature de jeunesse de l'autre se recompose, attestant la banalisation du scoutisme dans le vocabulaire des éducateurs. Baden-Powell meurt au Kenya en décembre 1941, Bovet cesse de diriger l'Institut Rousseau en 1944.

Les éditions de Baden-Powell en français font oublier l'entreprise suisse de traduction. Mais Bovet demeure peu connu en France hormis de rares cénacles de l'Education nouvelle. L'œuvre intellectuelle de l'interprète "si consciencieux" du fondateur a finalement peu en lien avec le mouvement scout. Outre un marché de plus en plus concurrentiel, les Eclaireurs, qui intéressent quelques philosophes, l'ignorent probablement pour cela. La construction scoute est rétive au regard savant. Les Français se désintéressent de la traduction de *Scouting for boys*, sauf dans la dixième édition d'*Eclaireurs* sortie avec l'aide du Scoutisme français en 1941.[64] On sait la place quasi officielle prise par le mouvement dans les politiques de jeunesse de Vichy. Etrange situation de janvier 1942 où les scouts français portent unanimement le deuil un pédagogue mort en décembre 1941, ressortissant d'un pays officiellement ennemi. C'est alors le double inversé de la situation qui prévalait en 1914. Ceux qui ne voulaient pas traduire Baden-Powell désirent alors améliorer la portée de son message, le contexte politique et diplomatique demeurant très différent. Dans ce premier XXe siècle, les frontières linguistiques s'ouvrent en pédagogie indépendamment du contexte politique international. Le scoutisme illustre ainsi le chassé croisé pédagogique entre pays voisins.

---

[64]Henri Bouchet, *Le scoutisme et l'individualité* (Paris: Alcan, 1933), 197. Préface d'Edmond Goblot. La première thèse de Bouchet, *L'individualisation de l'enseignement. L'individualité des enfants et son rôle dans l'éducation* (Paris: Alcan, 1933), 555, est préfacée par Adolphe Ferrière. Laurent Gutierrez, "L'individualisation de l'enseignement selon Henri Bouchet (1933)," *Vers l'éducation nouvelle* 546 (April 2012): 77.

Toiling together for social cohesion: International influences on the development of teacher education in the United States

Paul J. Ramsey

Eastern Michigan University, Ypsilanti, USA

> This article examines the ways in which the very idea of teacher education in the United States was transplanted from foreign lands. Teacher education, particularly normal school training, was based on a model imported from despotic Prussia, a model that was popularised by French and American visitors to the northeastern German land. Although normal schooling naturally was altered in the American context, the subsequent forms of teacher training, particularly in the emerging universities, owed a great debt to international models as well. This article also explores the ideology of the common school movement, which sought social cohesion, because that ideology helps explain why the Prussian model of teacher training became so attractive to conservative educational reformers in a democratic society.

Introduction

During his famous visit to the United States in the 1830s, Alexis de Tocqueville made note of Americans' isolationist tendencies. Drawing on the sentiments of George Washington and Thomas Jefferson, Tocqueville concluded that Americans had no desire to "meddle in the affairs of Europe" and that "[t]he foreign policy of the US is to wait and see; it consists in keeping away from things much more than in interfering".[1] Although the US certainly did limit its involvement in international affairs during its early history, the subsequent and widely held belief that Americans traditionally shunned foreign ideas and influences was undoubtedly a myth, especially with regard to education in general and teacher education in particular. In 1835, the same year that the first part of *Democracy in America* was published, J. Orville Taylor, an advocate for teaching training in the US, mirrored Tocqueville's view that Americans did not look outside their borders, but noted that, in the realm of education, neither did other countries. "On the subject of education," Taylor stated, "teachers and nations have had but little communication with each other – no exchange of views and sentiments – no mutual aid. Each one has toiled alone, and

---

[1] Alexis de Tocqueville, *Democracy in America and Two Essays on America*, trans. Isaac Kramnick (New York: Penguin, 2003), 266–267.

their *practical* knowledge has been buried with them."[2] Taylor and other like-minded educational advocates hoped to change this isolationism and noted that the "experimental knowledge [of other nations] is what we want".[3] "Toiling" together, in short, was what these influential reformers desired; they sought foreign models to improve public education, especially teacher education, in the US.

The myth that the US was largely free from international influences was subtly bolstered by the "consensus" historians of the mid-twentieth century who emphasised America's uniqueness. Although many of the tenets of the consensus scholars' worldview have been critiqued and rejected in recent decades, these historians' focus on America's "exceptional" status can still be seen, which, ultimately, reinforces the notion that the US is and has been a singularly "special" nation.[4] While avoiding many of the shortcomings of consensus scholarship, for instance, Herbert Kliebard's classic history of progressive education, *The Struggle for the American Curriculum*, ignores – as European critics have noted – the broader, international dimensions of progressive curricular trends.[5] Some scholars have observed that, excluding the well-known cases of the kindergarten and the university seminar, historians of education pass over the impact of foreign ideas on America's educational system.[6] There are, of course, exceptions to this scholarly neglect of the international influences upon US education. The foreign-born historian of education Jurgen Herbst, for example, has done much to demonstrate that particular models of schooling and teacher education were imported to the US, although these models certainly underwent dramatic transformations as they were embedded into the American soil.[7]

Following in the footsteps of Herbst, this article examines the ways in which the very idea of teacher education in the US – along with the models for conducting that form of training – was transplanted from foreign lands. The article notes that teacher

---

[2]J. Orville Taylor, "Preface", in M. Victor Cousin, *Report on the State of Public Instruction in Prussia; Addressed to the Count de Montalivet, Peer of France, Minister of Public Instruction and Ecclesiastical Affairs; with Plans for School of School Houses*, trans. Sarah Austin (New York: Wiley and Long, 1835), vi; John Lukacs, "American nationalism", *Harper's Magazine* 324, no. 1944 (2012): 56–58.
[3]Taylor, "Preface", vi.
[4]John Higham, "Changing paradigms: The collapse of consensus history", *Journal of American History* 76, no. 2 (1989): 460–466; Paul J. Ramsey, "Histories taking root: The contexts and patterns of educational historiography during the twentieth century", *American Educational History Journal* 34, no. 2 (2007): 350–354; Lukacs, "American nationalism", 56–58.
[5]Herbert M. Kliebard, *The Struggle for the American Curriculum, 1893–1958*, 3rd edn. (New York: Routledge Falmer, 2004); Kevin J. Brehony, "From the particular to the general, the continuous to the discontinuous: Progressive education revisited", *History of Education* 30, no. 5 (2001): 413–432; Hermann Röhrs, "Progressive education in the United States and its influence on related educational developments in Germany", *Paedagogica Historica* 33, no. 1 (1997): 45–68. For a brief survey of the US scholarship on progressive education, see David F. Labaree, "Progressivism, schools and schools of education", *Paedagogica Historica* 41, no. 1–2 (2005): 275–288.
[6]James C. Albisetti, "German influence on the higher education of American women, 1865–1914", in Henry Geitz, Jürgen Heideking and Jurgen Herbst, eds. *German Influences on Education in the United States to 1917* (New York: Cambridge University Press, 1995), 227.
[7]Jurgen Herbst, *And Sadly Teach: Teacher Education and Professionalization in American Culture* (Madison: University of Wisconsin Press, 1989); Henry Geitz, Jürgen Heideking and Jurgen Herbst, eds. *German Influences on Education in the United States to 1917* (New York: Cambridge University Press, 1995); Jurgen Herbst, "Teacher preparation in the nineteenth century: Institutions and purposes", in Donald Warren, ed. *American Teachers: Histories of a Profession at Work* (New York: Macmillan, 1989), 213–236.

education, particularly normal school training, was based on a model imported from despotic Prussia, a model that was popularised by French and American visitors to the northeastern German land. In 1891, William T. Harris, the US Commissioner of Education, distributed a report that noted that the American normal was, in essence, "a school with a French name and a Prussian curriculum".[8] Although normal schooling naturally was altered in the American context, the subsequent forms of teacher training, particularly in the emerging universities, owed a great debt to international models as well. The article begins with a brief overview and interpretation of the aims and growth of common schools in the US because, it argues, the ideology and agenda of American common schooling helps explain why the Prussian model of teacher training became attractive to conservative educational reformers in a democratic society during the nineteenth century.

The common school[9]

The dramatic growth of common schooling during the first half of the nineteenth century made teacher education, as its advocates argued, a central priority in the realm of education. This growth in American public education largely emerged as a means of addressing an anxiety that was coming to the fore because of social upheavals. The stable, hierarchical village of eighteenth-century America was on the wane; mobility and universal white suffrage were chipping away at those traditions. But, more important, the Industrial Revolution had come to the Northeast by the 1830s. Textile mills and other industries were becoming ubiquitous in states such as Massachusetts and New York. American agriculture was shifting away from subsistence farming to crop specialisation, making the idealised independent farmer an image of a by-gone era. The emerging transportation revolution made it possible to send agricultural goods to the mills and urban areas, thus facilitating industrial development. During the first half of the nineteenth century, therefore, the US had transformed into a modern capitalist society.[10]

The industrial development in the Northeast during the second third of the nineteenth century facilitated a massive population shift toward the urban areas. American-born rural folk, as well as vast numbers of immigrants, moved to the manufacturing centres for the potential economic opportunities. The majority of the immigrants came from the northern and western sections of Europe, and the newcomers, particularly the Irish, increasingly began to replace the native-born in the mills. The urbanisation that the Industrial Revolution fostered was simultaneously

---

[8]"The inception and the progress of the American normal school curriculum to 1880", in *Report of the Commissioner of Education for the Year 1888–89* (Washington, DC: Government Printing Office, 1891), 278.

[9]Although organised and worded differently, much of this section on the development of common schooling in the US is drawn from my recent monograph; see Paul J. Ramsey, *Bilingual Public Schooling in the United States: A History of America's "Polyglot Boardinghouse"* (New York: Palgrave Macmillan, 2010). While the title suggests that the monograph is a focused study on bilingual instruction, the text is context heavy and posits my interpretation not only of dual-language instruction, but also of American public education.

[10]Carl F. Kaestle, *Pillars of the Republic: Common Schools and American Society, 1780–1860* (New York: Hill and Wang, 2001), 63–66; Arthur M. Schlesinger, Jr., *The Age of Jackson* (Boston, MA: Little, Brown and Company, 1946), 144–158, 177–189, 334–349; Michael B. Katz, *The Irony of Early School Reform: Educational Innovation in Mid-nineteenth Century Massachusetts* (New York: Teachers College Press, 2001), 5–11, 222–223; Eric Hobsbawm, *The Age of Capital, 1848–1875* (New York: Vintage Books, 1996), 309–311.

seen as progress and depravity. Although the city had the potential of becoming a beacon of "civilisation", it also could destroy the cohesion of the nation if its ills were not quickly addressed.[11]

Public schools, therefore, were partially developed as a means of addressing the anxiety many Americans felt during this era of change. The school advocate Horace Mann, for instance, stated in 1848 that the common school will

> wield its mighty energies for the protection of society against the giant vices which now invade and torment it...[;] there will not be a height to which these enemies of the race can escape, which it will not scale, nor a Titan among them all, whom it will not slay.[12]

Not surprisingly, the common school movement began in the industrial Northeast, and gradually the newly created institutions began to reach more youngsters. Massachusetts developed nearly 1500 new public schools between 1840 and 1860. As the New England population moved westward, common schooling went with it, spreading to the new states and territories in the West. Common schooling, however, did not emerge in the South as rapidly, largely because of the low population density among whites and the planter class's resistance to change. Therefore, only a smattering of southern port cities had public school systems before the 1860s.[13]

The common school champions – Mann in Massachusetts, Henry Barnard in Connecticut, Calvin Stowe in Ohio and Caleb Mills in Indiana – were a relatively like-minded group; they were often middle-class Protestants with ties to the conservative Whig Party. As education officials for their respective states, the school reformers argued that public education would lead to social perfection; it would spur industrial growth and cure the problems related to urbanisation, particularly crime and pauperism.[14] This "implausible" ideology, as historian Michael Katz has called it, suggested that public schools would promote industry through the training of the younger generation in the "habits of regularity, punctuality, constancy and industry",

---

[11]Kaestle, *Pillars of the Republic*, 63–67; Katz, *Irony*, 222; Ronald Takaki, *A Different Mirror: A History of Multicultural America* (Boston, MA: Little, Brown and Company, 1993), 139–160; Thomas Bender, *Toward an Urban Vision: Ideas and Institutions in Nineteenth-century America* (Lexington, KY: University Press of Kentucky, 1975), 3–17; US Immigration Commission, *Statistical Review of Immigration, 1820–1910 – Distribution of Immigrants, 1850–1900* (Washington, DC: Government Printing Office, 1911), 4–5, 8–11; John Bodnar, *The Transplanted: A History of Immigrants in Urban America* (Bloomington, IN: Indiana University Press, 1985), 64.
[12]Horace Mann, "Tenth and Twelfth Annual Reports to the Massachusetts Board of Education", in James W. Fraser, ed. *The School in the United States: A Documentary History* (New York: McGraw-Hill, 2001), 54.
[13]Kaestle, *Pillars of the Republic*, 30–74; Katz, *Irony*, 224; William J. Reese, *America's Public Schools: From the Common School to "No Child Left Behind"* (Baltimore, MD: Johns Hopkins University Press, 2005), 26, 4344; John L. Rury, "Social capital and the common schools", in Donald Warren and John J. Patrick, eds. *Civic and Moral Learning in America* (New York: Palgrave Macmillan, 2006), 77–80.
[14]Merle Curti, *The Social Ideas of American Educators*, rev. ed. (Paterson, NJ: Littlefield, Adams and Co., 1959), 101–168; James W. Fraser, *Between Church and State: Religion and Public Education in a Multicultural America* (New York: St. Martin's Griffin, 2000), 23–47; John Wakefield, "'Whosoever will, let him come': Evangelical millennialism and the development of American public education", *American Educational History Journal* 39, no. 2 (2012): 289–306; Kaestle, *Pillars of the Republic*, 75–103.

while the ills of industrial society would be cured through the inculcation of Protestant morality and self-restraint.[15]

"Public behavior," historian Robert Wiebe has written, "once merely signifying the state of the soul, had become the substance of virtue," and fostering conformity to that public virtue became a primary function of the newly created common schools.[16] Of course, the public schools taught students the rudiments of reading, writing and arithmetic, but, moral training was the focus in the little red schoolhouse. As Americans during the nineteenth century came to the conclusion that "only absolute rules rigidly adhered to could provide a reliable guide to behavior and protect against the enormous temptations of the day", the common schools strictly enforced those rules, which largely mirrored pan-Protestant behaviour.[17] The common school teachers and curriculum emphasised this public morality by inculcating hard work, honesty, obedience and thrift. In their textbooks, students learned that God was all-seeing, which ensured children's "self-control". But that God was a Protestant God; students in the "common" schools, regardless of their faith, largely were indoctrinated in the pan-Protestant worldview and primarily read only the King James Version of the Bible.[18] Catholicism, in fact, was "depicted not only as a false religion, but as a positive danger to the state".[19]

The normal school

The growth of common schooling during the first two-thirds of the nineteenth century provided the impetus for the development of state-sponsored teacher training in the US. But, the common school and teacher-training movements were more than a drive to spread learning among the masses; the movements also promoted a particular ideology.[20] The central aim of the schooling ideology was social cohesion, a cohesion that, as the nineteenth-century teacher educator Catharine Beecher stated, called for "moral and religious restraints".[21] But developing an educational system that promoted social cohesion suggested that schooling be a "common" experience,

---

[15]Katz, *Irony*, 27–50, 159–160.
[16]Robert H. Wiebe, *The Segmented Society: An Introduction to the Meaning of America* (New York: Oxford University Press, 1975), 31. In Europe, virtue also came to be associated with external attributes, so much so that the physiognomic "scientists" claimed that they could determine the status of people's morality from their outward appearance; see Stuart Ewen and Elizabeth Ewen, *Typecasting: On the Arts and Sciences of Human Inequality* (New York: Seven Stories Press, 2006), 47.
[17]B. Edward McClellan, *Moral Education in America: Schools and the Shaping of Character from Colonial Times to the Present* (New York: Teachers College Press, 1999), 26.
[18]*By-laws of the School Officers and Trustees of the Nineteenth Ward, and Rules for the Government of Schools* (New York: J. Youdale, 1863), 4, 27, 30; Marcius Willson, *The Fourth Reader of the United States Series* (New York: Harper and Brothers, 1872), 21–22, 55–57, 117–118; Benjamin B. Comegys, ed. *A Primer of Ethics* (Boston,MA: Ginn and Company, 1891), 48, 124; Asa Fitz, *The American School Hymn Book* (Boston, MA: Crosby, Nichols and Company, 1854), 94; Ruth Miller Elson, *Guardians of Tradition: American Schoolbooks of the Nineteenth Century* (Lincoln, NE: University of Nebraska Press, 1964), 41–48, 226.
[19]Elson, *Guardians of Tradition*, 47.
[20]Kaestle, *Pillars of the Republic*, 75–103; Ramsey, *Bilingual Public Schooling*, 11–20.
[21]Catharine E. Beecher, "An essay on the education of female teachers for the United States, 1835", in *The School in the United States*, 62; Wakefield, "'Whosoever will, let him come'", 289–306; Annemieke van Drenth and Mineke van Essen, "'Shoulders squared ready for battle with forces that sought to overwhelm': West-European and American women pioneers in the educational sciences, 1800–1910", *Paedagogica Historica* 39, no. 3 (2003): 275–276.

which demanded a certain amount of centralisation and standardisation in education, including teacher training. The reformers' quest for centralisation – long an aim of the Whig Party – was frequently resisted; the US, since its founding, had been steeped in localism. Private schoolmasters, naturally, opposed the centralisation of schooling and teacher education, as did the growing Catholic population which saw the Protestant public schools as a threat to its faith.[22]

The Whig reformers, interestingly, were educational progressives and, at the same time, social conservatives, although the two positions were intimately intertwined. They sought to bring schooling to the masses – schooling that was imbued with the latest child-centred methods[23] – and to use public education to instil obedience, morality and self-restraint, skills and dispositions that were thought to be needed in an emerging industrial nation that was full of perceived social ills. Although the school reformers advocated for and implemented progressive pedagogical techniques, this adherence to the latest European teaching methods in no way threatened their vision of using public schooling for social cohesion; in fact, these reformers found much of their larger ideology echoed by the founders of the new methods, such as Johann Heinrich Pestalozzi. As historian Michel Soëtard has noted, Pestalozzi's method "can serve as an instrument of subjection as well as of liberation"; by and large, the American public school reformers chose the former. In *Pestalozzi and Pestalozzianism*, for example, Henry Barnard included in his two-volume edited collection an overview of the course of instruction from a London normal school that both utilised the Pestalozzian method *and* emphasised rigid moral training, a "training on a religious basis, showing how the Bible should be our guide".[24] Because common schooling was growing exponentially, educational reformers argued that what was needed was a system of public teacher training institutions to ensure conformity to the Whig gospel. The model for such a system to spread the reformers' ideals largely came from Prussia via sympathetic visitors.[25]

In the second quarter of the nineteenth century, a professor of philosophy at the University of Paris, M. Victor Cousin, was given the mission to tour various

---

[22] Katz, *Irony*, 19–62, 80–93, 115–160; Maris A. Vinovskis, *The Origins of Public High Schools: A Reexamination of the Beverly High School Controversy* (Madison, WI: University of Wisconsin Press, 1985), 79–82, 104–108; Fraser, *Between Church and State*, 49–65; Lloyd P. Jorgenson, *The State and the Non-public School, 1825–1925* (Columbia, MO: University of Missouri Press, 1987), 57–85; Ellwood P. Cubberley, *Public Education in the United States: A Study and Interpretation of American Educational History* (Boston, MA: Houghton Mifflin Company, 1919), 115–160.

[23] See, for example, Johann Heinrich Pesatlozzi, *Leonard and Gertrude*, trans. Eva Channing (Boston, MA: D.C. Heath, 1907); Johann Heinrich Pestalozzi, *How Gertrude Teaches Her Children: An Attempt to Help Mothers to Teach Their Own Children and an Account of the Method*, trans. Lucy E. Holland and Frances C. Turner (Syracuse, NY: C.W. Bardeen, 1894); Henry Barnard, ed. *Pestalozzi and Pestalozzianism: Life, Educational Principles, and Methods, of John Henry Pestalozzi, with Biographical Sketches of Several of His Assistants and Disciples*, 2 vols. (New York: F.C. Brownell, 1859); Maarten Bullynck, "The transmission of numeracy: Integrating reckoning in Protestant North-German elementary education (1770–1810)", *Paedagogica Historica* 44, no. 5 (2008): 563–585; Maria A. Laubach and Joan K. Smith, "Transatlantic dialogue: Pestalozzian influences on women's education in early nineteenth century America", *American Educational History Journal* 39, no. 2 (2012): 365–382.

[24] Michal Soëtard, "Johann Heinrich Pestalozzi", *Prospects* 14, no. 1–2 (1994): 297–310; Barnard, *Pestalozzi and Pestalozzianism*, vol. 2, 223; Katz, *Irony*, 115–160.

[25] Herbst, *And Sadly Teach*, 12–56.

German municipalities and states and to report on their educational endeavours for France's minister of public instruction, Count de Montalivet. Cousin wrote on the status of education in Saxony, Weimar and Frankfort, but it was his report on the Prussian schools that caught the attention of American reformers. Based on his 1831 visit to the northeastern Germanic lands, the professor's survey of education overviewed Prussian "normal" schools. In 1835, Cousin's report was translated by Sarah Austin and disseminated in the US; the teacher training institutions described by the French visitor quickly became the envy of Whig school leaders. The Prussian normal schools recruited men between the ages of 16 and 18, many of whom came from modest backgrounds. The students, Cousin noted, learned "the art of teaching" during their three-year course of study, a course of study that also required teaching practice in nearby schools. The teacher-training institutions emphasised academic and "character" training and, although publicly supported, were often affiliated with Protestant and Catholic churches. Because of the students' limited means, a stipend was given to pupils to cover their costs while receiving teacher training.[26]

Inspired by the favourable reports coming from Europe – including those of Americans such as Henry E. Dwight and William Channing Woodbridge – educational reformers in the US began to set out for the Old World to see its schools firsthand. Henry Barnard, the great public school champion of Connecticut, visited European schools from 1835 to 1837. During his travels, he became convinced that the Prussian model was the best and, therefore, proselytised on its merits in his *American Journal of Education*. Like Barnard, Alexander D. Bache – kin of Benjamin Franklin – made the voyage to Europe in order to survey its educational activities. Bache, who was taking up the presidency of the Girard College for Orphans in Philadelphia, was equally impressed with the schools in Prussia, and Barnard used and popularised Bache's observations in his own work.[27]

Following in Barnard and Bache's footsteps, Calvin Stowe, an advocate for public education in Ohio and the husband of Harriet Beecher Stowe, travelled to Europe in 1836 to purchase books and, at the request of the governor, to collect data on schools in order to improve education in the Buckeye State. In the early 1840s, Horace Mann, the first secretary of education in Massachusetts, also set off on a tour of the Old World's schools. Both Stowe and Mann were taken with the Prussian system of education, including its normal schools, and hoped to use it as a model of reform in their respective states. Stowe's observations were published in 1839, and Mann's became the well-known "Seventh Annual Report to the Massachusetts Board of Education"; both reports were widely disseminated, quoted and read in the US. Although situated in a despotic nation, the Prussian educational system was particularly

---

[26]Cousin, *Report on the State of Public Instruction in Prussia*, v–xvii, 62–67; "The inception and the progress of the American normal school curriculum to 1880", 278; B.A. Hinsdale, "Notes on the history of foreign influence upon education in the United States", in *Report of the Commissioner of Education*, vol. 1 (Washington, DC: Government Printing Office, 1899), 622–624; Herbst, *And Sadly Teach*, 21–24, 32–50; Donald Warren, "Waiting for teacher education", *Teacher Education Quarterly* 25, no. 4 (1998): 90–95.
[27]Hinsdale, "Notes on the history of foreign influence", 621–622; Barnard, *Pestalozzi and Pestalozzianism*, vol. 1, 150; Karl-Ernst Jeismann, "American observations concerning the Prussian educational system in the nineteenth century", in *German Influences on Education*, 21–41; Christopher J. Lucas, *Teacher Education in America: Reform Agendas for the Twenty-first Century* (New York: St Martin's Press, 1997), 16–28; Egbert R. Isbell, *A History of Eastern Michigan University, 1849–1965* (Ypsilanti: Eastern Michigan University Press, 1971), 2–3.

attractive because it paralleled many of the aims of the conservative Whig agenda, and both Stowe and Mann believed that it could be transplanted to the American soil.[28] Stowe, for instance, was impressed with "the excellent order and rigid economy with which all the Prussian institutions are conducted". He, as a devoted social conservative and the son-in-law of the famous Protestant minister Lyman Beecher, was struck by the "moral and religious character" of the German schools. The Prussian "system is no visionary scheme emanating from the closet of a recluse," Stowe stated, "but a sketch of the course of instruction now actually pursued by thousands of schoolmasters in the best district schools that have ever been organized." "If it can be done in Europe," Stowe concluded, "I believe it can be done in the United States; If it can be done in Prussia, I know it can be done in Ohio."[29]

These early surveys of education and teacher training in Europe generated a considerable amount of interest in publicly supported normal schools in the US, even though the Prussian model was rooted in and served a monarchy, not a democracy. Although the American normal schools were to be situated within a relatively young democratic nation, many of the leading teacher education advocates felt a certain amount of anxiety about the rise of popular democracy during the early decades of the nineteenth century. By the 1830s, suffrage was becoming nearly universal among white men, and the "common men" and immigrants, as it turned out, were casting their ballots for the Jacksonian Democrats – not for the Whigs – which, naturally, was unsettling for the conservative elites, many of whom were also educational reformers. In 1835, for example, the teacher education advocate Catharine Beecher noted her concern about popular democracy by stating that "these ignorant ... adults are now voters, and have a share in the government of the nation".[30] While the Prussian normal school model was not the product of a democratic society, the American Whig reformers – given their uneasiness with the spread of popular democracy – saw the European teacher education system as compatible with their educational and political vision.[31]

Although there had been a few teacher-education endeavours in some private seminaries – such as Beecher's Hartford Female Seminary – state normal schools began to be founded as the favourable reports from Europe started circulating among American reformers and legislators. Massachusetts opened its first public teacher-training institution in 1839. Located in Lexington (but later moved farther west) and

---

[28]Barnard, *Pestalozzi and Pestalozzianism*, vol. 1, 150; Hinsdale, "Notes on the history of foreign influence", 622; Jeismann, "American observations concerning the Prussian educational system", 21–41; Isbell, *A History of Eastern Michigan University*, 2–3; Horace Mann, "Seventh Annual Report", in Lawrence A. Cremin, ed. *The Republic and the School: Horace Mann on the Education of Free Men* (New York: Teachers College Press, 1957), 54–56.
[29]Calvin E. Stowe, "Report on elementary public instruction in Europe", in *The School in the United States*, 94–98.
[30]Schlesinger, *The Age of Jackson*, 36–44, 74–87, 210–226; James Oakes, "The ages of Jackson and the rise of American democracies", *Journal of the Historical Society* 6, no. 4 (2006): 491–500; Sean Wilentz, "Politics, irony, and the rise of American democracy", *Journal of the Historical Society* 6, no. 4 (2006): 537–539; Walter Dean Burnham, "Table I: Summary: Presidential elections, USA, 1788–2004", *Journal of the Historical Society* 7, no. 4 (2007): 530–537; David Nasaw, *Schooled to Order: A Social History of Public Schooling in the United States* (Oxford: Oxford University Press, 1981), 39–43; Beecher, "An essay on the education of female teachers", in *The School in the United States*, 62; Ramsey, *Bilingual Public Schooling*, 11–20.
[31]Stowe, "Report on elementary public instruction in Europe", in *The School in the United States*, 94–98; Barnard, *Pestalozzi and Pestalozzianism*, vol. 2, 217–227.

with Cyrus Peirce as its principal, the normal school's curriculum gave students a rehashing of the common school subjects as well as training in the latest pedagogical techniques, particularly those coming from Europe. A second normal school was authorised later in that same year, which was in Barre (later in Westfield). The following year, another publicly supported normal school opened in Bridgewater, and in 1854 the fourth state institution was established in Salem. Like the Prussian teacher-training schools and keeping in line with the Whig educational agenda, the normal schools in Massachusetts admitted only students of "good moral character", a quality, the reformers believed, that would foster social control in order to alleviate some of the anxiety regarding the fast-changing nation. As in the German states, the Massachusetts normal institutions were established as a means of supplying the right kind of teachers to the common schools of the state that were most in need, particularly the rural areas. Following the Prussian model, the state normal schools assisted their students financially by reducing or eliminating tuition costs, a move that was quite helpful since many of the Massachusetts students, like those in Prussia, were recruited from the lower orders, particularly from farming families.[32]

Normal schooling based on the Prussian model quickly spread beyond Massachusetts. New York, for instance, established a teacher-training institution in Albany in 1844; by the 1860s the state had opened its famous normal school in Oswego. Farther west, John D. Pierce, a congregational minister and a New Englander, emigrated to Michigan to found a church. As the territory was achieving statehood, Pierce – along with his fellow eastern transplant, Isaac Crary – emerged as Michigan's central champion of public education. Pierce had read Cousin's report on Prussian schools and took the model to heart. With the support of Crary and Governor Stevens T. Mason, Pierce became the first state superintendent of public instruction, making Michigan, as historian Egbert R. Isbell perhaps has exaggerated, "the first state to adopt the Prussian system of vesting the educational authority in a single individual".[33] Pierce, along with his like-minded successors, was concerned about teacher quality in the state's newly founded common schools. Initially, the University of Michigan was considered as a means of supplying teachers, but in 1849 the state legislature authorised the establishment of Michigan State Normal School (the forerunner to Eastern Michigan University), which, after some debate, was to be located in Ypsilanti. Headed up by Adonijah Strong Welch, the normal school had "the purposes of which shall be the instruction of persons, both male and female, in the art of teaching, and in all of the various branches that pertain to a good common school education".[34] "Normal", as it was colloquially called, offered two courses of study: a classical course for those preparing to teach in the state's

---

[32]"The inception and the progress of the American normal school curriculum to 1880", 277–278, 281–284; Herbst, *And Sadly Teach*, 65–86; Lucas, *Teacher Education in America*, 16–28.

[33]"The inception and the progress of the American normal school curriculum to 1880", 284–285, 287–288; Isbell, *A History of Eastern Michigan University*, 2–4; Lucas, *Teacher Education in America*, 25–28.

[34]*Catalogue of the Officers and Members of the Michigan State Normal School, State Teachers' Institute, and State Teachers' Association* (Detroit, MI: E.A. Wales, Printer, 1853), n.p.; "The inception and the progress of the American normal school curriculum to 1880", 287–288; Isbell, *A History of Eastern Michigan University*, 3–11; Ronald Flowers, *The Michigan State Normal School and the Preparation of Teachers: A History and Institutional Analysis* (Saarbrücken, Germany: VDM Verlag Dr. Müller Aktiengesellschaft & Co, 2008): 126–138, 166–179; Herbst, *And Sadly Teach*, 94–95; Lucas, *Teacher Education in America*, 26.

secondary "Union" schools and an English course for elementary teachers. Following Michigan's lead, Illinois adopted a state normal school in 1857, while Minnesota followed suit the next year. By the Civil War, however, there were still only a handful of these publicly supported teacher-training institutions in the US, but after the war normal schooling began to flourish.[35]

Although representing the premier system of teacher training, the Prussian model of normal schooling did not have to take root in the US. In fact, with the notable exception of the school reformers, many Americans were not fully convinced that teacher training was necessary. The conventional wisdom of the early nineteenth century suggested that good teaching emanated from solid content knowledge, not an understanding of pedagogy. Because of these lingering doubts concerning normal schools and because of the drastically different environment to which it was imported, the Prussian model was adjusted and redefined to suit the needs of the American context. The state normal schools in the US, for instance, emerged with a broader mission than mere teacher training. When it opened in 1853, the Michigan State Normal School had the additional purpose of providing "instruction in the mechanic arts, and in the arts of husbandry, and agricultural chemistry".[36] From the outset, then, and to the chagrin of reformers devoted to the Prussian model of teacher training, American normal schools were multipurpose institutions. Many students who had no yearning for the teaching profession enrolled nonetheless, primarily to receive a low-cost secondary education in order to prepare for white-collar positions or for colleges and universities.[37]

Besides the multiple functions, the Prussian normal model was altered in other significant ways to suit the American context. While the teacher-training institutions in Prussia enrolled only men, the American normal schools, from their inception, were largely either co-educational or admitted only women, a necessity because women had become the majority of the teaching corps by the time state-sponsored teacher education came to the US. The first normal school in Massachusetts (Lexington), for instance, allowed only women, as did the Salem school, which opened in 1854; the teacher-training institutions in Barre and Bridgewater enrolled both men and women. The length of the school term also differed from that of the Prussian model. While the normal schools in Prussia offered a three-year course of study, most students in the early state schools attended for a year or less. Partially because of the short amount of training and because of the female clientele in a patriarchal society, a professionalised body of teachers did not emerge from the normal schools in America, as it did in Europe. Teaching was still seen as a temporary position, one that was poorly paid and regarded as merely a brief occupational stint before marriage or, for men, until a better career was secured. The low status of the public school teacher unnerved the reformers, who, guided by the Prussian example, hoped that normal schools would lead to

---

[35]*Catalogue of the Officers and Members of the Michigan State Normal School*, 1853, n.p.; "The inception and the progress of the American normal school curriculum to 1880", 287–288; Herbst, *And Sadly Teach*, 94–98; Lucas, *Teacher Education in America*, 22–28.
[36]*Catalogue of the Officers and Members of the Michigan State Normal School*, 1853, n.p.; "The inception and the progress of the American normal school curriculum to 1880", 287–288; Flowers, *The Michigan State Normal School*, 166–179; Lucas, *Teacher Education in America*, 29–37.
[37]Herbst, *And Sadly Teach*, 92–139; Lucas, *Teacher Education in America*, 25–37; *Catalogue of the Officers and Members of the Michigan State Normal School*, 1853, n.p.

the development of highly skilled professionals willing to carry the banner of the Whig educational vision with authority.[38] In short, the normal school was "an immigrant institution", as one scholar recently called the preschool, because it, like the early education institution, "had to find its place in the socializing processes of [new] nations and neighborhoods".[39]

The lack of the development of teaching as a genuine profession – like medicine or law – also came from the existence of a variety of alternative routes into the field, some of which required little or no professional preparation. It was, for instance, not an uncommon practice for local school boards to hire an untrained community member's relative for an available teaching position. Additionally, teachers' institutes, which consisted of a few weeks of short courses and lectures on education and pedagogy, became the most popular form of training prior to the Civil War. Urban areas developed their own normal schools as a means of providing teachers for their municipal schools. Typically, the city normal schools were little more than secondary institutions (not professional schools) and sometimes merely catered to local conceptions of education. High schools, as they became more widespread in the second half of the nineteenth century, increasingly added normal departments or, in some instances, established or sought affiliations with municipal normal schools.[40]

While these forms of teacher preparation did little to add to the prestige of educators, the emergence of pedagogical departments in universities – for certain segments of the school folks – did bolster professionalism. Many American colleges – the colonists, naturally, used England's Oxford and Cambridge as guides – underwent a dramatic transformation during the nineteenth century. The English classical course of study broadened, and new ideas from continental Europe about the nature of higher education gradually began to have an impact. During the first half of the century, American scholars, such as George Ticknor of Harvard, travelled to the German states for graduate study, which was virtually unknown in the US. By the 1850s, numerous Americans had studied at Göttingen, Halle, Leipzig and the Royal Friedrich Wilhelm universities, and they brought back with them a desire for higher education reform. By the last quarter of the nineteenth century, a few institutions essentially grafted the German focus on graduate study and original research onto the American landscape, a task that worked best with newly created institutions, such as Johns Hopkins in Baltimore and Clark in Worcester. Older institutions in the US seeking university status attempted to fuse German scholarship with the traditional aspects of the colleges, which had long been based on the English model. For instance, Harvard, along with some state institutions, began to undergo the transformation as academic specialists, rather than ministers, were

---

[38]"The inception and the progress of the American normal school curriculum to 1880", 281288; Herbst, *And Sadly Teach*, 60–86; Lucas, *Teacher Education in America*, 12–15, 22–37.
[39]Roberta Wollons, "The immigrant preschool", *History of Education Quarterly* 49, no. 2 (2009): 241–243.
[40]Ramsey, *Bilingual Public Schooling*, 11–20, 56–62; Herbst, *And Sadly Teach*, 92–106; Lucas, *Teacher Education in America*, 21–29; Isbell, *A History of Eastern Michigan University*, 14–15.

appointed president.[41] When the ichthyologist David Starr Jordan was inaugurated as president of Indiana University in January 1885, he understood that the institution was "not yet a great university, not yet even a real university" because, as he had stated earlier, it did not yet have that "crowning function of a university": "original research".[42] But, before he took up the helm at Stanford, he, driven by visions of a new academic atmosphere and "original research", began to institutionalise German higher education ideals in Indiana.[43]

It was in this academic culture – a culture that held the German university model in high regard – that schools and departments of education began to form, particularly after the 1870s. Yet, this was a new era in American educational history, and new, "progressive" notions of how to promote social cohesion through education (often through "scientific" management) were fostered in the universities.[44] The leading American universities largely prepared the faculties for other institutions, thus creating a shared educational mission and vision of scholarship. Teachers College, for instance, trained Ellwood Cubberley, Jesse Sears and Lotus Coffman, while Stanford prepared David Snedden and Henry Suzzallo. The leading institutions also shared faculty with some of the normal schools. Richard Boone, for example, was part of Jordan's university-building endeavour at Indiana University, an endeavour that witnessed the hiring of numerous new faculty members; Dr Boone became the specialist in education at IU (as Cubberley was at Jordan's Stanford). In 1893, however, Boone moved on to Ypsilanti, Michigan, where he became the principal of Michigan State Normal School. Brought into the sometimes unwelcoming universities, educational scholars adopted their arts and sciences colleagues' vision of research and tried to demonstrate their worth by developing a "science" of education. Although the focus was on research, training in education was a lucrative business. By and large, therefore, a tiered system emerged; universities prepared education professors, normal school faculty, administrators and high school teachers, while the normal schools largely trained elementary teachers. Not fully content with this lowly status – because clientele conferred status, and elementary teachers were,

---

[41] Hermann Röhrs, *The Classical German Concept of the University and its Influence on Higher Education in the United States* (Frankfurt am Main: Peter Lang, 1995), 35–60, 75–87; Frederick Rudolph, *The American College and University: A History* (1962; reprint, with an introductory essay and supplemental bibliography by John R. Thelin, Athens, GA: University of Georgia Press, 1990), 118–122, 264–286; Frederick Rudolph, *Curriculum: A History of the American Undergraduate Course of Study since 1639* (San Francisco, CA: Jossey-Bass, 1977), 116–139; Laurence Veysey, *The Emergence of the American University* (Chicago, IL: University of Chicago Press, 1970), 121–179; Christopher J. Lucas, *American Higher Education: A History* (New York: St. Martin's Griffin, 1994), 170–174; John R. Thelin, *A History of American Higher Education* (Baltimore, MD: Johns Hopkins University Press, 2004), 110–154; Hinsdale, "Notes on the history of foreign influence", 591–594, 608–613; Paul J. Ramsey, "Building a 'real' university in the woodlands of Indiana: The Jordan Administration, 1885–1891", *American Educational History Journal* 31, no.1 (2004): 20–28.
[42] David Starr Jordan, *The Days of a Man: Being Memories of a Naturalist, Teacher and Minor Prophet of Democracy*, vol. 1 (Yonkers-on-Hudson, NY: World Book Company, 1922), 290; David Starr Jordan, *The Voice of the Scholar, with Other Addresses on the Problems of Higher Education* (San Francisco, CA: Paul Elder and Company, 1903), 31.
[43] Ramsey, "Building a 'real' university in the woodlands of Indiana", 20–28.
[44] Ramsey, *Bilingual Public Schooling*, 104–134.

unfortunately, on the bottom rung – normal schools gradually evolved into multipurpose universities throughout the first half of the twentieth century.[45]

Conclusions

For better or for worse, the development of teacher education in the US owes a great debt to international influence. The normal schools, so ubiquitous throughout the nineteenth century, were essentially Prussian institutions transplanted into the American soil. The earth in the new land, however, was manifestly different from that in Europe, and the normal schools – to the chagrin of their early advocates – blossomed into American hybrid institutions, institutions that had multiple aims, enrolled largely women and were plagued by a lowly status. By the end of the nineteenth century, universities also were quite involved in the field of education. Never fully shedding its English roots, the American college looked to the German lands for a model of reform, a model that helped pave the way for the American university. Universities held graduate training, specialisation and research in the highest esteem, and – after finding a home in these newly created institutions – so too did schools of education. Although at times on the periphery of the schools and departments of education's mission, teacher education in universities persisted and – especially with the transformation of normal schools into colleges and universities – even thrived.

The international influences on the *development* of teacher education in the US is an important topic, one to which many US historians, unfortunately, only pay passing attention (with the notable exception of the German influence on university development). There are numerous aspects of this international influence that need to be studied further. In some areas of the nation, for instance, a French influence was a powerful force in early education and teacher training, a topic that desperately needs further exploration.[46] In addition to the founding of teacher training in the US, a whole host of other aspects of teacher education that were impacted by international events and ideas require further research. The Scandinavian and German influences on vocational education (and its acceptance by teacher education faculty members), for instance, requires additional scholarship, as does the partial importation of the British informal school movement, which helped lay the foundation for alternative and free schools in the US during the 1960s and 1970s.[47] Hopefully, scholars soon will probe these and other issues in more depth.

---

[45]Geraldine Jonçich Clifford and James W. Guthrie, *Ed School: A Brief for Professional Education* (Chicago, IL: University of Chicago Press, 1988), 47–84; Ellen Condliffe Lagemann, "Whither schools of education? Whither education research?", *Journal of Teacher Education* 50, no. 5 (1999): 373–376; Isbell, *A History of Eastern Michigan University*, 141; Ramsey, "Building a 'real' university in the woodlands of Indiana", 20–28; David F. Labaree, *The Trouble with Ed Schools* (New Haven, CT: Yale University Press, 2004), 17–38; Lucas, *Teacher Education in America*, 29–47.

[46]Hinsdale, "Notes on the history of foreign influence", 594–603.

[47]Derek S. Linton, "American responses to German continuation schools during the progressive era", in *German Influences on Education*, 69–82; Richard Neumann, *Sixties Legacy: A History of the Public Alternative Schools Movement, 1967–2001* (New York: Peter Lang, 2003), 78–80. Linton points to the need for additional scholarship on German-influenced continuation schools, and Neumann's very brief treatment of the British informal schools suggests a substantial void in the (American) historical literature. Other international influences on education and teacher training, however, have received considerable attention from historians, such as demographic shifts (e.g. the mass immigration during the Progressive Era) and international conflicts (e.g. the First World War, the Second World War and the Cold War).

Acknowledgements

Different aspects of this article were presented at the Indiana University International Programs Committee Conference ("Toward a Research-based Approach to International Teacher Education", Bloomington, IN, 21–23 May 2009) and at the annual meeting of the International Standing Conference for the History of Education (Geneva, Switzerland, 27–30 June 2012); the author would like to thank the attendees for their invaluable feedback, as well as that of the reviewers and editors of *Paedagogica Historica*. The article was greatly facilitated by a research grant from the Eastern Michigan University Office of the Provost in 2012.

Fred Clarke and the internationalisation of studies and research in education

Gary McCulloch

Institute of Education, University of London, London, UK

Fred Clarke (1880–1952) was a key figure in the internationalisation of educational studies and research in the first half of the twentieth century. Clarke aimed to heighten the ideals and develop the practices of educational studies and research through promoting mutual influences in different countries around the world. He envisaged the Institute of Education at the University of London, England, as having a leading role, and was the director of the Institute from 1936 until 1945. His notion of internationalisation was reciprocal and transnational in nature, with aspirations for partnership within a common tradition. This built on the ideal of a "Commonwealth" that was current in the interwar years, and emphasised the affinities between the dominion nations and in particular Canada, South Africa, Australia and New Zealand. It also drew on the financial support and cultural influence of the Carnegie Corporation in New York. Two specific projects taken forward by Clarke to put these ideas into practice were his "world tour" of 1935 and his role as the "Adviser to Oversea Students" at the Institute of Education. These initiatives helped to convert strategic visions and policies into social practices, and to shape the subject of Education in higher education as a multi-disciplinary field in the generation after the Second World War.

Introduction

Fred Clarke (1880–1952) is perhaps best known for his work as the director of the Institute of Education, University of London (IOE), from 1936 to 1945, for his subsequent position as the chairman of the Central Advisory Council for Education (England), for his contributions to educational reform, especially in English secondary education, and for his elaboration of the "English tradition" of education in his book *Education and Social Change: An English Interpretation*.[1] According to

---

[1] Fred Clarke, *Education and Social Change: An English Interpretation* (London: Sheldon Books, 1940). See also, for example, Richard Aldrich, *The Institute of Education 1902–2002: A Centenary History* (London: Institute of Education, 2002), esp. chap. 5–6; and Gary McCulloch, *Failing the Ordinary Child? The Theory and Practice of Working Class Secondary Education* (Buckingham: Open University Press, 1998), chap. 4. On Clarke's approach to education reform in England, see also Hsiao-Yuh Ku, "Education for liberal democracy: Fred Clarke and educational reconstruction in England, 1936–1952" (unpublished PhD thesis, Institute of Education London, 2012).

Richard Glotzer, "The central theme of Fred Clarke's career was his commitment to British cultural ideas and institutions, articulated through educational ideas and practice".[2] Yet Clarke was a key figure in internationalisation in education, no less than in his assiduous pursuit of national ideals and reforms. He had a wide range of international experience, especially during his time as Professor of Education at the University of Cape Town, South Africa, from 1911 to 1929, and at McGill University, Montreal in Canada from 1929 to 1934. He was also actively involved both formally and informally in international associations for 40 years, from before the First World War through to the period after the Second World War.[3]

Clarke's approach to educational studies and research was an important aspect of his contribution as a whole, but has not as yet received full recognition from historians. Already known for his forthright views in this area by the early 1920s,[4] Clarke took part in the efforts of the British Association for the Advancement of Science to help to promote this field, and helped lead the establishment of the National Foundation for Educational Research and the Standing Conference on Studies in Education.[5] His short book *The Study of Education in England* is a key document in the history of educational studies and research.[6] He was indeed a key figure in "discipline building" in this domain of knowledge in higher education, as for example George Sarton was during the same period for the discipline of the history of science, but on an international as well as a national stage.[7]

Clarke was particularly concerned to internationalise educational studies and research. He perceived the IOE as a significant international centre for the study of education, and also drew on the experiences of other countries in assessing prospects for the future. His "world tour" of 1935, which he undertook just before his appointment as the IOE's director, had a significant bearing on his ideas about educational studies and research. The archive of Fred Clarke, held at the IOE, provides detailed insights into the development of his ideas about educational studies and research, and the nature of his engagement with groups and individuals based in different countries. This is also well reflected in the archives of other research organisations around the world, including the Carnegie Corporation, the New Zealand Council for Educational Research and the Australian Council for Educational Research, each of which had substantial involvement with Clarke. These sources permit insights into the views of contemporary educationists in different countries on Clarke and his activities. This article will appraise these ideas and contacts in detail to discern the ways in which Clarke contributed to internationalisation in educational studies and research during these years.

---

[2]Richard Glotzer, "Sir Fred Clarke: South Africa and Canada Carnegie Corporation philanthropy and the transition from Empire to Commonwealth", *Education Research and Perspectives* 22, no. 1 (1995): 13.
[3]For a general account, see Frank Mitchell, *Sir Fred Clarke: Master-Teacher* (London: Longman, 1967).
[4]Fred Clarke, *Essays in the Politics of Education* (Oxford: Oxford University Press, 1922).
[5]See also Gary McCulloch, "The Standing Conference on Studies in Education – sixty years on", *British Journal of Educational Studies* 60, no. 4 (2012): 301–316.
[6]Fred Clarke, *The Study of Education in England* (Oxford: Oxford University Press, 1943).
[7]On George Sarton and the history of science, see Arnold Thackray and Robert Merton, "On discipline building: The paradoxes of George Sarton", *Isis* 63, no. 4 (1972): 472–495.

Nearly 30 years ago, Goodenow and Cowen called for much greater historical and comparative attention to be given to the international relationships of institutes and schools of education.[8] Research on the history of educational studies has greatly developed over the past two decades with respect to a number of national contexts such as the US, Scotland, Switzerland and Australia.[9] Historical understanding of the processes by which educational studies and research became institutionalised in different countries has also been much enhanced. As Hofstetter and Schneuwly have discussed, these processes characteristically involve the creation of academic chairs, textbooks, institutions and posts for educational research, publications in specialised journals and public discourses on education.[10] Historians have also begun to explore the international dynamics involved in the history of educational studies and research[11] and it is clear that the field has developed in different ways in different contexts.[12] Much more detailed research is required, however, in order to develop the theme of internationalisation in this area in depth.

According to Ulrich Teichler, processes of internationalisation in higher education entail border-crossing activities between national systems, while globalisation denotes border-crossing activities of blurred national systems which reflect worldwide trends and growing global competition.[13] In relation to internationalisation, Teichler identifies different dimensions of this process in terms of the movement of knowledge across borders, the validation and recognition of teaching, learning and research results, issues of international homogeneity, the scope of actors' policies, and higher education steering as a whole. The last of these involves strategic action,

---

[8]Ronald Goodenow and Robert Cowen, "The American School of Education and the third world in the twentieth century: Teachers College and Africa, 1920–1950", *History of Education* 15, no. 4 (1986): 271–289.

[9]Ellen Lagemann, *An Elusive Science: The Troubling History of Education Research* (Chicago, IL: Chicago University Press, 2000); Martin Lawn, Ian Deary, David Bartholomew and Caroline Brett, "Embedding the new science of research: The organised culture of Scottish educational research in the mid-twentieth century", *Paedagogica Historica* 46, no. 3 (2010): 357–381; Rita Hofstetter, "The construction of a new science by means of an institute and its communication media: The Institute of Educational Sciences in Geneva (1912–1948)", *Paedagogica Historica* 40, no. 5–6 (2004): 657–683; Di Gardiner, Thomas O'Donoghue and Marnie O'Neil, *Constructing the Field of Education as a Liberal Art and as Teacher Preparation in Five Western Australian Universities: An Historical Analysis* (Lewiston, NY: Edwin Mellen Press, 2011).

[10]Rita Hofstetter and Bernard Schneuwly, "Introduction: Educational sciences in dynamic and hybrid institutionalisation", *Paedagogica Historica* 40, no. 5 (2004): 569–589; Rita Hofstetter and Bernard Schneuwly, "Institutionalisation of educational sciences and the dynamics of their development", *European Educational Research Journal* 1, no. 1 (2002): 3–26; Rita Hofstetter, "Educational studies: Evolutions of a pluridisciplinary discipline at the crossroads of other disciplinary and professional fields (20th century)", *British Journal of Educational Studies* 60, no. 4 (2012): 317–335.

[11]For example, Martin Lawn, ed., *An Atlantic Crossing? The Work of the International Examinations Inquiry, its Researchers, Methods and Influences* (Oxford: Symposium, 2008); Susan Middleton, "Claire Soper's hat: New Education Fellowship correspondence between Bloomsbury and New Zealand, 1918–1946", *History of Education* 42, no. 1 (2013): 92–114.

[12]Gert Biesta, "Disciplines and theory in the academic study of education: A comparative analysis of the Anglo-American and continental construction of the field", *Pedagogy, Culture and Society* 19, no. 2 (2011): 175–192.

[13]Ulrich Teichler, "The changing debate on internationalisation of higher education", *Higher Education* 48, no. 1–2 (2004): 5–26.

in recent times promoted most clearly by national governments and international agencies.[14] In the 1920s and 1930s, individuals and national organisations had key roles in this general process, and the development of educational studies and research provides a significant example of this. The activities of Clarke and his colleagues at the IOE and elsewhere also highlight the extent of international mobility to support these developments, and of changing practices within a specific higher education institution involving students, courses, curriculum and staff.

It is also most important to consider these issues in relation to their broader social and political contexts, especially as these impinged on the international arena of the time. These included the growing financial and cultural influence of the US, the shift from the British Empire to a British Commonwealth and its legacy of colonialism, and the growing international conflicts of the 1930s leading to the Second World War. Higher education institutions, philanthropic foundations and professors of education operated within these broad configurations and addressed immense challenges as they conspired and competed to change their world.

An Empire of influence?

Clarke's general vision of educational studies and research was already well developed by the First World War. The fundamental purpose of university departments of education, according to Clarke, was as "centres for the study of education".[15] This would mean the appointment of staff who would be able to specialise in particular aspects of education, such as history and organisation, methods of instruction and training, and the philosophy and psychology of education, and to engage in research in these areas.[16] Under the beneficent influence of such tutors, he concluded, the training of teachers would also be greatly elevated and improved.[17] It was these objectives that Clarke was determined to pursue further in the 1930s. In Clarke's view, a key means of promoting these aims was the internationalisation of educational studies and research. Through mutual influence in different countries around the world, Clarke aimed to heighten the ideals and develop the practices of educational studies and research in a number of ways. He hoped that at least some of the traditions of education in England might be adapted for use in other countries. At the same time, he argued that the educational ideas of other countries might also have a significant bearing on the changes that were taking place in the English context, and also that there should be an international market of students and staff to help to build up an enlarged role for educational studies and research in England as well as elsewhere. In all of these developments, Clarke saw the IOE as potentially having a crucial and leading role to play.

Clarke's notion of internationalisation was therefore reciprocal and transnational in nature, as opposed to proposing simply a uni-directional flow from "centre" to "periphery".[18] Clarke's ideas retained what the American historian of education

---

[14]Ibid., 19–22.
[15]Fred Clarke, "The university and the study of education", in Clarke, *Essays in the Politics of Education*, 136.
[16]Ibid., 140.
[17]Ibid., 144.
[18]See also Joyce Goodman, Gary McCulloch and William Richardson, "Introduction: 'Empires overseas' and 'empires at home': Postcolonial and transnational perspectives on social change in the history of education", *Paedagogica Historica* 45, no. 6 (2009): 695–706; Gary McCulloch, *The Struggle for the History of Education* (London: Routledge, 2011), 93–97.

Lawrence Cremin typified as "metropolitanism", involving the export of the culture and civilisation of a metropolitan nation to other nations and regions of the world.[19] Nevertheless, they were also symptomatic of a trend away from classical doctrines of the British Empire towards what were, in the context of the 1930s, more forward-looking and in some respects liberal internationalist ideals in the shape of the British Commonwealth.

The notion of a "Commonwealth" was central to the Statute of Westminster of December 1931. This built on the agreements of earlier conferences and the Balfour report of 1926 to recognise that the dominions of Canada, Australia, New Zealand, South Africa, Ireland and Newfoundland should control their own domestic and foreign affairs, establish their own diplomatic corps and be represented separately at the League of Nations. This effectively loosened the political bonds of the erstwhile British Empire, but highlighted the issues of how to retain effective collaboration and the nature of the common values that united the dominions with the metropolitan homeland. John Darwin has argued that these developments helped to create a constitutional compromise that bound the Dominions to Britain in a new form of "imperial nationhood". He concludes that this implied the continued dominance of the Mother Country, "as the 'Britishness' of their culture and institutions was reinforced by the modernisation of their political and economic life".[20]

These were key concerns in the shift from the former London Day Training College (LDTC) to the establishment of the IOE at the University of London in the 1930s.[21] For example, in July 1931 a British Commonwealth Education Conference took place at Bedford College, London, to discuss the nature of education in a changing Commonwealth under the auspices of the New Education Fellowship. Sir Percy Nunn, then-principal of the LDTC, used this conference to outline his aspirations for an IOE.[22] He proposed that there should be developed a permanent, strongly organised centre for continued discussion and enquiry into all educational problems that affected the welfare of the British Commonwealth, based on the provisions of the Statute of Westminster. Such an IOE, Nunn concluded, would be based in a university, and would provide a place for discussion and inquiry in which, he stated, "we stand to learn from you at least as much, probably much more than we can possibly teach", to facilitate "a mutual affair, in which we learn from each other".[23] These ideas were met favourably by the University of London, whose principal, Edwin Deller, recognised that, while the LDTC was already the most important and largest centre in England for advanced study and research in education, its position outside the university had "stood in the way of its development as an imperial and international centre for higher study and research,

---

[19] L. Cremin, *American Education: The Metropolitan Experience, 1876–1980* (New York: Harper Row, 1988).
[20] John Darwin, "A third British Empire? The dominion idea in imperial politics", in Judith Brown and William Roger Louis, eds., *The Oxford History of the British Empire: The Twentieth Century* (Oxford: Oxford University Press, 1999), 85–86.
[21] See also, for example, Aldrich, *The Institute of Education 1902–2002*, chap. 4–5; Aldrich, "The training of teachers and educational studies: The London Day Training College, 1902–1932", *Paedagogica Historica* 40, no. 5 (2004): 617–631; Aldrich, "The New Education and the Institute of Education, University of London, 1919–1945", *Paedagogica Historica* 45, no. 4 (2009): 485–502.
[22] Wyatt Rawson, ed., *Education in a Changing Commonwealth* (London: Report of British Commonwealth Education Conference, New Education Fellowship, 1931), iii.
[23] Ibid., 147.

which is emphatically the business of a university though not of a municipality to promote and encourage".[24]

The Carnegie Corporation and the Institute of Education

In the US, Isaac Kandel of the Teachers College at Columbia University in New York also noted with interest that the establishment of such a centre for the advanced study of education in England would be a highly positive development internationally,

> first, because it will give the subject itself a position which it has not hitherto enjoyed, and, secondly, because it may make the English articulate about the strength of their system and contribute to the progress of education generally.[25]

Nunn was able to pursue this substantial shared agenda with the support of the Carnegie Corporation of New York, which was active during this time in giving financial aid to educational research initiatives in different countries.[26] During 1934, Nunn negotiated a substantial grant from the Carnegie Corporation with the aim of developing what he called "the imperial and international, as distinguished from the domestic, side of the Institute".[27] He pointed out in private correspondence with Frederick Keppel, the president of the Carnegie Corporation, that these "imperial activities" would help to foster a common understanding among educational workers in England and in the self-governing Dominions, while also supporting the training of workers for the educational field in the colonies, provision of advanced and refresher courses for mature workers and research in the problems of colonial education.[28]

Under the terms of its charter, the Carnegie Corporation was not able to provide financial support directly to promoting education in England, but it could support initiatives in other parts of the world, including the British Dominions. It was this provision that it set out to exploit. Contact between the Carnegie Corporation and the University of London thus began to be fostered in the early 1930s, in anticipation of the establishment of the IOE, with both Keppel and Kandel proving pivotal in promoting these.[29] Kandel expressed strong support for a development of this kind, arguing in a letter to Keppel that, "Any new institution of this type will strengthen our own work".[30] Clarke,

---

[24]Edwin Deller (principal, University of London) to Frederick Keppel (Carnegie Corporation), 20 November 1931 (Carnegie Corporation papers, Columbia University, New York).
[25]Isaac Kandel to Frederick Keppel, 5 July 1932 (Carnegie Corporation papers).
[26]See also Ellen Lagemann, *The Politics of Knowledge: The Carnegie Corporation, Philanthropy, and Public Policy* (Chicago, IL: Chicago University Press, 1989).
[27]Sir Percy Nunn to Frederick Keppel, 28 May 1934 (Carnegie Corporation papers).
[28]Ibid.
[29]On Keppel's wider international contacts, see also Richard Glotzer, "A long shadow: Frederick P. Keppel, the Carnegie Corporation and the Dominions and colonies fund area experts, 1923–1943", *History of Education* 38, no. 5 (2009): 621648; Jenny Collins, "Creating women's work in the academy and beyond: Carnegie connections, 1923–1942", *History of Education* 38, no. 6 (2009): 791–808. On Kandel, see J. Wesley Null, *Peerless Educator: The Life and Work of Isaac Leon Kandel* (New York: Peter Lang, 2007).
[30]Isaac Kandel to Frederick Keppel, (day unknown) June 1932 (Carnegie Corporation papers).

at this time a professor of education at McGill University in Canada but forging a close relationship with Nunn, was enthusiastic about the "cultural possibilities of the English-founded lands", and emphasised that "without USA participation in its activities I feel that such an Institute cannot hope to be complete".[31] Kandel suggested that the most acceptable form of support for the IOE's further development would be in the form of fellowship grants for the dominions and colonies, with supplementary support for travel in England. The introduction of a professorship in comparative education was an additional proposal.[32] At a further meeting, in January 1933, Clarke urged that there should be a greater international exchange of ideas, with the US providing an important role in this and the IOE fitting into such a plan.[33] Letters and telephone contact ensued between the Corporation and the IOE, with a number of visits between them.

Clarke was admirably suited to liaising between the Carnegie Corporation and the IOE, and took his opportunity with vigour. He took his cue from Nunn in promoting international cooperation, and indeed was privately critical of Nunn and his generation for being "too little aware of the change that has come over the scene since 1919".[34] In an article for the *Oversea Education* journal in April 1932, when he was still based in Canada, he had set out what he described as "a Dominion view" of "an Education Institute for the Empire".[35] This pointed out the need for a more modern conception of empire than had been present before the First World War and at the height of the British Empire in the diamond jubilee of 1897. He argued that this should be encouraged through ideas that promoted the spirit of British institutions, channelled by a permanent organisation based in London. Such an "informing spirit", according to Clarke, should now be "concentrated at a central power-station and distributed by the transmitting lines of education for distant peoples to use according to their need".[36] By the same token, however, it was no less important for the old institutions rooting themselves in "new" societies now to be part of "a return movement from them to enrich the ancient sources".[37] This would motivate,

> a great back-and-forth movement of organised mental power and cultural achievement, contributing to mutual enrichment, and furthering both the separate integration of the members and the fruitful harmony of the whole group.[38]

It would also complement the growing cultural influence of the US, which should play a key part in any new educational scheme through agencies such as the Carnegie Corporation.

---

[31] Fred Clarke to Frederick Keppel, 14 June 1932 (Carnegie Corporation papers).
[32] Note of meeting between Keppel and Kandel, 16 July 1932 (Carnegie Corporation papers).
[33] Carnegie Corporation meeting with Fred Clarke and others, 19 January 1933 (Carnegie Corporation papers).
[34] Fred Clarke to Frederick Keppel, 8 December 1933 (Carnegie Corporation papers).
[35] Fred Clarke, "An education institute for the Empire: A Dominion view", *Oversea Education* 3, no. 3 (1932): 105–110.
[36] Ibid., 107.
[37] Ibid. See also, for example, Fred Clarke, "Canada and South Africa: An essay in comparative interpretation and a plea for an imperial institute of education", *Year Book of Education* (London: Evans Brothers, 1933), 500–518.
[38] Clarke, "An education institute for the Empire", 107.

Clarke's later published thoughts on these international developments, after he succeeded Nunn as the director of the IOE, took these ideas further to champion the prospect of being, in his terms, "British" with a small "b".[39] According to Clarke, the new Commonwealth would constitute

> not so much a unitary political structure as that whole philosophy of life and culture and social order which, with its roots and historical origins in these islands, has now re-rooted itself and grown to maturity in distant lands.[40]

Returning to England after many years of working in the Dominions, he suggested that there was a striking set of changes going on in British relations with the rest of the world. The previous supremacy of sovereign power, he proposed, was giving way to influence through the communication of ideas, which would depend on education to be effective:

> We have, in short, to take full account of the conditions that have been produced by popular education, by the wide dissemination of news and knowledge, and by facilities of communication which mean that men can now converse freely across the world.[41]

If a centre based in London could be organised, he contended that "a great temple of the common faith may result, in which the universal philosophy of *Res Britannica* can be formulated so as to become the potent sceptre of the new Empire of Influence".[42]

At the same time, Clarke found that the Carnegie Corporation was a useful source of educational ideas. For example, he congratulated Keppel for his Carnegie Centenary address in the *School and Society* journal at the end of 1935.[43] Clarke insisted to Keppel that:

> The case both for tightening the bonds of co-operation and, if possible, for extending our range grows stronger every day, and as you are right in the centre of the organism, nothing is more important than adequate understandings between yourself and those who are working with you.[44]

By now, Clarke was able to consolidate his close relationship with the Carnegie Corporation in his new position as the director of the IOE, and he was presented with a medal by the Corporation at this time.[45] At a meeting between Keppel and Clarke in London in July 1936, Keppel assured Clarke of further Corporation grants for the IOE, while Clarke for his part proposed that a small leadership team should be developed, including Kandel.[46] Carnegie's financial support had given Clarke a firm basis for extending activities and promoting the IOE's international profile.

---

[39] Fred Clarke, "'British' with a small 'b'", *The Nineteenth Century and After* 119, no. 710 (April 1936): 428–439.
[40] Ibid., 428.
[41] Ibid., 433.
[42] Ibid., 436–437.
[43] Fred Clarke to Frederick Keppel, 30 December 1935 (Carnegie Corporation papers).
[44] Fred Clarke to Frederick Keppel, 25 March 1936 (Carnegie Corporation papers).
[45] Edith Clarke to the President of the Carnegie Corporation, 29 January 1952 (Carnegie Corporation papers).
[46] Memorandum of Meeting of Frederick Keppel and Fred Clarke, 21 July 1936 (Carnegie Corporation papers).

The broad experience acquired as a professor of education in South Africa and Canada, as well as in England, led Clarke to be regarded as a leading authority on international issues in education, and especially on the nations of the new Commonwealth, by the time of his return to England. This was reflected, for instance, in an invitation from the Board of Education's consultative committee, during its preparation of a report on secondary education, to contribute an Appendix to its Report on aspects affecting secondary curricula in the Dominions.[47] He also gave active support to the *Year Book of Education*, which was taken over by the IOE in the later 1930s under his guidance, and provided a lead in helping to understand the common and differing problems of education in the Dominions and the US, including through active participation in the international conferences of the New Education Fellowship.[48]

In the later 1930s, as the international situation grew increasingly fraught, it also encouraged thoughts of an increasingly explicit political nature, with the US and Britain tied together in bonds of common traditions and values against the threat posed by the fascist dictators in Europe. Clarke proposed that they should combine to develop a democratic philosophy of education.[49] After the start of the Second World War, he returned to this theme.[50] Keppel was cautious but sympathetic, envisaging that "the union of this country and yours" would not disappear after the War, and that "post-war problems will, by their very nature, bring about an even stronger spirit of cooperation".[51]

There were limits to this relationship. Despite repeated requests from the IOE, Carnegie declined to provide financial support for the *Year Book of Education*, or to invest in its distribution across the US. Another rather grandiose proposal from Clarke for an international inquiry into how to control and limit post-war change also failed to win support. He argued that,

> If the ends and values towards which, with the Corporation's generous help, we have been working, win out in this context, I hope that the return of peace will find us much more effectively linked up with many forces of reconstruction which have been stirred into activity by the shock.[52]

To this end, a memo by Clarke in January 1940 argued that the "imposing of intelligent control" would be necessary in order to avoid losing "essential values".[53] Keppel and Walter Jessup of the Carnegie Foundation for the Advancement of Teaching discussed Clarke's scheme and could find nothing in it that could be supported,[54] and even Keppel felt obliged to tell Clarke that it was "premature".[55]

---

[47] Fred Clarke, "Appendix VI: Memorandum on Some Influences Affecting Secondary Curricula in the Dominions by Mr Fred Clarke, Professor of Education and Director of the Institute of Education, University of London", in *Secondary Education* (Spens Report), Board of Education, ed., (London: HMSO, 1938), 464.
[48] See for example the *Year Book of Education* (1937) for Clarke's "Introduction" and his role in Part Five on the education of the adolescent in the Dominions and the US.
[49] Fred Clarke to Frederick Keppel, 23 November 1938 (Carnegie Corporation papers).
[50] Fred Clarke to Frederick Keppel, 3 November 1939 (Carnegie Corporation papers).
[51] Frederick Keppel to Fred Clarke, 15 February 1941 (Carnegie Corporation papers).
[52] Fred Clarke to Frederick Keppel, 23 May 1940 (Carnegie Corporation papers).
[53] Fred Clarke, memorandum, "Education and the control of social change: Proposals for a survey of resources and possibilities", 4 January 1940 (Carnegie Corporation papers).
[54] Meeting of Isaac Kandel and Walter Jessup, 10 February 1940 (Carnegie Corporation papers).
[55] Frederick Keppel to Fred Clarke, 15 February 1940 (Carnegie Corporation papers).

Internationalisation abroad and at home

Two key projects that Clarke did take forward were outcomes of the agenda that Nunn had initiated and which, with the support of the Carnegie Corporation, he was able to bring to fruition. The first was what he described as his "world tour", in practice restricted to western Canada, Australia and New Zealand in 1935, which was also made possible through substantial financial assistance from the Carnegie Corporation for his travelling expenses and those of his daughter Mary who accompanied him. The second was his role as Adviser to Oversea Students, to which Nunn appointed him in 1934.

Clarke's "world tour" through a succession of journeys by ship and train lasted for 16 weeks, from May to September 1935. He considered that he already had sufficient experience of South Africa and eastern Canada, so concentrated his effort on western Canada, New Zealand and Australia. His initial purpose, as he confided to KS Cunningham of the Australian Council for Educational Research, was to "discover precisely what services a Central Institute in London might perform for students of Education from the Dominions, and in what form these services might best be discharged".[56] It was also an opportunity to develop personal contacts with key individuals such as CE Beeby in New Zealand and Frank Tate in Australia. As he commented, "More and more do I realise the importance of the two-way traffic of intercourse and especially that the key people should know one another personally".[57]

Clarke's discussions with Beeby, who had become Executive Officer of the New Zealand Council for Educational Research in November 1934 and later went on to be a long-serving director of education in New Zealand, highlighted the nature of this "two-way traffic of intercourse".[58] After his visit to New Zealand and having met with Beeby, Clarke raised serious concerns with him over some aspects of New Zealand education, including what he considered an excessive reliance on the State and loyalty to outdated English traditions.[59] Beeby acknowledged these difficulties, and suggested that in addressing them Clarke might develop his "considered opinion" as a "Royal command to the Dominions", becoming indeed "a much-needed Valuer-General". More specifically, Beeby argued, Clarke could help to "coordinate research in different parts of the Empire", with the support of his "arch-priests in London".[60] Clarke, however, preferred the idea of "translating" institutions and into different national environments rather than simply transplanting them, following a thorough study in each country of their own situations and problems.[61]

During his tour, Clarke interviewed the authorities of state departments of education, universities, teachers, leading citizens and others interested in education. He also made public addresses in Winnipeg, Auckland, Wellington, Christchurch, Dunedin, Brisbane, Melbourne, Adelaide and Perth, had discussions with informed groups in almost every centre that he visited, and gave interviews to newspapers in nearly every town along his route. He concluded in his formal report on the tour that there was an agreed need for considerable development of facilities in London for

---

[56] Fred Clarke to KS Cunningham, 14 February 1935 (Australian Council for Educational Research papers, Victoria, Australia).
[57] Fred Clarke to Frederick Keppel, 13 June 1935 (Carnegie Corporation papers).
[58] On Beeby's life and educational career, see Noeline Alcorn, *The Fullest Extent of his Powers: C.E. Beeby's Life in Education* (Wellington: Victoria University Press, 1999).
[59] Fred Clarke to Clarence Beeby, 25 July 1935 (NZCER papers, Wellington, New Zealand).
[60] Clarence Beeby to Fred Clarke, 5 August 1935 (NZCER papers).
[61] Fred Clarke to C. Beeby, 11 August 1935 (emphasis in original) (NZCER papers).

"advanced" cooperative studies, and also that priority should be given to mid-career men and women who showed promise to shape educational policy. He considered that the number of advanced students should be kept at a small size at present, while at the same time the Institute of Education should appoint a few men as professors with outstanding attainment and reputation in selected specialised areas, in particular educational philosophy, comparative education, history of education and the economics of education.[62]

These recommendations suggested a clear linkage being made between the creation of an international pool of researchers and fellows in educational studies, and the formation of a multi-disciplinary approach to the field as a whole that could draw on specialist expertise in a wide range of disciplines such as history, philosophy, sociology and comparative education. Indeed, in private, Clarke made this precise point when writing to Frank Tate in Australia, emphasising the importance of, first, creating two or three chairs for key people and, second, the increasing establishment and tightening of permanent bonds with people overseas that would establish a demand from overseas for advanced studies.[63] At the same time, he argued that, although the staff at the Institute should include individuals from around the world, they should not be selected on a territorial basis, "a sort of Joseph's coat, to include a patch for each land concerned in the scheme"; rather the Institute should be "constituted to represent diverse interests in education in general, different lines of approach to the problems".[64]

Clarke's public pronouncements during this tour revealed much about his priorities. For example, in a radio broadcast in Wellington, New Zealand, in July 1935, he noted his intention to help develop a "[h]igher School for the study of educational problems throughout the Empire and Commonwealth". This would focus especially on questions of "educational statesmanship", and on "the study of the bearings of educational organisation and methods on the maintenance and enrichment of our common British citizenship through all the diversities of form and expression that it assumes in the variegated whole to which we belong". He expressed hope that there would be organised in London,

> a well-equipped centre where men and women of weight and promise in their own educational world may assemble from all over the Empire and pursue common and co-operative studies of the common problems on a basis of complete equality and freedom.

Moreover, each nation involved would provide a distinctive contribution to this global vision, drawing on its own cultural and political traditions.[65]

This tour also provided opportunities for Clarke to prepare for his new position as the adviser to overseas students at the IOE. He began in this role in February 1935, and before embarking on his tour in May he organised a weekly seminar, had frequent discussions with individual students, and also arranged for visits by a number of students to schools outside London that offered useful features for them to

---

[62] Fred Clarke, Report on tour (1935) (Fred Clarke papers, Institute of Education London, FC/1/59).
[63] Fred Clarke to Frank Tate, 21 June 1936 (ACER papers).
[64] Fred Clarke to Frederick Keppel, 30 November 1934 (Carnegie Corporation papers).
[65] Fred Clarke, Wellington broadcast, 22 July 1935 (Clarke papers, FC/1/59).

observe.[66] In collaboration with Nunn, he instituted an "Oversea Division", with Clarke assuming a general responsibility for all students in this after he returned from his overseas visits for the academic year 1935–36. There were about 17 students in the Colonial Department of the Division and eight Carnegie Fellows recruited from the Dominions, together with several senior students engaged in special studies or registered for MA or PhD degrees. One of the Carnegie Fellows began a PhD course while another began a Teacher's Diploma course.[67]

After Clarke took over as director of the IOE, he decided to retain his position as adviser to overseas students as a mark of the importance that he attached to this role.[68] Overseas students were encouraged to spend their first few terms in London and then to travel so that they could acquire what Clarke regarded as "a real understanding of the general spirit and structure of English life and education".[69] By the end of the 1936–37 academic session there were 107 overseas students from all countries registered at the Institute, including 24 from India taking teacher's diploma courses.[70] Lengthy absences due to ill health obliged Clarke to pass further responsibility to others.[71] Nevertheless, further expansion of overseas provision was provided in the late 1930s, for example through the establishment of the Associateship of the IOE, which was open to any experienced senior student for a full session of relevant study. According to Clarke, the Associateship did not involve a set course, but would be based on individual students' own interests, although he insisted that work towards this would be carried out with "whole-hearted thoroughness" and that there would be "no rewards for joy-riders".[72] In 1939, the British Council also began to support overseas students from Europe.

Clarke's continued role as adviser to overseas students, combined with his position as director, also helped him to identify potential areas of specialist expertise that would require senior staff appointments. One such area was English as a foreign language, and once again he enlisted the support of the Carnegie Corporation to help take this forward.[73] Such assistance was envisaged as "getting the beginnings established in permanent form with good guarantees of growth and continuity".[74] Also in 1939, the IOE was rehoused in new buildings. This allowed provision of a special common room for overseas students, which promoted academic and social involvement, as well as separate tutorial rooms for all of the tutors in the Oversea Division, which allowed more scope for personal discussions with students from overseas.[75] Clarke reported that the presence of students from Egypt, India, Africa and else-

---

[66]Fred Clarke, Report of Adviser to Oversea Students, 30 September 1935 (Carnegie Corporation papers).
[67]Fred Clarke, Grant from Carnegie Corporation: Report of Adviser to Oversea Students, Session 1935–36 (Carnegie Corporation papers).
[68]Sir Percy Nunn to Frederick Keppel, 20 May 1936 (Carnegie Corporation papers).
[69]Fred Clarke to Mr Lester (Carnegie Corporation), 11 August 1937 (Carnegie Corporation papers).
[70]Fred Clarke, Grant from Carnegie Corporation: Report of Adviser to Oversea Students, Session 1936–37 (Carnegie Corporation papers).
[71]H. Hamley, Grant from Carnegie Corporation of New York: Report of the Acting Director of the Institute of Education, session 1937–38, 21 July 1938 (Carnegie Corporation papers).
[72]Fred Clarke to F. Tate, 24 November 1938 (ACER papers).
[73]Fred Clarke to Frederick Keppel, 30 June 1939 (Carnegie Corporation papers).
[74]Ibid.
[75]HR Hamley, report for 1937–38 (Carnegie Corporation papers).

where assisted in the development of a "healthy form of colour blindness".[76] The internationalisation of educational studies and research thus began to be reflected in everyday experience no less than in ideology and policy.

At the start of the Second World War, the IOE was temporarily relocated to University College Nottingham, and this, combined with wartime conditions, hampered overseas work to some extent. However, there continued to be "a considerable and varied oversea contingent, quite enough to maintain our character", in Clarke's view,[77] and by the end of the first term in 1939–40, numbers of overseas students at the Institute's temporary home reached 47. The buildings of the University College were crowded with the influx of staff and students from London and elsewhere, but the ground floor of a large house nearby was rented for the use of overseas students. According to Clarke's report to the Carnegie Corporation for 1939–40, this helped to encourage among overseas students "a corporate spirit and a common-room camaraderie which was most marked".[78] An overseas library was also gradually developed over this time, including official reports and a number of standard historical works to introduce students from different backgrounds and courses to systems of education around the world.[79] Meanwhile, growing interest in comparative education led to the US and the British Dominions being included in a well-attended optional course in the teacher's diploma, led by tutors with first-hand experience of education in different countries.[80]

In 1945, Clarke resigned from the directorship of the IOE in order to take up a national role as the first chairman of the Central Advisory Council for Education (England), but such was his continuing interest that he was invited to resume the part-time position that he had initially held as the adviser for overseas students. In the early postwar years, moreover, the number of overseas students at the Institute reached new levels as a result of the further development of British Council studentships from around the world, an increase in the number of students from India (from 24 in 1939 to 50 in 1946–1947), and a large number of students from Africa. Weekly seminars were held involving students from a number of nationalities and addressing postwar problems in different countries, and also to "describe and explain the different aspects and institutions of English education", with the help of outside speakers.[81] Clarke noted with evident satisfaction that a high number of overseas students were studying for MAs and PhDs and that these were being catered for by seven full-time professors of education at the University of London who specialised in different areas: philosophy, psychology, sociology, history (at King's College London), comparative education, education in the colonies and English as a foreign language.[82]

---

[76]Ibid.
[77]Fred Clarke to Frederick Keppel, 29 October 1939 (Carnegie Corporation papers).
[78]Fred Clarke, Report on the Work of the Oversea Division, 1939–40, 18 October 1940 (Carnegie Corporation papers).
[79]Fred Clarke, Report to the Carnegie Corporation of New York on the Session 1940–41, 21 November 1941 (Carnegie Corporation papers).
[80]Fred Clarke, Some Recent and Current Activities [n.d.; 1941] (Carnegie Corporation papers).
[81]GB Jeffrey, Progress Report Submitted to the Carnegie Corporation of New York on the Administration of the Carnegie Benefaction and the Work of the Overseas Divisions Generally, Session 1946–1947, 28 August 1947 (Carnegie Corporation papers).
[82]Fred Clarke, Report to the Carnegie Corporation, 1948–49 (Carnegie Corporation papers).

Conclusions

Internationalisation was clearly a key theme for Fred Clarke, and he made use of his wide range of international experience and expertise to provide the basis for the emergence of a new Institute of Education located in London, comparable in its international stature and reputation to the Teachers College at Columbia University, New York, and the International Bureau of Education in Geneva. These are the historical origins of the IOE's long-term institutional strategy for internationalisation that was to be maintained and developed further in changing circumstances into the twenty-first century.[83] It was indeed Clarke's approach to internationalisation that helped to create the conditions for his contribution to what Thackray and Merton describe as "discipline building".[84] In the case of educational studies and research, it was perhaps a multi-disciplinary field of study rather than a discipline as such that Clarke helped to build at the IOE, with its emphasis on specialisation in particular disciplines such as philosophy, history, sociology, psychology and comparative studies applied to the critical study of educational problems. This was to provide a dominant model for the social organisation of educational studies in Britain in the generation after the Second World War.[85]

In Teichler's terms, the internationalisation or border-crossing activities between national systems that developed in the interwar years was on this evidence highly strategic in nature, based as it was on the cooperation of well-placed individuals and institutions in pursuit of common strategic goals. The financial support of the Carnegie Corporation, the opportunities offered by the transition to the British Commonwealth, the new role of the IOE in London, all of these were instrumental in the rapid institutionalisation of educational studies and research. Clarke's own ability to liaise with such figures as Keppel, Kandel, Beeby and Tate, taken further as it was by his "world tour" of 1935, promoted the movement of ideas across international borders, the mobility of students and staff, and the establishment of new courses. These resulted also in novel interactions within specific institutions, in this case the IOE, as the introduction of students and staff from different countries began to encourage new educational and social practices. In the period before national governments and international agencies came to occupy a central and decisive position in internationalisation and globalisation, these individuals and institutions were already providing significant impetus to these continuing processes.[86] Their work also had broader social and political significance, as they promoted, on the one hand, a leading place for Britain in a post-imperial context and a changing world order and, on the other hand, common traditions and values against the international threat posed by fascism and war.

---

[83]See also Aldrich, *The Institute of Education*, chap. 11.
[84]Thackray and Merton, "On discipline building".
[85]See, for example, John William Tibble, ed., *The Study of Education* (London: Routledge and Kegan Paul, 1966); also Gary McCulloch, "'Disciplines contributing to education?' Educational studies and the disciplines", *British Journal of Educational Studies* 50, no. 1 (2002): 100–119.
[86]See, for example, Peter Scott, ed., *The Globalization of Higher Education* (Buckingham: Open University Press, 1998). Also see Felix Maringe and Nick Foskett, eds., *Globalization and Internationalization in Higher Education: Theoretical, Strategic and Management Perspectives* (London: Continuum, 2010) on the rise and development of governmental and international agency activities by the end of the century.

Acknowledgements

I am most grateful to the Society for Educational Studies for the support it provided for the National Award project, "The social organisation of educational studies: Past, present and future", on which this article is based; to my colleagues in this project, Gemma Moss, James Thomas and Steven Cowan for their advice and support; to Logan Moss for his generous sharing of archival data; and to delegates at the 2012 ISCHE conference in Geneva and at the AERA conference in 2013 in San Francisco for their helpful comments on earlier versions of the article.

"A miniature League of Nations"[1]: inquiry into the social origins of the International School, 1924–1930

Leonora Dugonjić

École des hautes études en sciences sociales (CESSP-CSE), Paris, France

Today, the International School of Geneva is known as the world's oldest and largest private international school, having opened in 1924 under the name "International School". Many schools have attempted to foster an international environment in a general sense; this school is the first to claim an *inter-national* identity with reference to a specific political ideology. In this article, I argue that neither student statistics, nor official discourse, nor the individual experience of consecrated School founders can account for this claim. After careful analysis of different forms of capital invested in the School, its founding no longer appears to be a simple response to a "need" or a "demand" but a complex process of social distinction.

Why combine historical and sociological methods of analysis? This was – in a nutshell – the theme of a symposium held at ISCHE 34. Historians often confront sociological issues without knowing it; conversely, sociologists encounter materials that are traditionally associated with historical research, yet may be critical in generating hypotheses. However, historical sociology should not be reduced to the study of times past or to working with archives.[2] Durkheim, Weber, Marx and Bourdieu all professed that understanding social reality requires inquiry into how it is historically constructed. While the history of educational institutions necessitates considering their social origins, it concurrently involves tackling the problem of identity formation.[3] Historians thus encounter a key question in sociology: how does objective reality shape subjective identities and meaningful action?

---

[1] Adolphe Ferrière, "Une Société des Nations en miniature: l'École internationale de Genève", Épreuve corrigée (Genève, 1925), AIJJR: Fonds Ferrière, E.IV.9 bis, 2.3. Articles, Coupures de presse.
[2] Craig Calhoun, "The Rise and Domestication of Historical Sociology", in *The Historic Turn in the Human Sciences*, ed. Terrence J. McDonald (Ann Arbor: University of Michigan Press, 1996), 305–28.
[3] Detlef Müller, Fritz Ringer, and Brian Simon, *The Rise of the Modern Educational System: Structural Change and Social Reproduction 1870–1920* (Cambridge: Cambridge University Press, 1989).

In highly differentiated societies, where social reproduction is school-mediated, education is a prime factor in the construction of social identity as difference.[4] As Mills contends, "the less important the pedigreed family becomes in the careful transmission of moral and cultural traits, the more important the private school".[5] Many schools have attempted to foster an international environment in a general sense;[6] the International School is the first to claim an *inter-national* identity with reference to a specific political ideology. Its internationalist ideology is embodied in the League of Nations and symbolised by the American president Woodrow Wilson (1913–1921). For this reason, the International School is a stimulating object of analysis for denationalising the history of education.[7]

Why did international civil servants newly settled in Geneva in the 1920s feel a "need" to create an "international" school? How can we explain this need? Following Berger and Luckmann's constructivist approach, I seek to understand identity as a specific case of socially legitimating theories that explain observable facts. According to these scholars, theories about identity, or "psychologies", as they call them, contribute to the social definition of reality and should be analysed regardless of their validity.[8] From this theoretical and methodological perspective, the question of whether, or to what extent, the International School is truly international is beside the point. Rather, I focus on the School's founding and the simultaneous construction of a "psychology of internationalism" in the interwar period; thus developing a genetic approach to categories of perception and appreciation that is characteristic of historical sociology.[9] In the Durkheimian tradition, I analyse internationalism as an ensemble of social representations generated by the founding of a specific institution.[10] Following Bourdieu's critique of constructivism, I define identity as proclamation of difference emerging from the correspondence between social and mental structures.[11] On the one hand, I examine official discourse and statistics; on the other, I consider various forms of capital[12] invested in the School along with the social trajectories of its founders.

I show how official discourse on the "need", or the "demand", for an international school and the ranking of students – by geographic origin, speaking language

---

[4]Pierre Bourdieu, *The State Nobility: Elite Schools in the Field of Power* (Stanford: Stanford University Press, 1996).
[5]Charles Wright Mills, *The Power Elite* (New York: Oxford University Press, 1957), 64.
[6]Robert Sylvester, *The Sage Handbook of Research in International Education*, ed. Mary Hayden, Jack Levy, and Jeff Thompson (London: Sage, 2007).
[7]Christophe Charle, Peter Wagner, and Jürgen Schriewer, *Transnational Intellectual Networks: Forms of Academic Knowledge and the Search for Cultural Identities* (Frankfurt: Campus, 2004).
[8]Peter L. Berger and Thomas Luckmann, *The Social Construction of Reality: A Treatise in the Sociology of Knowledge* (Garden City, NY: Anchor Books, 1967).
[9]For examples of this approach to educational institutions see Bourdieu, *The State Nobility*; Dominique Damamme, "Genèse sociale d'une institution scolaire", *Actes de la recherche en sciences sociales* 70, no. 1 (1987): 31–46; Francine Muel-Dreyfus, *Le Métier d'éducateur: les instituteurs de 1900, les éducateurs spécialisés de 1968* (Paris: Minuit, 1983); *Vichy et l'éternel féminin: contribution à une sociologie politique de l'ordre des corps* (Paris: Seuil, 1996); Gisèle Sapiro, "Défense et illustration de 'l'honnête homme': les hommes de lettres contre la sociologie", *Actes de la recherche en sciences sociales* 153, no. 3 (2004): 11–27.
[10]Émile Durkheim, *L'Évolution pédagogique en France* (Paris: Alcan, 1938).
[11]Bourdieu, *The State Nobility*.
[12]Pierre Bourdieu, "Forms of Capital", in *Handbook of Theory and Research for the Sociology of Education*, ed. John G. Richardson (New York: Greenwood Press, 1986).

and national examination – contribute to the social construction of the School's reality as *inter-national* in a political context marked by unprecedented institutional development in the field of international organisations. Due to the limitations of available data, the analysis is restricted to the interwar period between 1924 and 1930. In addition to secondary sources that compile primary materials, I have reviewed archives from the Jean-Jacques Rousseau Institute (AIJJR), the Foundation of the International School of Geneva (FEIG) and the International Labor Organization (ILO).[13]

The international civil service and the market for private education

The historical originality of the International School lies in different forms of capital invested by individuals of distinct geographic origin, which defines its position as being at the intersection of two long-term processes: the rise of an international public sector and the renewal of a declining local private education market.

During the interwar period, Geneva was at the centre of unprecedented institutional development in the political sphere. The creation of the League of Nations (LON) and the International Labor Office (ILO) was aimed at restoring the liberal utopia of an international self-regulating market system, which prospered in the nineteenth century and had been weakened by the war.[14] Scholars have identified this development as a novel political order characterised by an "organized peace interest"[15] and a "space of institutional positions".[16] This space generated a new category of intellectual work[17] – international civil service.[18] Consequently, the occupational group of international civil servants may be conceived as a *Stände* from a Weberian perspective. As demonstrated by its recruitment – based on social and symbolic capital rather than on specific skills[19] – the group rested on usurpation of these institutional positions, which is the origin of most "status honor", according to Weber.[20]

In contrast to local staff, international civil servants were represented by an international lifestyle. Education was not conceived as a defining aspect of this lifestyle;

---

[13]The research presented in this article is part of my doctoral dissertation, subsidized by the Swiss National Fund for Scientific Research (FNRS) and provisionally entitled Elitist Internationalism. A Historical Sociology of *IB Schools*. I am grateful for access to the archives and the kind help of archivists at the AIJJR, FEIG and ILO.
[14]Karl Polanyi, *The Great Transformation. The Political and Economic Origins of Our Time* (Boston: Beacon, 1944), 26.
[15]Polanyi, *The Great Transformation*.
[16]Guillaume Sacriste and Antoine Vauchez, "La 'Guerre hors-la-loi' 1919–1930. Les origines de la définition d'un ordre politique international", *Actes de la recherche en sciences sociales* 151–152, no. 1–2 (2004): 91–5.
[17]On the professional organisation of intellectual workers in the interwar period see Gisèle Sapiro, "L'internationalisation des champs intellectuels dans l'entre-deux-guerres: facteurs professionnels et politiques", in *L'Espace intellectuel en Europe. De la formation des États-nations à la Mondialisation XIXe-XXe siècle*, ed. Gisèle Sapiro (Paris: La Découverte, 2009), 111–46.
[18]Georges Langrod, *La Fonction publique internationale: Sa genèse, son essence, son évolution* (Leyden, Netherlands: Sythoff, 1963).
[19]Véronique Plata, "Le Recrutement de fonctionnaires du Bureau international du travail en 1920: une approche prosopographique" (mémoire d'histoire, Université de Genève, 2010).
[20]Charles Wright Mills and Hans Heinrich Gerth, *From Max Weber: Essays in Sociology* (New York: Oxford University Press, 1946).

expatriation was. In the legal statutes of the League personnel – where privileges and immunities were codified – the question of education appears only in 1931 with regard to local staff. Inside the League and the ILO, reflection on international education was subsequently limited to the practice of allocating educational allowances. For this purpose, an international school was defined as one in which programs corresponded to the nationality of the civil servant.[21] International governmental organisations encouraged "peace education" or "international education" but were reticent to get involved, given that national systems of education were strongly related to the construction of nation-states and national identities.[22] Like other international educational institutions in the interwar period[23] the International School was a private initiative; yet, traces of its first project can be found in the ILO archives.[24]

Before the First World War, private schools were founded on the basis of social class or religion rather than on national identity. The sixteenth-century *Compagnie de Jésus*, for instance – the first worldwide network of secondary schools – was founded on the principle of religious identity.[25] In the Geneva region, the process of nationalisation began with the Radical Revolution of 1846. Liberal policies of education generally encouraged the creation of private schools from the eighteenth century to the middle of the nineteenth century, when the state progressively constrained the freedom to establish schools, thereby favouring the public school system.[26] Before 1846, private schools took the form of either elite institutions or charitable organisations according to the social origins of their students. While the price of elite schooling varied from one institution to another, in 1843 – for example – it excluded 87% of the active population.[27] Amongst the institutions catering to the Genevan *grande bourgeoisie*, boarding schools such as the *Château Haccius* (1853–1919) recruited, almost exclusively, members of the European aristocracy: 13 out of 1791 students studying at the *Château* between 1853 and 1919, i.e. less than 1%, were locals.[28]

In contrast with the elite institutions that preceded it, the International School does not bear the name of a "founding father". Its origins are attributed to a group of international civil servants, and their wives, initially recruited following the First World War to hold executive positions at the LON and the ILO. Members of the professions (doctors, lawyers, journalists) holding degrees from different countries (United States, Great Britain, France, Poland), designated themselves and were

---

[21] ILO Archives: Children's Allowances and Education Grants, International Officials, P/9/6/1/1, 1937–1953.

[22] Anne-Marie Thiesse, *La Création des identités nationales: Europe XVIIIe-XXe siècle* (Paris: Le Grand livre du mois, 1999).

[23] Eckhardt Fuchs, "The Creation of New International Networks in Education: The League of Nations and Educational Organizations in the 1920s", *Paedagogica Historica* 43, no. 2 (2007): 199–209.

[24] ILO Archives: Butler Cabinet Files, XI 10/2, "Foundation of the International School in Geneva, including names and ages of children of members of Office Staff, 1924–1929".

[25] Victor Karady, "L'Émergence d'un espace européen des connaissances sur l'homme en société: cadres institutionnels et démographiques", in *L'Espace intellectuel en Europe. De la formation des États-nations à la Mondialisation XIXe-XXe siècle*, ed. Gisèle Sapiro (Paris: La Découverte, 2009), 43–67.

[26] Rita Hofstetter, *Les Lumières de la démocratie. Histoire de l'école primaire publique à Genève au 19e siècle* (Berne: Peter Lang, 1998).

[27] Rita Hofstetter, *Le Drapeau dans le cartable. Histoire des écoles privées. Genève XIXe siècle* (Carouge, Switzerland: Zoé, 1994), 154.

[28] Ibid.

perceived as belonging to an international "elite".[29] Adhering to the reformist movement commonly known as *progressive education*,[30] and consulting specialists of new fields (such as sociology, psychology, and pedagogy) at the *Institut Rousseau*,[31] endowed them with the authority necessary for pedagogic action.[32] According to Else Hartoch, secretary to Adolphe Ferrière at the International Bureau of New Schools, the School was "born" out of this group's "long talks" with Ferrière. She writes: "I remember very well the frequent visits of several gentlemen from the League of Nations, who, as Mr. Ferrière told me, had a project to found a School, a School responding to the most modern demands of pedagogy: a good progressive school".[33]

Conceived as "a miniature League of Nations",[34] the School was bilingual, using the two official languages of the League (French and English); coeducational (boys and girls); and "international", according to the self-professed criterion of "nationalities represented" by its first students (four Swiss, four American, one French) and teachers (one American, one German/Russian, one Swiss).[35] The miniature League to which the founders aspired was opposed point by point to the *Institut Privat* (1814–1960), where reference values were country and family tradition.[36] This elite institution, which alone survived the Radical Revolution and the two world wars, reveals educational possibilities in the interwar period as being profoundly nationalistic. In this context, international educational endeavours seemed doomed to fail;[37] yet the International School succeeded and still exists today. If the term 'international' designates diplomatic relations between nation-states, its social origins are better described as *transnational*, meaning that they transcend states.[38]

Forms of capital invested in the International School

The year 1924/1925 was a "test year" and the International School was but a gathering of several children and professors from the *Institut Rousseau* at Ferrière's *châlet*. Three primary teachers were recruited: Paul Meyhoffer, a Swiss citizen with

---

[29]I use the term elite in quotation marks to designate the process of self-definition and self-consecration of this social group. See Christophe Charle, *Les Élites de la République (1880–1900)* (Paris: Fayard, 1987).
[30]Lawrence A. Cremin, *The Transformation of the School. Progressivism in American Education 1876–1957* (New York: Alfred A. Knopf, 1961).
[31]Rita Hofstetter, "The Construction of A New Science by Means of an Institute and Its Communication Media: The Institute of Educational Sciences in Geneva (1912–1948)", *Paedagogica Historica: International Journal of the History of Education* 40, no. 5 (2004): 657–83.
[32]Pierre Bourdieu and Jean-Claude Passeron, *Reproduction in Education, Society and Culture* (London: Sage, 1990).
[33]Else Hartoch, "Écolint 20 Ans 1924–1944". FEIG Archives: Stereva Archives, XVII Student Magazines & Newspapers, 1944. My translation of the French original.
[34]Ferrière, "Une Société des Nations en miniature".
[35]Marie-Thérèse Maurette et al., *École Internationale de Genève. The First Fifty Years/Son Premier Demi-siècle* (Genève: École Internationale, 1974), 20. AIJJR.
[36]Hofstetter, *Le Drapeau dans le cartable*.
[37]Damiano Matasci, "L'École républicaine et l'étranger. Acteurs et espaces de l'internationalisation de la 'réforme scolaire' en France 1870-première moitié du XXe siècle" (thèse de doctorat d'histoire, Université de Genève et École des hautes études en sciences sociales, 2012).
[38]Patricia Clavin, "Defining Transnationalism", *Contemporary European History* 14, no. 4 (2005): 421–39.

a degree in theology from the University of Geneva and a certificate in pedagogy from the *Institut Rousseau*; Else Hartoch, a Russian citizen who had studied with Maria Montessori; and Florence Fake, an American with a PhD in educational sciences from the University of Chicago, who had studied with Carlton Washburn. Founded in 1925, the School was legally a private association – the Association for the International School of Geneva. It united international civil servants, professors, schoolteachers, lawyers, bankers and diplomats with "common needs". Members included the former heads of the *Château Haccius*, Charles Haccius and his grandson, Lucien Brunel, director of the School's boarding house.

Those who are consecrated as School "founders" today[39] invested different types of capital according to their geographic origin. Arthur W. Sweetser (1888–1968) was an American journalist who had worked for the Springfield Republican (1912–1913), United Press (1914) and Associated Press (1916–1917). A Harvard graduate and attendee at the Paris Peace Conference (1918–1919) within the American Commission for the Organization of Peace, he was recruited as deputy director to the League's Information Section.[40] Sweetser was an ardent admirer of Wilson.[41] He worked with Walter Lipmann at the Paris Peace Conference and was a member of the Council on Foreign Relations.

Ludwig W. Rajchman (1881–1965) was a Polish medical doctor and graduate of the University of Krakow. He was assistant bacteriologist at the *Institut Pasteur* in Paris (1906–1908), senior lecturer at the University of Krakow (1909–1910), chief bacteriologist at the Royal Institute of Public Health in London (1910–1913) and a researcher at King's College in Cambridge (1913–1914) and the Medical Research Council in London (1914–1919). Sir Eric Drummond nominated him as director of the League's Hygiene Section because he was familiar with the western scientific milieu.[42]

Fernand Maurette (1878–1937) was a French economist, a graduate of the *École normale supérieure* and *agrégé*[43] in history and geography. Before being nominated director of ILO's Research Division by Albert Thomas in 1924, he had been secretary (1904–1924) and lecturer (1910–1914) at the *École normale supérieure*, professor of economic geography at the *École des hautes études commerciales* (1910–1924) and assistant to the Minister of Colonies at the Paris Peace Conference in 1919. He also held the position of deputy director (1933–1937) at the ILO. He collaborated in the development of all scientific publications and had taken charge of international missions. He represented the ILO at the International Commission for Intellectual Cooperation and in most economic divisions of the League.[44]

---

[39]Established probably in the 1940s, a marble plaque carries nine names under "Founders" – Arthur and Ruth Sweetser, Ludwig and Marie Rajchman, Fernand and Therese Maurette, Dr. Adolphe Ferrière – and five names under "First Collaborators": Paul Mayhoffer, Else Hartoch, Florence Fake, Lucien Brunel and Paul Dupuy.
[40]Warren F. Kuehl, *Biographical Dictionary of Internationalists* (London: Greenwood Press, 1983).
[41]Maurette et al., *École Internationale de Genève*, 16.
[42]Martha A. Balinska, *Une vie pour l'humanitaire - Ludwik Rajchman (1881–1965)* (Paris: La Découverte, 1995).
[43]The *agrégation* is a college-level examination (*concours*) qualifying the candidate to teach in a *lycée* or in certain university faculties in France.
[44]*Journal de Genève*, August 4, 1937, http://www.letempsarchives.ch/

Finally, Adolphe Ferrière (1879–1960) was a Swiss sociologist of Leplaysian tradition, a graduate of the University of Geneva, a professor at the *Institut Rousseau* and the founder of the International Bureau of New Schools. As "expert in new schools",[45] he was the "technical counsellor" of the School and the guarantor of its scientific legitimacy. Moreover, Ferrière helped the Association assert its internationalism. Publishing in the International League for New Education's journal *Pour l'ère nouvelle*, where he was editor-in-chief, the founders of the International School adhered to the progressive education movement.

Sweetser was the strongest bearer of social capital. Through him, American industrial capitalists such as John D. Rockefeller, his son John D. Rockefeller III and the Rockefeller Foundation largely financed the International School. The challenge was to present the School to them as a "good progressive school" serving Americans abroad. Moreover, the biggest share of donations came from the family of Sweetser's spouse, Ruth Gregory – members of the industrial grand bourgeoisie residing in the wealthiest part of Chicago.[46] These women made donations by way of the American Foundation for the International School of Geneva, created and presided by Sweetser in memory of his son, a pupil at the School before his premature death in 1927.

In recognition of their group interest, the founders brought to the School not only the patronage of institutions within which they held leading positions, but also the *domestic work* of their wives within their marriage contracts.[47] The case of Marie-Thérèse Maurette (1890–1989), teacher and spouse of Fernand Maurette, who directed the School for 20 years (1929–1949), is a good example. She notes: "(…) my directorship did not cost anything since I never received any salary; only my maintenance at the *Grande Boissière* [the name of the property occupied by the School] after the death of my husband in 1937".[48] Indeed, the School survived not only due to the patronage of American philanthropy but also, in large part, due to the voluntary labour of women.

In the struggle for recognition of the School by the "Genevan core",[49] who feared "innovation" and advanced their own means of social reproduction ("the *Collège* has a past"[50]), the founders' strategy was to hire Paul Dupuy, who had a solid past in bourgeois teaching institutions. Dupuy was secretary of the *École normale supérieure* and a professor of geography at the *École normale supérieure de Fontenay-aux-Roses* and *Collège Sevigné*. He arrived in Geneva in 1925 to join his two daughters, Marie-Thérèse Maurette and Françoise Viguier, who were both married to international civil servants. Aged 70 upon arrival, he directed the School's secondary section until 1929 and taught human geography under the title of "International Culture" until 1948. A

---

[45]Hartoch, "Écolint 20 Ans 1924–1944".
[46]William H. Tyre, *Chicago's Historic Prairie Avenue* (Charleston, SC: Arcadia Publishing, 2008).
[47]Christine Delphy, *L'Ennemi principal. L'Économie politique du patriarcat* (Paris: Syllepse, 1998).
[48]Maurette et al., *École Internationale de Genève*, 63.
[49]Adolphe Ferrière, "Réunion du 17 Novembre 1926 avec un groupe genevois d'amis de l'École internationale", PV (Genève, 1926). AIJJR: Fonds Ferrière, E.IV.9, 1.3 Comptes-Rendus.
[50]Ibid.

French citizen and committed Dreyfusard[51] involved in reformist socialist circles,[52] Dupuy embodied the human ideal of the International School; he was its "illustration"[53] according to Ferrière. Having graduated from the *École normale supérieure*, Dupuy was not only a product of the French educational system but also "its tradition made man",[54] according to Paul Mantoux, director of the political section at the League. Almost 40 years of French symbolic (academic) capital were thus invested in the School and its "international" identity.

A psychology of internationalism

Two conflicting logics characterise the establishment of the International School: the economic and the ideological. On the one hand, social capital enabled the recruitment of predominantly American boarding students who generated profit; on the other, institutional structures enacted by French and English bilingualism and what I call a "psychology of internationalism" provided the School with symbolic capital to attract "international" day students. This is how the founders created a "demand" for "international education".

Originally, the School sought to serve the children of foreigners working for international organisations and residing in Geneva; it was geared to students issued from and destined for membership in this "elite": "(…) it [the School] is aimed at an 'elite': elite men's children – [elite] in their respective countries, representing them on Geneva's international forum. When they return to their countries, most of these youngsters will become members of the elite of their nation".[55] Thus, contrary to most elite institutions that preceded it, the International School began as a day school for international civil servants residing in Geneva. In 1924, the School enrolled nine students: four American, four Swiss and one French.[56] The number of students doubled in the course of the year. To ensure its survival, the School added a boys' boarding section in 1925. The income brought by a boarder (3900 CHF), which was almost eight times greater than that of a day student (500 CHF), accounted for the School's only source of profit.[57] Nevertheless, the founders denied this economic dimension and justified the opening of the boarding school by invoking the "need" of families who did not reside in Geneva but were "grouped around international institutions" abroad.[58]

---

[51] He took an active part in the Dreyfus Affair and published articles on the subject. His tomb in Geneva bears the inscription "An old *dreyfusard*". Marie-Thérèse Maurette, *Paul Dupuy (1856–1948)* (Coulomiers; Paris: Brodard et Taupin, 1951), 2.
[52] Christophe Prochasson, "Entre science et action sociale: le 'réseau Albert Thomas' et le socialisme normalien, 1900–1914", in *Laboratoires du nouveau siècle: la nébuleuse réformatrice et ses réseaux en France, 1880–1914*, ed. Christian Topalov (Paris: École des hautes études en sciences sociales, 1999), 141–58.
[53] Adolphe Ferrière, "L'École internationale de Genève: dix ans d'activité", *Pour l'ère nouvelle* 100 (September 1934): 2.
[54] Marie-Thérèse Maurette, *Paul Dupuy (1856–1948)*, 142.
[55] Ferrière, "L'École internationale de Genève: dix ans d'activité", 2.
[56] Maurette et al., *École Internationale de Genève*, 20.
[57] École internationale de Genève, "Rapport pour les sixième et septième années scolaires 1929–1930 et 1930–1931", 1931, 52. AIJJR: Fonds Ferrière, E.IV.9, 1.2.1 Rapports à diffusion externe.
[58] École internationale de Genève, "Premier rapport annuel 1925–1926", 1926, 10. AIJJR: Fonds Ferrière, E.IV.9, 1.2.1 Rapports à diffusion externe.

Table 1. Number and percentage of students by country in 1929/1930.

Country	Students (n=202)	%
USA	79	39.1
Switzerland	24	12.0
France	19	9.4
UK	16	8.0
Germany	12	6.0
Netherlands	10	5.0
Russia	6	3.0
Japan	5	2.4
Austria	4	2.0
Canada	4	2.0
Colombia	4	2.0
Spain	2	0.9
Mexico	2	0.9
Poland	2	0.9
Uruguay	2	0.9
Albania	1	0.5
Bulgaria	1	0.5
Denmark	1	0.5
Egypt	1	0.5
Greece	1	0.5
Hungary	1	0.5
Italy	1	0.5
Lithuania	1	0.5
Romania	1	0.5
Sweden	1	0.5
Czechoslovakia	1	0.5

Source: École internationale de Genève, "Rapport pour les sixième et septième années scolaires 1929–1930 et 1930–1931", 45.

The first official school year (1925/1926) began with 62 students and ended with 90,[59] of whom only 15 were boarders "… who came either through the Sweetsers' family connections or those of Mr. and Mrs. Brunel".[60] A year later, in 1926, the School opened another boarding section, this time for "all American"[61] girls, for "the propaganda which Mr. and Mrs. Sweetser were doing in the United States created a new demand".[62] Thus, the supply generated through social capital precedes the "demand" for an international school; yet this is rarely explicit in the founders' discourse, as it is here.

This recruitment of boarders put the School's "international character"[63] into question. Expressed in terms of "European" and "American" national groups, this "problem" was obviously related to economic inequality ("for the Europeans, the cost of boarding was sometimes high enough to be prohibitive").[64] On the one hand, statistics on the number of students by country and by region in the year 1929/1930

---

[59] École internationale de Genève, "Rapport pour la troisième année scolaire 1926–1927", 1927, 11. AIJJR: Fonds Ferrière, E.IV.9, 1.2.1 Rapports à diffusion externe.
[60] Maurette et al., *École Internationale de Genève*, 30.
[61] Ibid., 32.
[62] Ibid.
[63] Ibid., 57.
[64] École internationale de Genève, "Rapport pour les sixième et septième années scolaires 1929–1930 et 1930–1931", 7.

Table 2. Number and percentage of students by region in 1929/1930.

Region	Students (n=202)	%
Europe	105	52.0
North America	83	41.1
South America	8	3.9
Asia	5	2.5
Africa	1	0.5

Source: École internationale de Genève, "Rapport pour les sixième et septième années scolaires 1929–1930 et 1930–1931", 45.

Table 3. Number and percentage of students by national exam graduating between 1929 and 1931.

National exams	Students (n=39)	%
College Board Examination	26	67
Baccalauréat français	8	20
Maturité fédérale suisse	3	8
Canadian matriculation	2	5

Source: École internationale de Genève, "Rapport pour les sixième et septième années scolaires 1929–1930 et 1930–1931", 43.

indicate a strong hierarchy in "nationalities represented"). American students were best represented not only as boarders but also in day school. They accounted for 40% of the total number of students while students of other nationalities amounted to less than 10%, with the exception of the Swiss (see Table 1 above). On the other hand, the number of students by region indicates that the share of "Europeans" was greater in 1929/1930 than that of Americans and Canadians together – 52% and 41% respectively (see Table 2 above).

The weight of economic forces and the resulting creation of a boarding section, which recruited mainly Americans, put the School's "international character" into question as soon as it opened formally in 1925. Its internationalist mission was asserted the same year, paradoxically on the occasion of the opening ceremony for the boarding section. Pronounced by Paul Dupuy, it was published four months later in Adolphe Ferrière's journal, *Pour l'ère nouvelle*, under the title "The International Spirit at the International School of Geneva":

> There are various ways of being *international*. Internationalism from without is easy enough to achieve. It certainly has been – and already several times so – in Switzerland, and in particular in this beautiful city of Geneva, where old educational traditions have attracted and gathered children or young people belonging to the most diverse nationalities who have come from countries furthest apart, in a number of excellent institutions. (…) This, the International School will accomplish as well; it will do so by definition. But the school aspires to something else – something even more precious. It does not expect it from chance and does not have to receive it only from outside; rather, the School conceives of it as a fruit of its will and it wishes above all that it should emanate from its soul, from its spirit – something that comes from its innermost self. It is *from within* that its internationalism must act: it should not be superficial embroidery, but the tissue itself of the mind that we wish to shape. (…) The International School has hope founded on faith, and it is this hope and this faith that gather us here today, at the threshold of a new school year. The hope is one which, born amongst ruins, loomed out of the worst of disasters humanity has known, took hold of President Wilson's great soul, raised it, penetrated it, became its principle of

action, and – in spite of doubt, sarcasm, suspicion, hostility – gave birth to the international organism, already so vigorous, in whose shade we hope our school will grow.[65]

This proclamation of "international" identity advances a "pure theory"[66] of internationalism, dissociating the idea of school as merchandise from the portrayal of the International School as an institution for the cultivation of pure "spirit". The notion of "internationalism from within" introduces a social distinction through the use of a spatial metaphor as opposed to "internationalism from without".

Political references are implicit when given negative connotation and explicit when given positive overtones. The implicit reference here is, of course, Vladimir Lenin, the first leader of the Soviet Union (1918–1924), inspirer of communist internationalism, and key to understanding the origins of what today are widely known as "Wilson's ideas" as symbolised by his *Fourteen Points*. While Lenin was systematically censured in the immediate postwar period, Wilson briefly emerged as the champion of people's self-determination and the subject of immense hope.[67] Thus, Wilson became recognised as a fervent democrat working to spread democracy throughout the world, when in reality he had seized Lenin's notion of national self-determination and adapted it to both a liberal and a racist vision of the world. For Lenin, self-determination was an immediate necessity for all peoples; for Wilson, it was a process of liberal reform reserved mainly for white Europeans.[68] Along with the "great soul of President Wilson", symbols of the School's internationalism are "offices of the League and the ILO" and the metaphor of "elite brains".

It is in the idea that the founders had of themselves, and of those who were socially similar enough to aspire to their "international spirit", that they find the calling of the International School – its *raison d'être*. Thus, truly "symbolic logics of distinction"[69] lie at the heart of this transnational educational institution. Internationalism "from within" clearly designates the cultural capital of the "elite" for whom the School is explicitly destined. Indeed, the particularity of this form of capital is that it appears as if it were innate to its bearer. The "spirit" and "will" ("from within") that Dupuy contrasts with "chance" and "matter" ("from without") are not things that can be acquired. One must *be* international; clearly, one has to belong to a certain *Stände* and be thus disposed for the School's *pedagogic action* to accomplish its mission.

The mission of the International School – at its origin – was to "prompt, in the students, the development of a truly international mind and to create an *atmosphere*

---

[65]Paul Dupuy, "L'Esprit international à École internationale de Genève", *Pour l'ère nouvelle* 18 (January 1925): 3–5 (my italics).
[66]Berger and Luckmann, *The Social Construction of Reality*, 95.
[67]Existing historical literature suffers greatly from this censorship. Thus, historians of international organizations rarely combine the histories of communist and liberal internationalism. Outstanding examples are Arno J. Mayer, *Political Origins of the New Diplomacy, 1917–1918* (New Haven: Yale University Press, 1959) and Erez Manela, *The Wilsonian Moment. Self-Determination and the International Origins of Anticolonial Nationalism* (New York: Oxford University Press, 2007).
[68]Manela, *The Wilsonian Moment*. On the ideological origins of the League, see Mark Mazower, *No Enchanted Palace: The End of Empire and the Ideological Origins of the United Nations* (Princeton: Princeton University Press, 2009).
[69]Pierre Bourdieu, "L'identité et la représentation", *Actes de la recherche en sciences sociales* 35, no. 1 (1980): 63–72.

around them, which fosters the development of such a mind".[70] At that time, before the school moved to *La Grande Boissière* in 1929, students and teachers switched languages freely during class. With the increase in the number of students, "the School hardly presented moral unity".[71] To resolve this "problem", assemblies during which teachers and guest speakers gathered and addressed the "international and social questions" appeared during the 1930/1931 school year. These daily assemblies were limited to secondary school students and aimed to "orient (…) towards an international life".[72] They took place in the morning; speakers were mostly parents and members of the Association.

The School's educational techniques – the assemblies in particular –aimed to transmit "general culture otherwise than by traditional means"[73] thus valued most of all the inherited cultural capital of the students. Furthermore, the founders contrasted contact with ideas, facts and people belonging to "Geneva's international *milieu*" and contact with the "pages of a textbook", the latter being the mode of learning *par excellence* in "national schools". However, in a world divided into nation-states – each with their system of elite education[74] – training students involved preparing them for national exams, borrowing content from already existing languages and cultures and, above all, from curricula and textbooks used in "national schools". Consequently, internationalism as expressed in the School's curriculum corresponded with the juxtaposition of several national exams in both the English and French-speaking traditions: the College Board Examination, the Cambridge entrance exam, the Canadian matriculation, the French *baccalauréat* and the Swiss *maturité*. These exams were ranked through students' choices: the American exam had the highest demand, followed from afar by the French *baccalauréat*.

Before 1929, exam preparation was provided by a "tutorial system of almost all individual lessons". The School had a family character to it: the relationship between the directorate, the teachers and the students was "personal". As the total number of students doubled in 1930/1931, the experience had to be "normalised" and the teaching of languages "rationalised" by grouping the children according to their command of French or English either on the "French side" or on the "English side". The students were then divided according to their level in a given language and put either in "normal" or in "special" classes.[75] "Normal" French classes prepared secondary school students for the French *baccalauréat* and the Swiss *maturité*, while "special" French classes prepared them for the College Board Examination. On the "French side", French literature was taught for students of both the *baccalauréat* and Swiss *maturité*. On the "English side" either English literature or American literature was taught.

French and English-speaking students were certainly the most numerous: of 226 registered students in 1930/1931, 46% were English speakers, 24% were French speakers and 30% spoke other languages.[76] However, it was not the number of

---

[70]École Internationale de Genève, "Premier rapport annuel 1925–1926", 12.
[71]École Internationale de Genève, "Rapport pour les sixième et septième années scolaires 1929–1930 et 1930–1931", 36.
[72]Ibid., 39.
[73]Ibid., 54.
[74]Victor Karady, "La Migration internationale d'étudiants en Europe, 1890–1940", *Actes de la recherche en sciences sociales* 145, no. 1 (2002): 47–60.
[75]Ibid., 35.
[76]Ibid., 23.

students by language that determined the choice of languages for instruction. The value placed upon English and French as the School's official languages along the ideological model of the League led to the devaluation of all the other languages and national cultures "represented" by the students, and to the consecration of the two chosen ones as those most deserving to be transmitted and acquired.

Towards a historical sociology

The social significance of the School's internationalism is difficult to grasp because usual explanations of socio-historical phenomena postulate the existence of "needs" or "demands", thus naturalising them or making them seem self-evident. Historical sociology helps unveil how such explanations are historically constructed. Yet internationalism is empirically observable through individual trajectories, daily experience or student statistics; hence the psychology of internationalism developed at the School appears to be empirically adequate. However, this only confirms Bourdieu's theory of correspondence between social and mental structures. Neither individual experience nor trajectories can account sociologically for the School's claim to an international identity. As Mills contends, they cannot be adequately understood without reference to the institutions and to larger social structures within which individual biography is enacted.[77]

As I have shown, the founding of the International School may be explained according to Weber's definition of *Stände* and with reference to Bourdieu's theory of capital. Class stratification slowed down in the interwar period, which led to the growth in the importance of social honour as a principle of social distinction.[78] Growing awareness of international civil servants as a specific group inclined them to preserve prestige by institutionalised transmission of cultural capital. Thus, the founding of the International School may be interpreted as an essential element of larger group action involving the usurpation and monopolisation of symbolic and material goods. Moreover, the form of internationalism advocated by School founders was clearly related to political stakes. Their trajectories predisposed them to the liberal internationalism symbolised by Wilson – as opposed to the communist internationalism represented by Lenin – while their institutional connections guaranteed their claim to an international identity. The psychology of internationalism developed at the School in the process of its founding may therefore be an indicator of larger structural change.

---

[77]Charles Wright Mills, *The Sociological Imagination* (New York: Oxford University Press, 1959), 161–2.
[78]Mills and Gerth, *From Max Weber*, 194.

Transnational treaties on children's rights: Norm building and circulation in the twentieth century

Zoe Moody

University of Teacher Education Valais, St-Maurice, Switzerland

During the twentieth century, the socio-legal status of the child changed dramatically. The adoption of three international treaties specific to the rights of the child – namely, the Geneva Declaration (1924), the United Nations Declaration of the Rights of the Child (1959) and the United Nations Convention on the Rights on the Child (1989) – increasing at each stage the number and different types of rights, is a remarkable illustration of this state of fact. National socio-legal developments have, of course, greatly inspired the authors of these treaties. However, the rights of the child assumed a new dimension in intergovernmental and non-governmental organisations, exchange platforms par excellence. This article seeks a better understanding of the circulation of children's rights during the twentieth century, within the three above mentioned treaties. From an interdisciplinary and transnational perspective, the study aims to analyse the multiple facets of children's rights and the origins of non-domestic influences in this international process. The article appraises the role of international and intergovernmental organisations. Based on archival data, it identifies the concepts, the institutions, the agents and the contexts that influenced the evolution of children's rights. It shows how the genesis, the diffusion and the promotion of international treaties, as well as their subsequent regimes, structured the circulation of children's rights.

Introduction

At first glance, children's rights appear to be one of the most successful twentieth-century international projects. General agreement on promoting the child's best interests and well-being, whilst specifically implementing his right to education and participation,[1] seems to have emerged within the international community. The translation of the human rights of children into international hard law and the near universal ratification of the United Nations Convention on the Rights of the Child (1989, hereafter the UNCRC)[2] can be viewed as the culmination of this process. However, the standing of children's rights varies considerably across nations and regions, suggesting significant diversity in the interpretation and monitoring of the UNCRC as well as of the broader concept of children's rights.

---

[1] The masculine case refers to both the masculine and feminine genders and is used for conciseness only.
[2] To date, only the United States, Somalia and South Sudan have not ratified the Convention, bringing the number of states parties to 193 out of 196.

The universalisation of children's rights, through the endorsement of international charters, could be construed as a relatively straightforward process. It began with the adoption, in 1924, of the so-called Geneva Declaration of the League of Nations. This led to the Declaration of the Rights of the Child endorsed by the United Nations in 1959, which was itself completed, in 1989, by the legally binding Convention. However, and as will be argued within the scope of this article, the production and promotion of children's rights is a dynamic and open process. It has to be considered beyond single or regional socio-historical contexts, and should not be analysed on the basis of the simple juxtaposition of several of them. In order to best reflect the interrelations between the three international and institutionalised discourses – both in their specificities and in their common nature – the circulation of ideas and of agents through nations, cultures and time have to be examined. Moreover, children's rights have to be considered within the socio-cultural space established by international organisations.

This article seeks a better understanding of the *circulation* of children's rights, understood as their flow or transmission through spaces, time, different channels, routes and agents, at various rhythms, transforming them to a greater or a lesser degree.[3] It argues that this process created an intrinsically transnational object. This analysis is conducted from an interdisciplinary and transnational perspective. An interdisciplinary approach is required to take into account the multiple facets of children's rights, which cannot be solely considered as a legal concept, an educational evolution or a social construction. The complexity of children's rights as a subject must be recognised and evaluated on a three-tiered basis: the socio-historical, educational and legal.

Furthermore, a transnational perspective is particularly promising for historicising inter-dependences and interrelations between societies and beyond nation-states. Indeed, a transnational approach presents an enhanced capacity to highlight origins of non-domestic inputs in international processes, which are numerous in the history of children's rights. In addition, this is especially true for informal networks, international associations and intergovernmental organisations that expand their action beyond official borders and play, as will be shown, a central role in the internationalisation of children's rights.[4]

The article will first sketch the socio-historical context(s) leading to the adoption of the three above-mentioned institutionalised discourses. The various forms and interpretations of the rights of the child, as well as the perceived necessity of translating them into international law, will be highlighted in so doing. Second, and on the basis of sources collected in the archives of international (non-/inter-)governmental organisations, the main agents implicated in the genesis of the three discourses on children's rights will be identified. Their use of the platforms and channels,

---

[3]See Frédéric Darbellay, "The circulation of knowledge as an interdisciplinary process: Travelling concepts, analogies and metaphors", *Issues in Integrative Studies* 30 (2012): 1–18; ISCHE34-SHCY-DHA, *Internationalization in Education (18th–20th Centuries)*, Call for papers (2011).
[4]Pierre-Yves Saunier, "Les Régimes circulatoires du domaine social 1800–1940: projets et ingénierie de la convergence et de la différence", *Genèses* 71, no. 2 (2008): 4–25. See also Saunier, "Circulations, connexions et espaces transnationaux", *Genèses* 57, no. 4 (2004): 110–126; Jean-Paul Zúñiga, ed., *Pratiques du transnational, terrains, preuves, limites* (Paris: Centre de recherches historiques, 2011).

which contributed to their circulation, will also be scrutinised, in order to substantiate the processes.

Children's rights in context

During the twentieth century, children's rights and other related concepts, such as the best interests of the child, the right to education and autonomous rights, circulated widely transnationally. As will be argued in this article, the institutionalisation of children's rights by supranational agencies greatly contributed to their diffusion and *internalisation* – defined as the moment when "norms acquire a taken-for-granted quality and are no longer a matter of broad public debate"[5] – as well as to the dramatic growth of the target population.[6] However, we have to make it clear prior to this that children's rights cannot be strictly considered a twentieth-century "invention", crowning the so-called Century of the Child.[7] In fact, and as will be discussed hereafter, most of the constitutive dimensions of children's rights, as constructed by international law, arose within post-industrial developments and expanded thanks to the peace-building activities following the two world wars.[8]

Long-debated issues

As Dekker has highlighted, nineteenth-century "at risk" children, such as delinquents, orphans and other endangered children, were treated in Europe according to the guiding principle of their best interests.[9] Kohm argues that this principle came to be established at the same time as a part of American family law and juvenile justice jurisprudence, giving a firm grounding for adults to decide how best to protect children through legal means.[10] It was indeed commonly accepted that children's perfectibility – postulated by Enlightenment philosophy and corresponding romantic constructions of childhood – preordained them to be saved from appallingly poor living conditions. The "best interests of the child" was a guiding principle in the Western world in order to prioritise children's need to be protected.

---

[5]Martha Finnemore and Katheryn Sikkink, "International norm dynamics and political change", *International Organization* 52, no. 4 (1998): 895.
[6]Jeroen J.H. Dekker, "Children at risk in history: A story of expansion", *Paedagogica Historica* 45, no. 1 (2009): 17–36.
[7]Ellen Key's expression has almost become a common name for the twentieth century amongst childhood historians and more widely.
[8]The rights of children were indeed addressed by codes of law before the Industrial Revolution. However, within the scope and the limits of this article, this fact will not be further developed. For an insightful analysis of the rights of the child under Roman law, for instance, see Dominique Youf, *Penser les droits de l'enfant* (Paris: Presses universitaires de France, 2002).
[9]Jeroen J.H. Dekker, *Educational Ambitions in History: Childhood and Education in an Expanding Educational Space from the Seventeenth to the Twentieth Century* (Berlin: Peter Lang, 2010). See also Eckhardt Fuchs, "Children's rights and global civil society", *Comparative Education* 43, no. 3 (2007): 393–412; Ingrid Lohmann and Christine Mayer, "Lessons from the history of education for a 'Century of the Child at Risk'", *Paedagogica Historica* 45, no. 1–2 (2009): 1–16; Annemieke van Drenth and Kevin Myers, "Normalising childhood: Policies and interventions concerning special children in the United States and Europe (1900–1960)", *Paedagogica Historica* 47, no. 6 (2011): 719–727.
[10]Lynne M. Kohm, "Tracing the foundations of the best interests of the child standard in American jurisprudence", *Journal of Law & Family Studies* 10 (2008): 337–376.

Underpinning this notion lay, according to Cunningham, "a conviction that the way childhood was spent was crucial in determining the kind of adult that the child would become, and an increasing awareness that childhood had rights and privileges of its own".[11] He argues that this assumption led to the voicing of the rather incongruous right of children "not to work at all"[12] and to the first laws limiting children's working hours in the 1830s in Europe and North America. These national legislations were soon reinforced by the parallel drive to introduce compulsory schooling. The rise of democracies and corresponding egalitarian ideals indeed resulted in an expansion of states' responsibility for all children, whether at risk or not.[13] Henceforth, children had a universal right to education. Yet, as Hofstetter has shown, far from promoting a solely standardising education, public schools also intended to cultivate the autonomy of future enlightened citizens as well as their freedom.[14]

Ideas about what childhood was or should be dictated the way children spent this specific period of their life long before these ideas were standardised through the adoption of treaties on an international level. Additionally, numerous legislative actions were taken on both the national and international levels. However, international recognition of such norms was by no means obvious and straightforward. Creating legal responsibilities for states on a national level requires a certain degree of persuasion and of political lobbying from various agents. Authorising the state to enter the private family sphere in order to take care of children in accordance with national standards is undoubtedly a sensitive issue, as national histories of child protection have indicated.[15] However, persuading governments to relinquish national sovereignty to international authority on the issue of the "Children of the Nation"[16] is particularly controversial. This explains to a certain extent how difficult it may have been to come to a general agreement.[17]

Emergence of a transnational childhood

Beyond these outlined legislative, social and educational long-term evolutions, it is certain that the ever-broader circulation of children's rights and their advent on the international scene has to be read in the very specific twentieth-century historical context. Some events have indeed greatly favoured the adoption of treaties concerning children's rights. As Fass has made clear, the two devastating major armed conflicts in Europe – the First and Second World Wars – were definitive triggers for the almost

---

[11]Hugh Cunningham, *Children and Childhood in Western Society since 1500*, 2nd edn. (Harlow: Pearson Education, 2005), 41.
[12]Ibid., 142.
[13]Dekker, "Children at risk".
[14]Rita Hofstetter, *Genève: creuset des sciences de l'éducation* (Genève: Droz, 2010).
[15]See, for instance, Harry Hendrick, *Child Welfare, Historical Dimensions, Contemporary Debate* (Bristol: Policy Press, 2003); Judith Sealander, *The Failed Century of the Child: Governing America's Young in the Twentieth Century* (Cambridge: Cambridge University Press, 2003).
[16]Hendrick, *Child Welfare*, chap. 2.
[17]Joëlle Droux, "L'Internationalisation de la protection de l'enfance: acteurs, concurrences et projets transnationaux (1900–1925)", *Critique Internationale* 52, no. 3 (2011): 17–33; Lawrence J. LeBlanc, *The Convention on the Rights of the Child: United Nations Lawmaking on Human Rights* (Lincoln: University of Nebraska Press, 1995); Philip E. Veerman, *The Rights of the Child and the Changing Image of Childhood* (Dordrecht: Martinus Nijhoff Publishers, 1992).

immediate adoptions of the Geneva Declaration and the UN Declaration of the Rights of the Child, in 1924 and 1959, respectively.[18] They amplified the child-saving movement, rooted in the nineteenth century, and the related ideals of protection and education. Moreover, by picturing the child as an innocent victim of adults' warring tendencies, the international community settled on a common feature among all societies by defining standards "in the interests ... of humanity at large".[19] The former Children of the Nation, for which the state was responsible on behalf of his parents, forthwith became the Children of the World, "because they are not aware of the divisions of parties and nations and ... because they are the hope of humanity", as Eglantyne Jebb, linchpin of the drafting process of the Geneva Declaration, worded it in 1919.

This view of children as the repositories of pacifism was broadly shared among national and international organisations, whether or not their concerns were related to children. If Jebb is famous for having publicly stated after the First World War that she did not have any enemies below seven years of age, the chairman of the *Miners' Federation of Great Britain*, Robert Smillie, defending the British Labour Party who had provided huge financial support to the child-saving operations in Central Europe, used similar arguments. He specified that this action was taken "with no distinction between 'friend' and 'enemy', giving children a new ideal of internationalism and solidarity, which shall prevent to a large extent any future conflict between peoples such as the one we have just emerged from", perfectly synthesising this new transnational philosophy.[20]

A child is henceforth considered a child before being a citizen, and such an assertion has dual implications. On the one hand, if he is not a citizen, the child has a right to be protected from adults' conflicts and problems. On the other hand, if adults succeed in preserving his childhood and educating him for peace, that child can eventually prevent future outbursts of violence. Similar discourses were held after the Second World War. Léon Blum, delegate of France at the Conference for the Establishment of the United Nations Educational, Scientific and Cultural Organisation (UNESCO), held in 1945, argued that, "[p]opular education ... must be steered in the direction of that 'ideology' of democracy and progress which is the psychological basis of international solidarity and peace".[21] The double trauma of the use of children and youth by the Nazis in political campaigning and that of the children put to death in concentration camps reinforced the sense of the need to take action on behalf of children and for the sake of humanity. Furthermore, Adam Lopatka, Polish delegate at the UN Human Rights Commission and chairman of the working group for the drafting of the UNCRC, argued that the traumas of the

---

[18]Paula S. Fass, "A historical context for the United Nations Convention on the Rights of the Child", *Annals of the American Academy of Political and Social Science* 633 (2011): 17–29.

[19]Dominique Marshall, "The construction of children as an object of international relations: The Declaration of Children's Rights and the Child Welfare Committee of the League of Nations, 1900–1924", *International Journal of Children's Rights* 7 (1999): 108, quoting the assistant to the Secretary General of the LoN.

[20]Archives of the State of Geneva, International Union for Child Welfare Fund (ASG-IUCW), M1.2, Tri/71.1, Historique de l'UISE, mémorandum, publications de l'UISE de 1929-1939, Texte préparé pour le Xe anniversaire de l'UISE, 5. Translated from French.

[21]UNESCO Online Archives (UNESCO-OA), http://unesdoc.unesco.org, "1946–1950: First steps in a war-devastated world" (Conference for the Establishment of the United Nations Educational, Scientific and Cultural Organisation, Institute of Civil Engineers, London, 1–16 November 1945), ECO/CONF/29:27.

Second World War still acted as triggers for "Polish authorities to undertake action to improve the situation of children" when they initiated the process of the Convention in 1978.[22] Standardising the conditions to promote the ideal of a transnational childhood, developing both between states but also above and beyond these, was thus perceived as imperative throughout the twentieth century; stating children's rights appeared to be a powerful lever for action.

Children's rights norm building

Children's rights and their institutionalisation on an international level owe a great deal to the exchange platforms offered by the establishment of the League of Nations (LoN), then of the United Nations Organisation. Although these organisations were those that made the idea of adopting children's charters possible, the drafting of the latter involved almost systematically non-governmental organisations (NGOs), literally flourishing around the agencies. The geographical proximity and the increased accessibility of numerous national delegations facilitated the circulation of ideas as well as of norms, strategies of persuasion and intensive lobbying. The platform created as a direct result of the co-presence of intergovernmental organisations (IOs) and NGOs spurred on the diffusion of children's rights.

Five principles for the rights of the Children of the World

The case of the Geneva Declaration is illustrative. Its adoption by the LoN in 1924, as Droux argues, was somehow unexpected.[23] Indeed, there had been no political intention to come to a general agreement concerning children in particular. On the contrary, the League had adopted a resolution in 1920 stating that its responsibilities did not include humanitarian actions taken on the behalf of children. The LoN General Assembly considered that:

> Le travail était déjà fort bien réalisé par des organisations volontaires et qu'il n'y avait pas lieu pour la Société des Nations, d'examiner la question de savoir s'il lui incombait de prendre une part active à cette grande œuvre philanthropique [The work was already very well carried out by voluntary organisations and that there was no need for the League of Nations to consider whether it was its duty to take an active part in this great philanthropic work].[24]

It nevertheless requested the General Secretary to undertake a study in order to define how the LoN could support the humanitarian cause of children and the work realised by NGOs. Although the Secretariat did not produce ground-breaking conclusions, this specific resolution was on several occasions invoked in order to remind the General Assembly of its will to intervene in favour of NGOs dedicated to children. This was the case in September 1924 when two competing international NGOs, the

---

[22] Adam Lopatka, introduction to *Legislative History of the Convention on the Rights of the Child*, Office of the High Commissioner for Human Rights (OHCHR) (Geneva: United Nations, 2007), 37.
[23] Joëlle Droux, "La Première Déclaration des droits de l'enfant (1924): acte de naissance d'un nouveau contrat social transnational?" (computer printout, Institut européen, Université de Genève, 2010).
[24] League of Nations Archives (LoNA), 12e Session du Conseil de la SDN, 21/41/15, Annexe 161 – Secours aux enfants des pays éprouvés par la guerre, rapport présenté par M. Balfour, délégué de l'Empire britannique et adopté par le Conseil dans sa séance du 23 février 1921.

International Association for Child Welfare (IACW) and the Save the Children International Union (SCIU), attempted to obtain official LoN recognition of their actions.

The first, founded in 1920 by early supporters and reformers of the juvenile justice system in Brussels, had attempted almost since its creation to transfer part of its activities to the LoN Secretariat.[25] As Droux indicated, this takeover appeared to be very threatening to the SCIU.[26] The Geneva-based umbrella organisation – created in 1919 by two British women, Eglantyne Jebb and her sister Dorothy Buxton, to save European children affected by the war – believed it was the leading organisation acting on behalf of children and therefore the first in line to pursue its activities in the name of the LoN. Moreover, the humanitarian crisis overcome, the SCIU was seeking to expand its activities, from child-saving to the broader field of child welfare.[27] Since the domain was partly occupied by the IUCW, and the SCIU was funded solely by private donations, this endeavour required something of a master stroke. When Jebb suggested drafting a children's charter, as an international guideline for child welfare, the Executive Committee thought it could be an effective lever for action. Its president was enthusiastic:

> Ce sera un appel au monde en faveur de l'enfant, fruit des réflexions et expériences faites, depuis quatre ans, par des personnalités ou des institutions qui après s'être consacrées à l'activité que réclamait l'urgence de l'heure, veulent dès maintenant prévoir l'avenir [It will be an appeal to the world, the fruit of reflections and experiences made over the past four years by personalities or institutions that, after devoting their time to the emergency of the war period, now want to anticipate and plan for the future]. [28]

Such a declaration was indeed considered a promising tool for propaganda.[29] Members of the Committee believed it "could yield significant results, especially from a financial point of view" and "could also facilitate ... membership recruitment".[30] The SCIU wanted the Declaration to be signed by "the most influential notables in the field of philanthropy worldwide",[31] translated in numerous languages and printed in various formats (cards, posters and so on) in order to diffuse it broadly and quickly. This process culminated when the idea of having the Declaration proclaimed by the LoN General Assembly actually transpired. One year after the SCIU, the LoN endorsed the Geneva Declaration and invited its state members "to be guided by its principles in the work of child welfare".[32]

The process leading to the proclamation of the Geneva Declaration by the LoN was thus almost exclusively held outside IOs. Yet, although this event was unforeseen by the LoN and occurred in an astonishingly smooth manner, its unexpected nature stops

---

[25] LoNA, 21e Session du Conseil de la SDN, Annexe 419, Relations entre l'AIPE et la SDN.
[26] Droux, "La Première Déclaration des droits de l'enfant".
[27] ASG-IUCW, M1.5, Tri/71.1, (Histoire) Exposé des buts de l'UISE (circa 1925): 9.
[28] ASG-IUCW, AP 92.2.2, Tri/65-3, PV du IVe Conseil Général, jeudi-vendredi 22–23 février 1923.
[29] ASG-IUCW, AP 92.1.3, Tri/65-3, PV de la 87e séance du Comité Exécutif de l'Union, jeudi 1er mars 1923, Nomination d'une commission de rédaction de la charte de l'enfant.
[30] ASG-IUCW, AP 92.1.3, Tri/65-3, PV de la 95e séance du Comité Exécutif de l'Union, jeudi 28 juin 1923, Déclaration de Genève.
[31] ASG-IUCW, AP 92.1.3, Tri/65-3, PV de la 87e séance du Comité Exécutif de l'Union, jeudi 1er mars 1923, Nomination d'une commission de rédaction de la charte de l'enfant. Translated from French.
[32] LoNA, PV de la Ve Commission, 12e séance (vendredi 18 (sic) septembre 1924, à 15h30), Suite de la protection de l'enfance.

at this point. Indeed, the treaty had been written in an extremely consensual manner in order to maximise its possibility of acceptance. The five principles of the Declaration – referring mainly to protection aims and basic provisions – were considered by their authors as "chapter headings", giving freedom to national initiatives to develop them.[33] The norm they translated was already considered as such by most of the delegates and was partly internalised by member states, which for the most part had national laws addressing these issues. Consequently, the Geneva Declaration and its content did not raise any opposition, within or outside the LoN. Moreover, a declaration is not legally binding; member states were thus free to implement it as they saw fit.

The internalisation of the norm is also reflected in the great acceptance and diffusion of the Geneva Declaration before the outbreak of the Second World War. Indeed, when the UN undertook a study to decide if it should reaffirm the treaty, its conclusions were clear. It observed that:

> There was a very general acceptance and warm approval of the Declaration of Geneva by organizations interested in child welfare; by persons prominent in this field all over the world; by the press of the world; by many leaders of religious communities in all parts of the world; by statesmen and by heads of states, some of whom officially specified the Declaration as the basis for their future systems of child welfare.[34]

Although this fact can be read as partly resulting from the uncontroversial nature of the Declaration and the pre-existence of the regime it established,[35] it also has to be noted that the intensive activities conducted by the SCIU to make the Geneva Declaration known worldwide, as well as the symbolic weight given to it by the LoN, played an important part in the Declaration's popularity. As mentioned before, the SCIU translated the Declaration into over 35 languages before the Second World War, and got many philanthropists and other personalities to sign it. The Declaration was read on the radio from the Eiffel Tower in Paris, as well as in Belgium and Czechoslovakia,[36] and drawing contests for children were organised so that they could discover its five principles. The LoN for its part adopted in 1933 a resolution requiring governments to send reports concerning the measures taken in the field of child welfare, defined by the Declaration.[37] It also seized the opportunity of the tenth anniversary of its adoption in 1934 to reaffirm its principles.[38]

---

[33] ASG-IUCW, AP 92.2.2, Tri/65-3, PV du Ve Conseil Général, jeudi-vendredi 28–29 février 1924, Commission de la "Déclaration de Genève".
[34] United Nations Organisation General Secretariat Archives (UNOGS-A), 19485-Child Welfare-Declaration on the Rights of the Child-Information from Member Governments (part A 1946-1948) Documentation Relating to the "Declaration of Geneva" Including Declarations and Charters Concerning Children's Rights Adopted by Various Bodies Subsequent to 1924: 7.
[35] For a definition of a regime, see Jack Donnelly, "International human rights: A regime analysis", *International Organization* 40, no. 3 (1986): 599–642; see also Michael Freeman, *Human Rights* (Cambridge: Polity Press, 2010).
[36] ASG-IUCW, M1.2, Tri/71.1, Historique de l'UISE, mémorandum, publications de l'UISE de 1929–1939, Texte préparé pour le Xe Anniversaire.
[37] Human Rights Commission Archives (HRC-A), S-0916-0009-0011 - Social Questions - Division of Social Activities - Protection of Youth - Child Welfare - Annual Reports, Interoffice Memo from Milhaud to Laugier, Objet: Projet de lettre circulaire à adresser à certains gouvernements membres, 6 December 1946.
[38] LoNA, PV de la Ve Commission Questions humanitaires et générales, Rapport de la Ve Commission à l'Assemblée, Annexe 2, no. officiel A.52.1934.IV.

According to Debos and Goenheix, "the formation of transnational militant networks enables broad dissemination of information on the causes espoused but also socialisation of actors to the standards produced".[39] The work achieved by the SCIU in collaboration with the LoN is exemplary in this respect. Children's rights as defined by the Geneva Declaration were broadly diffused and used as a basis for the development of new legislation; for instance, the 1931 Spanish Constitution explicitly drew on the Declaration for issues related to child welfare.[40] Furthermore, the specific concept of children's rights it proposed survived its redrafting, as will be discussed below.

"So large an area of agreement"

The regime symbolised by the Geneva Declaration was relatively strong between the two wars and still largely supported when the United Nations Organisation was founded. The adoption of numerous other treaties of international law, consolidating social security, raising the age of minimum employment and so on, also contributed to the internalisation of this specific children's rights norm and legitimised its related regime.[41] With the wind in its sails, the SCIU's offspring, the International Union for Child Welfare (IUCW), started to lobby the UN immediately after the Second World War in order to get the Geneva Declaration re-endorsed. Despite the UN's public distancing from the work of the LoN and its perceived failure, the Temporary Social Commission explicitly supported that idea. It stated in 1946 that the principles of the Declaration "should bind the peoples of the world today as firmly as it did in 1924".[42] However, the content of the treaty was challenged because it was considered out-dated.[43] Having heard about the UN's will to "transform"[44] the Declaration into a UN Children's Charter, the IUCW made a clear statement:

> The Union regards the Declaration as its property and [considers that] no amendment can be made without its consent, ... nevertheless, appreciating the significance of the UN action and recognizing the evolution in Child welfare concept, [it] is prepared to envisage some amendments.[45]

Since the IUCW agreed to add principles related to non-discrimination, social security and the family to its Declaration, it expected the UN to adopt a "slightly

---

[39] Marielle Debos and Alice Goheneix, "Les ONG et la fabrique de 'l'opinion publique internationale'", *Raisons politiques* 3, no. 19 (2005): 74. Translated from French.
[40] UNOGS-A, 19485-Child Welfare-Declaration on the Rights of the Child-Information from Member Governments (part A 1946-1948), Documentation Relating to the "Declaration of Geneva".
[41] For an analysis of other international treaties on the rights of the child see Anna Holzscheiter, *Children's Rights in International Politics, The Transformative Power of Discourse* (Basingstoke: Palgrave-Macmillan, 2010).
[42] UNOGS-A, S-0445-0077, Draft Declaration on the Rights of the Child (1958-1967), Inter-office Memoranda from J.P. Humphrey to Sir Humphrey Trevelyan (17 April 1958) and from J. Henderson to J.P. Humphrey (5 May 1958).
[43] AUNOG-S, 19485-Child Welfare-Declaration on the Rights of the Child-Information from Member Governments (part A 1946-1948), Letter from Delegation of Czechoslovakia, 2 September 1948.
[44] ASG-IUCW, N.1.3, Tri/71.3, Letter from G. Thélin to M. Milhaud, 22 June 1948.
[45] AUNOG-S, 18795-NGO-IUCW (part A-1937-1951), Memo from M. Milhaud to R. Cilento (Director of Division of Social Activities), 27 May 1948.

revised [version] in order to take new developments into account", as the UN Secretariat had planned in 1948.[46] Despite the IUCW's goodwill as well as its privileged contacts at Lake Success, it did not succeed in obtaining a mandate to redraft the treaty. Moreover, the Human Rights Commission (HRC), busy drafting the Universal Human Rights Declaration (UDHR), left the project undeveloped for the next decade.

The second phase of the drafting process of what would become the UN Declaration of the Rights of the Child stayed very much in the intergovernmental sphere and never restored the IUCW's status as a norm entrepreneur. After a consultation process conducted from 1957 to 1958 accepting input from member states, UN specialised agencies, as well as a few IGOs and NGOs, one of which was the IUCW, the final project was adapted and then directly transmitted to the UN General Assembly.[47] A debate about the relevance of endorsing a specific instrument while the UDHR already recognised human rights for every human being, children included, did however arise.[48] Nevertheless, the General Assembly had not produced any treaty for some time and the outlook on the HRC, struggling with the drafting of the Covenants on Human Rights, was "rather dim".[49] Therefore, some agents found it to be the right moment to "come up with an accomplishment",[50] thanks to an unproblematic treaty. The point was – as the Temporary Social Commission had announced – to get everyone to agree on an already accepted general agreement. The *New York Times* editorialist, covering its imminent adoption, perceived this very clearly:

> Drafting a UN Declaration on the Rights of the Child was not an unusually difficult task because there is so large an area of agreement. ... [T]here is no great variation in the regard for the child and for his needs. Almost every society cherishes its children.[51]

The wording of children's rights changed but the related norm and regime did not radically evolve with the adoption of the UNDCR, despite the fact that scientific study of the child had produced an enormous amount of new knowledge about children's psychology, socialisation, learning abilities and so on.[52] Retrospectively, one can say that the lack of consultation during the drafting process induced in the Declaration the seeds of its own inaccuracy. Indeed, many influential states believed the UDHR was sufficient to guarantee the rights of the child, to the detriment of the

---

[46] AUNOG-S, S-0445-0077, Draft Declaration on the Rights of the Child (1958–1967), Interoffice Memorandum, To J.P. Humphrey from J. Henderson, director, Bureau of Social Affairs, ESA, Subject: Declaration of the Rights of the Child, 5 June 1958.
[47] Office of the High Commissioner for Human Rights [OHCHR], *Legislative History of the Convention on the Rights of the Child* (Geneva: United Nations, 2007).
[48] UNOGS.A, S-0445-0077 Draft Declaration on the Rights of the Child (1958–1967), Interoffice Memorandum from J. Henderson to J.P. Humphrey (5 May 1958).
[49] ASG-IUCW, M.4.4, Tri/71.1, Confidential Letter to Miss Moser from Frieda S. Miller (2 September 1959).
[50] Ibid.
[51] ASG-IUCW, M.4.5, Tri/71.1, Coupures de presses, Editorial, *New York Times*, 18 October 1959.
[52] See, in particular, Hofstetter, *Genève*; Dominique Ottavi, *De Darwin à Piaget, pour une histoire de la psychologie de l'enfant* (Paris: CNRS Editions, 2009).

UNDCR. Also, the fact that it mixed general and specific principles, halfway between soft and hard law, rendered it inapplicable according to jurists.[53]

The gap between legislation and social reality might explain why the actions taken to diffuse the UNDCR, mainly by UNESCO and IUCW, achieved limited success. The UNDCR was indeed translated into numerous languages, an information pamphlet for teachers was printed and travelling exhibitions on human rights as well as on the rights of the child were organised. The Declaration was also broadly distributed through networks of international organisations. However, the archives show that by the mid-1960s, most of the IOs neither referred to the treaty nor promoted it, and many NGOs also drafted their own children's charters.

Additionally, new norms recognising children's human rights as equal to adults' – such as the ban on corporal punishment in Sweden and the Supreme Court's decisions concerning children's constitutional rights in the US – were partly institutionalised at a national level.[54] Internationally, UNESCO was also conducting research on youth rights and responsibilities together with youth associations. The children's rights regime based on the UNDCR and children's protection needs was thus progressively losing its coherence.[55] Renewal was a necessary condition for its survival; the drafting of the UNCRC, taking into account scientific advancements as well as new practices and social realities, was an imperative.

A consensual treaty

While the Geneva Declaration was purely an NGO product and the Declaration on the Rights of the Child, in contrast, a strictly UN document, the working group for the UNCRC – created after the Polish delegation proposed a renewed version of the UNDCR in 1978 – succeeded in combining the two approaches. One could say that the UN learnt from its mistakes and the fate of its unpopular Declaration of the Rights of the Child. Nevertheless, it is within the successful partnership with NGOs, during the organisation of the International Year of the Child (IYC) (1979) and throughout, that one should look for an explanatory factor. Active notably through their own central secretariat, NGOs played a central role in the co-construction of children's rights as they emerged internationally in the late 1970s. The Secretary-General of the United Nations, Kurt Waldheim, at the closing ceremony of the IYC, underlined the importance of this collaboration:

> At both international and national levels, NGOs not only provided the impetus but also sponsored innovative projects that enlivened and enriched the Year. ... I hope that the process of which the International Year of the Child marked only the beginning will be an important part of policies and programmes of social development throughout the world.[56]

---

[53] See, in particular, Jordi Cots, "Le BICE et les Droits de l'Enfant: le message de la Convention et le message du BICE", *BICE, l'Enfance dans le Monde* (1996): 4–7.
[54] Bengt Sandin, "Children and the Swedish welfare state: From different to similar", in Paula S. Fass and Michael Grossberg, eds., *Reinventing Childhood after World War II* (Philadelphia, PA: University of Pennsylvania Press, 2012), 110–138.
[55] For a definition of regime coherence, see Donnelly, "International human rights".
[56] UNOGS-A, S-0910-0016-01 UN. SG Waldheim-IYC-UNICEF (1980-1981), Secretary General's Message at the Opening of Final Plenary Session of NGO/IYC Committee, 15 May 1980: 2.

Since the UN had planned to build the new legally binding treaty devoted to the rights of the child on the information and knowledge harvested during the IYC,[57] undoubtedly the latter allowed NGOs to stand out on the horizon of the drafting process. However, as Price and Cantwell recall, NGOs did not immediately seize this opportunity. During the first sessions of the working group, the NGOs were uncoordinated and found it difficult to get propositions passed.[58] The drafting of a legally binding instrument is unusual in that it requires adhesion of every potential member state to all of the rights contained in the treaty. Therefore, the working group took all its decisions on the principle of general consensus. NGOs understood this issue and in 1983 organised themselves as a pressure group to bring new issues into the debates and to promote coordinated positions among the delegations.

The group pursued its actions with increasing success under the auspices of the UN International Children Emergency Fund (UNICEF), which was progressively more involved in the process. The latter's Executive Board had at first stated that it was highly undesirable to "involve UNICEF in 'rights' issues which would clash with [its] 'needs' mandate",[59] Nevertheless, in 1980, UNICEF's new Assistant Director for External Relations showed interest in taking part in Human Rights committees, which pleased the HRC in return as well as NGOs "outside the UN Family".[60] The change of course was made explicit in 1986 when the Executive Board asked "UNICEF to participate in the work of the drafting of the Convention as appropriate".[61] Ultimately, the NGO Group found an influential and a "very active"[62] ally to spur on the drafting process and to obtain necessary support for unanimous adoption of the Convention.

After having submitted the working group's draft convention to a technical review within the UN Secretariat, as well as holding a broad consultation process among the member states, the HRC transmitted the document to the UN General Assembly. The NGO Group had for its part secured the agreement in principle of a majority of states; in this way, when the Convention was adopted, 10 years after the beginning of the drafting process and 30 exactly after the promulgation of the UN Declaration of the Rights of the Child, NGOs were already in the lead, organising its ratification and dissemination.

As a result of the specific juridical character of a Convention that makes it legally binding – unlike Declarations, which can remain catalogues of goodwill – member states not only adhere to the norm but also have to make it part of their national

---

[57] Veerman, *Rights of the Child*.
[58] Cynthia Price Cohen, "The role of nongovernmental organizations in the drafting of the Convention on the Rights of the Child", *Human Rights Quarterly* 12, no. 1 (1990): 137–147; Nigel Cantwell, "The origins, development and significance of the United Nations Convention on the Rights of the Child", in Sharon Detrick, ed., *The United Nations Convention on the Rights of the Child: A Guide to the "Travaux Préparatoires"* (Dordrecht: Martinus Nijhoff Publishers, 1992), 19–30.
[59] UNICEF Online Archives (UNICEF-OA), Executive Board Decisions 1978–1979, E/ICEF/L.1309/Add., 2–11 September, 1979: para. 72.
[60] HRC-A, G/SO 214 (28) Part 2 [Folder 1] File begins January 1979, ends March 1982, Notes for the Record Approved by Participants, Meeting 17 December 1980 "On the importance given to the child maltreatment question within the UN system".
[61] HRC-A, G/SO 214 (28) Part 2 [Folder 2] File begins March 1982, ends December 1986, Resolution Adopted by the Executive Board of UNICEF E/ICEF/1986/CRP.37.
[62] HRC-A, G/SO 214 (28) Part 6 bis Begins December 1985, ends November 1989, Briefing Note, T. McCarthy Meeting with Mr James Grant.

juridical system. They are obliged to "make the principles and provisions of the Convention widely known, by appropriate and active means, to adults and children alike".[63] They are also required to demonstrate the progress achieved in the realisation of the obligations undertaken to a specific and specialised UN committee, that of the Rights of the Child. These provisions partly guarantee the spread of the norm. Still, the NGO Group also undertook important acts of communication in order to urge ratification of the Convention. For instance, on the day of its adoption, a torch-light march was organised in Geneva after a child received a phone call from New York announcing the adoption of the UNCRC.[64] In January 1990, a successful signature ceremony was held, as a result of which the minimum 20 signatures threshold was rapidly reached, allowing the Convention's entry into force less than one year after its adoption.

A *New York Times* journalist described the UN Convention as "a careful fabric of compromises and unresolved moral issues, drafted by a 42-nation working group".[65] If the first statement was correct, it should be specified that the nations did not write the Convention by themselves. Indeed, civil society took an active part in both the production and the promotion of the document. The Third Committee of the UNGA stated that, "such a process represents an ideal fusion of the ideals of nations, and those of the international community".[66] This highlights the transnational nature of the treaty, written by a network including states as well as international agents.

Conclusion

This analysis indicates that the issue of children's rights circulated widely and internationally during the twentieth century. Children's rights successive translations into international charters underline the transnational nature of the idea. Children's rights treaties are built-up and influenced by various agents, legal frameworks, cultures and historical events. They are partly constructed on the basis of local or regional habits and legal norms and thus take into account local particularities. But they are also generated within international interactions and transnational platforms of agents. As Kott emphasised, studying transnational networks and organisations highlights how the "international"[67] is built. Children's rights standards can in this respect be considered as the lowest common denominator likely to assemble the international community in a particular world context, rather than solely an extension of Western norms. The universality of the underlying arguments can of course be discussed, as well as the degree of legitimation sought by the states that ratify the treaties (*versus* their actual will to comply with the norm). However, socio-historical, legal and

---

[63] United Nations, *Convention on the Rights of the Child*, General Assembly, Resolution 44/25, 1989, UN doc. A/44/25: article 42.

[64] HRC-A, G/SO 214 (28) Part 6 bis Begins December 1985, ends November 1989, Letter to delegates, NGO representatives, etc. from the NGO committee on UNICEF.

[65] HRC-A, G/SO 214 (28) Part 7 [Folder 2], Begins September 1989, ends February 1990, *New York Times*, 29 October 1989.

[66] General Assembly, *Official Records*, 14th Session, Plenary Meetings (841st Meeting on November 20, 1959), item 64: Draft Declaration of the Rights of the Child, Report of the Third Committee, A/4249 and Corr.2, paragraph 42.

[67] Sandrine Kott, "Dynamiques de l'Internationalisation: l'Allemagne et l'Organisation Internationale du Travail (1919–1940)", *Critique internationale* 52, no. 3 (2011): 70.

educational constructions of the Children of the World as well as that of a transnational childhood do make sense in a globalised world.

The study of the history of children's rights does however question the durability of the agreement. Indeed, a norm close to being institutionalised has to find the right balance between minimum shared values and maximum authorised variation to take into account socio-historical evolutions. Children's rights regimes arising from the proclamation of the treaties seem to have frozen the rights of the child at three different moments, thereby neutralising their transnational and "trans-historical" character. The progressive incoherence of the children's rights regimes stabilised within international organisations, as a result of their incapacity to take into account controversies or new world contexts, as their history has shown, leads to an inescapable need for a redefinition of minimum standards. This situation offers an interesting area of analysis for the future evolution of children's rights.

The Century of the Child was marked from its beginning by an unprecedented production of knowledge concerning the child and childhood. This huge production of knowledge, which was not examined within the scope and limits of this article, also acted as a trigger, continuously providing new information about how best to raise, treat and help children and consequently define what the needs of the child are. This emulation made the circulation of knowledge possible and meaningful at an international level as well as between actors and institutions (civil society, academy, governments).

However, if science is considered a normative framework, incessantly progressing more rapidly than related and subsequent pieces of legislation, how long will the UNCRC, partly based on the scientific documentation harvested during the IYC as well as on scientific breakthroughs that occurred in the 1980s, stay up to date? And will the possibility of extending the UNCRC with optional protocols, general comments and days of discussion be sufficient to adapt it to contemporary issues? The evolution of children's rights indicates that the process is by no means straightforward. The complexity of this dynamic and open concept as well as its transnational nature might require a corresponding regime; that is, one more concerned with how children's rights circulate through time, space and culture, thanks to various agents and institutions, rather than focusing on the stabilisation of a progressively but inexorably out-dated norm.

L'éducation sexuelle, entre médecine, morale et pédagogie: débats transnationaux et réalisations locales (Suisse romande 1890–1930)[1]

Anne-Françoise Praz

Department of Contemporary History, University of Fribourg, Switzerland

Autour de 1900, la question de l'éducation sexuelle de la jeunesse émerge dans plusieurs pays d'Europe occidentale. Tous sont confrontés au processus de déclin de la fécondité maritale, qui suscite de nouvelles préoccupations relatives à la dépopulation et à la dégénérescence. Avec la prise de conscience médicale de la gravité et de la contagiosité des maladies vénériennes, ces inquiétudes prennent la dimension d'un péril national. La nécessité de contrer ces dangers autorise un discours respectable sur la sexualité, qui devient l'objet d'un savoir à diffuser, voire à enseigner dans les écoles. Bien plus qu'une information, l'éducation sexuelle est davantage comprise comme l'imposition de normes, en particulier l'abstinence prémaritale, très largement prônée. Un tel consensus pourrait favoriser la mise en place de projets; or, malgré la profusion de discours, les réalisations concrètes restent rares et controversées, surtout dans le cadre scolaire. Comment expliquer ces difficultés? Cet article analyse les dynamiques entre le niveau transnational (conférences, congrès) et le niveau local, en comparant les discours et mobilisations autour de l'éducation sexuelle dans deux cantons suisses francophones (Vaud et Genève). Nous attachons une attention particulière à la manière dont ces projets sont légitimés scientifiquement et sur quelles disciplines leurs défenseurs s'appuient; nous examinons aussi le rôle du genre dans ces mobilisations, étant donné que les femmes et les féministes s'invitent dans ces débats.

The issue of sex education emerged in Western Europe around 1900. The region was experiencing a decline in fertility that raised new concerns related to depopulation and degeneration. The finding of the severity and contagiousness of venereal diseases reinforced these fears to the dimension of a national peril. In an effort to fight these dangers, sexuality entered the public debate and became an object of knowledge that was disseminated and even taught in schools. Sex education in the early twentieth century had more to do with imposing norms of behaviour than communicating information: premarital abstinence was widely advocated. Such a consensus should have facilitated the implementation of projects. Yet, although discourses were profuse, concrete achievements remained rare and controversial, particularly for schools. How can we explain such difficulties? Could the general consensus vanish because of conflicts opposing competing experts? Did this consensus come up with serious resistances to implementation that were related to local political contexts? Did public policies interfere with the scientific debate? This article uses research on the dynamics between the transnational (conferences and congresses) and the local level,

---

[1] Ce texte est la version remaniée d'une conférence donnée au congrès ISCHE34-SHCY-DHA 2012. Je remercie Christian Schiess pour une première lecture critique, ainsi que les évaluateurs/trices anonymes dont les remarques ont permis de restructurer et d'enrichir le texte.

comparing the Swiss Protestant cantons of Vaud and Geneva. It examines the discourses and mobilisations around sex education, combining two patterns of analysis. First, the composition of networks engaged in its promotion (professional groups, activist orientations) and the disciplinary knowledge that is referred to in the debate are considered. Second, this mobilisation is questioned in a gender perspective. As women and feminists were involved in this debate, how did this participation, historically unprecedented, influence the content of the projects and the patterns of mobilisation?

Autour de 1900, l'éducation sexuelle de la jeunesse surgit comme préoccupation nouvelle dans les pays occidentaux. Les recherches sur cet objet d'études récent[2] attribuent la simultanéité de cette émergence à la perception commune de périls sanitaires et sociaux, à commencer par les maladies vénériennes, dont les médecins soulignent la contagiosité et la dangerosité. Le déclin de la fécondité maritale suscite des inquiétudes plus diffuses, relatives à la dépopulation, à la dégénérescence et au déclin des nations dites "civilisées". Le silence coutumier sur la question sexuelle n'est plus possible. Outrepassant les tabous, la sexualité doit entrer dans le débat public, devenir un objet de connaissance à diffuser, voire même à enseigner dans les écoles.

Les historien(ne)s ont souligné la fonction normative de l'éducation sexuelle à l'époque: davantage qu'une information, c'est une dissuasion sexuelle qui est prônée par tous les milieux. Un tel consensus, conforme à la morale dominante, devrait favoriser la mise en œuvre des projets. Or, si l'on assiste à une prolifération de discours, les réalisations concrètes restent rares et controversées, notamment dans le cadre scolaire. Comment expliquer ces difficultés pour un programme à première vue si peu subversif? Diverses hypothèses sont examinées ci-après. Le consensus général sur la nécessité d'une éducation sexuelle se dilue-t-il dans les conflits de concurrence entre spécialistes? Face à l'importance des enjeux sociaux et sanitaires, plusieurs réseaux scientifiques, professionnels et associatifs font en effet valoir leurs compétences, présageant des chances d'obtenir une reconnaissance publique ou un tremplin pour leurs idées. Les résistances lors de la concrétisation des projets relèvent-elles de logiques politiques indépendantes des débats de spécialistes? Ces logiques interfèrent-elles avec les débats scientifiques?

La réponse à ces questions nécessite de confronter deux échelles d'analyse, transnationale et locale. Le terme transnational est utilisé ici pour définir "un espace où les individus de différentes nationalités circulent, se rencontrent, échangent des idées, regardent les réformes et les expériences dans un autre pays, reviennent et les adoptent ou les transforment".[3] Pour l'histoire de l'éducation sexuelle, ce concept est doublement pertinent. D'abord, le débat sur la nécessité d'une telle éducation est lancé dans l'enceinte des congrès internationaux autour

---

[2]Un premier ouvrage collectif permet d'intéressantes confrontations: Lutz D. H. Sauerteig and Roger Davidson, eds., *Shaping Sexual Knowledge: A Cultural History of Sex Education in Twentieth Century Europe* (London and New York: Routledge, 2009).
[3]Christophe Capunao, "L'internationalisation des milieux natalistes et familialistes durant l'entre-deux guerres: un échec?," in *Pratiques du transnational, terrains, preuves, limites*, ed. Jean-Paul Zúñiga (Paris: Centre de recherches historiques, 2011), 37.

de 1900, moment "organisateur" avec la mise en place de structures plus formelles encadrant ces congrès.[4] Ensuite, le transnational implique l'abandon de l'Etat-nation comme unité d'analyse. Or, le débat sur l'éducation sexuelle se déroule au-delà de l'initiative des Etats, entre représentant(e)s d'associations professionnelles, scientifiques et militantes; si les délégués des administrations publiques sont invités aux congrès, c'est davantage comme récepteurs d'un transfert de savoirs spécifiques, à répercuter auprès de leurs gouvernements. Les initiatives sur le terrain n'impliquent généralement pas l'Etat comme acteur principal. Sans disparaître totalement, le national est ici transcendé.[5]

La confrontation entre l'échelle transnationale et locale s'impose par la nature même des principaux protagonistes, à savoir les membres des diverses associations. Celles-ci sont ancrées dans le transnational par la circulation des personnes et des écrits, mais aussi au niveau local ou national par le biais de leurs filiales. Les acteurs jouent d'ailleurs de ces différents terrains, s'appuyant sur le transnational pour faire progresser leur cause au niveau local ou prétendant représenter leur nation alors qu'ils ne constituent qu'une tendance. Surtout, le niveau local s'avère crucial pour analyser la réception et l'appropriation des débats. Comprendre les difficultés de concrétisation des projets d'éducation sexuelle oblige à identifier précisément les acteurs locaux, leur inscription dans différents réseaux, l'adéquation de leurs discours et stratégies au contexte. A ce titre, la Suisse constitue un laboratoire de recherche idéal: les débats transnationaux ont des impacts différenciés d'un canton voire d'une ville à l'autre, étant donné le système fédéraliste (en particulier l'autonomie en matière scolaire), combiné avec la diversité politique et culturelle.

Aux niveaux transnational et local, nous adoptons deux grilles d'analyse. La première s'intéresse à la composition des réseaux actifs dans la promotion de l'éducation sexuelle, ainsi qu'aux disciplines sollicitées pour la légitimer, la contester et en esquisser le contenu. Au-delà d'une histoire des idées désincarnée, cet effort pour restituer le débat "dans les contextes institutionnels de son énonciation"[6] permet de mieux saisir cet objet hybride qu'est alors l'éducation sexuelle. Il n'existe en effet aucun congrès international spécifiquement consacré au sujet, et l'on peut difficilement parler de l'émergence d'un champ disciplinaire. En revanche, la thématique est convoquée par différentes disciplines qui se profilent sur le terrain scolaire: médecine, hygiène, sciences naturelles, éducation morale, pédagogie, psychologie. Ce constat suscite plusieurs interrogations. L'éducation sexuelle constitue-t-elle, pour certains groupes professionnels ou scientifiques, un terrain pour visibiliser de nouveaux savoirs? Ces savoirs sont-ils instrumentalisés par les mouvements d'obédience politique, religieuse ou philanthropique?

La deuxième grille d'analyse questionne ces discours et mobilisations dans une perspective de genre. Certains travaux ont analysé les contenus genrés de l'éducation

---

[4] Anne Rasmussen, "Tournant, inflexions, ruptures: le moment internationaliste," *Mille neuf cent, Revue d'histoire intellectuelle* 19 (2001): 27–41.
[5] Robert Frank, conclusion à *Les relations culturelles internationales au 20e siècle: de la diplomatie culturelle à l'acculturation*, ed. Anne Dulphy et al. (Brussels: Peter Lang, 2010), 672.
[6] Marco Cicchini, "Un bouillon de culture pour les sciences de l'éducation? Le congrès international d'éducation morale (1908-1934)," *Paedagogica Historica* 40, no. 5-6 (2004): 636.

sexuelle.[7] Notre analyse se focalise sur la place des femmes dans les réseaux étudiés et sur l'impact d'une telle présence sur l'orientation féministe de cette éducation. Ce terrain est en effet tout désigné pour mettre en œuvre un objectif sur lequel convergent les féminismes: la contestation de la construction normative artificielle de la séparation privé/public. Les questions prétendument privées ne cessent en effet d'être l'objet de débats et de politiques publiques, qu'il s'agisse de maternité, de mariage, de famille, d'illégitimité, de prostitution, de maladies vénériennes. Les féministes se sont efforcées de "rendre ces liens privé/public plus explicites ... et de s'attaquer sans détour au noyau socio-politique des sociétés humaines: les relations entre les sexes".[8] L'utilisation plurielle du terme féminisme indique ses orientations plus ou moins radicales, qu'il est intéressant de croiser avec les savoirs sollicités dans le débat. Ceux-ci participent-ils à la subversion ou au renforcement des normes de genre? Dans ce dernier cas, comment l'innovation scientifique se concilie-t-elle avec le conservatisme en termes de rapports sociaux de sexe?

La première partie du texte analyse le débat transnational sur l'éducation sexuelle à partir de l'émergence et de la circulation du thème dans divers congrès internationaux entre 1899 et 1930. Le matériel est constitué par les actes de ces congrès (programmes, intervenants, conférences, résolutions, etc.), ainsi que par diverses publications éditées par les milieux qui s'y retrouvent. En seconde partie, nous proposons une analyse de la concrétisation de ce débat au niveau local, en confrontant les discours, mobilisations et réalisations dans les cantons suisses protestants[9] de Genève et Vaud. Nous disposons ici des archives de deux associations locales de relèvement moral (rapports annuels, listes de membres, budgets, bulletins, publications diverses, conférences), complétées par le dépouillement de la revue *L'Educateur*, à quoi s'ajoutent des sondages dans des revues locales et nationales d'hygiène et dans les Archives de l'Institut Jean-Jacques Rousseau de Genève.

L'éducation sexuelle au niveau transnational: débats d'experts

Médecins et réformateurs moraux: alliance stratégique autour de la morale

La première impulsion d'un débat transnational sur l'éducation sexuelle est donnée par deux Conférences internationales pour la prophylaxie de la syphilis et des maladies vénériennes, organisées à Bruxelles en 1899 et 1902 à l'instigation de l'Académie belge de médecine.

Lors de la conférence de 1899 (près de 400 médecins et responsables nationaux de santé publique de 29 pays), un réseau spécifique émerge: les syphiligraphes et vénérologues, qui entendent renforcer l'institutionnalisation de leur spécialité. Ainsi,

---

[7] Virginie De Luca Barruse, "Le genre de l'éducation à la sexualité des jeunes gens (1900–1940)," *Cahiers du Genre* 49 (2010): 155–82; Mary Lynn Stewart, "Sex Education and Sexual Initiation of Bourgeois French Girls, 1880–1930," in *Secret Gardens, Satanic Mills. Placing Girls in European History 1750–1960*, ed. Mary Jo Maines, Birgitte Soland et Christina Benninghaus (Bloomington: Indiana University Press, 2005), 164–77.

[8] Karen Offen, "'Flux et éruptions': réflexions sur l'écriture d'une histoire comparée des féminismes européens, 1700–1950," in *Histoire comparée des femmes. Nouvelles approches*, ed. Anne Cova (Lyon: ENS Editions, 2009), 48.

[9] Dans les cantons catholiques, le débat public sur la sexualité est réprimé jusque vers 1920, puis évoqué avec une extrême discrétion: Anne-Françoise Praz, "Religion, Masculinity and Fertility Decline : A Comparative Analysis of Protestant and Catholic Culture (Switzerland 1890–1930)," *History of the Family* 14 (2009): 88–106.

la résolution V "recommande instamment aux Gouvernements d'assurer la création de médecins vraiment compétents en la matière par l'institution, dans chaque université, de cours complets et obligatoires dont les matières figureraient au programme des examens d'Etat".[10] Toutefois, étant donné l'absence de moyens thérapeutiques efficaces, les médecins reconnaissent l'utilité des mesures non médicales, au-delà de la seule réglementation de la prostitution (maisons closes, contrôles sanitaires et isolement des prostituées). Ils invitent les Etats à "saisir toutes les occasions favorables pour attirer l'attention du public et surtout celle des jeunes gens sur les dangers que la prostitution fait courir à la santé des personnes de l'un et l'autre sexe, et sur les suites funestes des maladies vénériennes".[11] Ce tournant prophylactique légitime le lancement d'un débat sur l'éducation sexuelle, la prévention vénérienne constituant l'objectif minimal de tous ses promoteurs. Autre innovation, ces maladies ne sont plus associées aux seules prostituées; les politiques de prévention ne peuvent plus ignorer la gent masculine.

La conférence de 1902 (env. 250 participant(e)s de 27 pays) sollicite ainsi, aux côtés des médecins et fonctionnaires étatiques, des juristes, des philanthropes, des représentants d'associations de relèvement moral (réformateurs moraux). Ce dernier groupe comprend une forte présence féminine, suscitant de vives critiques de la part d'une majorité de médecins, qui accusent ces non spécialistes, en particulier féminins, d'incompétence.[12] Parmi les associations invitées, la *Fédération abolitionniste internationale* (FAI) est représentée par son secrétaire général (Henri Minod, Genève), des dirigeants nationaux (Alfred de Morsier, Genevois installé à Paris pour la France), et plusieurs médecins hostiles à la réglementation aux côtés de militant(e)s. La fondatrice, Joséphine Butler (1828–1906), s'est illustrée par sa campagne (1869–1886) pour l'abolition des lois réglementaristes en Angleterre. Alors que les médecins continentaux font pression sur leurs collègues britanniques et que des congrès médicaux envisagent d'internationaliser le système réglementariste, Butler décide de modifier l'opinion en Europe. Au terme d'une série de voyages, elle organise en 1877 le premier congrès international abolitionniste à Genève, qui devient le siège du secrétariat de la FAI dès 1886, avec un comité mixte, selon la volonté de la fondatrice.[13]

Ce mouvement est une agrégation d'associations nationales ou locales dont l'orientation (libéralisme, féminisme, moralisme) varie.[14] Les sections se retrouvent sur un message central, le refus de la double morale sexuelle, autorisant aux hommes tous les écarts, alors que les femmes doivent rester des fiancées vierges et des épouses fidèles; à l'exception bien sûr des prostituées, contraintes à des

---

[10] Dubois-Havenith, ed., *Conférence internationale pour la prophylaxie de la syphilis et des maladies vénériennes, Bruxelles, septembre 1899, vol. 2* (Bruxelles: H. Lamertin, 1899), 43.
[11] Ibid.
[12] Dominique Puenzieux and Brigitte Ruckstuhl, *Medizin, Moral und Sexualität. Die Bekämpfung der Geschlechtskrankheiten Syphilis und Gonorrhöe in Zürich 1870–1920* (Zurich: Chronos, 1994), 126.
[13] Anne Summers, "Which Women? What Europe? Josephine Butler and the International Abolitionist Federation," *History Workshop Journal* 62 (2006): 216. Les liens de Butler avec la Suisse sont facilités par les réseaux protestants (parmi lesquels de généreux banquiers genevois) et par le mariage de sa sœur dans une famille italo-suisse, installée sur la Riviera vaudoise.
[14] Christine Machiels, "Dealing with the Issue of Prostitution; Mobilizing Feminisms in France, Switzerland and Belgium (1875–1920)," *Women's History Review* 17, no. 2 (2008): 200.

contrôles sanitaires humiliants pour satisfaire les pulsions soi-disant irrépressibles des hommes. Pour les abolitionnistes, les problèmes sociaux comme les maladies vénériennes s'expliquent par l'abandon des hommes à leurs pulsions. La solution consiste à exiger d'eux le même comportement que celui préconisé pour les femmes: continence prénuptiale, modération sexuelle. Cette morale sexuelle unique participe au combat pour l'égalité des sexes. Toutefois, cette utopie égalitaire reste prisonnière d'une vision négative de la sexualité, comme pulsion néfaste à combattre, de pair avec une vision essentialiste de la différence des sexes:[15] les hommes seraient par nature des êtres charnels entraînés par leurs pulsions, les femmes des créatures morales et spirituelles, qui doivent néanmoins être instruites de sexualité:

> La force du jeune homme sera en raison directe de la libération de la jeune fille des préjugés et des ignorances où elle végète. La femme non sachante et non consciente sur ces questions est le plus grand obstacle à la moralisation du jeune homme. Voilà la valeur du féminisme.[16]

La promotion de l'éducation sexuelle ne figure pas au programme initial de la FAI mais les abolitionnistes s'en emparent, profitant de l'orientation prophylactique du débat médical, un argument en faveur de la continence prénuptiale masculine. Ce consensus explique l'alliance nouée au congrès de 1902 entre médecins et réformateurs moraux. L'incitation de la jeunesse masculine à la continence figure dans la résolution IV, déposée par Henri Minod et deux médecins.[17] La résolution VI, première résolution officielle en faveur de l'éducation sexuelle dans les écoles, souhaite que "le problème de l'éducation rationnelle et progressive des questions d'ordre intersexuel, au point de vue hygiénique et moral, soit posé auprès des instituteurs et éducateurs de la jeunesse à tous les degrés".[18] Elle est défendue par trois membres de la FAI (de Morsier, le médecin français Louis Fiaux, l'avocat belge Louis Franck), associés à l'éminent biologiste allemand Albert Neisser.

Le savoir médical est ici convoqué dans un double but: comme caution scientifique des injonctions morales et comme langage respectable pour évoquer les organes et fonctions sexuelles.[19] Lors de son allocution à Bruxelles, de Morsier se présente comme "un modeste sociologue". Sans doute se réfère-t-il à l'enseignement donné à l'époque à Genève, davantage apparenté à une ébauche de philosophie sociale, teintée d'évaluation normative, de jugements éthiques, proche

---

[15]Anne-Marie Käppeli, *Sublime croisade. Ethique et politique du féminisme protestant 1875–1928* (Genève: Zoé, 1990).

[16]Bibliothèque publique et universitaire de Genève, Manuscrits de Morsier, MS fr. 6939/20, *Fragments d'une conférence concernant l'instruction de la morale sexuelle* [s.d.]. De Morsier est de retour à Genève dès 1902.

[17]"Il faut enseigner à la jeunesse masculine que non seulement la chasteté et la continence ne sont pas nuisibles, mais encore que ces vertus sont les plus recommandables du point de vue médical," *IIe Conférence internationale*, vol. 2, 514.

[18]Ibid. Ces deux résolutions sont votées à l'unanimité.

[19]Des tabous persistent: le premier manuel d'éducation sexuelle publié en français (par une abolitionniste genevoise) décrit les organes sexuels, la reproduction, la grossesse, l'accouchement, mais occulte soigneusement l'acte sexuel; Emma Pieczynska, *L'Ecole de la pureté. Aux mères de famille* (Paris: Fischbacher, 1898).

du protestantisme social.[20] En revanche, les écrits de la FAI et ses interventions au congrès ne se réfèrent jamais à la pédagogie dans cette phase initiale; ils critiquent les travaux de psychologues de l'époque, accusés de négliger la "question intersexuelle", d'entériner l'infériorité des femmes et de réduire leur destinée à la maternité.[21]

Vers une éducation sexuelle scientiste: le moment eugéniste

La pédagogie s'invite progressivement comme discipline de référence, aux côtés de la médecine et des sciences naturelles, dans une seconde phase du débat sur l'éducation sexuelle, repérable dès 1904. Le sujet figure dans les premiers congrès internationaux d'hygiène scolaire (Nuremberg 1904, Londres 1907 et Paris 1910), auquel s'ajoute le Congrès international de propagande et d'hygiène sociale de Paris (1923), qui y consacre une importante section. L'éducation sexuelle est aussi traitée dans les Congrès internationaux d'éducation morale (CIEM) qui connaissent six éditions entre 1908 et 1934.[22]

Les congrès d'hygiène scolaire participent de "l'exacerbation de la question hygiénique" au tournant du 20ème siècle et de sa spécialisation en sous disciplines.[23] L'identité des médecins traitant d'éducation sexuelle signale l'influence des associations nationales de lutte contre le péril vénérien. Mais les congrès de Nuremberg et Londres ne parviennent à aucun consensus sur la pertinence d'une éducation sexuelle scolaire, son contenu ou sur la personne (médecin, enseignant(e)) le mieux à même de la dispenser.[24]

L'impulsion des congrès internationaux d'éducation morale (CIEM) est donnée en Angleterre par la *Moral Instruction League*, une société pédagogique liée à l'*International Union of Ethical Societies*, qui s'efforce de définir les bases d'une éducation morale distincte de l'éducation religieuse. L'identité des intervenants qui s'expriment sur l'éducation sexuelle au premier CIEM (Londres 1908) révèle une autre influence. Ce sont de fervents partisans du savant Francis Galton (1822–1911), fondateur d'une science nouvelle, l'eugénique, qu'il a lui-même définie comme "l'étude des facteurs soumis au contrôle social et susceptibles d'augmenter ou de

---

[20] Le premier enseignement de sociologie en Suisse est donné entre 1885 et 1922 à Genève, par Louis Wuarin, journaliste, formé en théologie, spécialisé dans les questions sociales (et membre du comité exécutif de la FAI). Giovanni Busino et Sven Stelling-Michaud, "Esquisse d'une histoire des sciences sociales à Genève," *Cahiers Vilfredo Pareto* 6 (1965): 28–33.

[21] Dans *Le Droit des femmes et la morale intersexuelle* (Genève: Kundig, 1903), de Morsier critique ainsi l'ouvrage d'Henri Marion, *Psychologie de la femme* (Paris: Librairie Armand Colin, 1900).

[22] Marco Cicchini, "Un bouillon de culture," 633–56; Rita Hofstetter, *Genève, creuset des sciences de l'éducation, fin du 19e–première moitié du 20e siècle* (Genève: Droz, 2010), 267–73. Ces congrès ont lieu successivement à Londres, La Haye, Genève, Rome, Paris et Cracovie.

[23] Anne Tschinart, "Rôle et évolution de l'hygiène scolaire dans l'enseignement secondaire de 1800 à 1910," *Carrefours de l'éducation* 26 (July–December 2008): 204; Anne Rasmussen, "L'hygiène en congrès (1852–1912): circulation et configurations internationales," in *Les hygiénistes, enjeux, modèles et pratiques*, ed. Patrice Bourdelais (Paris: Belin, 2001), 213–39.

[24] L'opposition entre le médecin et le pédagogue est thématisée dans différents comptes-rendus du congrès de Londres. Par exemple: Charles Chabot, "Hygiène et pédagogie," *L'Année psychologique* 14 (1907): 345.

diminuer les qualités soit physiques, soit mentales des futures générations". L'historiographie a démontré le large écho de cette pensée, à une époque où les perspectives d'une dégénérescence biologique de l'espèce humaine étaient sérieusement redoutées.[25] En Grande-Bretagne cependant, les mesures prônées par Galton pour contrer la détérioration de la santé des classes populaires (notamment la stérilisation) se heurtent à de vives oppositions; aux facteurs héréditaires, les médecins hygiénistes opposent les conditions économiques.[26] Dès lors, Galton recherche d'autres moyens pour promouvoir ses idées. Il se rapproche des milieux de l'éducation, en particulier la *Moral Instruction League*, avec un double objectif: introduire l'eugénique dans l'enseignement afin de forger une opinion plus favorable, profiter des réseaux de cette association pour internationaliser son combat. En 1908, Galton et des membres de cette ligue s'associent pour fonder l'*Eugenics Education Society*,[27] qui publie *The Eugenics Review* dès 1908 et organise le premier Congrès international eugéniste (Londres 1912). Quelques mois plus tard, la Société relance le débat sur le terrain britannique par une conférence nationale sur l'éducation, où plus de 900 enseignant(e)s débattent de l'introduction de l'hygiène sexuelle dans les écoles en lien avec l'idéal eugénique.[28]

L'orientation eugénique du débat sur l'éducation sexuelle, très présente aux CIEM de 1908 et de 1912, s'atténue en 1922 puis disparaît, un mouvement que l'on retrouve dans les congrès d'hygiène scolaire. Au congrès de Paris (1910), l'éducation sexuelle figure en séance plénière et trois rapporteurs sur quatre s'inscrivent dans l'eugénisme; au Congrès international de propagande et d'hygiène sociale de 1923, il n'y a plus qu'une seule oratrice liée à ce courant parmi les dix rapporteurs traitant d'éducation sexuelle.[29]

Quel est donc l'objectif d'une éducation sexuelle eugéniste? La lecture des communications indique la primauté de l'enjeu biologique – qualité de la descendance – inspiré d'une morale scientiste: "L'utilité sociale et le devenir de l'espèce doivent être le critérium de la morale individuelle." A ce titre, il n'existe pas de clivage entre instruction et éducation sexuelle: c'est sur la base de connaissances

---

[25] Daniel Kelves, *Au nom de l'eugénisme. Génétique et politique dans le monde anglo-saxon* (Paris: PUF, 1995); Paul Weindling, *L'hygiène de la race. Hygiène raciale et eugénisme médical en Allemagne, 1870–1933* (Paris: La Découverte, 1998); Anne Carol, *Histoire de l'eugénisme en France* (Paris: Seuil, 1995). Les solutions proposées étaient très variées, selon qu'on admettait la toute puissance de l'hérédité ou l'action possible du milieu et de l'éducation.

[26] Sur l'opposition entre hygiénistes et eugénistes, cf. Simon Szreter, *Fertility, Class and Gender in Britain 1860–1940* (Cambridge: Cambridge University Press, 1996), 182–246.

[27] Robert Bérard, "Frederick James Gould and the Transformation of Moral Education," *British Journal of Educational Studies* 25, no. 3 (1987): 233–47; Roy Lowe, "The Educational Impact of the Eugenics Movement," *International Journal of Educational Research* 27, no. 8 (1998): 648.

[28] Dans son discours inaugural, le major L. Darwin lance un appel aux enseignants: "The benefit resulting from your wise teaching will in part appear in the form of sound eugenic legislation; for legislation now springs out of the opinion of the many, which it embodies.... In short, the conclusion I wish to urge with all my force is that by implanting the eugenic ideal in the mind of children of to-day, you will be taking a definite step towards ensuring the racial progress of our nation in the future," *Eugenics Review* 5, no. 1 (April 1913): 8–9.

[29] Au congrès de 1910, il s'agit du Dr Jean-Jacques Doléris (Paris, obstétricien et gynécologue renommé), de Mlle Raquel Camana (Argentine), de Mlle Freda Kerry (Glasgow). En 1923, il s'agit de la Dr Paulina Luisi (Uruguay), première femme médecin de son pays, militante féministe et socialiste, membre de la FAI.

scientifiques que les enfants doivent être conscientisés à leurs responsabilités procréatives. Si certains intervenants restent soucieux du consentement parental, d'autres estiment que les enjeux pour "l'avenir de la race" justifient pleinement une éducation sexuelle obligatoire.[30]

A propos du risque de choquer les élèves, les eugénistes sont confiants dans l'effet neutralisant du discours scientifique. "A scientific fact is uncoloured by emotion", déclare une oratrice.[31] Les intervenant(e)s se réfèrent prioritairement aux sciences naturelles et à la biologie de l'hérédité. Cependant, la pédagogie n'est pas négligée. Les eugénistes vont au-delà des réformateurs moraux qui se contenaient de conseiller "tact, prudence et élévation d'esprit". Plusieurs orateurs et oratrices développent un programme scolaire complet: notions élémentaires sur la transmission de la vie chez les animaux et les plantes (avant 10 ans), mécanismes de la reproduction humaine et de l'hérédité (10–14 ans), pour terminer à l'adolescence avec des enseignements sur l'hygiène sexuelle, les maladies vénériennes et l'eugénique. Cette attention à la progression des contenus va de pair avec une réflexion sur les modalités de transmission. L'éducation sexuelle scolaire est préférée à l'éducation familiale, jugée "timide, maladroite, et faussée par la réserve ou l'ignorance".[32] L'enseignement collectif est jugé supérieur à l'enseignement individuel, car il participe à la "désérotisation" de la sexualité en présentant celle-ci au même titre que n'importe quel sujet.

Cette éducation sexuelle eugéniste inscrit-elle l'égalité entre les sexes à l'horizon de la société idéale qu'elle projette? Les eugénistes destinent cette éducation aux deux sexes, mais la jeune fille est davantage l'objet de leur attention. La qualité de la génération future dépend en effet de sa capacité à maintenir son corps en santé et de son discernement dans le choix du père de ses enfants.[33] Alors que les réformateurs moraux tentaient d'abolir la différence sexuelle au nom d'une égale dignité morale, les eugénistes soulignent cette différence, ancrée dans la biologie, et insistent sur l'assignation des femmes à la reproduction. "La femme est faite pour la maternité et uniquement pour la maternité, c'est là son objectif biologique et tout le reste n'est que contingence", déclare le Dr Doléris (Paris 1910).[34] Au nom de cette finalité biologique, des orateurs et même des oratrices en viennent à critiquer le féminisme:

> Devant les résultats pratiques, individuels, collectifs, les jeunes filles opposeront au féminisme actuel, qui tend à les masculiniser, l'éternel féminin qui fait de chaque femme une mère en n'importe quelle occasion de la vie … les jeunes filles apprendront que … « femme » et « homme », ce sont deux êtres différents, inverses, complémentaires, équivalents; qu'il y a progrès sexuel lorsqu'on approfondit les différences entre les deux sexes par l'accentuation des caractères spécifiques; et que le caractère spécifique de la femme, c'est la maternité.[35]

---

[30]Interventions de Mlle Raquel Camana, Argentine. *IIIe Congrès international d'hygiène scolaire, Paris, 2–7 août 1910* (Paris: impr. de Chaix, 1910) vol. 1, 157, 159.
[31]Intervention de Mlle Freda Kerry, Glasgow. *IIIe Congrès international d'hygiène scolaire*, vol. 1, 168.
[32]Selon le Dr Doléris au Congrès d'hygiène scolaire de Paris en 1910. Emile Durkheim, *Sur l'éducation sexuelle* (Paris: Payot & Rivages, 2011), 123.
[33]Par ce choix, la jeune fille "is or may be partly responsible for the future of mankind". Intervention du Dr C. W. Saleeby (London) au IIe Congrès international d'éducation morale (La Haye, 1912), 581.
[34]Virginie de Luca, préface to *Sur l'éducation sexuelle*, Durkheim, 28.
[35]*IIIe Congrès international d'hygiène scolaire*, vol. 1, 161 (Mlle Raquel Camana).

Education nouvelle et remise en cause de l'éducation sexuelle

La disparition du thème de l'éducation sexuelle dans les CIEM après 1922 s'explique-t-elle par le transfert de leur organisation au Bureau international d'éducation inauguré en 1925 à Genève, en lien avec l'Institut Jean-Jacques Rousseau et placé sous la direction de Pierre Bovet?[36] Des réticences face à l'éducation sexuelle sont déjà perceptibles avant la guerre dans certaines publications liées au mouvement de l'Ecole nouvelle, dont l'Institut Rousseau devient l'ambassadeur à partir de 1912.[37] A la lumière des psychologues de l'adolescence, ces pionniers considèrent l'instinct sexuel de manière positive, comme facteur de créativité, d'émotion esthétique, d'intérêt pour autrui. Le rôle du pédagogue consiste, par une éducation du caractère et de la volonté, à préparer l'élève à gérer ces pulsions à l'adolescence. Or, l'éducation sexuelle se révélerait incompatible avec cet objectif: elle comporte en effet le défaut de concentrer l'attention des élèves sur la sexualité, alors qu'il faudrait justement la dériver.

Pierre Bovet, directeur de l'Institut Rousseau dès 1912, traduit en 1909 l'ouvrage de Frederick W. Foerster, *L'Ecole et le caractère*. Dominique Ottavi a souligné la "conversion spectaculaire" intervenue dans le parcours de ce pédagogue allemand, professeur de philosophie et d'éducation morale à Zurich, membre des CIEM. D'abord adepte d'une morale scientiste, il en vient à douter des conséquences ultimes de la libre-pensée. N'est-il pas préférable de conserver les traditions et règles morales pour "alléger l'individu du poids de son moi" et ne pas l'inciter à se chercher de nouveaux maîtres?[38] Il prône ainsi une pédagogie sexuelle indépendante du scientisme et de l'hygiénisme. Précédant l'éveil de l'instinct, celle-ci doit consister en "une éducation complète du caractère ... qui mette en lumière la force inépuisable dont l'esprit dispose pour se rendre maître des désirs et des dispositions du corps". Selon lui, l'instruction sexuelle va à l'encontre de toute prudence pédagogique.[39] Foerster se réfère également au psychanalyste allemand Wilhelm Stekel, pour qui l'instruction sexuelle collective est "une monstruosité qui amènerait des traumatismes innombrables".[40] Pédagogie, psychologie et psychanalyse remettent en cause l'éducation sexuelle scolaire.

Dans son ouvrage de 1916 consacré à l'hygiène dans les Ecoles nouvelles, Adolphe Ferrière s'inscrit dans une même méfiance. Il insiste sur l'enseignement individuel de l'hygiène sexuelle, ainsi pratiqué dans les écoles nouvelles de Suisse. Si la reproduction des animaux et des plantes est intégrée au cours de sciences naturelles, la reproduction humaine fait l'objet d'une "instruction *en tête à tête*, par le père, la mère, le directeur d'école, le médecin ou même le pasteur". C'est tout aussi

---

[36] Marco Cicchini, "Un bouillon de culture," 640.
[37] Rita Hofstetter, *Genève*, 277–319.
[38] Dominique Ottavi, "Allemagne, Friedrich W. Foerster et le défi de l'éducation sexuelle," in *Les jeunes et la sexualité. Initiations, interdits, identités (19e–20e siècle)*, ed. Véronique Blanchard, Régis Revenin, and Jean-Jacques Yvorel (Paris: Autrement, 2010), 49–59.
[39] "Les instincts sexuels sont par nature suffisamment conscients, c'est une aberration que de les projeter, pour ainsi dire, dans les hémisphères cérébraux, de façon à leur donner sur l'âme une emprise plus grande encore. Une fois l'attention portée sur ces sujets, l'imagination travaille, la curiosité et le désir s'excitent et la raison est tout à fait incapable de leur tenir tête." F. W. Foerster, *L'Ecole et le caractère. Le problèmes moraux de la vie scolaire* (Neuchâtel: Delachaux et Niestlé, 1911, 1st ed. 1909), 104.
[40] Wilhelm Stekel, *Nervöse Angstzustände und ihre Behandlung* (Berlin: [s.n.], 1906), 310, cité par Foerster.

discrètement qu'il s'agira, vers 16–18 ans, d'ouvrir les yeux au jeune homme et à la jeune fille sur "le côté pathologique du sujet".[41]

Au lendemain de la guerre, cette prudence pédagogique évolue vers un certain conservatisme. Si le sujet de l'éducation sexuelle disparaît dans les CIEM, les rares exposés encore prononcés dans les "communications diverses" offrent un espace aux représentants les plus conservateurs des mouvements moralistes.[42] Au Congrès international d'éducation nouvelle de 1924, le sujet est confié à Georges Bertier, directeur de l'Ecole des Roches promoteur de l'Ecole nouvelle en France, et ancré dans une idéologie conservatrice.[43] Son exposé reprend les traditionnelles injonctions à la continence et la seule innovation pédagogique consiste à signaler l'intérêt du scoutisme pour la dérivation de l'instinct sexuel.[44] Quant à la promotion de l'égalité des sexes, elle a totalement disparu des discours, nous y reviendrons.

L'éducation sexuelle au niveau local: interactions politiques

Comment ce débat transnational influence-t-il les mobilisations locales en faveur de l'éducation sexuelle? Comment les enjeux scientifiques se combinent-ils avec le contexte politique? L'analyse comparée des cantons de Vaud et Genève servira ci-après de révélateur.

Education sexuelle à l'école, expérience pionnière et blocages

En Suisse romande protestante, les associations locales issues de la FAI se saisissent du tremplin de l'éducation sexuelle pour promouvoir leur combat moral et social. Dans le canton de Vaud, la *Société vaudoise pour le relèvement de la moralité* (SVRM, fondée en 1896) fait œuvre de pionnier. Elle compte à ses débuts 67% de femmes, pour atteindre la parité en 1905; on note la présence conjointe de pasteurs et de médecins et une forte représentation des enseignant(e)s.[45]

En 1896 déjà, dans le cadre des Facultés de médecine et de théologie de Lausanne, un médecin de la SVRM propose quinze leçons sur "l'hygiène sexuelle".[46] La SVRM intervient auprès des autorités par le biais de pétitions sur les questions de mœurs (une action politique autorisée aux femmes) et organise des conférences, destinées surtout à un public masculin, pour dénoncer la double morale et affirmer les vertus médicales et morales de la continence. Mais pour transformer les mentalités masculines ne faudrait-il pas intervenir avant l'âge adulte, suggère le rapport de

---

[41]Adolphe Ferrière, "L'hygiène dans les Ecoles nouvelles," *Annales de la Société suisse d'hygiène scolaire*, 16 (1916): 320–25, http://dx.doi.org/10.5169/seals-91251; en italique dans le texte.

[42]A l'exemple de Emile Pourésy, de la Ligue française pour le relèvement de la moralité publique, en 1926 au congrès de Rome.

[43]Nathalie Duval, "L'Ecole des Roches, phare français au sein de la nébuleuse de l'Education nouvelle (1899–1944)," *Paedagogica Historica* 42, no. 1–2 (2006): 74.

[44]L'exposé est rapporté dans: "La Semaine de Villebon," *Pour l'Ère nouvelle. Revue internationale d'éducation nouvelle* 4, no. 13 (1924): 5–8.

[45]Entre 1895 et 1905, la Société passe de 107 à 461 membres; en 1895, le comité compte 10 hommes et 6 femmes (dont la présidente); en 1905, 12 hommes et 5 femmes. Parmi les membres de 1905 dont les professions sont indiquées, les pasteurs dominent (55), puis les enseignants (26) et médecins (20); les professions féminines indiquées relèvent de l'enseignement (20 enseignantes ou directrices d'école), 1 sage-femme, 1 pharmacienne.

[46]Archives de la Ville de Lausanne, *Rapport de la Société vaudoise pour le relèvement de la moralité pour l'année 1897*, 10.

1903. L'année suivante, un médecin de la Société donne une première conférence à des garçons de 13–16 ans dans le collège d'une petite ville. A l'heure où les congrès internationaux échouent à trouver un consensus sur l'éducation sexuelle scolaire, l'initiative est reconduite dans plusieurs localités selon la même démarche: contact avec les autorités scolaires pour l'organisation de leçons, informations aux parents qui peuvent retirer leur enfant s'ils le souhaitent.[47] Ces conférences débouchent sur une légitimation de l'éducation sexuelle à l'école publique. En 1909, la Société lance une vaste enquête auprès des enseignants des écoles secondaires.[48] Le rapport, approuvé par la *Société vaudoise des maîtres secondaires* et transmis au gouvernement cantonal, conclut que l'éducation sexuelle, "n'étant qu'une des formes de l'éducation générale", entre dans la mission confiée par l'Etat à l'école. Face à la négligence de nombreux parents à cet égard, l'Etat est légitimé à utiliser l'école "pour former des hommes et des femmes ... plus conscients de leurs responsabilités".[49] Le texte propose d'introduire "les lois de la propagation de la vie" dans le cours de sciences naturelles, ainsi qu'un cours spécial d'hygiène aux jeunes des deux sexes en fin de scolarité; à cet effet, une formation spéciale devrait être dispensée aux enseignants secondaires et primaires.

A Genève, aucun projet d'éducation sexuelle n'aboutit. Le contexte politique et les stratégies militantes expliquent cet échec, à commencer par la division sexuée des abolitionnistes. Des femmes se retrouvent au sein de l'*Association du Sou pour le relèvement moral* (fondée en 1889) pour récolter des fonds et diffuser les idées abolitionnistes. Leur revue *Feuilles volantes* maintient la séparation privé/public en matière sexuelle, en affirmant que l'éducation morale et sexuelle est une prérogative de la mère dans l'espace privé de la famille.[50] Des hommes abolitionnistes fondent en 1892 un parti politique (*Groupe national d'études et de réformes sociales*, une dissidence de la droite conservatrice), qui place des élus au parlement cantonal dès 1895 (un type d'action politique excluant les femmes). Ce parti essuie une cuisante défaite en 1896, lorsque les citoyens genevois refusent son projet de fermeture des maisons closes; l'affrontement s'inscrit dans la lutte entre conservateurs et radicaux au pouvoir et ces derniers se réjouissent de "l'écrasement du piétisme malfaisant".[51] Dès lors, les hommes du mouvement abolitionniste sont politiquement marginalisés et suscitent la méfiance des autorités cantonales en charge de l'instruction publique.

Dans le canton de Vaud en revanche, les abolitionnistes ont réussi à s'intégrer dans la conjoncture politique marquée dès 1892 par l'alliance des forces de droite (libéraux et radicaux) contre le Parti socialiste. Sur le terrain brûlant de la question sociale, les réformateurs moraux proposent des solutions réformistes bienvenues (juridiques, philanthropiques), à l'heure où les élites bourgeoises s'effraient des options révolutionnaires d'un mouvement ouvrier en pleine ascension.

---

[47]Cette expérience est facilitée par une large autonomie communale en matière scolaire. Dès 1906, la SVRM s'efforce de toucher la jeunesse ouvrière non scolarisée par des conférences à la Maison du peuple de Lausanne.
[48]La gratuité des écoles secondaires vaudoises (payantes à Genève) les rend plus accessibles aux enfants des classes moyennes et populaires. Ces écoles sont également mixtes dans la plupart des localités.
[49]Léon Robert, *L'Ecole a-t-elle un rôle à jouer dans l'éducation sexuelle? Rapport présenté à la Société vaudoise des maîtres secondaires en 1911* (Vevey: Klausfelder, 1911).
[50]Lydia Cuenca, *La société de la fin du 19e et du début du 20e sous le regard moralisateur d'une association féminine, l'Association du Sou* (mémoire de licence, Université de Genève, 1990).
[51]Alexandre Guillot, *L'Etat et la moralité publique* (Genève: Jeheber, 1896).

L'éducation sexuelle eugéniste en Suisse romande, une menace morale?

Une menace commune va contribuer à rapprocher les stratégies des réformateurs moraux vaudois et genevois. En 1907, la fondation du *Groupe néo-malthusien de Genève* porte sur le sol genevois et suisse la propagande en faveur du contrôle des naissances.[52] Le néo-malthusianisme, né en Grande-Bretagne, prône la limitation des naissances par les méthodes contraceptives, et s'écarte ainsi de la seule modération sexuelle et du mariage tardif préconisés par Malthus. En passant d'Angleterre en France, le mouvement prend une connotation anticapitaliste, antimilitariste, et s'engage dans la promotion et la vente de contraceptifs. Résolument féministe, il s'adresse aux ouvrières pour alléger leurs tâches, améliorer leur santé, et les munir d'une prévention efficace contre l'irresponsabilité sexuelle de certains hommes. Pour les néo-malthusiens, l'égalité des sexes passe par l'octroi aux femmes de moyens d'autonomie sexuelle, plutôt que par la seule responsabilisation des hommes. Par ailleurs, cette branche intègre une composante eugénique, le contrôle volontaire des naissances étant censé éviter la venue d'individus porteurs de "tares".[53]

Les thèses eugénistes sont vigoureusement défendues en Suisse par le Dr Auguste Forel. L'éminent psychiatre vaudois demeure très controversé en raison de sa libre-pensée et de son ouvrage *La Question sexuelle* (1905), qui connaît une diffusion internationale. Forel y décrit précisément les maladies vénériennes et tous les moyens de s'en protéger, de la continence au préservatif. Il avance une morale sexuelle audacieuse, présente la sexualité comme un facteur d'épanouissement, préconise le contrôle des naissances dans un but eugénique et se déclare partisan d'une éducation sexuelle précoce. A ses yeux, "si on habitue l'enfant à considérer innocemment les rapports sexuels comme quelque chose de tout naturel, ces derniers exciteront plus tard beaucoup moins sa curiosité et son érotisme".[54] Telle est l'option également défendue par *La Vie intime*, journal du *Groupe néo-malthusien de Genève*. Il juge l'éducation sexuelle particulièrement utile aux jeunes filles des classes populaires pour éviter les naissances illégitimes et les drames de l'avortement. Le journal organise des cours mixtes de physiologie sexuelle à l'intention des adultes, pour que les mères instruisent leurs filles, en attendant que "sur les bancs de l'école, des professeurs autorisés renseignent notre jeunesse sur le sujet".[55]

Ce féminisme néo-malthusien se révèle incompatible avec le féminisme abolitionniste: comment les femmes pourraient-elles moraliser les hommes si elles s'adonnent à une sexualité sans risque? Pour contrer la propagande néo-malthusienne, jugée immorale, les réformateurs moraux genevois s'allient aux conservateurs.[56] Effrayés par des thèses qu'ils assimilent à un encouragement à la licence, les réformateurs moraux de Vaud et Genève délaissent alors la promotion de l'éducation sexuelle pour combattre vigoureusement le néo-malthusianisme.

---

[52] Emmanuelle Allegra, *La propagande néo-malthusienne à Genève à travers son organe: la Vie intime (1908–1914)* (mémoire de licence, Université de Genève, 1996).
[53] Francis Ronsin, "Malthusianisme, néo-malthusianisme, birth control et planning familial, des oppositions plus politiques que morales," in *Démographie et politique*, ed. Hervé Le Bras (Dijon, France: Editions universitaires de Dijon, 1997), 67–79. Les néo-malthusiens refusent cependant les solutions eugénistes autoritaires.
[54] Auguste Forel, *La Morale sexuelle* (Lausanne: Editions de la Libre Pensée, 1907), 546.
[55] *La Vie intime* 8 (avril 1909): 2.
[56] Auguste de Morsier, député du *Groupe national* au parlement genevois, intervient contre les néo-malthusiens dans un projet de loi sur l'outrage à la morale publique. *Mémorial du Grand Conseil* (27 mai 1908), 1375–78.

Une instrumentalisation politique des sciences de l'enfant ?

Que pensent les enseignant(e)s romands de l'éducation sexuelle? A l'exception de l'enquête vaudoise déjà citée, ces milieux interviennent peu dans le débat avant la guerre. Mais au cours des années vingt, une controverse surgit dans *L'Educateur*, la revue des enseignants de la Suisse romande protestante, alors en étroite proximité avec l'Institut Jean-Jacques Rousseau de Genève.[57]

Cet échange oppose sur plusieurs numéros un enseignant vaudois et une collègue genevoise.[58] Le premier justifie l'éducation sexuelle à l'école et suggère un programme selon le modèle eugéniste, suscitant de vives critiques de la part de l'enseignante genevoise. Avant 17–18 ans, affirme-t-elle, l'initiation aux "mystères de la vie" doit être strictement individuelle; il faut laisser à la jeunesse "la possibilité de rester ignorante le plus longtemps possible" au lieu de stimuler précocement et dangereusement son imagination. Elle s'insurge contre des prémisses scientifiques et physiologiques "qui ravalent l'homme au rang des bêtes". Son projet consiste à fortifier chez les élèves la volonté et à leur insuffler un idéal de pureté morale, différencié selon le sexe: développer le respect de la femme chez les garçons, l'instinct maternel chez les filles. Son discours s'appuie sur des références scientifiques proches de l'Ecole nouvelle: Stanley Hall, pionnier américain de la psychologie de l'adolescence et hostile à toute instruction sexuelle collective, Frederick W. Foerster et Wilhelm Stekel, déjà mentionnés. Et c'est encore un argument propre à l'Ecole nouvelle qu'elle invoque pour dénier à l'école la capacité de donner un enseignement sexuel: dans un grand nombre de classes "règne encore la discipline militaire, très peu favorable à la culture morale, qui serait avantageusement remplacée par le self-gouvernement".

Ce même discours, appuyé sur la pédagogie et la psychologie, est repris à l'époque par un autre réseau qui entend monopoliser le débat sur l'éducation sexuelle et représenter la Suisse dans les congrès internationaux. Il s'agit du *Cartel romand d'hygiène sociale et morale*, une association faîtière qui regroupe dès 1918 tous les milieux intéressés "à la lutte contre l'immoralité" (abolitionnistes, sociétés contre le péril vénérien, contre les mauvaises lectures, l'alcoolisme, etc.).[59] Un objectif commun fédère les combats de ces nouveaux moralistes: soutenir la famille, menacée par l'individualisme, la dénatalité, l'avortement, les loisirs modernes, la décadence des mœurs. L'élargissement du réseau aux cantons catholiques est un indicateur supplémentaire de son orientation conservatrice.

Cette insistance nouvelle sur la vie de famille s'inscrit dans les inquiétudes liées à la dénatalité, qui relèguent au second plan le débat sur la prostitution ou la dégénérescence. Les résultats du recensement fédéral de 1920, attestant d'un recul marqué de la fécondité, sont commentés de manière catastrophiste aussi bien dans

---

[57]Hofstetter, *Genève*, 357–60.

[58]L'enseignant vaudois, Jules Laurent, est un orateur des conférences de district du corps enseignant vaudois de 1921, où le sujet de "l'attitude du maître en face des questions sexuelles" a été proposé par le Département de l'instruction publique. De sa collègue genevoise, on ne connaît que ses initiales (M.B.) et son célibat, avancé par un contradicteur pour suggérer de manière quelque peu blessante son incompétence. La controverse s'étend sur six ans: 29 octobre 1921, 7 janvier 1922, 24 avril 1922, 8 juillet 1922, 21 janvier 1924, 8 mars 1924, 22 mars 1924, 1er novembre 1924, 24 novembre 1924, 24 janvier 1925, 1er mai 1926, 14 août 1926, 15 septembre 1926, 9 juillet 1927.

[59]Geneviève Heller, "Psychiatrie et société: de quelques associations pour l'hygiène mentale, morale et sociale," *Revue historique vaudoise* 103 (1995): 115–37. La SVRM devient en 1921 la Société vaudoise de moralité publique et fusionne ensuite avec *Pro Familia*, ligue pour la protection de la famille.

les publications officielles,[60] que dans la presse romande de toute obédience. A cette question brûlante, le Cartel entend apporter une réponse avant tout morale, et observe avec une certaine méfiance l'évolution du monde médical à l'égard des questions sexuelles. Certains médecins affichent en effet une attitude plus pragmatique envers le péril vénérien: vulgariser des moyens préventifs individuels, inciter les malades à se soigner rapidement grâce à de nouveaux traitements efficaces en cas d'utilisation précoce, diffuser une large information, notamment par le biais de l'école. C'est la position défendue par le médecin genevois Charles Dubois:

> Grâce à l'instruction publique obligatoire, l'Etat peut atteindre chacun; il doit en profiter et faire bénéficier garçons et filles d'une éducation aussi complète que possible dans ce domaine. C'est tout un programme nouveau et spécial à intercaler dans le programme général des études. Réparti sur plusieurs années et bien établi, il aboutirait au résultat merveilleux de faire passer un examen de prophylaxie sociale et médicale à tout élève quittant les écoles.[61]

Que deviendrait l'éducation morale dans un tel programme? Ne risque-t-on pas de prendre acte de la "décadence des mœurs", alors qu'il faudrait engager une action énergique pour "assainir le climat moral" dans lequel grandissent les enfants? Les nouveaux moralistes du Cartel se méfient dès lors de l'éducation sexuelle à l'école publique, et légitiment leur attitude par la psychologie et la pédagogie. Dans les congrès internationaux, c'est en invoquant la critique de l'institution scolaire propre à l'Ecole nouvelle que les représentants du Cartel refusent l'éducation sexuelle scolaire:

> L'Ecole? Tant que le système d'éducation sera basé sur le seul accomplissement d'un programme d'enseignement, l'école ne pourra que fort peu de chose. Elle pourra enseigner la biologie du sexe ... elle pourra fort peu pour le fondement même de toute éducation sexuelle, la formation du caractère. Toute autre est la perspective de réussite dans les écoles nouvelles, les écoles de plein air, et partout où l'on cherche à sortir de l'ornière où s'est embourbée trop longtemps l'école officielle.[62]

Le rapprochement entre le *Cartel d'hygiène sociale et morale* et les pédagogues de l'Institut Jean-Jacques Rousseau est attesté par plusieurs indices. Les publications du Cartel sont régulièrement annoncées dans *L'Educateur*; son président, le juriste lausannois Maurice Veillard, y signe des articles, où il se déclare hostile à un enseignement sexuel obligatoire. Moralistes et pédagogues collaborent dans ce qui apparaît comme une parade à l'éducation sexuelle scolaire: l'organisation de cours de "pédagogie sexuelle" à l'intention des éducateurs: parents, enseignants, pasteurs, animateurs de sociétés de jeunesse, mais aussi les médecins, invités à se familiariser avec les sciences de l'enfant. En 1929, sous l'égide de *Pro Juventute* et de la *Société pédagogique romande*, le Cartel organise un tel cours à Lausanne. Le professeur Bovet figure parmi les intervenants et *L'Educateur* en propose un long compte-rendu. Selon ce texte, les objectifs consistent à aider les éducateurs à éclairer les

---

[60] Anne-Françoise Praz, *De l'enfant utile à l'enfant précieux* (Lausanne: Antipodes, 2005), 337–40.
[61] Charles Du Bois, "Du rôle de l'Etat dans la lutte contre les maladies vénériennes," Rapport présenté à la réunion des Directeurs sanitaires suisses, Berne, 5 juin 1921, *Revue médicale de la Suisse romande* 41 (1921): 535.
[62] Robert Chable, "Sur l'éducation sexuelle," in *Congrès international de propagande d'hygiène sociale et d'éducation prophylactique sanitaire et morale, Paris, 24–27 mai 1923* (Paris, 1923), 339.

jeunes de manière individualisée, mais également à susciter parmi les adultes un consensus "quant aux points essentiels d'une morale sexuelle".

Dans ce credo conservateur et familialiste, la question de l'égalité des sexes, à l'horizon des réformateurs moraux d'avant-guerre, disparaît. Est-ce en raison de l'échec des votations cantonales sur le suffrage féminin en 1919–1920 (Zurich, Bâle et Genève) que certaines féministes réorientent leur action? Dans ses brochures et conférences, Emma Pieczynska, très engagée en faveur de l'éducation sexuelle scolaire avant la guerre,[63] se concentre sur l'éducation sociale de l'instinct maternel, à l'instar de sa communication au Congrès international d'éducation morale de Genève (1922). Elle n'est pas la seule, dans ces enceintes internationales, à assimiler l'éducation sexuelle des jeunes filles à l'éducation maternelle. La contribution des pédagogues à cette insistance sur la différence des sexes mériterait une analyse plus approfondie. Cette sexuation est très marquée dans les conférences de Pierre Bovet et dans ses cours à l'Institut Rousseau sur l'éducation sexuelle. Il invite à faire appel chez le jeune homme à son courage, son sentiment chevaleresque, familial et patriotique; pour la jeune fille, il s'agit de recourir à son sentiment maternel et à "l'instinct de plaire" qui peut avoir des fins très hautes: "développer en soi les qualités qu'apprécieraient un homme dont elle voudrait pour le père de ses enfants".[64]

Conclusion

Cette histoire de l'éducation sexuelle montre l'intérêt de combiner les différentes échelles d'observation pour comprendre les décalages entre les discours et leur mise en œuvre. La concrétisation des idées émises au niveau transnational dépend en effet surtout des contraintes et opportunités locales. Ceci est particulièrement vérifiable pour la Suisse: même des cantons voisins relevant des mêmes langue et culture religieuse (Vaud et Genève) n'offrent pas les mêmes possibilités.

Sur la question des savoirs disciplinaires, plusieurs mécanismes sont observables. Certains groupes professionnels s'emparent du thème de l'éducation sexuelle pour promouvoir un savoir dont ils maîtrisent le maniement. Telle est la stratégie des médecins vénérologues, initiateurs des premiers congrès internationaux; telle est celle des médecins eugénistes, avec une approche basée sur les sciences de la nature. De même, les psychologues et pédagogues de l'Ecole nouvelle motivent l'injonction à la continence juvénile en invoquant la nature du développement psycho-sexuel de l'enfant, légitimée scientifiquement par la nouvelle psychologie de l'adolescence. En revanche, la faiblesse des réformateurs moraux du début du siècle et des nouveaux moralistes d'après-guerre réside dans leur incapacité à générer une théorie qui leur soit propre, les obligeant à se référer à d'autres disciplines.

Toutefois, cette faiblesse est compensée par leur capacité à s'inscrire dans les préoccupations sociopolitiques du moment. Car l'affirmation de certains savoirs ne relève pas seulement des réseaux professionnels et scientifiques capables de les promouvoir. Elle est tout aussi est aussi dépendante du contexte historique qui favorise telle approche, en fonction de sa capacité à répondre aux inquiétudes des élites.

---

[63] Emma Pieczynska, *Education sexuelle. Le rôle de l'école* (Saint-Blaise, Switzerland: Foyer solidariste, 1910).
[64] Pierre Bovet, *Le pasteur et l'éducation sexuelle de la jeunesse. Notes pédagogiques* (Lausanne: Secrétariat romand d'hygiène sociale et morale, 1921), 24–6. Archives de l'Institut Jean-Jacques Rousseau, Bovet B.I. – dossier semestre d'hiver 31–32, Education sexuelle (le dossier contient aussi des pièces issues du même cours donné les années précédentes).

Dans l'après-guerre, lorsque les questions de reproduction sont dominées par le souci de dénatalité, les nouveaux moralistes conservateurs parviennent à présenter la défense des valeurs familiales comme une solution adéquate. Ils sont à la recherche d'une légitimation scientifique étayant la primauté de la famille sur l'Etat et du privé sur le public dans certains domaines sensibles. La critique de l'éducation sexuelle par certains psychologues, également soucieux de limiter l'emprise des médecins sur l'école, constitue un recours utile. C'est ainsi que les tendances idéologiques les plus traditionnelles de l'Ecole nouvelle sont sollicitées. Sans surprise, elles sont également les plus conservatrices en matière de rapports sociaux de sexe, assimilant l'éducation sexuelle des jeunes filles à l'éducation maternelle et la coéducation à la préservation morale des jeunes hommes. Cette réflexion suggère tout l'intérêt d'une analyse genrée de l'Education nouvelle qui reste à l'agenda de prochaines recherches.

Braille, amma and integration: the hybrid evolution of education for the blind in Taiwan, 1870s–1970s

Tasing Chiu

Department of Medical Sociology and Social Work, Kaohsiung Medical University, Kaohsiung, Taiwan

Industrialisation and mass education have long been considered two main determinants in the emergence of special education, but in many formerly colonised countries, such as Taiwan, historical development did not follow along these lines. In Taiwan, schools for the blind were initially set up by missionaries and colonisers, and were primarily designed to meet the latter's preconceptions and needs. However, pedagogic knowledge and techniques were unexpectedly displaced and transformed as they crossed borders. This study examines the emergence and development of education for the blind in Taiwan from the 1870s to the 1970s. Documentary sources, government statistics and proclamations and oral histories were used in the analysis; they reveal how in Taiwan, education for the blind was shaped under different foreign and domestic influences within specific historical–social contexts.

In the middle decades of the eighteenth century, special education emerged in a number of western nations. Industrialisation brought dramatic social changes and efficient and cost-effective labour became the norm. As a result, people with disabilities were unable to make a living by traditional means. They became special members of mass education systems under which they could, depending on one's view, gain access to literacy and numeracy so as to develop their human potential, or be socially set aside and kept out of the way. The human potential perspective assumed that special education was underpinned by humanitarian values that could enlighten disabled students.[1] It also reflected an historical shift in western social attitudes towards a growing acceptance of disabled people's developmental potential. The social control perspective, on the contrary, regarded special education as a strategy to ensure order and stability both inside and outside educational institutions.[2] According to this view, as compulsory education became a reality in the 1890s in western countries, those deemed to be unfit for the regular education system were to

---

[1] Felicity Armstrong, "The Historical Development of Special Education: Humanitarian Rationality or 'Wild Profusion of Entangled Events'?," *History of Education* 31, no. 5 (2002): 437–56.
[2] Ted Cole, "The History of Special Education: Social Control or Humanitarian Progress?," *British Journal of Special Education* 17 (1990): 101–7.

be sent to special education. Thus, mass education would run smoothly by keeping atypical students from interfering with the education of their peers in ordinary schools.³ This view emphasised the utility of special education in meeting the interests of professionals and "normal" people rather than those of the disabled.

Yet missionaries and colonial settlers exported the ideas of special education and set up schools for the disabled in non-western societies long before the beginnings of industrialisation or mass education. Missionary and colonial government records regarding the "birth" of special education in these societies usually begin with statements about the "barbaric" treatment of the disabled, followed by mention of the benevolent works done by missionaries or colonisers. Thus, disability functioned as a representative borderline between the limitless potentialities of the colonisers and the inevitable suffering and limited existence available in the colonised societies prior to colonial intervention.⁴ Special education practitioners would then provide colonised countries with a channel through which to perpetuate the paternalistic hierarchy between underdeveloped and developed nations. Furthermore, the contemporary literature documenting the emergence of special education tends to concentrate on pedagogic ideas, practices, programmes and instruments, within the assumption that more provision equals progress. However, the dichotomy of coloniser/colonised was elastic⁵ and pedagogic knowledge and techniques were often transferred through discontinuous and multilateral processes which frequently transcended territorial borders, not subject to the control of any sort of governmental jurisdiction.⁶ According to Werner and Zimmerman's approach, known as *histoire croisée*, all elements of society are affected by their coming into contact with each other, although not necessarily in the same manner, and they could also affect their local or remote environment and manifest themselves at a later moment. Accordingly, objects of research should be considered not merely in relation to one another but also through one another, in terms of relationships, interactions and circulation.⁷ This is the approach followed here. The study uses documentary sources, including missionary records, government statistics and proclamations and oral histories, to reconstruct the development of education for the blind in Taiwan between 1870s to the 1970s.

Chinese Braille invented by British missionaries

In the early nineteenth century western colonial expansion occurred at the same time as an evangelical revival in Britain, leading to a dramatic rise in overseas missionary

---

³Sally Tomlinson, "The Radical Structuralist View of Special Education and Disability: Unpopular Perspectives on Their Origins and Development," in *Disability and Democracy: Reconstructing (Special) Education for Postmodernity*, ed., Thomas M. Skrtic (New York: Teachers College Press, 1995), 122–34.
⁴Michelle Jarman, "Resisting 'Good Imperialism': Reading Disability as Radical Vulnerability," *Atenea* 25, no. 1 (2005): 107–16.
⁵Hiroko Matsuda, "Becoming Japanese in the Colony: Okinawan Migrants in Colonial Taiwan," *Cultural Studies* 26, no. 5 (2012): 688–709.
⁶Gabriela Ossenback and Maria del Mar del Pozo, "Postcolonial Models, Cultural Transfers and Transnational Perspectives in Latin America: A Research Agenda," *Paedagogica Historica* 47, no. 5 (2011): 579–600.
⁷Michael Werner and Bénédicte Zimmermann, "Beyond Comparison: Histoire Croisée and the Challenge of Reflexivity," *History and Theory* 45, no. 1 (2006): 30–50.

activity. The Protestant Churches of Scotland accelerated their involvement in attempts to spread the Christian message to Africa, India and China.[8] William Campbell (1841–1921), a Scottish Presbyterian missionary, thus began his mission in southern Taiwan in 1871 and was stationed in Tainan. His account tells of a great number of Taiwanese suffering from ophthalmia, and many nearly blind from want of proper treatment.[9] Since native doctors could not heal these eye diseases, many people turned to westerners for the preservation or restoration of their eyesight. Missionary medical work, like educational projects, was not merely philanthropic but also effective in spreading the gospel. Such work brought the missionary into contact with many people and provided potential for the development of a wide sphere of influence. Blind and vision-impaired patients who visited the mission hospitals were encouraged to learn to read embossed books of scriptures.[10] Campbell noted the means of livelihood of the Chinese blind:

> [T]he blind in China seem to be mostly engaged as beggars or as fortune-tellers. Some gain a living at pounding rice, or in treading the water-wheels which are used for purposes of irrigation, and I know one man who supports himself by making and repairing baskets. I think the beggars are the most numerous class, and their lot is certainly a very unenviable one.[11]

In 1891, Campbell started a school in Tainan called "Training Blind Hall" (訓瞽堂) to provide courses such as tactile reading, writing, counting and vocational training for the blind (see Figure 1). At that time, the British education system for the blind was quite distinct from its counterparts on the Continent. The French system, for example, offered a broad range of literary texts, whereas the British system consisted in excessive hours of training for a trade.[12] Campbell's approach was closer to the British view; he noted that skills in reading, writing and arithmetic would not help the blind to make a living.[13]

In order to create jobs for the blind and to prevent them from being burdens to their families, he proposed to train them to make handicrafts such as strings and cords, straw-sandals, fish-nets, little baskets and shoes.[14] The courses Campbell offered were similar to those offered by other western missionaries at the time. Since these jobs could hardly be considered a great improvement on the choices already

---

[8]Susan Thorne, *Congregational Missions and the Making of an Imperial Culture in Nineteenth-Century England* (Stanford, CA: Stanford University Press, 1999).
[9]Author Unknown, "Formosa—Missionaries," *The Messenger and Missionary Record* (September 2, 1872): 204.
[10]William Gauld, "Medical Missions," *The Messenger and Missionary Record* (October 1, 1877): 247; Author Unknown, "Formosa—From Dr. Matthew Dickson," *The Messenger and Missionary Record* (August 2, 1875): 198; George Ede, "Story of the Blind Hospital-Porter in Taiwanfoo," *The Messenger and Missionary Record* (December 1, 1887): 6; William Campbell, "Formosa: A Survey," *The Monthly Messenger* (October 1898): 268.
[11]William Campbell, *An Account of Missionary Success in the Island of Formosa* (London: Trübner & Co., 1889), 654–5.
[12]Simon Hayhoe, *God, Money, and Politics: English Attitudes to Blindness and Touch, from the Enlightenment to Integration* (Charlotte, NC: Information Age Publishing, 2008).
[13]William Campbell, *Sketches from Formosa* (1915; repr., Taipei, Taiwan: SMC, 1996), 259.
[14]There is little record showing who taught the blind handicrafts or how to teach craft-making. Since it was unlikely that missionaries did either, it is very possible that local craftspeople were paid to teach in the beginning. See William Hanks Levy, *Blindness and the Blind: Or, A Treatise on the Science of Typhlology* (London: Chapman and Hall, 1872).

Figure 1. A teacher and students in Training Blind Hall. The man sitting at the table was Lim-Ang, teacher of the Blind School. In-a and Chhun-á, on either side of him, were knitting. Toa-in, second from the teacher on the left, was reading a book. Khe, second from the teacher on the right, was doing sums on a board. He used pins stuck into the board instead of a pencil. Ki-ko, with the turban, on the extreme right, was making nets with string; Chhin-á, with the wooden frame before him, was plaiting grass into shoes. See George Ede, "Formosa: Blind Chhin-A," *Our Own Missions*, 1895, 60–2.
Note: Image courtesy of Church History Committee of the Presbyterian Church in Taiwan.

available, the blind went to missionary school at great cost, for they had to relinquish the most profitable part of their profession – namely, fortune-telling and legend chanting – as both were considered idolatrous and superstitious and could interfere with Sunday-keeping.[15] Therefore, the ability to read became the chief attraction of schools for the blind.

> The boys in our school can make a very good firm shoe, but they are still rather slow at the process to depend on it entirely. So far our experience inclines us to favour knitting as a means of livelihood for the Chinese blind. It has this good feature that it preserves the sensitiveness of the touch for reading, and it is quite as remunerative as any of the other handicrafts we have experimented with.[16]

Scotland, where Campbell came from, was a nation more concerned with popular education than England was at that time, and Scottish philanthropists felt a strong

---

[15] Mary Darley, *Cameos of a Chinese City* (London: Church of England Zenana Missionary Society, 1917).
[16] William Campbell, "Formosa," *Our Own Missions* (1895): 255.

impulse to provide the sightless with direct access to God's word through raised print.[17] In Europe there were at least 20 different forms of raised print in use, and five distinct systems were in everyday use in British institutions. Of these, at least eight different versions of tactile types were introduced to China in the nineteenth century.[18] In 1842, Agnes Gutzlaff (1836–1869), a Chinese-native blind girl named after her missionary benefactor, was sent to England to be educated.[19] After her return to China in 1956, she started to teach the blind how to read Lucas Type, then Moon script, a system suited to the hardened fingers of the manual worker and older blind people.[20] William Moon, the inventor of Moon script, also adapted his alphabet to different Chinese dialects.[21] Braille, which took up less space and was suitable for musical notation and mathematics, was introduced later but became widespread towards the end of the nineteenth century.

> The simplicity of Braille's system, superimposed upon the phonetic spelling of the vernacular, is striking as compared with the complexity and abstruseness of the native Chinese written language. The latter offers the gravest difficulty even to those who see; while a little blind boy in [blind] school, who had only been there a week, was already, with the most joyous face, spelling out simple words in the adapted Braille spelling-book.[22]

To many of the western missionaries, the Chinese characters appeared to be an instrument in the hands of the ruling classes to oppress the people and keep them away from the Christian faith.[23] The "complexity and abstruseness" of the native Chinese written language offered the gravest difficulty not only to the blind, but also to those who could see. To link the Chinese language with Braille would be a very arduous task because the Chinese language is written using tens of thousands of characters that cannot be represented by the 63 possible combinations of dots used in six-dot Braille. William Hill Murray (1843–1911), a Scottish missionary stationed in Beijing (then known as Peking), created a "numeral-type" system which "brailled" all of the 408 syllables of Mandarin. It was hoped that the system would increase Chinese literacy for both blind and sighted people by using the same symbols – embossed dots for the blind and printed outlines of dots in black for the sighted. It took between six weeks and two months for the blind to be acquainted with both reading and writing under this system, while the average person took six years or more to recognise distinct characters in the ordinary Chinese writing system.[24] After learning this reading system, the blind could become teachers for

---

[17]John Oliphant, "Touching the Light: The Invention of Literacy for the Blind," *Paedagogica Historica* 44, no. 2 (2008): 67–82.
[18]Author Unknown, "The Blind in China," *The Chinese Recorder* (May 1889): 220.
[19]Author Unknown, "London Society for Teaching the Blind to Read," *The Illustrated London News* (1842): 129.
[20]Levy, *Blindness and the Blind;* William Moon, *Light for the Blind: A History of the Origin and Success of Moon's System of Reading (Embossed in Various Languages) for the Blind* (London: Longmans & Co., 1877).
[21]John Rutherfurd, *William Moon, LL.D., F.R.G.S., F.S.A., and His Work for the Blind* (London: Hodder and Stoughton, 1898).
[22]Author Unknown, "New from Our Own Missions," *The Monthly Messenger of the Presbyterian Church of England* (July 1, 1893): 157–8.
[23]Elisabeth Kaske, *The Politics of Language in Chinese Education, 1895–1919* (Leiden, Netherlands and Boston: Brill, 2008).
[24]Author Unknown, "The Blind in China," *The Chinese Recorder* (May 1889): 219–20.

both the sighted and the sightless. Advocates of Murray's system claimed that "the Chinese all have a natural liking for numerals"[25] and suggested the system could "open the doors to 150,000,000 secluded Chinese women".[26] Nevertheless, the typical missionary stationed in southern China was teaching the illiterate lower classes in a local dialect, for which Murray's numeral system might not have been suitable, because the number of sounds in southern dialects was much greater than that in Mandarin.[27] Amoy, highly similar to "Taiwanese" (Hokkien – the language of Fujian Province, China, the ancestral home of most Taiwanese), was the first Chinese subdialect to be systematically Romanised. This script had been widely utilised for the Bible and other Christian texts. The alphabetic method of phonetically adapting Braille to the Chinese language was thus preferred by missionaries in Taiwan as well as southern China.[28]

Education for the blind, for many western missionaries, referred to notions of social equity where all citizens should have access to literacy, as well as the possibility of studying further if they showed the talent. Yet Braille literacy for the blind was not quite the same thing as literacy for the sighted. For one thing, Braille readers could not create written documents readable by sighted people, which created a communication barrier between blind and sighted. Moreover, the blind could not even write their full name to sign a document – a basic criterion of literacy for the sighted.[29] Opportunities for further study and employment for the blind in Taiwan were also limited at that time. While a wider range of secular literature had been made available in the USA, France and Belgium, the greater share of British teaching materials comprised religious texts.[30] Many of the blind in Taiwan who were acquainted with Braille could only be put in charge of a missionary school or in service of a church. Blind students were often in charge of preparing stereotype plates and Braille books of scriptures, which were sent to blind readers in different parts of the country.[31] Campbell occasionally took one or two of the blind pupils to read the scriptures as a form of open-air preaching, because "the sight of a blind man reading a book is no doubt an evangelizing agency".[32] Some blind school graduates were stationed in

---

[25] C.F. Gordon Cumming, *The Inventor of the Numeral-Type for China by the Use of Which Illiterate Chinese Both Blind and Sighted Can Very Quickly be Taught to Read and Write Fluently* (London: Downey, 1899).
[26] Author Unknown, "The Blind in China," *The Chinese Recorder* (May 1889): 221.
[27] There were 408 sounds in Mandarin but there were 846 sounds in Amoy. See William Campbell, *The Blind in China: A Criticism of Miss C.F. Gordon-Cumming's Advocacy of the Murray Non-Alphabetic Method of Writing Chinese with Additional Remarks* (London: Sampson Low, Marston & Co., 1897), 1–3.
[28] The dispute between the "alphabetic method" and the "numeral method" went on for years and was eventually brought to the second General Missionary Conference convened at Shanghai in 1890, but was not totally settled.
[29] R.A. Houston, "The Development of Literacy: Northern England, 1640–1750," *The Economic History Review* 35, no. 2 (1982): 199–216.
[30] John Oliphant, "Touching the Light: The Invention of Literacy for the Blind," *Paedagogica Historica* 44, no.1–2 (2008): 67–82.
[31] Author Unknown, "The Gospel in China," *The Monthly Messenger of the Presbyterian Church of England* (May 1, 1892): 7; George Ede, "Formosa: Blind Chhin-A," *Our Own Missions* (1895): 61.
[32] George Ede, "Story of the Blind Hospital-Porter in Taiwanfoo," *The Messenger and Missionary Record* (December 1, 1887): 7.

hospitals to speak to patients and get them to join the worship.[33] In response to their limited options, some blind men probably took up their old professions, such as fortune-telling and legend chanting, after several years in Braille institutions.[34]

Japanese amma intermixed with western anatomy

After Japan's victory over China in 1894–1895, Taiwan became a colony of the Empire of Japan. In 1887, Training Blind Hall was closed following financial difficulties and turmoil at the beginning of Japanese occupation. In order to re-open the blind school and continue his missionary work, Campbell was open to collaboration with the Japanese colonial government. In the early days of Japanese colonial rule, little was done to curtail western missionary activities among the Chinese population. Christian schools and hospitals posed little challenge to the Japanese colonial government or its policies at that time, and missionaries did not publicise the negative aspects of colonial rule in their reports.[35] Relations between foreign missionaries and the Japanese Government-General in Taiwan thus remained good for the most part until the mid-1930s, when Japan joined the Axis.

In 1900, Campbell took advantage of a holiday to travel to Japan. After visiting Tokyo School for the Blind and Deaf-Mutes, Campbell received an invitation from Count Kabayama Sukenori (樺山資紀, 1837–1922), then the Japanese Minister of Education and the first Governor-General of colonial Taiwan, to confer with him about continuing work for the blind in Taiwan. Later that year, the Tainan County magistrate arranged for the Tainan Cihui Institute (慈惠院), a private welfare organisation, to re-open Campbell's blind school. Mr. Akiyama Enzou (秋山衍三) from the Mission Middle School was appointed as the first headmaster of the blind school. Enzou himself was a Christian, so the lady missionaries were free to go down to the blind school to give Bible lessons or to teach Christian hymns after school hours.[36] The Christian blind students were able to attend their nearest place of worship. In 1905, the Tainan Cihui Institute Curriculum for the Blind (臺南慈惠院盲生教育規程) was issued, establishing a five-year general curriculum and a three-year skill-based curriculum teaching students morality, Japanese, physical education, singing and amma. In 1922, the Tainan State School for the Vision- and Hearing-Impaired (臺南州立盲啞學校) was established, providing general vocational education (including acupuncture, moxibustion, massage and electrotherapy) for people with visual and hearing deficits, and also teaching skills necessary in daily life (see Figure 2). Another major school for the blind, the Taipei State School for the Visually and Hearing Impaired (臺北州立盲啞學校), was established in 1928. The school was organised into departments for the vision-impaired and for the hearing-impaired. Both schools had a six-year general

---

[33] Author Unknown, "Formosa," *The Monthly Messenger of the Presbyterian Church of England* (August 1, 1892): 7.
[34] Homer S. Wong, "The Work Done by and for the Blind in China," *The China Critic* (April 2, 1936): 12–7.
[35] A. Hamish Ion, "Missions and Empires: A Case Study of Canadians in the Japanese Empire, 1895–1941," in *Canadian Missionaries, Indigenous Peoples: Representing Religion at Home and Abroad*, ed., Alvyn Austin and Jamie S. Scott (Canada: University of Toronto, 2005), 177–202.
[36] Campbell, *Sketches from Formosa*, 257.

Figure 2. Amma training in the Tainan State School for the Vision- and Hearing-Impaired, 1920s.
Note: Authorisation for use of image provided by National Central Library, Taiwan.

curriculum, a two- to five-year handicrafts curriculum and a specialised curriculum of two to three years.

Although manual treatment of the body had been found all over the world since ancient times, Japan was the first society in which the blind monopolised a massage speciality, amma.[37] Theories and practice of Japanese amma, which originated from China,[38] were quite different from those in modern orthodox western medicine. Japanese traditional amma focused on maintaining a proper flow of "energy" ("ki" in Japanese) through the body, and the task of the practitioners was to help the patient achieve a balance of this "energy" in the body.[39] Blind amma practitioners were regarded as medical practitioners, and the majority of Japanese indulged in amma for relief of fatigue and to cure illness. Rich and poor alike were served by the blind masseur/masseuse, such that even the smallest village could boast one.[40] Thus, amma has long been considered one of the most effective and important

---

[37] Author Unknown, "Medicine in Japan," *The British Medical Journal* (June 11, 1887): 1292; Author Unknown, "The Portrayal of the Blind in Japan," *The British Medical Journal* (February 9, 1913): 301.
[38] 肖永芝, "日本古代針灸醫學源流概論," 中國針灸 5 (1999): 309–12.
[39] UA Casal, "Acupuncture, Cautery and Massage in Japan," Folklore Studies 21 (1962): 221–35.
[40] Author Unknown, "Massage by the Blind," *The British Medical Journal* (November 10, 1906): 1322; Author Unknown, "The Portrayal of the Blind in Japan," *The British Medical Journal* (February 8, 1913): 301.

means by which the blind in Japan have been able to achieve occupational independence.[41]

Campbell frowned on the amma courses included in the blind schools because he thought Taiwanese knew little about amma, and there were comparatively few Japanese residents living in Taiwan at the time.[42] Although some amma practitioners were able to obtain fairly good fees, continuous graduation from the Tainan Blind School would soon bring about serious changes – i.e. oversupply – in the practice.[43] Moreover, Campbell thought that only boys would be able to start their own businesses; blind girls who had finished the four-year course might still struggle to make a living as masseuses. However, schools for the blind did provide their students with a better chance to learn Japanese, so Campbell suggested that local governments hire blind graduates as interpreters for public offices in Taiwan, but this suggestion was not adopted.[44] According to the Taiwan Household Survey conducted in 1905, agriculture was the main source of revenue for the blind in Taiwan. The majority of the blind (60.1%) were engaged in agriculture, with 10.1% in technical industries and 7.8% in trade, while 2.4% were unoccupied. Compared to the high unemployment rate in western countries at the time,[45] the unemployment rate of the blind in Taiwan was relatively low. There was little pressure for the Japanese colonial government to worry about the blind. It did not nationalise blind schools until 20 years after its occupation of Taiwan. As Taipei (then Taihoku-shi) developed into a modern city, professionals and unskilled or semi-skilled migrants flocked into certain areas of Taiwan, an Outer Territory, from places just within the Japanese Inner Territory (内地).[46] In the 1930s, Japanese migrants accounted for 29.27% of the total population of Taipei. The large number of Japanese settlers and seasonal migrants resulted in a huge increase in the demand for amma, and gradually changed the vocational pattern of the blind in cities of Taiwan.

Although Campbell disagreed with the inclusion of amma courses in blind schools in Taiwan, the idea of blind massage training had already reached Europe. In the early nineteenth century, Dutch medicine became widely accepted in Japan, and both acupuncturists and doctors tried to study Dutch medical books. Knowledge of anatomy and physiology from the west started to be incorporated into the system of Japanese amma. At the same time, Japanese amma and acupuncture were introduced into Europe via Holland.[47] Massage did not become popular in England until the 1880s, owing to the influence of Swedish medical gymnasts and masseurs. For those unused to intimate physical contact, massage was a highly sensual

---

[41]中山太郎, 日本盲人史 (東京市: 昭和書房, 1934).

[42]By 1904, those of Chinese origin numbered over 2,800,000, aborigines about 135,000 and Japanese officials and colonists, excluding the military, some 50,000.

[43]Campbell, *Sketches from Formosa*, 259–60.

[44]Campbell, "Formosa: A Survey," *The Monthly Messenger* (October 1898): 268; Author Unknown, "Work for the Blind: Formosa," *The Presbyterian Messenger* (March 1915): 98.

[45]For example Occupation Census of the Blind in England and Wales, which reported an unemployment rate for the blind as high as 84.5% in 1851.

[46]Hiroko Matsuda, "Becoming Japanese in the Colony: Okinawan Migrants in Colonial Taiwan," *Cultural Studies* 26, no. 5 (2012): 688–709.

[47]Akiko Kobayashi, Miwa Uefuji and Washiro Yasumo, "History and Progress of Japanese Acupuncture," *eCAM* 7, no. 3 (2010): 359–65.

experience.[48] In 1894, an editorial titled "Immoral 'massage' establishment" published by the *British Medical Journal* implied that many masseurs and masseuses were simply using massage as a euphemism for prostitution. This report led to widespread interest in massage practices on the part of the national press in England. The Society of Trained Masseuses (STM) was formed in response to massage scandals and established a clear practice model for massage which effectively regulated the sensual elements of contact between therapist and patient. In 1900, the Committee of Gardner's Trust for the Blind started to consider the desirability of taking steps to organise the work of "massage" by the blind in England.[49] In 1901, Tadasu Yoshimoto (好本督), a pioneer of services for the blind in Japan,[50] visited Europe and published an article introducing blind massage to westerners.[51] In 1906, an experiment was carried out by Eggebrecht at Leipzig, Germany, teaching massage to blind pupils. A capable sightless man or woman, once trained, could earn nearly enough to make a comfortable living.[52] In 1918 the British Masseurs Union was established, and with it also a school training blind and partially sighted people as masseurs. In 1934, the school opened a clinic, where blind masseurs could gain work practice and a reputation among the general public.[53]

In the colonial period, education in Taiwan was mostly carried out in the Japanese language, with the goal of having the colonised abandon their mother culture and adopt that of their colonial rulers. Although Japanese writing includes Kanji (Chinese characters), the standardised syllabary written in Kana (the phonetic scripts of Katakana and Hiragana) obviated the need to attempt to introduce Japanese into Braille using Kanji.[54] Therefore books featuring raised characters for the blind were mostly in Kana.[55] While Japanese Braille, tenji (点字), was taught in schools for the blind, Amoy Braille continued to be used in missionary churches and schools. Missionaries thought that in this way the local people would better understand their evangelical messages. With help from Westminster College Missionary Society, Campbell continued his outdoor mission to the blind by providing Christian books and corresponding with them or visiting them in their own homes. Campbell issued an Amoy vernacular periodical in raised type to supply blind readers in Taiwan and mainland China with Church news and Christian instruction.[56] While Amoy Braille was only available for the Bible, Japanese Braille opened a gateway for the blind to a wide range of knowledge with relatively

---

[48]David A. Nicholls and Julianne Cheek, "Physiotherapy and the Shadow of Prostitution: The Society of Trained Masseuses and the Massage Scandals of 1894," *Social Science & Medicine* 62 (2006): 2336–48.
[49]Editor, "Notes," *The Blind: Occasional Paper*, no. 11 (July 20, 1900): 188.
[50]森田昭二, "近代盲人福祉の先覚者好本督—『真英国』と『日英の盲人』を中心に," 人間福祉学研究 2, no. 1 (2009): 61–72.
[51]Tadasu Yoshimoto, "Massage by the Blind in Japan," *The Blind: Occasional Paper*, no. 16 (October 19, 1901): 292–3.
[52]Author Unknown, "Massage by the Blind," *The British Medical Journal* (November 10, 1906): 1322.
[53]A. Lee, "Physiotherapy," *RNIB, Royal National Institute of the Blind*. New Beacon, June, 78 (1994): 921.
[54]宮村健二, "視覚障害者と漢字," 筑波技術短期大学テクノルポート 1 (1994): 1–3.
[55]Author Unknown, "The Deaf and Dumb and Blind in Japan," *The Chinese Recorder* (January 1889): 34.
[56]William Campbell, "Work for the Blind: Formosa," *The Presbyterian Messenger* (March 1915): 97.

abundant Japanese translations. After the Meiji restoration, a political and social revolution in 1866–1869, Japan's growing acceptance of western medicine led to the adoption of western massage, anatomy and physiology in blind schools, while retaining traditional Chinese meridian theory and meridian points.[57] Since there was no concept of physical therapy, massage was done by blind amma practitioners in community hospitals. Opening to western civilisation also led to rapid social and economic changes, with the result that some sighted people sought to become involved in occupations hitherto monopolised by the blind. In Tokyo, in the early twentieth century, half of all shampooers and masseurs were already sighted people.[58] Even so, according to sources of oral history, many blind people in Taiwan were already making a decent living by performing amma and acupuncture at the end of the Japanese colonial period.

UNESCO funding and AFOB advisors

In 1945 Japan, having been defeated in the Second World War, was forced to cede all overseas possessions, including Taiwan. Chinese Braille started to be used in blind schools but Japanese colonial-era education policies and vocational courses, for the most part, continued to be followed for a number of years. Schoolteachers were recruited from among blind school graduates, and vocational teaching materials were adapted directly from those of the Japanese colonial period. Although blind people were largely employed as fortune-tellers in traditional Chinese societies, this trade was regarded as superstition and forbidden by the Chinese Nationalist Government in 1929. Thus, even though the monopoly of amma had been removed from the blind in Japan since the early twentieth century, after moving from China to Taiwan the Chinese Nationalist Government reserved it for the blind; this resulted in the stabilisation of massage as a major vocation for the blind in postwar Taiwan.

From the 1950s onwards, the medical system and educational policies in Taiwan were influenced greatly by developments in America. With the outbreak of the Korean War, the China Aid Act and the Chinese-American Joint Commission on Rural Reconstruction were put in place to ensure that Taiwan would not succumb to Communist forces. As the poliomyelitis epidemic also broke out in the 1950s, care for children who had become ill and survived the epidemic led to a strong demand for physical therapy. American aid and United States Military Advisory members thus contributed to the initial development of the physical therapy profession in Taiwan. Moreover, many spouses of United States Military Advisory members served as physical therapists to these children, and offered training courses to meet the requirements of local physical therapy personnel.

The emergence of physical therapy as a profession changed the fate of the Taiwanese blind. In 1957, the government of Taiwan started to limit the range of clinical practice conducted by the blind. In 1967, a law recognising rehabilitation therapy was enacted as part of a statute for the new allied health profession. Medical

---

[57] Nozomi Donoyama, "Introduction of Traditional Japanese Massage, Amma, and its Education for the Visually Impaired, the Past and the Present," *TCT Education of Disability* 3, no. 1 (2004): 41–7.
[58] International Conference on the Blind, "Past, Present, and Future of the Blind in Japan," *Report of the Second Triennial International Conference on the Blind and Exhibition* (Manchester, UK: "Guardian" Printing Works, 1908), 174–81.

courses in schools for the blind were cancelled in the same year, and work limitations were further added for blind masseurs and masseuses.

Many of Europe's essential services for the blind had been disrupted and needed reconstruction after the Second World War. In the 1960s, as egalitarian and humanist ideology created a new climate in the US, the educational integration of students with disabilities became the central theme of special education.[59] At the invitation of the United Nations Children's Fund (UNICEF), the American Foundation for Overseas Blind (AFOB), which was reborn from the American Braille Press, began the practice of assigning on-the-spot consultants to countries in all parts of the world to help establish services for local blind populations.[60] In 1967, with financial support from UNICEF and technical support from AFOB, a program called the Integrated Project for the Blind Students was started in Taiwan.[61] This project aimed at keeping blind children in a "normal" family environment within society, so that they could learn to live in a sighted world.[62] AFOB consultants participated in the selection of participating elementary school teachers (who had to have a good knowledge of English), assisted in conducting the training courses, and supervised the implementation of the field programme. AFOB also provided special aids and equipment, reference books and so on for the first training course for the specialised teachers.

In the 1960s, Taiwan's economy began to take off, and rapid industrial growth was maintained for the following three decades. At the same time, education for those with special needs attained legal status, while the Regulation for a Nine-Year Compulsory Education went into effect in 1968. Additionally, blind students finally started to attend regular classes in "normal" school, where no massage or vocational courses were provided. The elementary school teachers, on completion of the necessary training, were qualified to become "specialised teachers", whose duties included the instruction of the blind child in reading and writing skills and in using special aids and equipment, such as Braille slates, writers and arithmetical frames. They also needed to prepare special materials required by the blind child in class, such as Braille test papers. Nevertheless, many of the blind could not find jobs after finishing six years of regular school, and had to go back to the school for the blind to learn massage.

Conclusion

Modern special education was brought to Taiwan long before industrialisation or mass education. That is, special education did not emerge in response to social changes brought by industrialisation or by demands for order within mass education; instead its advocates, holding certain preconceptions, actively intervened in the lives of the blind. In traditional Chinese societies, the blind were mostly engaged in fortune-telling and legend chanting, which were considered idolatrous and

---

[59]Margret A. Winzer, "Confronting Difference: An Excursion through the History of Special Education," in *The SAGE Handbook of Special Education*, ed., Lani Florian (Thousand Oaks, CA: Sage, 2007), 21–33.
[60]Frances A. Koestler, *The Unseen Minority: A Social History of Blindness in America* (New York: D. McKay Co., 1976).
[61]毛連塭, "盲童走讀計畫在亞洲," 師友月刊 3 (1967): 16–7; 張紹焱, "特殊教育的意義理念與目標," 師友月刊 42 (1970): 6–9.
[62]UNICEF Project Preview No. TN-PP/23 (April 20, 1965).

superstitious by most western missionaries. The blind in the missionary schools were thus trained to make handicrafts for a wage so low as to reach almost the point of starvation. Braille literacy did not improve opportunities for further study and employment for the blind either; therefore the blind were used in preaching and many of them, after having learned to read and write, worked for the church. As such, education for the blind in effect led to the removal and continued separation of the blind from family and community. Japanese administrators as a whole were less eager to educate the Taiwanese blind. The main purpose of colonial-era education for the blind was to train them to meet the Japanese migrants' demands for amma, since amma was the traditional occupation of the blind in Japan. Yet while amma gradually became a major vocation of the blind in Taiwan, within the Japanese Inner Territory the monopoly over amma had already been taken away them. After western medical systems and knowledge moved in, the range of clinical practice conducted by the blind was restricted and eventually reduced to non-medical massage. Integration programmes were instituted with the aim of helping the blind to live and work in a sighted world, but since no massage courses were provided in regular schools, they became unable to support themselves. Pedagogic knowledge and techniques were displaced and transformed as they crossed borders and new combinations thus resulted from and developed within these historical processes, which led to unexpected consequences.

De Genève à Belo Horizonte, une histoire croisée: circulation, réception et réinterprétation d'un modèle européen des classes spéciales au Brésil des années 1930

Regina Helena de Freitas Campos and Adriana Araújo Pereira Borges

Faculdade de Educação, Universidade Federal de Minas Gerais, Belo Horizonte, Brasil

L'organisation des classes homogènes selon le niveau de développement mental des élèves et celle des classes spéciales pour les enfants en retard scolaire eut lieu dans les écoles élémentaires de Belo Horizonte, au Brésil, pendant les années de 1930, dans le cadre d'une réforme du système d'éducation, à laquelle participèrent des spécialistes étrangers, et en spécial la psychologue russe Helena Antipoff (1892–1974). Le projet des classes spéciales alors établies et leurs transformations dans le contexte brésilien sont étudiés à partir de données documentaires publiées entre 1930 et 1940. Née en Russie, Antipoff a fait des études supérieures en France (1910–1911), comme stagiaire dans le laboratoire Binet-Simon, et à Genève (1912–1914), à l'Institut Jean-Jacques Rousseau, où elle exerça ultérieurement les fonctions d'assistante d'Édouard Claparède (1926–1929). Notre hypothèse est que les classes spéciales créées à Belo Horizonte le furent sur le modèle genevois, et constituèrent un important exemple de circulation et diffusion de connaissances au niveau international, ainsi que de construction de repères dans le domaine de l'éducation spéciale au Brésil. Ainsi, la division des classes par niveau intellectuel mesuré par des tests d'intelligence, l'idée de "l'école sur mesure" proposée par Claparède, le dialogue avec les méthodes suggérées par Alice Descouedres démontrent les relations avec le modèle genevois. En même temps, l'interprétation des résultats des tests comme manifestation d'une forme d' "intelligence civilisée" et les adaptations des exercices d'orthopédie mentale pour développer cette intelligence demandée par l'école montrent les transformations du modèle dans le contexte brésilien.

The circulation of knowledge and educational innovations at the beginning of the twentieth century followed the growth of public educational systems. It led to complex exchanges and configurations due to the crossing of different national traditions, ideas and practices. The organisation of homogeneous classrooms according to the mental development of students and of special classes for children with learning difficulties and personality troubles are examples of this process. In the elementary schools of Belo Horizonte, Brazil, special classes for the "mentally retarded" were part of a reform of the public educational system promoted by the local government in 1927. The reform was implemented during the 1930s under the supervision of the Belo Horizonte Teachers Training College, where foreign specialists were hired to head the Laboratory of Psychology and to help in the organisation of homogeneous classrooms. The Laboratory of Psychology was established in 1928 by the French psychiatrist Théodore Simon (1873–1961), who had been invited for the task, and its directorship was assumed subsequently by two Russian psychologists who had worked as assistants to Claparède at the Rousseau Institute in Geneva (Léon Walther [1889–1963], in the first semester of 1929, and Helena Antipoff [1892–1974] from 1929 till 1944). The purpose of this paper is to study the project of special classes that were established at the time, using as sources articles published by Antipoff and her students in the periodical *Infância Excepcional* (Exceptional Children), edited in Belo Horizonte during the 1930s and 1940s, the correspondence Antipoff maintained with her master Édouard Claparède (1873–1940), the Swiss psychiatrist and psychologist, and a founder of the Rousseau Institute of the Sciences of Education in Geneva, and other documents concerning the works of the Belo Horizonte Teachers Training College. This article looks at how these special classes, based on the guidelines proposed by Helena Antipoff, were established, adapted and transformed within the Brazilian context. Born in Russia, Helena Antipoff studied in France (1910–1911), where she was an intern at the Binet-Simon laboratory of psychology, and Geneva (1912–1914), where she completed her studies in the sciences of education at the Jean-Jacques Rousseau Institute, where she subsequently worked as teaching assistant and researcher (1926–1929). The authors' hypothesis is that the special classes established in Belo Horizonte were designed on the basis of the European, especially the Genevan model; that they represented an example of the international flow and dissemination of knowledge, and of the building of a benchmark in the field of special education in Brazil; that they subsequently contributed to the social construction of professions related to the field of special education and of the circulation and modelling of what came to be labelled as "learning and personality troubles" in children. Special classes for the education of "retarded" children and of children with learning difficulties were established in Geneva in the beginning of the twentieth century, where Claparède had supervised the examination and selection of students and the training of schoolteachers for special education since 1901. With the foundation of the Rousseau Institute in 1912, the training of teachers and the development of methods for the examination and education of special children were assumed by the Institute's team, including Claparède, the medical doctor François Naville and Alice Descoeudres, who was responsible for the development of several methods for special education. In Belo Horizonte, the establishment of special classes for the education of "retarded" children was part of a school reform launched in 1927, inspired by New Education ideals. Under Antipoff's leadership, the Laboratory of Psychology promoted the organisation of homogeneous classrooms and of special education classes in local elementary schools, starting in 1930. Intelligence tests were adapted for the measurement of the mental development of students. In the interpretation of the results, Antipoff emphasised the role of the social environment in shaping students' cognitive abilities, and developed the concept of "civilised intelligence" to explain differences in students' performances with regard to the social level of their families. "Civilised intelligence" referred to intellectual abilities already polished by society and culture, present in mental test results. She discussed with Claparède the possibility of including a "social factor" in the interpretation of test results. In the organisation and supervision of educational activities in the special classes of Belo Horizonte, the laboratory of Psychology team adapted mental orthopaedic exercises developed in Paris by Alfred Binet and in Geneva by Alice Descoeudres. Books written by Claparède and Descoeudres were translated into Portuguese, and educational practices recommended for special classes based on their suggestions were spread among teachers who came from other Brazilian states and even from other Latin American countries to attend the Belo Horizonte Teachers College. In 1932, under Antipoff's leadership, a group of teachers, doctors and intellectuals established the Belo Horizonte Pestalozzi Society for the purpose of better developing the examination and the education of mentally "retarded" and troubled children, and of giving support for the work done in special classes in Belo Horizonte schools. The approach to special education developed at the Laboratory of Psychology and at the Pestalozzi Society became known in Brazil for its "Active school" perspective, inspired by the

Genevan experience. Reports written by Antipoff's students such as Naytres Rezende show that most students who attended special classes presented normal levels of intelligence, but were psychologically disturbed. The majority of those students came from low-income families. Mental orthopaedic exercises were then adapted for the development of the "civilised intelligence" required by schools. Concerning the development of special education in Belo Horizonte, one can see that the division of classes by intellectual level, the use of intelligence tests for diagnosis, the reference to the idea of a "student tailored school" proposed by Claparède, and the dialogue with methods suggested by Alice Descoeudres provide evidence of its close relationship with the Genevan model. The ideal of a scientific pedagogy, as proposed by Claparède, was remarkable in the Belo Horizonte experience, under the leadership of the Teachers College Laboratory of Psychology. At the same time, the interpretation of mental test results as manifestations of a type of "civilised intelligence" and the adaptations of mental orthopaedic exercises in order to develop this kind of intelligence required by schools show the transformations of the model within the Brazilian context. Although the model proposed for Belo Horizonte special classes can be interpreted as deriving from the Genevan approach, more research is needed to better describe how these ideas were put into practice within the highly complex institutional context of existing schools. It is important to observe what the consequences were of the organisation of special classes for children with learning or personality troubles for the future development of the local school system and for the targeted population, i.e. children with difficulties of adaptation to a highly centralised and hierarchical school system.

Introduction

Les classes spéciales pour les enfants en difficulté scolaire sont une invention du tournant du XIXe au XXe siècle et une conséquence de l'expansion des systèmes d'éducation publique dans les pays dits les plus développés, en Europe et en Amérique du Nord. Les différences individuelles entre les enfants, du point de vue de leur développement intellectuel et socio-moral, devenaient plus visibles dans les grands établissements scolaires, mis sur pieds à la fin du XIXe siècle pour favoriser l'accès à l'éducation publique et garantir la modernisation de la gestion des politiques sociales d'État. D'après les suggestions des éducateurs et des professionnels liés au domaine de la santé – médecins, psychologues, psychopédagogues – les classes spéciales obéissaient au modèle de normalité–anormalité issu des pratiques médicales et asilaires. Les "anormaux" scolaires, inadaptés à l'école, sont les enfants qui vont être éduqués dans ces classes spéciales, avec des méthodes spécifiques, développées soit par des médecins, soit par des pédagogues ou pédo-psychologues.[1] Certains auteurs, comme le médecin et psychologue genevois Édouard Claparède ou le psychologue brésilien Lourenço Filho, importants leaders du mouvement de l'Éducation nouvelle, considéraient les classes spéciales et, plus

---

[1] Sur l'histoire des classes spéciales, voir Martine Ruchat, *Inventer les arriérés pour créer l'intelligence: L'arriéré scolaire et la classe spéciale – Histoire d'un concept et d'une innovation pédagogique* (Berne: Peter Lang, 2003); pour une histoire de la formation des enseignants aux méthodes actives dans l'éducation spécialisée "pour l'enfance déficiente ou inadaptée" voir Jacqueline Roca, "La formation de maîtres spécialisés, un terrain d'expérimentation pour l'Éducation nouvelle 1930–1964," in *Réformer l'école. L'apport de l'Éducation nouvelle (1930–1970),* ed. Laurent Gutierrez, Laurent Besse et Antoine Prost (Grenoble: Presses universitaires de Grenoble, 2012), 305–16.

généralement, le groupement des élèves par niveau intellectuel dans les écoles, comme l'une des innovations les plus importantes de la pédagogie moderne. Ce groupement serait compatible avec l'idée d'une "école sur mesure" (comme le préconisait Claparède) qui devrait adapter les activités et programmes éducationnels aux différences individuelles et aux caractéristiques psychologiques singulières des élèves.[2]

La littérature critique des années 1970 et 1980 analysa les processus d'homogénéisation des classes et l'établissement des classes spéciales comme une manière de faire reproduire et approfondir, par le biais de l'école, les différences sociales et culturelles entre les élèves issus de familles de conditions socioéconomiques inégales.[3] Malgré les critiques, ces innovations se sont toutefois répandues comme un signe de modernité dans les systèmes d'éducation publique. Pour les intellectuels et éducateurs inspirés du mouvement de défense des droits des enfants et du droit à l'éducation, surtout pendant l'entre-deux-guerres, l'homogénéisation des classes était vue comme une manière rationnelle de promouvoir le développement physique et intellectuel des élèves en tenant compte de leurs différences psychologiques et psycho-sociales.[4] Simultanément, la séparation des classes par niveau intellectuel aida à construire, dans chaque milieu social, les représentations des enfants et des jeunes considérés comme normaux et anormaux, à travers la description même produite par les professionnels chargés de leur éducation ou de leur traitement, dans un processus de construction sociale.[5] C'est ainsi que se sont conjointement établies les représentations des élèves considérés comme hors norme par rapport à leur tranche d'âge, et les professions qui les prirent en charge. L'hypothèse du contrôle social unidimensionnel fut alors remplacée par l'idée que les politiques et les interventions ciblant les enfants et jeunes qui présentent des handicaps ou du retard scolaire auraient déclenché des relations dynamiques entre élèves et maîtres, clients et professionnels de santé ou d'éducation, avec des moments de tension, de contraintes et de libération.[6]

Pendant les années 1930, dans l'État de Minas Gerais (région centrale du Brésil), une expérience bien documentée fut mise en place: elle consistait en une homogénéisation des classes des écoles primaires, et en une organisation de classes

---

[2]Édouard Claparède, *A escola sob medida* (Rio de Janeiro: Editora Fundo de Cultura, 1959); Manoel Bergstrom Lourenço Filho, *Introdução ao Estudo da Escola Nova: bases, sistemas e diretrizes da pedagogia contemporânea* (Rio de Janeiro: EDUERJ, 2002).
[3]Voir par exemple Pierre Bourdieu et Jean-Claude Passeron, *La reproduction: éléments pour une théorie des systèmes d'enseignement* (Paris: Minuit, 1970); Christian Baudelot et Roger Establet, *L'école capitaliste en France* (Paris: Maspéro, 1971); Noëlle Bisseret, *Les inégaux et la sélection universitaire* (Paris: Presses universitaires de France, 1974); Maria Helena Souza Patto, *A produção do fracasso escolar* (São Paulo: T. A. Queiroz, 1990).
[4]Helena Antipoff, "Organização das classes nos grupos escolares de Belo Horizonte," in *Coletânea das Obras Escritas de Helena Antipoff*, vol. 1, ed. Centro de Documentação e Pesquisa Helena Antipoff (Belo Horizonte: Imprensa Oficial, 1992), 131–50.
[5]Sur ce processus de construction sociale de "l'enfant-problème", voir Joëlle Droux et Martine Ruchat, "L''enfant-problème' ou l'émergence de figures problématiques dans la construction d'un dispositif de protection de l'enfance (Genève, 1890–1929)," *Carnets de Bord* 14 (2007): 14–27.
[6]Annemieke Van Drenth et Kevin Myers, "Normalising Childhood: Policies and Interventions Concerning Special Children in the United States and Europe (1900–1960)," *Paedagogica Historica* 47, no. 6 (2011): 719–27.

spéciales et d'institutions d'accueil et d'éducation des enfants "exceptionnels"[7] – c'est-à-dire intellectuellement sur- ou sous-doués, ou mal adaptés au milieu scolaire. Le mot "exceptionnel", qui devait désigner les individus dont les caractéristiques psychologiques s'éloignaient de la norme de leur âge, fut introduit vers 1932 dans le lexique éducationnel brésilien par la psychologue russe Helena Antipoff, dans le but de prévenir les effets stigmatisants des qualificatifs "anormal" ou "arriéré". L'expérience se développa à partir de la fondation de l'École de perfectionnement des enseignants de Belo Horizonte, établie en 1928 dans le cadre de la Réforme Francisco Campos qui visait une expansion du système scolaire public en y diffusant les idéaux du mouvement de l'Éducation nouvelle.

Dans cet article, nous nous intéressons surtout à la réception et aux transformations des concepts et pratiques concernant la réorganisation des classes scolaires coordonnée par le Laboratoire de psychologie de l'École de perfectionnement, qui fut à l'origine de la création des classes spéciales dans le système d'enseignement primaire public de l'État. Nous posons l'hypothèse suivante: les classes spéciales créées à Belo Horizonte à l'époque le furent sur le modèle européen, et plus spécifiquement sur le modèle genevois, et elles constituèrent un exemple important de circulation et de diffusion de connaissances au niveau international ainsi que de construction de repères dans le domaine de l'éducation spéciale au Brésil.

Cette expérience de circulation de connaissances entre l'Europe et le Brésil peut être analysée, en outre, comme une histoire croisée.[8] C'est une étude de cas dans laquelle les concepts, instruments analytiques et pratiques de travail avec les "anormaux", alors proposés, sont le résultat de processus de croisement complexes, où les différentes traditions nationales et disciplinaires apparaissent amalgamées selon diverses configurations. Au lieu d'analyser la diffusion des idées et pratiques à partir d'entités individuelles, considérées en soi sans lien avec le contexte, la perspective de l'histoire croisée exige une approche multidimensionnelle, "donnant droit de cité à la pluralité et aux configurations complexes qui en découlent".[9] Les institutions, pratiques et sujets affectés par le croisement subissent ainsi des transformations dues à leur interaction. Cependant, leurs relations peuvent être asymétriques, comme c'est souvent le cas dans l'histoire des sciences, quand les inventions conceptuelles et techniques sont diffusées selon une logique d'autorité.

Dans le cas de l'histoire de l'éducation, surtout dans le cadre de l'expansion mondiale de l'école moderne, avec son arsenal scientifique de mesures et procédures standardisées, le modèle suggéré est celui d'une approche culturelle, concentrée sur la production de différences dans les processus de réception, de réinterprétation et de réarticulation des idées et institutions. Ce sont les nouveaux signifiants – sur lesquels l'analyse se focalisera – qui sont produits dans les processus de croisement par les acteurs engagés dans l'interaction. La réalité du "vécu" de chaque acteur prend ainsi une place proéminente. D'après Caruso et Vera,[10] l'étude de ces

---

[7]Sergio Domingues, "Conceito de excepcional na obra de Helena Antipoff: diagnóstico, intervenções e sua relação com a educação" (master's thesis, Universidade Federal de Minas Gerais, 2011).
[8]Michael Werner et Bénédicte Zimmermann, "Penser l'histoire croisée: entre empirie et réflexivité," *Le Genre Humain* 42 (2004): 15–49.
[9]Ibid., 22.
[10]Marcelo Caruso et Eugenia Roldán Vera, "Pluralizing Meanings: The Monitorial System of Education in Latin America in the Early Nineteenth Century," *Paedagogica Historica* 41, no. 6 (2005): 645–54.

processus d'internationalisation dans le domaine de l'éducation exige de porter une attention particulière à la construction des "internationalités", c'est-à-dire à "la production de modèles de progrès et de références qui sont profondément sélectifs et qui sont liés à des groupes d'intérêt, à des traditions héritées et aux facteurs endogènes de réception".[11] Les classes spéciales constituent l'une de ces "internationalités" produites dans le processus de diffusion des modèles scolaires du XXᵉ siècle.

Les sources utilisées pour notre analyse sont constituées de la biographie d'Helena Antipoff, principale responsable du *design* des classes spéciales adopté à l'époque sous la supervision du Laboratoire de psychologie qu'elle dirigea à l'École de perfectionnement des enseignants de Belo Horizonte entre 1929 et 1944; des rapports sur l'examen médical, psychologique et pédagogique des enfants accueillis dans les classes spéciales, publiés par le Secrétariat d'éducation et de santé publique de l'État de Minas Gerais;[12] de la législation de l'époque; des écrits d'Helena Antipoff; et de la correspondance entre Antipoff et Claparède, éditée par Martine Ruchat.[13]

A propos de la circulation de connaissances qui donnèrent naissance aux classes spéciales établies à Belo Horizonte pendant les années 1930, nous cherchons à savoir dans quelle mesure le modèle suggéré par Antipoff, inspiré de celui de Genève et qui fut adopté par ses collaborateurs brésiliens, a été adapté au contexte local. Pour répondre à cette question, nous allons observer comment Antipoff utilisa son expérience préalable à Paris, à Genève et en Russie pour répondre aux demandes de son nouveau poste et, sur la base des données fournies par nos sources, comment cette utilisation reconfigura le modèle.

Les classes spéciales à Genève

La création des classes spéciales à Genève fut une initiative de la fin du XIXᵉ siècle et était liée à trois grandes questions politiques et sociales: l'application de la loi constitutionnelle de 1874 sur l'obligation d'instruction; le repérage des récalcitrants qui est intimement lié au niveau pédagogique des recrues militaires et à la distinction entre "retardés" scolaires, illettrés et idiots; et le recensement de l'enfance démunie réalisé en Suisse en 1896.

La nomenclature "classes spéciales" apparaît à Genève en 1878 dans le but d'héberger les "indisciplinés". L'indiscipline était comprise comme une résistance à l'ordre et passible de punition. La première classe spéciale pour enfants "peu dotés" ou "retardés dans leur développement" fut créée en 1895 à Lausanne. A Genève, la classe spéciale apparaît en 1898, avec l'idée d'adapter les méthodes pédagogiques

---

[11]"By 'construction of internationalities' is meant the production of models of progress and references that are deeply selective, and that are linked to interest groups, inherited traditions and endogenous factors of reception." Ibid., 649.

[12]Le premier volume date de 1933, avec le titre "Enfance Exceptionnelle". S'en suivirent le Bulletin numéro 16 de 1934 et le Bulletin numéro 20 de 1937, également dénommés "Enfance Exceptionnelle", édités sous la responsabilité de la Société Pestalozzi de Minas Gerais. Le quatrième volume analysé est celui de 1944 et il contient une compilation des rapports annuels de la Société Pestalozzi couvrant les années 1932 à 1941.

[13]Helena Antipoff, *Coletânea das Obras Escritas de Helena Antipoff*, ed. Centro de Documentação e Pesquisa Helena Antipoff, 5 vols (Belo Horizonte: Imprensa Oficial, 1992); Martine Ruchat, ed., *Édouard Claparède – Hélène Antipoff – Correspondance (1914–1940)* (Firenze: Leo Olschki Editore, 2010).

aux aptitudes des enfants et d'homogénéiser les classes par niveau intellectuel. Dès le début des classes spéciales, le médecin eut un rôle important, celui de répondre aux demandes ponctuelles d'examen de cas individuels.

C'est en fait l'année 1901 qui fut déterminante dans l'histoire du fameux "retardé scolaire". Durant cette année-là, les régents des classes spéciales demandent une formation et le médecin et psychologue Édouard Claparède est invité à y contribuer. C'est à partir de ce travail auprès des enseignants des classes spéciales que se développa son intérêt pour la psychopathologie de l'enfant. Toujours en 1901, Claparède rencontre Ovide Decroly, neuropsychiatre belge, "fondateur en 1905 de la Société de Pédotechnie, lequel va influencer fortement ses conceptions d'organisation et de pédagogie des classes spéciales genevoises".[14]

La création des classes spéciales à Genève entraînera donc le besoin d'étudier les élèves individuellement et de former les instituteurs; par la suite, de nouvelles représentations sur les "enfants-problèmes" et de nouvelles professions pour s'en occuper émergeront.[15] Claparède fut l'un des responsables de la formation des enseignants pour l'expertise psychologique (ou étude anamnestique) et pour l'enseignement spécial depuis 1912, après la fondation de l'Institut Jean-Jacques Rousseau, École des sciences de l'éducation. L'Institut réunit le médecin genevois, son collègue Pierre Bovet et un groupe d'éducateurs et éducatrices associés autour du mouvement de l'Éducation nouvelle, avec le but de devenir un centre de recherches et d'études de la psychologie de l'enfant, de la pédagogie expérimentale et de la réforme scolaire. La devise *Discat a puero magister* (Que le maître apprenne de l'élève), inspirée de Jean-Jacques Rousseau, exprimait le désir de promouvoir la connaissance scientifique de l'enfant pour mieux diriger son éducation. En 1929, l'Institut fut rattaché à la Faculté des lettres de l'Université de Genève.[16]

Dans le groupe fondateur de l'Institut Rousseau, on retrouve l'éducatrice Alice Descoeudres. Depuis 1909, elle s'occupait d'une classe pour enfants "arriérés" dans une école genevoise et sous la supervision de Claparède, et avait fait un stage auprès de Decroly en Belgique. Descoeudres fut chargée des cours dans le domaine de l'éducation spécialisée. L'Institut proposait un enseignement théorique et pratique des sciences de l'éducation. Les cours sur les anormalités mentales étaient articulés à des exemples pratiques grâce à la Consultation médico-pédagogique et durant le stage que les étudiants pouvaient faire dans une classe spéciale, avec l'autorisation du Département de l'instruction publique de Genève. L'enseignement des méthodes d'éducation des "anormaux" se concentrait sur les déficits d'intelligence et sur les troubles de caractère relevant de l'éducation morale. La seconde décennie du XXe siècle verra ainsi la question des "retardés" scolaires revenir dans le domaine médical. Dans ce contexte, le médecin genevois François Naville eut aussi un rôle fondamental et la prévention devint objet de recherche en psychologie appliquée. Il défendait les classes spéciales et l'enseignement spécial comme la meilleure manière pour les enfants en retard de pouvoir accéder à un travail et à l'autonomie financière.

---

[14]Ruchat, *Inventer les arriérés*, 117.
[15]Pour l'histoire de l'implantation de la consultation médico-pédagogique des enfants considérés "difficiles à éduquer" à Genève au début du XXe siècle, voir Droux et Ruchat, L''enfant-problème'.
[16]Rita Hofstetter, Marc Ratcliff et Bernard Schneuwly, *Cent ans de vie (1912–2012)* (Genève: Georg, 2012); aussi Rita Hofstetter, *Genève: creuset des sciences de l'éducation* (Genève: Librairie Droz, 2010).

Naville soutenait que tous les élèves pouvaient profiter des classes spéciales s'ils étaient regroupés selon leurs capacités et non par tranches d'âge. L'organisation des classes homogènes d'après le développement mental serait donc une manière d'étudier les enfants et d'acquérir le savoir qui permettrait de créer une science des anomalies mentales, à partir de la collaboration entre la médecine générale et infantile, la neurologie, la psychiatrie et la pédagogie. Dès le début du XXe siècle, les enfants "difficiles à éduquer" (selon l'expression de Pierre Bovet) seront donc soumis à un examen médico-pédagogique systématique pour sélectionner ceux qui seront envoyés dans une classe spéciale. Les enfants classés comme violents, intraitables, brutaux, avec tendances à dérober, vicieux, fugueurs, moralement abandonnés, avec des comportements inadéquats étaient alors ciblés, dans le but de prévenir la future délinquance. Leur problème était plutôt d'ordre moral, et la prophylaxie de leurs troubles devait promouvoir leur réadaptation.[17]

Selon Hofstetter, depuis la fondation de l'Institut Rousseau, "la classe spéciale de Descoeudres devient un véritable lieu de pèlerinage et de formation, jouant aussi un rôle décisif pour hisser Genève au statut de référence suisse, voire internationale, pour la formation et la recherche des enfants arriérés".[18] Après la Première Guerre mondiale, Descoeudres, impressionnée par les évènements qui bouleversaient l'Europe, s'était dédiée aussi à étudier le développement socio-moral des enfants et faisait des recherches sur leur pensée concernant la guerre, l'argent, le travail et la famille. Travaillant avec les "arriérés" dont elle voyait grandir le nombre à cause des troubles sociaux, elle voulait stimuler leurs sentiments altruistes et leur humanité.[19]

C'est ainsi que l'établissement des classes spéciales à Genève put compter sur la collaboration fondamentale du psychologue Edouard Claparède et de l'Institut Rousseau. Claparède et ses collègues stimulèrent l'intérêt des politiques et des pédagogues à propos du sujet dans leur pays et au niveau international. Leur dialogue avec Helena Antipoff, élève de l'Institut et ultérieurement assistante de Claparède, fut aussi décisif pour élaborer un modèle de classes spéciales adopté dans l'État de Minas Gerais, comme nous le verrons par la suite.

Le contexte de l'homogénéisation des classes scolaires et l'établissement des classes spéciales à Belo Horizonte

Avec l'avènement du XXe siècle, et comme dans le reste du monde, l'école va également assumer un rôle fondamental dans la société brésilienne. La précarité du système éducatif devient objet de discussion, la qualité de l'enseignement un objectif politique.

La figure du technicien prend alors de l'importance. Dans l'État de Minas Gerais, une École de perfectionnement des enseignants, dont l'objectif était de garantir une approche scientifique de la question éducationnelle, fut créée; elle devait jouer un rôle fondamental dans la formation des enseignants. L'École fut inaugurée en 1928 dans le cadre d'une importante réforme éducative coordonnée par le juriste Francisco Campos, chargé de l'administration du système d'instruction publique.

---

[17]Droux et Ruchat, L'"enfant-problème".
[18]Rita Hofstetter, *Genève: creuset*, 280.
[19]Helena Antipoff, préface à *A Educação das Crianças Retardadas,* par Alice Descoeudres (Belo Horizonte: Imprensa Oficial, 1968).

L'institution avait pour but de transmettre aux élèves – enseignantes choisies pour leurs compétences techniques – des connaissances en matière d'organisation de contenus et de gestion scolaire dans l'esprit du mouvement de l'Éducation nouvelle. Il fallait surtout améliorer l'efficacité et promouvoir la démocratisation de l'accès à l'école élémentaire, pour faire face aux demandes croissantes de la population concernant l'éducation.

Pour équiper l'École d'un corps enseignant connaisseur des nouvelles tendances en éducation, en 1926 déjà un groupe de normaliennes avait été envoyé à l'Université de Columbia de New York pour un stage de deux ans auprès des leaders du mouvement progressiste américain en éducation – tels John Dewey et William Kilpatrick. A la même époque, une mission fut envoyée en Europe pour sélectionner et inviter des professeurs pour la réalisation du projet. La mission se rendit à Paris et rencontra le médecin Théodore Simon, collaborateur d'Alfred Binet pour le développement des tests d'intelligence, qui fut invité à installer un Laboratoire de psychologie à Belo Horizonte.[20] Le Laboratoire serait ensuite chargé de promouvoir les mesures objectives des capacités intellectuelles des enfants et d'appuyer le processus d'homogénéisation des classes scolaires – y compris les classes spéciales – par niveau mental.

Les travaux du Laboratoire débutèrent avec le médecin français et continuèrent avec deux psychologues russes venus de l'Institut Rousseau de Genève: Léon Walther, invité au premier semestre 1929, et Helena Antipoff, qui remplaça Walther à partir du second semestre de la même année. A cette époque, l'Institut Rousseau était déjà reconnu mondialement comme un centre important d'études des sciences de l'éducation et de la psychologie de l'enfant. Le contrat d'Antipoff, signé par le Consul du Brésil à Genève le 5 janvier 1929, fut renouvelé plusieurs fois pendant les années 1930 et 1940. Elle décida finalement de rester au Brésil et de devenir citoyenne brésilienne en 1952.

Entre la Russie, Paris, Genève et Belo Horizonte: Helena Antipoff, citoyenne du monde[21]

Née à Grodno en Russie en 1892, Antipoff fit ses études primaires et secondaires à Saint Pétersbourg. Elle s'installa à Paris en 1909 pour des études universitaires, d'abord en médecine, ensuite en psychologie. Elle fréquenta des séminaires à la Sorbonne ainsi qu'au Collège de France et, en 1911, pendant un stage auprès du Dr Simon dans le Laboratoire de psychologie pédagogique de la rue Grange-aux-Belles, elle participa au travail empirique de validation des nouveaux tests psychologiques de mesure de l'intelligence.

C'est encore dans ce laboratoire qu'elle rencontra le médecin suisse Edouard Claparède, qui l'invita à poursuivre ses études à Genève. Elle partit donc en Suisse et fit partie de la première classe de l'Institut Rousseau, composée de 22 élèves. Elle fréquenta, entre 1912 et 1914, les cours de psychologie de l'enfant et de psychologie

---

[20]Anamaria Casasanta Peixoto, "A reforma educacional Francisco Campos – Minas Gerais, governo Presidente Antônio Carlos" (master's thesis, Universidade Federal de Minas Gerais, 1981).

[21]Pour une biographie intellectuelle d'Helena Antipoff, voir Regina Helena de Freitas Campos, *Helena Antipoff, uma biografia intelectual* (Rio de Janeiro: Fundação Miguel de Cervantes, 2012); aussi "Helena Antipoff: A Synthesis of Swiss and Soviet Psychology in the Context of Brazilian Education," *History of Psychology* 4, no. 2 (2001): 133–58.

expérimentale de Claparède et suivit, en outre, les cours d'autres pionniers de l'Institut tels que Pierre Bovet, François Naville, Alice Descoeudres et Mina Audemars, ce qui lui permit d'obtenir des connaissances plus complètes sur l'approche fonctionnelle en psychologie de l'intelligence et sur les méthodes actives en éducation.

En 1916, Antipoff retourna en Russie pour s'occuper de son père, blessé pendant la guerre. A cette époque, elle travailla comme psychologue au laboratoire fondé par Alexander Nechaev à Saint Pétersbourg et participa à des recherches sur les effets des troubles sociaux (guerre mondiale, guerre civile et révolution) sur le développement mental des enfants. Les résultats de ces recherches montrèrent que, malgré leur faiblesse physique, les enfants russes âgés de quatre à neuf ans – surtout ceux issus de famille d'intellectuels[22] – présentaient des résultats supérieurs à ceux des petits Parisiens.

A cette époque-là, en Russie, les conséquences de la guerre de 1914–1918 et de la Révolution de 1917 provoquaient le chaos dans le pays. Des milliers d'enfants, selon Antipoff, erraient dans les rues des grandes villes russes. Le gouvernement communiste créa alors des institutions pour trier, accueillir, abriter et acheminer les enfants au bon endroit. Helena Antipoff fut admise comme psychologue dans l'un de ces foyers à Saint-Pétersbourg, où elle utilisa dans son travail les connaissances acquises à Paris et à Genève.[23]

Au sein de l'institution, sa tâche était d'appliquer les examens psychologiques aux enfants et de programmer leur rééducation. Pour l'évaluation psychologique, elle utilisa les tests qui lui étaient déjà familiers, comme l'échelle de mesure de l'intelligence proposée par Alfred Binet et Théodore Simon. Outre les tests, elle travailla sur la technique d'étude de la personnalité développée par le psychologue russe Alexandre Lazourski et appelée "expérimentation naturelle". Il s'agissait d'observer les enfants et les adolescents dans leurs activités quotidiennes sur le terrain pour décrire leurs caractéristiques psychologiques.[24] Entre 1922 et 1924, Helena Antipoff travailla aussi dans une station médico-pédagogique dans la ville de Viatka où elle était chargée, en tant que psychologue, d'organiser les activités éducatives des jeunes internes. En 1924, elle quitta la Russie et passa brièvement par Berlin – où habitait son mari, exilé par la Révolution russe – et, en 1926, retourna à Genève comme assistante de Claparède à l'Université et à l'Institut Rousseau. Ses travaux à cette époque concernaient l'étude des aptitudes motrices, la constance des résultats dans les tests d'intelligence et de motricité. Elle contribua aussi à la diffusion de la méthode Lazourski en Suisse et collabora avec Claparède sur des recherches concernant l'intelligence et la genèse de l'hypothèse dans le processus de raisonnement, dont les résultats furent publiés en 1933.[25]

---

[22]Helena Antipoff, "O nível mental das crianças russas nas escolas infantis," in *Coletânea das Obras Escritas de Helena Antipoff*, Vol. 1, ed. Centro de Documentação e Pesquisa Helena Antipoff (Belo Horizonte: Imprensa Oficial, 1992), 9–10.

[23]Helena Antipoff, "L'expérience russe. L'éducation sociale des enfants," *Semaine Littéraire*, 32 (1924): 592–94.

[24]Helena Antipoff, "A experimentação natural – Método psicológico de A. Lazursky," in *Coletânea das Obras Escritas de Helena Antipoff*, Vol. 1, ed. Centro de Documentação e Pesquisa Helena Antipoff (Belo Horizonte: Imprensa Oficial, 1992), 29–42.

[25]Édouard Claparède, "La genèse de l'hypothèse," *Archives de Psychologie* 24 (1933): 1–155.

Le travail à l'École de perfectionnement des enseignants à Belo Horizonte, Brésil

Dotée de ces expériences d'études de l'intelligence et de la psychologie des enfants à risque social dans différents pays, Antipoff arriva au Brésil en 1929 pour enseigner la psychologie et la pédologie, et diriger le Laboratoire de psychologie de l'École de perfectionnement des enseignants de Belo Horizonte, où elle travailla entre 1929 et 1944. A cette époque, Antipoff écrivit à son maître Claparède:

> Il s'agit de prouver que l'École (de perfectionnement) n'est pas une utopie, qu'elle n'est pas un organisme parasitaire et inutile, mais au contraire, qu'elle est en train de faire une besogne considérable et que son succès garantit en quelque sorte le succès de la Réforme scolaire, puisqu'elle a pour but de préparer des spécialistes en matière d'enseignement, et de hausser le niveau général et professionnel des instituteurs scolaires.[26]

En 1929 déjà, l'équipe du Laboratoire, sous la direction d'Antipoff, avait fait une enquête sur les idéaux et les intérêts des enfants de Belo Horizonte. La recherche, un questionnaire établi sur un modèle proposé par Descoeudres à Genève, ciblait les activités préférées à la maison et à l'école, les modèles adultes choisis et les projets pour le futur et avait pour but, d'après Antipoff, de l'aider à connaître la nouvelle population avec laquelle elle allait devoir travailler.[27] En 1930, le Laboratoire commença le travail d'adaptation des tests d'intelligence qui seraient utilisés pour l'homogénéisation des classes scolaires: le test d'intelligence et de vocabulaire du Dr Simon, le test Dearborn, le Ballard et le test du dessin de la figure humaine développé par Florence Goodenough.[28] Pour interpréter les résultats, Antipoff considéra surtout l'influence du milieu social et culturel de l'enfant. Elle observa que l'intelligence évaluée à travers les tests serait le résultat d'une combinaison de tendances innées et de caractéristiques dues à l'action de la société et de la culture dans lesquelles est élevé l'enfant. C'est ainsi qu'elle a repris au Brésil le concept d'*intelligence civilisée*, déjà observée en Russie, pour décrire les capacités évaluées par les tests.

Ce concept lui avait été suggéré à partir de son travail en Union soviétique, quand elle examinait les enfants abandonnés sous sa responsabilité dans les foyers de Saint-Pétersbourg et de Viatka. Selon ses observations, les enfants en situation de risque social qui y étaient reçus avaient des difficultés pour répondre aux questions plus abstraites des tests, malgré l'intelligence concrète qu'ils démontraient pour subvenir à leurs besoins vitaux dans les rues des grandes villes russes.

Les études du développement mental des enfants de Belo Horizonte menaient à des conclusions similaires. Les limitations du milieu culturel des familles plus pauvres, associées aux besoins de faire face aux difficultés de la vie quotidienne, conditionnaient des résultats inférieurs dans les tests, sans que la majorité des enfants puissent être classifiés comme moins intelligents. Antipoff pense alors que le

---

[26] Ruchat, *Édouard Claparède – Hélène Antipoff*, 95.
[27] Helena Antipoff, "Ideaes e interesses das creanças de Bello Horizonte e algumas sugestões pedagógicas," *Boletim de Educação e Saúde Pública de Minas Gerais* 6 (1930): 61–100.
[28] W. Dearborn (1878–1955), PhD, Université de Columbia (EUA); P. B. Ballard (1865–1950), psychologue et éducateur né au Pays de Gales; Florence Goodenough (1866–1959), PhD, Université de Stanford (EUA). Les trois auteurs sont connus par leurs travaux en psychologie de l'éducation et développement d'instruments de mesure de l'intelligence.

concept d'*intelligence civilisée* serait plus adapté pour décrire les résultats des tests; elle le décrit ainsi:

> ... cette intelligence qui se construit et se discipline à travers le contact avec l'exemple au sein du régime réglé et des exigences imposées par la vie conventionnelle, la famille et l'école, cette intelligence civilisée que nous recherchons à travers nos tests dits d'intelligence générale.[29]

Antipoff a peut-être choisi l'adjectif "civilisée" à partir de son expérience à l'Institut Rousseau. Entre 1926 et 1929 – elle est alors l'assistante de Claparède – Jean Piaget avait déjà débuté ses études sur le développement du raisonnement chez les enfants et adoptait le qualificatif "civilisé" pour se référer à la société moderne, dans la tradition des études d'Émile Durkheim et de Lévy-Bruhl. Piaget faisait également référence à l'action de deux facteurs dans la promotion du développement: le facteur biologique et le facteur social, qui agiraient de façon intégrée durant le développement.[30] L'approche historique et culturelle de la psychologie soviétique considérait aussi, à la même époque, que les fonctions psychologiques supérieures étaient construites à partir des interactions sociales et culturelles. L'éducation et la culture étaient donc vues comme les médiateurs entre l'individu et son milieu.[31]

Ces observations ont suggéré à Antipoff la proposition d'un "coefficient social" pour mesurer l'influence du milieu sur les résultats des tests d'intelligence. À ce propos elle écrit à Claparède:

> Lorsqu'il s'agit de tous nos tests d'intelligence générale, qui sont des tests d'intelligence civilisée (je vous envoie par le même courrier notre travail sur le développement mental des enf. de Belo Horizonte) – le facteur social, le milieu et son influence entre en jeu bien plus encore. Donc surtout pour les fins pratiques, de diagnostic individuel, mais aussi en vue de solution d'ordre théorique, il nous faut avoir des C.S. (coeff. sociaux) pour interpréter aussi bien à sa juste valeur l'examen d'intelligence de tel ou autre enf., que comprendre tout ce que l'intelligence doit aux dispositions innées et ce qu'elle est en fonction du milieu où elles se réalisent.[32]

La proposition était de calculer ces coefficients sociaux à partir de la profession des parents, conforme à leur situation dans l'échelle sociale, et corriger les résultats de chaque enfant d'après le niveau de la famille d'origine. Antipoff envisageait aussi la possibilité que ces coefficients sociaux soient plus forts à l'entrée à l'école, et que les différences entre enfants de parents avec ou sans instruction supérieure se réduisent ensuite par l'influence de l'école. Claparède a salué l'idée du coefficient social, qui lui a paru intéressante.[33] L'échange de perceptions entre les deux psychologues, d'un côté et de l'autre de l'Atlantique, concernant l'action du milieu social sur le

---

[29]Helena Antipoff, "O desenvolvimento mental das crianças de Belo Horizonte – 1931," in *Coletânea das Obras Escritas de Helena Antipoff*, Vol. 1, Ed. Centro de Documentação e Pesquisa Helena Antipoff (Belo Horizonte: Imprensa Oficial, 1992), 73–130, 79.

[30]Jean Piaget, *Le jugement et le raisonnement chez l'enfant* (Neuchâtel: Délâchaux et Niestlé, 1924).

[31]Lev Vygotski, Alexander Luria et Aléxis Leontiev, eds., *Linguagem, desenvolvimento e aprendizagem* (São Paulo: Icone Editora, 1988). A propos, Édouard Claparède, Jean Piaget et Alexander Luria étaient parmi les auteurs les plus cités par Antipoff dans ses classes à l'École de perfectionnement de Belo Horizonte.

[32]Ruchat, *Édouard Claparède – Hélène Antipoff*, 122.

[33]Ibid., 125.

développement mental des enfants, montre un cas concret de croisement de différentes traditions de recherche, et le mouvement de transformation des connaissances dû à la circulation d'observations scientifiques dans différentes cultures.

Il fut alors possible d'observer des similarités entre les résultats des tests appliqués aux enfants russes et ceux des enfants brésiliens issus des milieux pauvres. C'est ainsi qu'Antipoff, en prise avec les problèmes de la société où elle avait choisi de vivre, s'est engagée dans la supervision du processus d'homogénéisation des classes scolaires, ainsi que dans l'organisation et l'orientation des classes spéciales dans les écoles de Belo Horizonte. A ce propos, elle écrit à Claparède:

> La nouvelle du jour pour le travail exécuté est la suivante: tous les enfants des écoles de B. H. sont, grâce à nos élèves diplômées, triés, d'après les résultats des tests et de l'observation. Il s'agit actuellement surtout des enfants de première année scolaire qui, à eux seuls s'élèvent à plus de 4 mille. Sur ces quatre mille un millier environ se trouvent dans les classes faibles ou pour retardés (classes C et D; classes A – constitués par les enfants bien doués et les plus nombreuses classes B – classes pour enfants communs).[34]

Des classes spéciales (les classes D) furent alors créées, environ 50 classes pour l'année 1931. Pour faire l'orientation du travail, il y avait tous les jeudis des réunions avec le personnel du Laboratoire, les médecins scolaires et les enseignantes:

> C'est avec ces classes C et D que nous avons le plus grand travail: tous les jeudis matins – réunion avec les professeurs (d')*une cinquantaine* de ces classes. Aidé par les médecins scolaires, notre Laboratoire leur fait des causeries sur les enfants arriérés et insuffisants sous divers rapports. Organise des cours de perfectionnement pour l'enseignement spécial, des matières scolaires, travaux manuels, gymnastique. Et surtout, voilà un beau morceau pour les psychologues! dirige l'enquête et l'observation de ces professeurs afin qu'ils nous apportent au Laboratoire les données les plus exactes et fidèles sur la conduite de ces enfants faibles et anormaux.[35]

C'est ainsi que les descriptions des enfants inadaptés ont commencé à être produites pour alimenter la réflexion et la pratique des nouvelles professions concernant l'éducation spécialisée. Le modèle adopté pour les classes spéciales dans l'État de Minas Gerais correspond par de nombreux aspects au modèle genevois, une "internationalité", d'après le concept proposé par Caruso et Vera,[36] qui atteint le système local en voie de modernisation.

Classes homogènes et classes spéciales à Belo Horizonte

La proposition de réorganisation des classes scolaires et de création des classes spéciales figurait déjà dans le Règlement de l'enseignement primaire de 1927.[37] Selon l'article 367, ces classes seraient destinées à l'enseignement d'enfants d'âge scolaire considérés comme débiles soit par leur constitution organique, soit à cause d'infirmités ou d'insuffisance de nutrition.[38] Il faut noter que, d'après le document

---

[34]Ibid., 116.
[35]Ibid.
[36]Caruso et Vera, "Pluralizing meanings," 10.
[37]Decreto n. 7.970-A, 15 octobre 1927. *Regulamento do Ensino Primário*, Minas Gerais (Belo Horizonte: Imprensa Oficial, 1927).
[38]Ibid., 1242.

légal, les troubles présentés par les enfants étaient considérés surtout du point de vue médical. C'est seulement après l'entrée en scène du personnel du Laboratoire de psychologie de l'École de perfectionnement des enseignants que les troubles psychiques des enfants et l'action du milieu social sur leur étiologie commencèrent à être pris en compte.

La participation du Laboratoire, du point de vue intellectuel, dans le processus d'organisation des "classes homogènes" à travers l'application des tests d'intelligence commença à partir de 1931. Concernant les classes spéciales, c'est en juin 1932 qu'une classe pour "anormaux" avec 15 enfants présentant des troubles mentaux ou des handicaps fut ouverte par le Laboratoire de psychologie avec le but d'expérimenter de nouvelles méthodes pour l'éducation spéciale. La classe fut appelée "classe Descoeudres" et était coordonnée par Naytres Rezende, élève d'Antipoff.

Le nom d'Alice Descoeudres, attribué à la classe expérimentale, est le signe de l'étroitesse des liens entre le modèle de la classe spéciale à Belo Horizonte et le modèle de l'Institut Rousseau à partir de ce moment-là. Le livre de Descoeudres, *L'Éducation des enfants arriérés*, fut traduit en portugais en 1936 par la même Naytres Rezende, sous la supervision d'Helena Antipoff.[39] En 1933, Rezende déclare qu'il y avait déjà à Belo Horizonte 34 classes spéciales. Sur un total de 9272 enfants, 883 fréquentaient les classes spéciales, soit 9.5% de la population scolaire. Les classes furent sélectionnées selon les résultats des tests et l'observation des enfants. Les élèves des classes spéciales possédaient ainsi une fiche individuelle d'observation.

A partir de mai 1933, l'institutrice Naytres Rezende commença un travail d'orientation et de soutien matériel pour les classes D dans les réunions d'orientation des jeudis matins. Pendant ces réunions, des connaissances sur les exercices d'orthopédie mentale et sur le matériel préparé pour l'éducation des "anormaux" étaient transmises aux enseignantes.

Les exercices d'orthopédie mentale recommandés pour les classes spéciales étaient ceux proposés par Alfred Binet dans son livre *Les idées modernes sur les enfants*,[40] par Descoeudres à propos de l'éducation des "arriérés", par Maria Montessori, ou inventés par Antipoff et son équipe. Leur finalité était de "redresser, guider et fortifier les fonctions mentales",[41] en analogie avec l'orthopédie qui tente de corriger les difformités du corps. L'entraînement systématique et répétitif des fonctions mentales, dans le but de les améliorer, constituait la base des exercices d'orthopédie mentale. Binet partait du principe que si un muscle pouvait améliorer sa fonction à travers les exercices, il devait en être de même pour les fonctions mentales. Antipoff, par contre, était plus modeste et pensait que, dans l'état de la science psychologique à l'époque, il n'était pas possible de garantir que les fonctions et dispositions mentales puissent être développées. En tout cas, elle était sûre que "l'individu qui les pratique perfectionne l'art de s'en servir et, par conséquent, fait accroître nécessairement le rendement de ses facultés".[42] Les exercices

---

[39] Alice Descoeudres, *A Educação das crianças retardadas: seus principios, seus methodos, o que todas as crianças podem della aproveitar* (Belo Horizonte: Sociedade Pestalozzi, 1936).
[40] Alfred Binet. *Les idées modernes sur les enfants* (Paris: Flammarion, 1920).
[41] Helena Antipoff, "Da ortopedia mental," in *Coletânea das Obras Escritas de Helena Antipoff*, vol. 3, ed. Centro de Documentação e Pesquisa Helena Antipoff (Belo Horizonte: Imprensa Oficial, 1992), 67–74.
[42] Ibid., 67.

d'orthopédie mentale s'adressaient à plusieurs fonctions psychologiques et psychomotrices: les sens, la motricité, l'affectivité, la pensée, la volonté, et avaient pour but de développer la mémoire, l'intelligence, l'attention et l'imagination. Ils devaient être agréables et stimulants pour les enfants, leur durée courte pour ne pas les fatiguer. L'application était progressive, des plus faciles aux plus difficiles, pour stimuler les réussites et éveiller le désir de continuer.

Pour Antipoff, selon les propositions de Descoeudres, l'enseignement dans les classes spéciales devait suivre les principes suivants: 1) respecter l'activité propre de l'élève, sa liberté, éviter la discipline rigide, offrir l'opportunité de pratiquer des activités variées en classe, dans le jardin ou même durant des promenades et excursions à travers la ville; 2) cibler l'éducation sensorielle pour éveiller l'intelligence; 3) concentrer l'enseignement sur des sujets plus concrets, proches des intérêts des enfants; 4) individualiser l'enseignement pour prendre en compte les particularités physiques et mentales de chaque enfant; 5) l'enseignement devait être utile pour préparer l'enfant à la vie, développer ses aptitudes pour lui donner la possibilité d'être indépendant. Selon Antipoff, ces principes seraient les mêmes que ceux de la pédagogie moderne en général, basée sur les méthodes actives. La différence, dans l'enseignement spécial, était liée à la distribution des activités dans le temps. Ainsi, les proportions entre les exercices didactiques, les exercices psychologiques (orthopédie mentale), le travail manuel, les jeux éducatifs et l'occupation libre devaient être établies selon les possibilités des enfants. Dans ce programme, l'éducation – et non pas l'instruction – devait être la priorité. Il fallait mettre l'accent sur l'organisation de la personnalité, la formation d'habitudes pour fixer l'attention, observer, coordonner les actions, imiter, penser et réfléchir, dans la perspective de l'éducation fonctionnelle claparedienne.[43]

Le rapport de Naytres Rezende sur la situation des classes spéciales à Belo Horizonte en 1933 souligne que leur organisation avait été faite à partir des résultats des tests d'intelligence (Binet-Terman, Dearborn et Goodenough) et des tests scolaires. Beaucoup d'enfants étaient des redoublants. La majorité des élèves des classes D – 57.23% – présentaient des résultats normaux en ce qui concerne l'intelligence. Les problèmes les plus fréquents concernaient les troubles psychologiques (agitation, apathie, tristesse, comportements bizarres). Les enfants étaient classifiés par les enseignantes, dans leur majorité, comme désobéissants, agressifs, ou présentant des troubles de caractère (mensonge, vol). L'auteur observe qu'il y avait plus d'enfants assignés aux classes spéciales en provenance des milieux sociaux les plus pauvres de la ville.[44] Il manquait à une grande quantité de ces enfants l'*intelligence civilisée*, en conformité à ce qui avait été prévu par Antipoff. Pour cette raison, les exercices d'orthopédie mentale devaient leur apprendre à penser, à observer, à mieux organiser l'attention et la réflexion, c'est-à-dire à développer les aptitudes adaptées à l'environnement scolaire. Les enfants spéciaux, d'après Antipoff, présentaient soit

---

[43]Helena Antipoff, "O ensino nas classes especiais," in *Coletânea das Obras Escritas de Helena Antipoff*, vol. 3, ed. Centro de Documentação e Pesquisa Helena Antipoff (Belo Horizonte: Imprensa Oficial, 1992), 47–65.
[44]Naytres de Rezende, "Orientação do ensino nas classes especiais dos Grupos Escolares de Belo Horizonte, em 1933," *Boletim de educação e saúde pública de Minas Gerais* 16 (1934): 55–66.

un système nerveux affaibli, soit des difficultés qui pouvaient être attribuées à un environnement désorganisé et à une vie sans règles. Pour eux, l'éducation de l'attention et de la pensée devait être complétée par des moyens plus analytiques.[45]

Il est ainsi possible de voir que l'organisation par niveau intellectuel et les activités prévues pour les classes spéciales établies à Belo Horizonte au début des années 1930 suivirent globalement le modèle genevois proposé par l'Institut Rousseau, et spécialement par Claparède et Descoeudres. Outre le livre de Descoeudres, le livre de Claparède intitulé *Psychologie de l'enfant et pédagogie expérimentale* a été traduit en portugais à l'époque par l'équipe du Laboratoire de psychologie, publié à Belo Horizonte et distribué dans d'autres régions brésiliennes. En 1933, la traduction de l'*Éducation fonctionnelle*, du même auteur, fut stimulée par le groupe de Belo Horizonte et publiée à São Paulo par l'éditeur Companhia Editora Nacional, responsable de la diffusion d'une importante collection de titres en éducation et pédagogie parmi les éducateurs brésiliens de l'époque.[46] Claparède a visité Belo Horizonte en 1930, à l'invitation d'Antipoff et de l'équipe de l'École de perfectionnement, et le travail du Laboratoire de psychologie devint bien connu des éducateurs brésiliens comme un exemple remarquable d'éducation spéciale, surtout à partir de la fondation de la Société Pestalozzi de Belo Horizonte, en 1932, et de l'Institut Pestalozzi, en 1934, deux institutions établies par Antipoff et son équipe pour l'éducation des enfants exceptionnels, avec le soutien du gouvernement de Minas Gerais. Dans un rapport concernant l'examen médical des enfants indiqués aux classes spéciales, publié en 1934, le médecin Aureliano Tavares Bastos, qui faisait partie de l'équipe pestalozzienne, observa que l'État de Minas Gerais fut le premier, au Brésil, à promouvoir la création d'une institution spécifique pour le traitement et la rééducation des enfants exceptionnels d'après les principes de l'hygiène mentale.

Une marque importante de l'expérience d'éducation spéciale à Belo Horizonte fut, bien sûr, l'observation des effets du milieu social et culturel sur le développement des enfants venant des familles des classes populaires. Pour ces enfants, les exercices d'orthopédie mentale et les activités flexibles proposées par Antipoff pour enrichir leur expérience en ville seraient bien probablement une manière de leur offrir un accès plus aisé à l'intelligence "civilisée" demandée par l'école.

Dans les années suivantes, le Laboratoire de psychologie de l'École de perfectionnement des enseignants de Belo Horizonte accueillait des éducateurs venus d'autres États du Brésil et d'autres pays d'Amérique du sud, désireux d'apprendre les nouvelles techniques développées en psychologie de l'enfant et pour l'éducation des enfants "exceptionnels". En 1945, quand l'École fut annexée comme un cours d'administration scolaire à l'École normale de l'État de Minas Gerais, Antipoff accepta un poste de psychologue au Département national de l'enfant, au Ministère de la santé, à Rio de Janeiro. Pendant son séjour à Rio, elle réunit aussi un groupe d'éducateurs pour la fondation de la Société Pestalozzi du Brésil, avec le but de continuer le travail en éducation spécialisée. Les Sociétés Pestalozzi se sont répandues partout dans le pays, comme des organisations indépendantes associées en réseau (il

---

[45]Helena Antipoff, "Exercícios de atenção," in *Coletânea das Obras Escritas de Helena Antipoff*, vol. 3, ed. Centro de Documentação e Pesquisa Helena Antipoff (Belo Horizonte: Imprensa Oficial, 1992), 109–14.

[46]Édouard Claparède, *Psicologia da criança e pedagogia experimental*, trad. Aires M. M. Filho et T. Pereira, préface H. Antipoff (Belo Horizonte: Imprensa Oficial, 1934) et *Educação funcional*, trad. J. Grabois (São Paulo: Companhia Editora Nacional, 1933).

y a aujourd'hui au Brésil 156 Sociétés Pestalozzi). Les classes spéciales se sont aussi répandues dans le système d'enseignement public et l'influence des méthodes développées dans les Sociétés Pestalozzi pour l'enseignement des enfants "exceptionnels" a circulé partout au Brésil.[47] Cependant, il faut dire que les conséquences de l'adoption d'un modèle hybride d'évaluation des difficultés scolaires – dans lequel sont considérés les difficultés dues à la constitution organique et les problèmes découlant de la situation sociale et culturelle des familles – avec une forte participation de l'approche de la psychologie de l'enfant d'orientation fonctionnelle, sont encore à découvrir. Il est vrai également que la description des difficultés scolaires des enfants produite par le groupe d'enseignantes liées à Antipoff et les méthodes de traitement et d'éducation alors proposées ont influencé d'une manière profonde le développement ultérieur des professions concernées – psychologues, pédagogues, psychopédagogues, psychiatres – réunies dans les équipes des Sociétés Pestalozzi.

Conclusion

L'histoire de l'établissement de classes spéciales pour l'éducation d'enfants avec des troubles de développement dans la ville de Belo Horizonte pendant les années 1930 est étroitement liée à l'histoire d'Helena Antipoff et, par conséquent, au modèle établi à Genève – modèle qu'elle connaissait bien et auquel elle avait participé comme élève et assistante de Claparède, avant de migrer au Brésil. La division des classes par niveau intellectuel, le diagnostic des enfants à travers les tests d'intelligence, la référence à l'idée de "l'école sur mesure" proposée par Claparède, le dialogue avec les méthodes développées par Alice Descoeudres démontrent la présence au Brésil du modèle genevois. L'idéal d'une pédagogie scientifique qui pourrait traiter les cas d'enfants "anormaux" ou d'enfants dits "exceptionnels", comme l'a suggéré Antipoff, était présent dans le modèle prévu pour ces classes spéciales. En même temps, l'observation des caractéristiques singulières du contexte brésilien, et surtout l'existence de différences culturelles importantes entre les enfants venant de différents milieux sociaux, a provoqué la réflexion sur la possibilité d'interpréter les résultats des tests d'intelligence comme manifestations de l'action du milieu social et culturel sur le développement des enfants. L'une des suggestions fut alors d'aménager les pratiques éducatives d'orthopédie mentale comme un moyen de développer le type d'intelligence demandé par l'école.

Les résultats des travaux réalisés dans le domaine de l'éducation des individus exceptionnels dans le Minas Gerais à l'époque dépassèrent les frontières de l'État. De nouvelles études doivent être faites pour mieux comprendre comment la circulation de ces travaux a produit des repères pour l'histoire de l'éducation spéciale au Brésil; qu'elle fut l'influence réelle d'un modèle – fortement basé sur la psychologie – sur le développement ultérieur du système d'éducation publique, et des professions organisées autour de l'éducation et du traitement des difficultés d'apprentissage dans le pays.

Les classes spéciales furent l'une des nombreuses initiatives mises en œuvre dans le Minas Gerais par le groupe associé à Antipoff, à partir du dialogue avec l'équipe de l'Institut Rousseau. En même temps, la construction du concept d'*intelligence civilisée* pour traduire les différences culturelles entre les enfants montre les adapta-

---

[47]Elza M. S. Cataldo, "Politiques d'intégration: Aspects de l'éducation spécialisée au Brésil" (thèse de doctorat, Université de Paris René Descartes, 1986).

tions et réinterprétations que les concepts d'enfant spécial, d'école sur mesure et d'orthopédie mentale peuvent avoir subi dans le contexte brésilien.

Acknowledgements

Les auteurs remercient l'agence FAPEMIG – Fundação de Amparo à Pesquisa do Estado de Minas Gerais – pour le soutien fourni à la recherche et à la production de l'article.

Westward bound? Dutch education and cultural transfer in the mid-twentieth century

Nelleke Bakker

University of Groningen, Groningen, The Netherlands

This article discusses the transition from philosophy to psychology as the main source of inspiration for education during the mid-twentieth century in the Netherlands, situated between Germany in the east and the English-speaking world in the west. Claims have been made that educational theory in the Netherlands was dominated by German philosophy before 1945 and subsequently turned westward for inspiration. The transnational transfer of ideas and concepts to the Netherlands is studied using textbooks on childhood and education for teachers-to-be, published between 1925 and 1970, as sources. Did the Dutch indeed turn from the east to the west for inspiration, and if so when and along the lines of which theories? This article shows that the authors of the textbooks did not simply copy theories from abroad, but gave them a reading of their own and selected what they liked. A shift from the east to the west as a source of inspiration did not occur before the 1970s. Developmentalism, personalism, phenomenology, characterology and individual psychology were all imported from German-speaking countries. It is true that some of these theories were brought to the west as their founders fled Nazism, but that does not undo their continental European origins.

Introduction

Discussing the foundations of prevailing theories on education it has been suggested by several authors that the twentieth century witnessed a shift from educational philosophy, religion and bourgeois morality to academic psychology and psychiatry as major sources of inspiration. This transition is supposed to be fruit of the development of welfare states in the Western world, as well as an expression of a larger process called modernisation, individualisation, psychologisation or scientisation of society and culture.[1] From a more critical perspective authors have referred to this increased reliance on science as

---

[1] For example, Jeroen Jansz and Peter van Drunen, eds., *A Social History of Psychology* (Oxford: Blackwell, 2004); Barbara Beatty, Emily D. Cahan and Julia Grant, eds., *When Science Encounters the Child: Educating, Parenting, and Child Welfare in 20th-century America* (New York and London: Teachers University Press, 2006).

medicalisation or normalisation ("governing") of the individual and of interpersonal relationships.[2] Education is usually mentioned as one of the fields in which these processes can be recognised most particularly. Compulsory schooling as an aspect of nation building and a growing impact of school life on childhood appear as preconditions that have enabled these processes, next to the establishment and development of child care institutions like judicial child protection and child guidance clinics. Instead of future citizens, children became pupils who deserve proper schooling and actual but vulnerable citizens who deserve professional help when parents fail.[3]

As regards the everyday treatment of children in schools, these major processes of change are said to express themselves in a greater emphasis on happiness instead of conformity and obedience, on differences between individuals and between phases of development instead of uniformity (children of various types and ages instead of "the child"), as well as in a greater emphasis on mental health instead of "just" physical health and sheer survival into adulthood, and in an individualised approach to behavioural problems instead of collective disciplining. This transition is usually associated with a shift of staff among professionals involved, from teachers and preachers (focusing on conformity and obedience) and from paediatricians (focusing on physical health and growth) to psychologists and psychiatrists, who directed their attention at mental health and development in the widest sense. These shifts are said to have occurred in the middle of the century, after the preconditions had been fulfilled but before normal development and the absence of emotional and behavioural problems became the exclusive criteria for adequate parenting and education as they are today.[4]

In the Anglo-American literature it is, moreover, suggested that these processes have occurred across the Western world. On the basis of this literature a first historical line of development, focusing on individual development, is often drawn from Granville Stanley Hall as the pioneer of empirical, evolutionary child study and developmentalism, through John Watson's behaviourism and his focus on habit formation, to Arnold Gesell and his understanding of the particularities of children's

---

[2]For example, Peter Conrad, *The Medicalization of Society: On the Transformation of Human Conditions into Treatable Disorders* (Baltimore, MD: Johns Hopkins University Press, 2007); Nicolas Rose, *The Psychological Complex: Psychology, Politics and Society in England 1869–1939* (London: Routledge and Kegan Paul, 1985); André Turmel, *A Historical Sociology of Childhood: Developmental Thinking, Categorization, and Graphic Visualization* (Cambridge: Cambridge University Press, 2008).

[3]Depaepe recognises that the twentieth century shows an increase in institutional care for children, but prefers to see this as an aspect of a longer process of "educationalisation" starting in the eighteenth century. See Marc Depaepe, *Between Educationalization and Appropriation: Selected Writings on the History of Educational Systems* (Leuven: Leuven University Press, 2012). On the idea that the twentieth century showed a distinct increase in expert involvement in children's lives, see Beatty et al., *When Science Encounters the Child*; Marijke Gijswijt-Hofstra and Hilary Marland, eds., *Cultures of Child Health in Britain and the Netherlands in the Twentieth Century* (Amsterdam and New York: Rodopi, 2003).

[4]Peter N. Stearns, *Anxious Parents: A History of Modern Child Rearing in America* (New York: New York University Press, 2003); Turmel, *A Historical Sociology*; Sol Cohen, *Challenging Orthodoxies: Towards a New History of Education* (New York: Peter Lang, 1999); Theresa R. Richardson, *The Century of the Child: The Mental Hygiene Movement and Social Policy in the United States and Canada* (New York: New York State University Press, 1989); Nelleke Bakker, "Child guidance and mental health in the Netherlands", *Paedagogica Historica* 42 (2006): 769–791.

natural developmental phases, as described in the 1940s and 1950s, and the way the famous Doctor Benjamin Spock used his ideas. His *Common Sense Book on Baby and Child Care*, which first appeared in 1946, has become the icon of the modern, easy-going style of child-rearing that focuses on normal and healthy development and on the necessity of seeking professional help in the case of abnormal behaviour.[5] A second historical line of development is constructed around mental health by authors who discuss pedagogical pathology and institutions taking care of children with emotional or behavioural disorders, starting from William Healy's Juvenile Psychopathic Institute, meant to prevent juvenile crime by studying young criminals' personalities and hereditary predisposition, through the Mental Hygiene Movement and child guidance clinics, established from the 1920s, which quickly developed into popular, non-residential clinical institutions inspired by Sigmund Freud's psychoanalysis, to modern awareness of the multiple risks threatening a child's safety, secure attachment, and normal or healthy development, which can equally be recognised in Spock's *magnum opus* and its many adaptations from 1957 onward.[6]

In contrast to Anglo-American historiography's suggestion that a common road was taken across the Western world, I would like to propose that there is no reason to assume that the transformation process from educational philosophy, religion and bourgeois morality to developmentalism, psychoanalysis and a clinical approach as the main sources of inspiration in education has developed along identical lines and at the same pace outside the English-speaking world.

This article questions the assumption of a common road for one country, the Netherlands, which is situated in-between Germany in the east and England in the west. Claims have been made that educational theory in the Netherlands by and large took inspiration from German-speaking countries (the East) and their tradition of educational philosophy before the Second World War and has turned westward to Britain and the United States (the West) and their empirical research tradition in psychology and psychiatry ever since.[7] Although child guidance was modelled after the American example and parenting ideals were strongly influenced by British Freudianism after the war,[8] as regards schooling there are good reasons to put this assumption to the test of historical inquiry. First, more recent research into the history of the academic disciplines of education studies and psychology in the Netherlands has shown a considerable time lag between these disciplines as

---

[5]Alice Boardman Smuts, *History and Research in Child Development* (Chicago, IL: University of Chicago Press, 1986); John R. Morss, *The Biologising of Childhood: Developmental Psychology and the Darwinian Myth* (London: Lawrence Erlbaum, 1990); Turmel, *A Historical Sociology of Childhood*; Julia Grant, *Raising Baby by the Book: The Education of American Mothers* (New Haven, CT: Yale University Press, 1998); Benjamin Spock, *The Pocket Book of Baby and Child Care* (New York: Pocket Books, 1946). This version appeared shortly after the original, *The Common Sense Book of Baby and Child Care* (1946).
[6]Richardson, *The Century of the Child*; Cohen, *Challenging Orthodoxies*; Kathleen W. Jones, *Taming the Troublesome Child: American Families, Child Guidance, and the Limits of Psychiatric Authority* (Cambridge, MA: Harvard University Press, 1999); Alice Boardman Smuts, *Science in the Service of Children, 1893–1935* (New Haven, CT: Yale University Press, 2006); James M. Kauffman and Timothy J. Landrum, *Children and Youth with Emotional and Behavioral Disorders* (Austin, TX: Pro-ed, 2006); Spock, *The Pocket Book of Baby and Child Care*.
[7]Ernst Mulder, *Beginsel en beroep. Pedagogiek aan de universiteit in Nederland 1900–1940* (Amsterdam: Historisch Seminarium, 1989); Philip J. Idenburg, *Schets van het Nederlandse schoolwezen* (Groningen: Wolters, 1964).
[8]Bakker, "Child guidance and mental health in the Netherlands".

receivers of intellectual influences from the West and a difference in the extent to which continental European influences continued to be experienced. Whereas psychology had already turned away from the German tradition by the mid-1950s,[9] education studies did not do so until the 1970s and, even then, to a much lesser degree. Academic educationists continued to draw their inspiration from European continental phenomenology well into the 1960s.[10] Second, research into the intellectual orientation of Dutch universities, particularly their granting of honorary degrees and use of textbooks, during the post-war era has demonstrated that the universities were dominated by German intellectual influences up to about 1970, which is much longer than has commonly been assumed. In education, only two fields stand out as already fully "Americanised" in the 1960s, educational testing and school management, which have both been promoted by the American Fulbright Program. Educational reform, for example, was not orientated toward the West before the 1980s.[11] Therefore, it is not very likely that schooling, which was much more determined by education studies than by psychology, turned to the West for its inspiration immediately after the war.

Transnational circulation of pedagogical ideas and concepts has only recently become a field of historical study. Scholars who study transmission and transformation of culture over time and through institutions prefer the term "transmission" to "transfer", as it recognises the pedagogical and cultural processes involved and is more akin to sharing, as the knowledge and values transmitted are retained by the "source group" at the same time as they are gained by the "target group", whereas "transfer" suggests their loss by the former.[12] Those who study the transnational circulation of culture, on the other hand, consistently use "cultural transfer" as a conceptual tool to analyse the manifold interdependencies and entanglements between geographical and cultural spaces, its focus being pointed primarily at the processes and mechanisms of transmission that effect cultural transfer. "Transfer" pertains to the movement in space of both material objects like books, and their translations, and symbols and concepts. It refers, moreover, not so much to the will to export but to the desire to import particular aspects of a culture and, consequently, to selection by the receiving party. As ideas do not move on their own, cultural intermediaries or translators are involved in this process. This implies that the study of transnational circulation of ideas and concepts needs to take into consideration not only the context in which they arose, but even more particularly the conditions of their reception, which include not only selection but also adaptation or transformation in the process of their integration into the receiving culture. So,

---

[9] Pieter J. van Strien, *Nederlandse psychologen en hun publiek. Een contextuele geschiedenis* (Assen: Van Gorcum, 1993), 155–172.
[10] Marc Depaepe and Nelleke Bakker, "Een gemeenschappelijke studeerkamer. 75 jaar Pedagogische Studiën", in N. Verloop, ed., *75 jaar opvoeding en onderwijs – 75 jaar Pedagogische Studiën* (Groningen: Wolters-Noordhoff, 1998), 9–44; Ivo van Hilvoorde, *Grenswachters van de pedagogiek. Demarcatie en disciplinevorming in de ontwikkeling van de Nederlandse academische pedagogiek (1900–1970)* (Deventer: HB Uitgevers, 2002).
[11] Jan C.C. Rupp, *Van oude en nieuwe universiteiten. De verdringing van Duitse door Amerikaanse invloeden op de wetenschapsbeoefening en het hoger onderwijs in Nederland, 1945–1995* (The Hague: Sdu Uitgevers, 1997), 219–232.
[12] Peter Cunningham and Bruce Leslie, "Introduction", *History of Education* 40 (2012), 135–141.

paradoxically, a transnational perspective implies the need to focus attention on the national culture and the way it transforms as ideas and concepts cross borders.[13]

Everyday schooling has been determined much more by professional manuals and textbooks for teachers-to-be, suggesting particular attitudes towards children and their education, than by the academic outlook and orientation of studies in education and psychology.[14] Textbooks provided authoritative models of behaviour, which may have been influenced by theory from across borders directly, but the transfer may also have been mediated through cultural intermediaries or translators. This article discusses the cultural transfer of ideas and concepts from neighbouring countries and the United States to the Netherlands, as they became manifest in textbooks on childhood and education for teachers-to-be that were published between 1925 and 1970. Did the Dutch indeed turn from the East to the West for their inspiration in matters of education? If so, when and along the lines of which theories and concepts? Did the Dutch come to focus on individual development and mental health in the way that Anglo-American educators did? If so, were these foci indeed imported from across the North Sea and the Atlantic or did they come in from any other direction than the west? Which role was played in the process of selection and adaptation by cultural intermediaries and which elements of "Dutchness" were preserved in the process of cultural transfer? To answer these questions, this article discusses the theoretical foundations of the textbooks that were used in public and private-religious teacher training colleges.

Textbooks for public school teachers

Throughout this period, textbooks for teachers-to-be in public schools continued to consider child rearing in a traditional way that corresponded with the moderate Calvinism that prevailed in Dutch society. Children had to learn to obey the rules, to learn self-restraint, to develop their conscience and to become morally good, responsible and useful citizens of the nation. At the same time, however, child rearing was defined as "guiding a human being's growth" in the most authoritative textbook for public teacher training colleges, *Educational Studies: The Child* (*Paedagogiek: Het kind*), 10 editions of which were published between 1930 and 1953. The author of this textbook, Louis Bigot, the director of a teacher training college, warned his readers that the power of the educator was not unlimited, as heredity and given physical and mental characteristics of children were not to be

---

[13]Matthias Middell, "Kulturtransfer und historische Komparistik: Thesen zu ihrem Verhältnis", *Comparativ* 10 (2000), 4–7; Michel Espagne, "Kulturtransfer und Fachgeschichte der Geisteswissenschaften", *Comparativ* 10 (2000), 42–61; Maria del Mar del Pozo, "The transnational dimensions of pedagogical ideas: The case of the project method, 1918–1939", *Paedagogica Historica* 45 (2009), 561–584; Gabriela Ossenbach and Maria del Mar del Pozo, "Postcolonial models, cultural transfers and transnational perspectives in Latin America: A research agenda", *Paedagogica Historica* 47 (2011), 579–600; Christine Mayer, "Female education and the cultural transfer of pedagogical knowledge in the eighteenth century", *Paedagogica Historica* 48 (2012), 511–526.

[14]Depaepe et al. argue that educational journals as sources for historians of classroom history do not only show which issues were bothering teachers, but also their attitude towards teaching and children and consequently school practice. See Marc Depaepe et al., *Order in Progress: Everyday Educational Practice in Primary Schools: Belgium 1880–1970* (Leuven: Leuven University Press, 2008). Compared to journals, I conceive of textbooks as more condensed versions of shared attitudes among educational professionals.

denied. John Locke had made this mistake by thinking that the child was a *tabula rasa*, as had the behaviourist John Watson, who had focused too narrowly on learning by conditioning, he explained. The teachers' manual instead emphasised the limits of the power of education. A child's individual character had to be taken into account in a serious manner. Nevertheless, there was a strong emphasis on characteristics of "the" child as it passes through the different phases of development. As in the older German pedagogical pathology, behavioural problems were discussed as "children's faults", which varied from mental retardation to hysteria and shyness. Child guidance clinics, the first of which had been established in 1928 in Amsterdam,[15] were only briefly mentioned as institutions that could provide help to "difficult" children, who "used to be called naughty".[16]

Child study does not figure prominently in this textbook. Edouard Claparède's version of the recapitulation theory was, for example, mentioned but not subscribed to, whereas Maria Montessori's concept of the "sensitive period" in a child's development was presented as useful. Psychology was mentioned as one of four "supportive sciences" for educationists, next to physiology, ethics and history. Apart from cognitive training, the child was in need of physical, mental, emotional, moral, social, aesthetic and particularly religious education, according to the textbook. Because "inner peace" was mentioned as the ultimate goal of child rearing, both as an individual and as a member of the community, it is clear to the modern reader that the ideas of the foremost Dutch protagonist of academic education studies in the interwar years, Philip Kohnstamm,[17] have served as a major source of inspiration for this teachers' manual. This is not a coincidence, as he and an academic psychologist acted as scientific advisors for the textbook. Kohnstamm in turn was particularly under the influence of the German psychologist and philosopher Wilhelm Stern, who was a representative of philosophical personalism and one of the founders of both differential psychology and IQ theory.[18] However, whereas Kohnstamm's major study into personalism, subtitled *A Christian Pedagogical Theory* and published in 1929,[19] was based on a plethora of German academic psychological studies – such as developmental and psychoanalytic works – the teachers' manual gives only a very short reading list, mentioning primarily older Dutch work on moral upbringing, a few translated German books on child rearing and adolescence, and one early study of Karl Bühler, which has probably served as a source of inspiration for discussing the upbringing of toddlers, school children and adolescents in more detail in separate chapters.[20] By 1930, we must conclude, development was already an important line of thought in Dutch education and the inspiration clearly came from the East, although the Jewish Stern and Bühler moved to the United States, in 1933 and 1938 respectively.

---

[15] Bakker, "Child guidance and mental health in the Netherlands".
[16] Louis C.T. Bigot, *Het kind*, 3rd edn. (Groningen: Wolters, 1933), 101; Bigot, *Het kind*, 8th edn. (Groningen: Wolters, 1948), 120.
[17] Mulder, *Beginsel en beroep*, 89–128
[18] James T. Lamiell, *Beyond Individual and Group Differences: Human Individuality, Scientific Psychology, and William Stern's Critical Personalism* (Thousand Oaks, CA: Sage, 2003).
[19] Philip A. Kohnstamm, *Persoonlijkheid in wording. Schets ener christelijke opvoedkunde*, 3rd edn. (Haarlem: Tjeenk Willink & Zoon, 1959).
[20] Bigot, *Het kind* (1933).

The textbook was seriously revised only from the eleventh edition, in 1955, up to the fifteenth edition, in 1967, in which particularly the chapter on school children with learning disabilities was greatly extended. Child psychology was no longer presented as a "supportive science", but as a relevant field of knowledge on its own accord. As before, enlightened or romantic European philosophers such as Jean-Jacques Rousseau and Friedrich Froebel were mentioned as pioneers in the field, but contemporary psychologists were also briefly introduced to the students now, Jean Piaget, Stern, Ovide Decroly and Karl and Charlotte Bühler among them. Schools of thought that had influenced the study of childhood were mentioned as such, without any further explanation: behaviourism, individual psychology and Gestalt.[21] Nevertheless, the suggested reading list was still very limited. The 1967 list includes few titles of studies from abroad; those that are mentioned are mostly of German origin, such as the translation of Eduard Spranger's hermeneutic study on youth. Students apparently were not supposed to study scholarly books themselves, apart from Dutch ones.[22] They were referred to Dutch intermediaries such as the most authoritative professor of education and psychology in the post-war era, Martinus Langeveld, who embraced Edmund Husserls's phenomenology and the German hermeneutic educational philosophy and conceived of upbringing as helping a child to become morally autonomous.[23] Stern, Spranger, the Bühlers and German educational reformers were among the authors he most frequently referred to.[24] So, throughout the 1960s, European and especially German theory, particularly developmentalism and phenomenology, continued to be the dominant influence on this teachers' manual.

A parallel series on psychology by the same author accompanied the volume on child rearing. Between 1925 and 1967 16 editions of *Psychology* were published. Throughout these years the textbook continued to be organised along the lines of psychological functions, such as perception, memory, cognition, emotion and will. In the late 1950s the chapter on character was extended with information on German characterology, and brief chapters were added on psychoanalysis, individual psychology, behaviourism, German hermeneutics and Dutch phenomenology as developed by Langeveld, of which the latter was described with most sympathy.[25] There was no reading list and it was not made clear to the students how they could use the wisdom collected in these fields of knowledge, all of which had their origins on the European continent.

In 1951 sweeping reforms were made to teacher training with the aim of elevating it to a higher intellectual level and making it offer better preparation for school practice by means of a stronger emphasis on pedagogy and didactics.[26] To serve the new teacher training colleges, a series of textbooks entitled *The New*

---

[21] Louis C.T. Bigot and Gilles van Hees, *Het kind*, 15th edn. (Groningen: Wolters, 1967), 37–38.
[22] Ibid., 215–6.
[23] Jaap Bos, *M.J. Langeveld: pedagoog aan de hand van het kind* (Amsterdam: Boom, 2011).
[24] Martinus Langeveld, *Beknopte theoretische paedagogiek*, 2nd edn. (Groningen: Wolters, 1946), 137.
[25] Louis C.T. Bigot, *Psychologie. Hoofdzaken van de zielkunde ten behoeve van aanstaande onderwijzers en onderwijzeressen* (Groningen: Wolters, 1926); Bigot, *Psychologie. Hoofdzaken van de zielkunde ten behoeve van aanstaande onderwijzers en onderwijzeressen*, 13th edn. (Groningen: Wolters, 1958).
[26] Mineke van Essen, *Kwekeling tussen akte en ideaal. De opleiding tot onderwijzer(es) vanaf 1800* (Amsterdam: SUN, 2006), 274–282.

Teacher Training College (*De Nieuwe Kweekschool*) was issued from the late 1950s onwards. The volume *Educational Studies A* (*Opvoedkunde A voor openbare kweekscholen*, 1956) was even more particularly based on Langeveld's reading of contemporary psychology and phenomenology. At the same time in this series, as in post-war Dutch society,[27] there was a strong emphasis on education for society. Reading suggestions in the 1956 edition of this manual were extensive, whereas the third and final edition of 1967 no longer contained a reading list but included references to primarily Dutch studies, some of them based on psychoanalysis. The German Reform-educationist Georg Kerschensteiner's book on education for citizenship (*Staatsbürgerlichte Erziehung*) was mentioned, as was the psychoanalyst Erich Fromm's work on freedom and individual responsibility for society. Moreover, the list included several individual psychological studies by Alfred Adler, the founder of this major Freudian heterodoxy, and by pupils of his such as Fritz and Ruth Künkel and Rudolf Dreikurs.[28] Like Fromm, the Jewish Adler and Dreikurs had left Germany or Austria in the early 1930s and become American citizens, whereas the Künkels did so in 1939, but that does not undo the continental European origins of their individual psychology, in which – in spite of its name – service to the community figured as a key aim of child rearing. Like Freudian psychoanalysis, individual psychology considers unconscious feelings and their influence on development, but unlike orthodox psychoanalysis it does not focus on desire and sexual drives, but on feelings of inferiority and a compensatory urge to become powerful as determining or, in the case of disharmony, sickening forces.[29]

The series *The New Teacher Training College* also included volumes on *Psychology* (*Algemene Psychologie*, 1957) and *Characterology* (*Karakterkunde*, 1962). The textbook on psychology was organised in a traditional way, along the lines of mental functions such as cognition, memory, perception and will, and explained what a teacher could expect regarding children's mental functioning. In a second part a selection of ideas was presented from newer philosophies, particularly phenomenology and existentialism, focusing on the subjective experience of the self, on human existence and on encounters with "the other". There is no reading list attached, but the names of the German theologian Martin Buber and the French philosopher Jean-Paul Sartre show up, as do Langeveld and the Dutch phenomenological psychologist Frederik Buytendijk. In a third part of the textbook three schools of psychological thought were briefly introduced to the students, Gestalt, psychoanalysis and behaviourism, of which the latter was immediately criticised as not concerned with the human being as a subject (a psychology *ohne Seele*) and therefore not very useful. Freudianism was criticised for its reductionism; religion, for example, was said to be reduced to "sublimated incestuous father fixation" and smoking to "oral satisfaction". Moreover, Freudianism was blamed for being void of

---

[27]Kees Schuyt and Ed Taverne, *1950: Prosperity and Welfare* (Assen: Van Gorcum, 2004), 290–293; Nelleke Bakker, Jan Noordman and Marjoke Rietveld-van Wingerden, *Vijf eeuwen opvoeden in Nederland. Idee en praktijk 1500–2000* (Assen: Van Gorcum, 2006), 237–243.

[28]Jan D. Brinksma and Frank Daalder, *Opvoedkunde A voor openbare kweekscholen. Leergang voor opvoedkunde en psychologie* I (Groningen: Wolters, 1956); Brinksma and Daalder, *Opvoedkunde. Algemene uitgave*, 3rd edn. (Groningen: Wolters, 1966).

[29]Heinz L. Ansbacher and Rowena R. Ansbacher, eds., *The Individual Psychology of Alfred Adler: A Systematic Presentation in Selections from his Writings* (New York: Basic Books, 1956).

"responsibility" on the part of the subject. Though unwillingly, it was admitted that Freudian therapy was "often successful".[30]

The volume on *Characterology* (*Karakterkunde*, 1962) was meant to help teachers-to-be to become good observers of individual children in their classrooms. This might become important if a suspicion grew that "a child's behaviour or school work departs from what one can normally expect".[31] In that case teachers could adapt their approach to the particular child or provide relevant information to other professionals on the basis of at least some knowledge of the theory. They could also, moreover, apply the theory to a systematic observation of the "problem" child. To support the teacher-to-be in the process of understanding differences between children, information was provided on six systems of classification of characters: one based on classical concepts of inborn temperament (choleric, sanguine and so on) developed by the Dutch differential psychologist Gerard Heymans, one based on psycho-physical characteristics developed by Ernst Kretschmer (active, slow and so on), one based on mental functioning developed by the analytic psychologist Carl Jung (introvert, extravert), one based on individual psychology's classification of the effects of healthy or sickening parenting styles developed by Künkel (submissive, well-adapted, shy and so on) and, finally, Henry Murray's Freudian typology of children's various emotional needs and the possible consequences if they remained unfulfilled.[32] Of these taxonomies of character only the latter was of American origin; the others were German, Swiss or Dutch. The textbook does not show a preference for any of these classifications, nor does it explain how to use them.

Regarding this series of textbooks for teachers-to-be, published around 1960, we must conclude that it did introduce new, subject-orientated theory, based on clinical experiences to the students, particularly individual psychology and various characterologies, almost all of which had their intellectual roots in the German-speaking world.

Textbooks for orthodox Calvinist teachers

Throughout the period under study, Dutch society was deeply divided by religion. These were the heydays of the so-called "pillarisation". This implied that within one nation people lived in separate cultures, a constellation that had come into being at the end of the nineteenth century and continued well into the 1960s when secularisation ended it in many social fields.[33] Therefore, it is important to also consider textbooks for teachers-to-be that were used in orthodox Calvinist and Roman Catholic teacher training colleges. The majority of these colleges were founded after the principle of equal state financing of public and private-religious

---

[30]J. Jonges, *Algemene psychologie. Leergang voor opvoedkunde en psychologie II, eerste stuk* (Groningen: Wolters, 1957), 74–75, 84–85. He quoted Jan H. Van den Berg on Freud.
[31]Sipke D. Fokkema, *Karakterkunde. Leergang voor opvoedkunde en psychologie II, tweede stuk* (Groningen: Wolters, 1962), 78. The other volumes in this series concerned: Willem Bordewijk, H.E. Daamen, Dirk Fokkema and Hendrik Nieuwenhuis, *Kinderpsychologie en opvoedkundige psychologie. Leergang voor opvoedkunde en psychologie III, eerste stuk, verkorte uitgave* (Groningen: Wolters, 1960); Reinier Vedder, *Afwijkende kinderen in de school. Leergang voor opvoedkunde en psychologie IV* (Groningen: Wolters, 1958).
[32]Fokkema, *Karakterkunde*, 6–55.
[33]Piet de Rooy, *Republiek van rivaliteiten. Nederland sinds 1813* (Amsterdam: Mets & Schilt, 2002), 233–261.

schools was implemented in 1920. Calvinist colleges are known to have used textbooks for public school teachers until the 1930s, when they finally could obtain books of their own.[34]

One of the first textbooks for Calvinist colleges was a handbook on psychology, *Our Mental Life* (*Ons zieleleven*), edited six times between 1934 and 1948 and authored by the most influential orthodox Calvinist professor of education, Jan Waterink. This author was much quicker at integrating the newer psychology than the authors of the textbooks for public colleges. This greater receptivity towards the newer, subject-orientated psychology, particularly psychoanalysis, is not surprising if one realises that the empirical, function-orientated psychology, developed by Wilhelm Wundt and others in laboratories from the 1880s, had never been seen positively by orthodox Calvinists, as they declined any kind of human science that denied the unity of "the soul" (*Psychologie ohne Seele*) and welcomed theories that focused on personality or personality development.[35]

Unsurprisingly, religious and moral upbringing stood out as the prime goal of child rearing among orthodox Calvinists. However, as Waterink saw it, a child's emotional life counted just as much; an unhappy child could not live up to biblical rules. That is why from the first edition of his manual Waterink presented differential characterology in a positive light, discussing the taxonomies of character proposed by the German psychologist and graphologist Ludwig Klages, of the bio-psychologist Ernst Kretschmer and of the Dutch differential psychologist Heymans, and explaining the sickening effects of feelings of inferiority that remained uncompensated for, as described by the individual psychologists Adler and Künkel. The professor warned his readers that he consciously skipped Freudian psychoanalysis, which according to him did not consider "normal" people, whereas he claimed that Adler's individual psychology could be seen as a kind of characterology. From the third edition of his textbook, however, published in 1941, he did discuss Freud's "theory of lust" extensively in order to make sure that young Calvinists would understand the danger of Freud's "pansexualism", whereas Adler and Künkel were praised for providing a theory that could be used in the clinic to help explain the unconscious motives behind children's misbehaviours. The positive thing about Künkel's version of individual psychology was, the Calvinist professor insisted, that he allowed for a child's conscience and, consequently, for religion, as well as for a positive goal in child rearing, a life in harmony with one's family, the wider community, oneself and God.[36]

The first guide on education for Calvinist teacher training colleges, authored by Lucas van Klinken, a pupil of Waterink and himself a teacher in a Calvinist college, was published in 1936. His book put much more emphasis on authority in the

---

[34] Gerben E. de Vries, *De opleiding van de christelijke onderwijzer. Het karakter van de protestants-christelijke onderwijzersopleidingen, in het bijzonder in Friesland 1880–1980* (Leeuwarden: Fryske Academie, 2004), 120–133.

[35] Their intellectual leader during the early years of the century, professor of theology Herman Bavinck, explained this position in several studies. See Nelleke Bakker, *Kind en karakter. Nederlandse pedagogen over opvoeding in het gezin 1845–1925* (Amsterdam: Het Spinhuis, 1995), 177–180.

[36] Jan Waterink, *Ons zieleleven*, 3rd edn. (Wageningen: Zomer en Keuning's, 1941) 151–202; Waterink, *Ons zieleven*, 6th edn. (Wageningen: Zomer en Keuning's, 1948), 153–204. The pre-war edition had a different title: Jan Waterink, *Hoofdlijnen der zielkunde* (Wageningen: Zomer en Keuning's, 1934).

classroom than did other manuals and it devoted half of the text to the history of education, especially the tradition of Dutch Calvinist schooling with its strong emphasis on the Bible as the source of truth. As regards modern educational theory, Van Klinken was most critical of Decroly's and Montessori's biological-psychological or "naturalistic" perspective, which he accused of ignoring religion, authority and the child's higher destiny and of focusing too much on the senses. Kohnstamm and Stern, on the other hand, were praised for their interest in the individual and his conscience, in religion and in character building. Two German educationists stand out for receiving more positive attention than all others in this encyclopaedia of educational thought. One is the theologian Friedrich Foerster, whose books on moral and religious education used to be popular among Dutch liberal educationists in the 1910s. The other is the individual psychologist Künkel, several of whose books had been recently translated into the Dutch language. With Kohnstamm, Van Klinken was of the opinion that Künkel's *Einführung in die Charakterkunde* (1928) was one of the "deepest" studies into the essence of humanity. What he liked most was its normative assumption that a child had to reach the goal of a sense of belonging to the community through an "inner revolution", which could just as well be read as a religious conversion.[37] Again, in the index of this textbook German names far outnumber all others. What is even more remarkable is that almost no English or American authors were mentioned.[38]

Alongside the volume *Educational studies A* for public school teachers two different volumes on the theory of education for orthodox Protestant schools were published in the series of textbooks for the reformed post-war teacher training colleges: *Educational Studies B* (*Opvoedkunde B voor protestants-christelijke kweekscholen*, 1959) and *Textbook on Education* (*Leerboek der pedagogiek voor protestants-christelijke kweekscholen*, 1968).[39] Like Van Klinken's "encyclopaedia", these textbooks were much more traditional than Waterink's manual on psychology. The authors frequently referred to the Bible and to respected Dutch Calvinist theologians and educationists next to a whole range of German philosophers and educationists, such as Dietrich Bonhoeffer and Theodor Litt. The 1959 Calvinist textbook latched on to Langeveld's concept of autonomy as the final goal of all education, but added "being ready" for the acceptance of one's "assignment" in life. As expected, religion and authority played a more important role in these manuals than in the textbooks for public schooling, although it was emphasised that, for a Calvinist teacher, punishment should also be the last resort and "trust and friendship" were to dominate teacher–child interaction.[40]

The 1968 Calvinist textbook shows a very high level of Dutchness, as transnational influences were almost exclusively mediated through Langeveld's phenomenology and his reading of developmentalism and Freudianism. Not even the preferred definition of education was of orthodox Calvinist origin, as the two authors preferred to conceive of it in the same way that the first Roman Catholic

---

[37] Lucas van Klinken, *Hoofdlijnen en hoofdpunten van de opvoedkunde* (Meppel: Stenvert & Zoon), 212–217.
[38] Out of 167 names of educationists, only five were Anglo-American; all others were continental European. See van Klinken, *Hoofdlijnen en hoofdpunten van de opvoedkunde*, 465–468.
[39] Dirk Fokkema, *Opvoedkunde B voor protestants-christelijke kweekscholen* (Groningen: Wolters, 1959); Johan W. van Hulst and Ijsbrand van der Molen, *Leerboek der pedagogiek voor protestants-christelijke kweekscholen* IB (Groningen: Wolters-Noordhoff, 1968).
[40] Fokkema, *Opvoedkunde B*, 88.

professor of education, Johannes Hoogveld, had done: "helping a child to autonomously accomplish his assignment in life". The authors explicitly stated that "helping" instead of "moulding" had become the new keyword in their profession.[41] Even by the late 1960s British and American child psychology had not yet reached Calvinist schooling. Developmentalism and mental health had, but they came in late and even in the 1960s they did not yet dominate Calvinist education, which stuck to Dutchness much more than did public school teaching.

Textbooks for Roman Catholic teachers

How about the Roman Catholics? They may have been much more internationally orientated than the Dutch Calvinists, as French and German theologians such as the bishop Félix Dupanloup and Friedrich Foerster have been identified as sources of inspiration for the first educational theories they developed in the early years of the century as an intellectual foundation for the rapidly growing network of Catholic schools.[42] Unlike what one would expect, the authoritative textbook *The Child* (*Het kind*), which was part of the *Roman Catholic Educational Studies* (*Katholieke pedagogiek*) series for Roman Catholic teachers-to-be, issued between 1931 and 1950, was from the first edition saturated with the newest theories in the field of child studies, primarily from Germany. Although religious education stood out as most important, the author, the congregational priest and college teacher Sigebertus Rombouts, explained that he had deliberately included "all which is good" from the newer and newest psychologies, particularly those of Montessori, Stern, Spranger, the Bühlers and Adler, as he aimed to present not just a Catholic book but a "modern" one too. Although their work was not discussed extensively, the author claimed that their subject-orientated theories were useful for Roman Catholic teachers, if only for the enlightening concepts they had introduced, such as "a sensitive period" (Montessori), "a phase of opposition" (Charlotte Bühler's *Trotzalter*) or "feelings of inferiority" (Adler).[43]

A separate textbook by the same author, *The Educators* (*De opvoeders*), issued between 1933 and 1956, made it very clear that the aim of all education was still "to serve God". Like the book on the child, it was used in all Roman Catholic teacher training colleges. Here, Rombouts provided a more functional definition of a teacher's task: "to enable young people to reach the goal of their life autonomously".[44] He used Stern to explain that development was the outcome of nature and nurture and agreed with the international educational reform movement that school was threatened by intellectualism and too much passivity on the part of pupils. Children, he insisted, could profit from more active and individualised ways of learning, more freedom, more cooperation and a stronger sense of community in the classroom. This, he disagreed with progressive educationists, could only be realised in a

---

[41]Van Hulst and van der Molen, *Leerboek*, 17.
[42]Bakker, *Kind en karakter*, 197–214; Hans de Frankrijker, *De katholieke onderwijzersopleiding. Organisatie en ideologie 1889–1984* (Meppel: Krips Repro, 1988), 38–40.
[43]Fr. Sigebertus Rombouts, *Het kind. Katholieke pedagogiek* (Tilburg: R.K. Jongensweeshuis, 1931), 6, 37–44.
[44]Fr. Sigebertus Rombouts, *De opvoeders. Katholieke Pedagogiek*, 8th edn. (Tilburg: R.K. Jongensweeshuis, 1956), 7–15.

Roman Catholic school by a teacher who was aware of his duty to love and understand children and conceived of his task as if it were "a priestly vocation".[45]

Parallel to his textbooks on childhood and education, which remained remarkably silent on development, Rombouts also published two series of introductions into psychology for students who wanted to become headmasters between 1925 and 1956. In each case, the reading list included almost exclusively German and Dutch publications, some of the latter translated from German, and but a few French titles. One of his series on psychology was particularly meant to discuss the relevant new ideas originating from the newer, subject-orientated psychology: *New Lanes in Psychology and Education Studies* (*Nieuwe banen in psychologie en pedagogiek – Nieuwste banen*).[46] Like his Calvinist counterpart, the author appeared very happy with the new winds that were blowing in the world of psychology, particularly with Spranger's hermeneutic educational philosophy, which he called "structural psychology", and with Künkel's version of individual psychology. In 1931 Rombouts published an overview of the most interesting psychologies he thought were relevant for teachers. In this book, Rombouts presented Spranger's psychology as an antidote to a "naturalistic" or "experimental" scientific psychology *ohne Seele*, because it included an "ethics" of personality. Spranger's theory, Rombouts happily explained, focused on souls, who experienced and created values and were living in a meaningful cultural and social world. It could best be seen as a "protest" against the naturalistic *Seelenkunde ohne Seele* and, consequently, as a "rehabilitation of the human autonomy, that was driven away or denied by the empiricists" and their narrow focus on separate functions of the mind, he insisted.[47] Stern's personalism had likewise restored human individuality to science, he explained.[48] The one element he missed in these theories was God, the priest revealed in a post-war edition of his textbook. Fortunately, God had been restored to His Almighty position as the source of an ethics for teachers by the Dutch Protestant educationist Kohnstamm's "correction" of Stern's personalism: "What one still misses abroad, we already have in our country", a personalism with God, Rombouts claimed in 1949.[49]

Psychoanalysis could be useful in therapy or in finding out what was troubling a child, the priest Rombouts agreed, unwillingly, with the orthodox Calvinist Waterink. However, he declined Freudian psychoanalysis for its "pansexualism" and Adlerian individual psychology for its uncritical acceptance of an egoistic desire for power as the driving force in a child. And there was much more he did not like about depth psychology. Essentially, Adlerian psychology was no more than "medical pedagogy", "a pedagogy for the sick, to regain health from their illnesses, not for the normal", he explained. There were, moreover, no "Christian principles"

---

[45] Ibid., 132–169, esp. 165.
[46] Fr. Sigebertus Rombouts, *Zielkundige begrippen* (Tilburg: R.K. Jongensweeshuis, 1925); Rombouts, *Zielkundige begrippen*, 5th edn. (Tilburg: R.K. Jongensweeshuis, 1939); Rombouts, *Nieuwe banen in psychologie en pedagogiek* (Tilburg: R.K. Jongensweeshuis, 1925); Rombouts, *Nieuwe banen in de psychologie*, 9th edn. (Tilburg: R.K. Jongensweeshuis, 1949), continued as Rombouts, *Psychologie voor opvoeders: algemene psychologie*, 2nd edn. (Tilburg: R.K. Jongensweeshuis, 1956).
[47] Fr. Sigebertus Rombouts, *Nieuwste Banen in psychologie en pedagogiek* (Tilburg: R.K. Jongensweeshuis, 1931), 27. Parts of this volume were later integrated into the newer editions of *Nieuwe banen in de psychologie*.
[48] Ibid., 40.
[49] Rombouts, *Nieuwe banen* (1949), 212.

in it and "happiness", to be pursued by human instinct, was its highest goal, he complained. Instead of following, he insisted, mastering and control of the instincts should be the goal of child rearing: "If compensation for feelings of inferiority was to be found anywhere, it was in religion".[50] In a post-war edition of his textbook on psychology, the priest's denunciation of the Vienna School of thought was even more pertinent. He called it "hedonistic" and "immoral". He explicitly stated that Freud himself was much worse than Adler and Jung. By the 1940s he had to face the reality that across the world Roman Catholic child psychologists embraced elements of these theories. "Freudianism still has not stopped spreading disease, ... not just in England, but also here", he warned his readers in 1949. Instead of Künkel, he now appreciated Jung's reading of psychoanalysis, which he considered more positive, more optimistic and least focused on sexuality.[51]

In 1954 an extended and updated version of Rombouts' *Psychology for Educators* (*Psychologie voor opvoeders*) was published, to which a long reading list was added. Almost all publications mentioned were in German and Dutch. In this textbook the priest held on to the traditional, "thomistic" organisation of the information on mental capacities according to their functions, for "a system that had survived seven centuries" should not be discarded easily. After a systematic overview of what psychologists had stated about cognitive and voluntary functions, he briefly discussed recent developments in psychology, such as mass psychology, differential psychology, social psychology, psychological testing, educational psychology and child psychology, all on the basis of German and Dutch studies. In four chapters he discussed a small number of schools of psychology more extensively. He consistently approved of all approaches that conceived of human beings as subjects, such as Gestalt, Spranger's structural psychology, Stern's personalism and Langeveld's phenomenology. As before, he was very negative about American behaviourism: "it is typically American to see the human being as ... only slightly above the animal".[52] In a separate chapter he now discussed three characterologies in detail, those of Heymans, Kretschmer and Jung. Likewise, he presented a number of tests and their founding theories as useful for teachers. The chapter on psychoanalysis was slightly less negative than in previous books, as he now conceived of Adler's individual psychology as useful in education, although he still disapproved of its "egotism". The more benevolent treatise on Freudianism was probably inspired by the Dutch translation of the Swiss-American, Roman Catholic psychoanalyst Rudolf Allers' critical study of the theory, *The Successful Error* (*Succes van een dwaling*, 1949). Instead of debunking Freud, the priest now deplored most of all the omission of "higher values" in all varieties of depth psychology.[53]

Whereas Rombouts' textbooks continued to put the Roman Catholic religion on a pedestal, a new textbook authored by two, recently appointed, lay professors of education at the Roman Catholic University of Nijmegen, broke with this tradition. Their *Basic Principles of a Theory on Education* (*Grondbeginselen ener opvoedkunde voor de tweede leerkring*, 1955) was in print until 1969 and soon became popular at

---

[50]Rombouts, *Nieuwste banen* (1931), 72.
[51]Rombouts, *Nieuwe banen* (1949), 219.
[52]Fr. Sigebertus Rombouts, *Psychologie voor opvoeders*, 2nd edn. (Tilburg: R.K. Jongensweeshuis, 1956), 250.
[53]Ibid., 279–355.

Catholic teacher training colleges. It was a practical introduction into all basic concepts used in German and Dutch theories on childhood and education. Religious education was now only a part of a larger task and the Church was only one of the environments that impacted upon the child, whereas God's grace was reduced to a precondition for the effectiveness of other means. According to this textbook, a child had to be educated to become a "virtuous person" with the help and encouragement of the teacher. It was made clear to the students that "naturalism, biologism and evolutionism" would not contribute to their understanding of the child as a person in the making. Langeveld's phenomenology, on the other hand, was often referred to in a positive way; for example, his emphasis on "moral autonomy" as the goal of all education and on a trustful and cordial educational relationship as a precondition for effective authority. These authors still took their inspiration largely from German and Dutch Roman Catholic authors, but there was room for other influences as well. The importance of positive encouragement of pupils instead of punishment was, for example, underpinned by a reference to Adler's and Künkel's individual psychology.[54]

A second volume for students who wanted to become headmasters, authored by the same lay professors and issued in 1957, provided theoretical reflection on a wide range of educational concepts and conditions, including "neurotisising" elements in modern culture such as radio, film and television. Developmentalism and mental health were fully included and determined part of the organisation of the information. Although children were still raised to reach their supernatural destiny, teachers also had to "help" them to become "morally autonomous persons", along the lines of Langeveld's concept of education. Distinct chapters on children's mental health and the way teachers could promote it, on behavioural problems and their causes and on childhood abnormalities and their preferred treatment made Roman Catholic teachers finally enter the world of child guidance clinics and of psychoanalytic treatment and interpretations of child behaviour. References now were more often made to non-religious authors, mostly of German origin, than to Roman Catholic educationists and psychologists. The liberals Kohnstamm and Langeveld were frequently referred to, always in a positive sense, and they easily beat Roman Catholic Maria Montessori in this respect.[55] Students learned to discriminate between characters and normal and abnormal behaviour, how to recognise a disorder and when to refer to a child guidance clinic. They were, moreover, reassured that most behaviour and learning problems had their origin in the family. Parents might be too strict or neglect their children, or they might not be capable of stimulating their development. Bad children no longer existed; family conditions were to blame if a child failed at school. Disciplining had to be mild and always individualised, the two authors insisted. This wisdom came invariably from the East and it was often mediated through non-Catholic Dutch cultural intermediaries such as Kohnstamm and Langeveld. Catholicism had been exchanged for Dutchness.

---

[54] Jos J. Gielen and Stephan Strasser, *Grondbeginselen ener opvoedkunde voor de tweede leerkring*, 2nd edn. ('s-Hertogenbosch: Malmberg, 1956), 189.

[55] Gerard Heymans and Philip Kohnstamm were referred to seven times, Martinus Langeveld six times and Maria Montessori four times. All other theorists were referred to less often. See Jos J. Gielen and Stephan Strasser, *Leerboek der opvoedkunde voor de derde leerkring* ('s-Hertogenbosch: Malmberg, 1957), 221–223.

Conclusion

Textbooks on childhood and education for teachers-to-be reflect, we must conclude, a high level of cultural transfer during the years of transition from a purely philosophically based concept of education to an interpretation that was founded on the principles of developmentalism and mental health. Schooling was not a pioneering field in these respects, as the newer ideas and concepts arrived relatively late in these textbooks. The authors did not simply copy theories from abroad, but gave them a reading of their own and selected what they liked and ignored the rest. Behaviourism and orthodox Freudianism were, for example, ignored or objected to. In this process Dutch intellectual leaders in education such as Kohnstamm and Langeveld, who themselves studied those theories in great depth, acted as cultural intermediaries. They preferred subject-orientated theories such as personalism and phenomenology and this is reflected in the textbooks for teacher training colleges of all denominations. A shift from the East to the West as the main source of intellectual inspiration did not occur before the 1970s, whereas denominational authors do not particularly stand out for arriving late, as their dislike of a psychology "without a soul" stimulated an interest in the newer subject-orientated psychologies. Developmentalism, personalism, phenomenology, characterology and individual psychology consistently influenced Dutch education from the 1920s onwards, but they were all imported from the German-speaking world. It is true that during the 1930s some of these theories were taken to the New World in a suitcase by their founders as they fled Nazism, but that does not undo their continental European origins.

L'Association internationale des éducateurs de jeunes inadaptés (AIEJI) et la fabrique de l'éducateur spécialisé par delà les frontières (1951–1963)

Samuel Boussion

CIRCEFT, Université Paris 8, Saint-Denis, France

Cet article aborde l'histoire de l'Association internationale des éducateurs de jeunes inadaptés (AIEJI), une organisation méconnue dans l'histoire de l'éducation spécialisée. Créée en 1951, elle devient un lieu d'échanges pour des éducateurs en recherche de modèles. Elle est constituée dans le contexte de rapprochement franco-allemand, par le biais de rencontres annuelles, notamment initiées par les éducateurs français, qui existent depuis le début des années 1940, exerçant dans des internats récemment ouverts pour accueillir enfants et adolescents placés. De nombreux voyages d'étude structurent les échanges entre éducateurs de pays différents et forment les contours d'une organisation dont l'axe se situe rapidement entre Pays-Bas et France. L'AIEJI contribue aux débats sur le rôle de l'éducateur, entre pédagogue et thérapeute, ce qui ne se déroule pas sans tension ni résistances. Ils rendent compte des évolutions de la conception de l'éducateur et des pratiques et savoirs qui le fondent. L'AIEJI est le lieu où circulent les conceptions issues du *case-work*, du *group-work*, de la psychologie sociale, de la sociométrie. Là, se confrontent une vision praticienne du métier d'éducateur, axée sur le groupe et une vision plus technicienne, basée sur la psychologie et les approches psychanalytiques, davantage tournée autour de la prise en charge individuelle. L'AIEJI s'est enfin insérée dans les nouvelles organisations internationales, réussissant à faire reconnaître l'utilité sociale des éducateurs, y compris dans les pays où ils n'existent pas. Ainsi, à la fin des années 1950, l'AIEJI obtient le statut consultatif auprès de l'UNESCO et devient un acteur de l'expertise internationale en matière de jeunesse inadaptée, ce qui correspond à l'extension de son audience.

This article aims to address the history of the International Association of Workers for Maladjusted Children (IAWMC), which is an organisation often ignored in the field of history of transfers and circulations in the international specialised education. Yet this organisation, which was officially created in 1951 in the post-Second World War reconstruction period, quickly became a forum for exchange of experiences between *éducateurs* who were focused on the quest for models and methods. The IAWMC was created first during the beginning of the early Franco-German reconciliation, through annual meetings, especially initiated by French *éducateurs*. These existed in France from the early 1940s, working in the recently created institutions to support children and adolescents placed by the Justice and Child Care administration, and were looking for *alter egos* across borders. For example, many collective study tours structured such exchanges between *éducateurs* from different countries and shaped an organisation based in the Netherlands and France – where the first two Presidents, D. Q. R. Mulock-

Houwer and Henri Joubrel, came from – and then in Belgium and Germany. In its own way, the IAWMC contributed towards debates on the role of the specialised *éducateur* in the institution, among pedagogues and therapists, which did not come without tension or resistance. The technical discussions of the association, held at conferences and annual workshops, reflected changes in the general design of the *éducateur* and in practices and knowledge upon which it was based. The IAWMC was a forum for clinical concepts from case-work and group-work, but also social psychology, sociometry and more generally methods inspired by the human and social sciences, which were expanding in international social work in the 1950s and 1960s. This was done through debates even within the international association, between a practitioner vision of the *éducateur* role, based on the group and whose leaders are French *éducateurs*, and a more technical vision based on psychology and psychoanalytic approaches more focused on personal interview and individual care. This contribution focuses finally on how IAWMC on the one hand was included in international organisations, e.g. UNESCO, and on the other hand forged the public recognition of the utility of *éducateurs*, even in the case of developing countries where they did not exist. Thus, in the late 1950s, the IAWMC was accredited consultative status by UNESCO and played an important role in the international expertise on maladjusted youth. This timing corresponds to the final extension of its audience, after decolonisation, to emerging countries and to what is termed the "Third World".

C'est sur les cendres d'un monde traumatisé par la Seconde Guerre mondiale et à partir des urgences de la reconstruction que l'"international", en tant qu'idée, voire concept, mais aussi invite à la mise en œuvre de relations apaisées entre pays, prend une acuité nouvelle et se régénère. Ceci est particulièrement édifiant dans le champ de l'enfance et de la jeunesse, populations cibles qu'il faut soigner, protéger et éduquer, parce qu'elles ont eu à souffrir du conflit mais aussi parce qu'elles sont porteuses d'avenir. La prise de conscience se traduit d'abord par une efflorescence d'institutions de sauvegarde de l'enfance dans beaucoup de pays. Mais aussi par de nombreuses organisations intergouvernementales nées dans le giron de l'ONU (Organisation des Nations unies), dont l'UNESCO (Organisation des Nations unies pour l'éducation, la science et la culture) paraît la plus représentative.[1] Cette problématique est tout aussi vive dans certaines organisations non gouvernementales, nées à la même période dans le but d'organiser secours, assistance et éducation, le plus souvent vers l'enfance dite "victime de la guerre": SEPEG (Semaines internationales d'études pour l'enfance victime de la guerre) en 1945, UIPE (Union internationale de protection de l'enfance) en 1946, BICE (Bureau international catholique de l'enfance) en 1948, FICE (Fédération internationale des communautés d'enfants) constituée aussi en 1948, jusqu'à des groupements plus spécifiques comme l'Association internationale des juges des enfants, créée en 1928 mais remise sur pied en 1949. C'est dans cette litanie d'acteurs collectifs et cette progressive segmentation de l'action internationale que prend place l'AIEJI quand elle est officiellement constituée en 1951, dans le but "d'unir tous les éducateurs de jeunes inadaptés ... quelles que soient leur fonction ou nationalité" et "de contribuer à

---

[1] L'UNESCO a été fondée en 1945. Il faudrait aussi inclure l'UNRRA (Administration des nations unies pour les secours et la reconstruction), l'UNICEF (Fonds international du secours à l'enfance), l'OMS (Organisation mondiale de la Santé) ou encore le TICER (Conseil international provisoire pour le relèvement de l'éducation).

l'organisation de la profession d'éducateur de jeunes inadaptés en liaison avec les organismes à caractère national ou international".[2]

C'est ce nouveau chantier que nous ouvrons, souhaitant éclairer ce qui constitue encore un angle mort de la recherche et ainsi participer à un mouvement s'intéressant à l'internationalisation dans ce domaine.[3] Non pas que l'histoire de la protection de l'enfance n'ait pas tenu compte jusque-là de la dimension transnationale, loin de là, par exemple à l'aide de perspectives comparatives,[4] ou encore par l'étude des précoces et nombreuses circulations et transferts depuis la fin du XIXe siècle,[5] qui ont contribué à forger davantage encore la "dimension fondamentalement transnationale du domaine social".[6] Mais si ce processus est maintenant mieux connu pour l'entre-deux-guerres,[7] la période qui s'ouvre dans les années 1940 reste encore peu étudiée. Des travaux en cours s'intéressent à certaines organisations non gouvernementales, par exemple la FICE[8] et le BICE[9] ou à l'usage des références prises à l'international,[10] mais l'AIEJI, quant à elle, bien que souvent évoquée,[11] reste encore méconnue.

Dans cette perspective, nous souhaitons restituer l'histoire de cette association, bien vivante aujourd'hui,[12] depuis sa genèse à la fin des années 1940 jusqu'au congrès de 1963 qui, nous semble-t-il, marque une rupture, ce découpage resserré permettant en outre de saisir avec plus de finesse ses scansions. Ce travail se propose de comprendre la montée à l'échelon international de nouveaux acteurs de la protection de l'enfance, les éducateurs spécialisés. En creux, il s'agit de retracer sous un autre angle l'histoire d'un nouveau métier, installé dans quelques pays à partir du début des années 1940, qui consiste à prendre en charge l'éducation d'enfants et

---

[2] Statuts de l'AIEJI, 1951 (ANMT, fonds Jacques Guyomarc'h 2002040 / 633).
[3] En témoigne le congrès de l'ISCHE à Genève en juin 2012, particulièrement: "Les communautés d'enfants victimes de la guerre. Transferts, diffusions, circulations de modèles XIXe-XXe siècles," symposium coordonné par Mathias Gardet, Charles Heimberg et Martine Ruchat et "La fabrication internationale de la jeunesse inadaptée: circulations, traducteurs et formes de réception dans le champ de l'éducation surveillée au XXe siècle," symposium coordonné par Joëlle Droux.
[4] Marie-Sylvie Dupont-Bouchat et Eric Pierre, eds., *Enfants et justice au XIXe siècle. Essai d'histoire comparée de la protection de l'enfance 1820–1914, France, Belgique, Pays-Bas, Canada* (Paris: PUF, 2001).
[5] David Niget, *La naissance du tribunal pour enfants. Une comparaison France-Québec (1912–1945)* (Rennes: Presses Universitaires de Rennes, 2009).
[6] Pierre-Yves Saunier, "Les régimes circulatoires du domaine social 1800–1940: projets et ingénierie de la convergence et de la différence," *Genèses* 71 (2008): 13.
[7] Dominique Marshall, "Dimensions transnationales et locales de l'histoire des droits des enfants. La Société des Nations et les cultures politiques canadiennes," *Genèses* 71 (2008): 47–63; Joëlle Droux, "L'internationalisation de la protection de l'enfance: acteurs, concurrences et projets transnationaux (1900-1925)," *Critique internationale*, 52 (2011): 17–33.
[8] Symposium "Républiques, villages et communautés d'enfants: un idéal concerté de l'après Seconde Guerre mondiale," congrès de l'AREF, Genève, septembre 2010.
[9] Lucia Ferretti et Louise Bienvenue, "Le Bureau international catholique de l'enfance: réseau et tribune pour les spécialistes québécois de l'enfance en difficulté (1947–1977)," *Revue d'histoire de l'enfance "irrégulière"* 12 (2010): 155–76.
[10] Lucia Ferretti et Louise Bienvenue, "Usages des références françaises et internationales dans le développement et la promotion d'une expertise québécoise: la psychoéducation (1940–1970)," in *Violences juvéniles sous expertises XIXe-XXe siècles*, ed. Aurore François, Veerle Massin et David Niget (Louvain: Presses Universitaires de Louvain, 2010), 131–56.
[11] Par exemple Maurice Capul, ed., *L'invention de l'enfance inadaptée. L'exemple de Toulouse Saint-Simon (1950–1975)* (Toulouse: Erès, 2011), 551.
[12] Voir: http://www.aieji.net.

d'adolescents placés par les tribunaux, les services de l'assistance à l'enfance ou d'autres organismes selon les pays, dans des institutions spécialisées et avec des méthodes éducatives renouvelées, chargées de faire oublier le passé disciplinaire de nombre d'entre elles.

Nous serons attentifs à la constitution de l'AIEJI, aux réseaux mobilisés et à l'investissement de ses acteurs. Dépassant la stricte dimension comparative, nous tenterons de comprendre comment s'agrègent les différentes composantes nationales, comment elles tentent de fabriquer un langage commun ainsi que la teneur des circulations, des échanges de pratiques et de techniques propres au champ de l'éducation spécialisée. L'internationalisation ne se présente pas comme un processus linéaire propre à subvertir à tous les coups les spécificités et n'échappe pas aux tensions nées de concurrences externes (avec d'autres organisations) et de résistances internes. Une attention spécifique doit enfin être portée à la place de l'AIEJI dans le concert des organisations internationales, notamment l'UNESCO, tandis que l'obtention de son statut consultatif en 1958 semble consacrer son expertise, développée par la suite vers de nouveaux pays.

Ce regard posé sur l'AIEJI ne dissocie pas non plus l'international du national, bien au contraire tente d'approcher les interactions. La dimension importante des relations internationales dans la structuration du métier d'éducateur spécialisé en France nous était ainsi déjà apparue dans des recherches antérieures, tandis que l'AIEJI est largement redevable à l'investissement de certains spécialistes français de l'éducation spécialisée ainsi qu'à leur association nationale, l'ANEJI (Association nationale des éducateurs de jeunes inadaptés).[13] Les archives invitent elles-mêmes à ces allers et retours. Plusieurs fonds concernant l'AIEJI sont déposés au CNAHES (Conservatoire national des archives et de l'histoire de l'éducation spécialisée et de l'action sociale), conservés aux ANMT (Archives nationales du monde du travail) à Roubaix et ont constitué une grande part de nos matériaux.[14] Si la revue *Rééducation* ouvre régulièrement ses colonnes aux comptes rendus exhaustifs des congrès, les archives de l'association et des militants (notes, correspondance ou divers rapports) permettent de mieux travailler sur les temps entre chaque grand événement et de comprendre ce qui se joue hors-champ. Elles sont aussi une manière de retrouver les acteurs, souvent effacés dans ce type d'organisation derrière une production très discursive voire bavarde, redondante même sous les effets des multiples traductions empilées dans les synthèses.

Une association internationale sur fond de réconciliation franco-allemande

La genèse de l'AIEJI relève de dynamiques convergentes, depuis les prémices dès 1948 jusqu'à son lancement en 1951. Elle doit d'abord beaucoup à la reconstruction post-conflit, à l'idée de réparation aussi et, plus concrètement, au processus de

---

[13] Samuel Boussion, *Les éducateurs spécialisés et leur association professionnelle: l'ANEJI (Association nationale des éducateurs de jeunes inadaptés) de 1947 à 1967. Naissance et construction d'une profession sociale* (thèse de doctorat d'histoire, Université d'Angers, 2007).

[14] Le fonds d'archives de l'AIEJI a été déposé par Daniel Dupied en 1998, en tant qu'ancien président de l'ANEJI et de l'AIEJI. Il est encore à l'heure actuelle vice-président de l'association. D'autres fonds déposés au CNAHES ont constitué nos matériaux: les fonds Jacques Guyomarc'h, ANEJI, Serge Ginger-Jacques Leblanc, Jacques Gauneau. Voir: http://www.cnahes.org.

rapprochement franco-allemand. C'est au cœur des zones d'occupation française en Allemagne que sont initiées les premières rencontres internationales d'éducateurs. Dans cet espace de "l'entre-deux", propice aux expériences et aux échanges, l'enfance victime de la guerre devient une préoccupation pour les milieux spécialisés, l'attention étant notamment portée sur une population juvénile "mobile" ou "flottante"[15] ainsi que sur les jeunes Allemands détenus pour raisons politiques. Ainsi, en 1948, la sous-direction "Jeunesse et Sports" de la direction de l'Education publique au Gouvernement militaire français ouvre un centre de rééducation pour jeunes Allemands à Gau-Algesheim, près de Bingen. Se voulant novateur, cet établissement rappelle néanmoins le modèle des institutions françaises, dans son encadrement (des éducateurs chargés des adolescents en dehors des heures de classe et d'atelier), mise à part la sous-direction bicéphale franco-allemande, dans ses méthodes comme dans son choix architectural (le château des ducs de Mayence, Schloss Ardeck).[16] La direction en est confiée à une figure de la rééducation en France, Henry Van Etten (1893–1969). Connu depuis le début des années 1930 comme un des propagandistes les plus en vue du champ de la protection de l'enfance, depuis qu'il a été secrétaire général du Comité d'étude pour la diminution du crime puis de la revue qui en est l'émanation, *Pour l'enfance coupable*; personnage clé, il fait alors lien entre les courants réformateurs,[17] les générations et les pays. Né à Paris, ce fils d'un commerçant hollandais et d'une mère française cultive ses diverses origines, s'amusant de s'être trouvé une lignée familiale écossaise, tout en entretenant une culture internationale, depuis ses études londoniennes jusqu'à sa conversion au Quakerisme, ce qui l'amène à devenir homme de missions et de voyages dans l'entre-deux-guerres (Angleterre, Allemagne, Etats-Unis), en passant par sa fréquentation des milieux pacifistes et espérantistes.[18]

Rien d'étonnant donc à constater que c'est depuis ce petit morceau de France en Allemagne que se forgent les premières rencontres entre éducateurs de ces deux pays. Henry Van Etten en est l'entremetteur, qui sollicite dès 1948 Henri Joubrel (1914–1983), ancien avocat et magistrat, alors commissaire spécialisé à la sauvegarde de l'enfance pour les Eclaireurs de France et fondateur l'année précédente de l'ANEJI, pour réunir une délégation française en vue d'une rencontre franco-allemande. Cette dernière se tient finalement la semaine de Pâques 1949, au Centre d'action pédagogique et culturelle de Spire,[19] dans le Palatinat, et regroupe une

---

[15]Pierre Gulphe, "Les *unaccompanied children* en Allemagne occupée," *Revue de l'Education surveillée* 5 (1946): 3–12.
[16]Samuel Boussion et Mathias Gardet, eds., *Les châteaux du social XIXe–XXe siècle* (Paris: Beauchesne-Presses universitaires de Vincennes, 2010).
[17]Nagisa Mitsushima, "L'expertise criminologique au sein de la revue *Pour l'enfance coupable* (1935–1942): une expertise en action" (IIe session de l'école thématique Cnrs Pacte / Latts / Epfl, "Les nouvelles controverses de l'action publique," 2010, http://www.pacte.cnrs.fr/IMG/html_Mitsushima_Action_publique_et_expertise.html, consulté en novembre 2010).
[18]Henry Van Etten, *Journal d'un Quaker de notre temps (1893–1962)* (Paris: éd. du Scorpion, 1962).
[19]Ce centre a été ouvert en 1948 et a été l'occasion de réaliser diverses rencontres internationales spécialisées pour des responsables de mouvements féminins, des journalistes de la presse de jeunesse, des assistantes sociales, des auteurs de manuels d'histoire et des professeurs d'histoire, des dirigeants de mouvements de jeunesse, etc. Présentation de la Session internationale sur les méthodes de pédagogie nouvelle appliquées à l'enfance en danger moral, 9 au 15 avril 1949 (ANMT, Fonds Jacques Guyomarc'h, 2002040 / C 660).

vingtaine de Français et une quarantaine d'Allemands, ainsi que quelques spécialistes d'Autriche, de Suisse, des Pays-Bas et de Belgique. La semaine d'échanges bénéficie alors des énormes moyens dont dispose l'action culturelle française en Allemagne à cette période,[20] sous l'impulsion de Joseph Rovan.[21] Le titre général de la rencontre montre les opportunes connexions avec l'éducation populaire et l'éducation nouvelle, qui constituent il est vrai une part du bagage pédagogique des premiers éducateurs: "Session internationale d'étude sur les méthodes de pédagogie nouvelle appliquées à l'enfance en danger moral".[22] C'est à Spire (Speyer) que les diverses délégations se mettent d'accord sur le principe d'une association internationale d'éducateurs et qu'est prise la décision de pérenniser ces rencontres. Celles-ci, dites "internationales" malgré leur fort accent franco-allemand, se ritualisent en se tenant chaque année à la même période, tout en migrant dès 1950 à Bad-Dürckheim, sous les auspices du Service des rencontres internationales du Haut-commissariat de la République française, puis à Fribourg à partir de 1951.[23] Les rencontres internationales, sous l'égide de l'AIEJI à partir de 1951, se tiennent chaque année en République fédérale d'Allemagne jusqu'en 1962, quand elles sont délocalisées une première fois, à Vienne.

Si l'AIEJI s'affiche franco-allemande, elle est largement une création française. Elle s'appuie sur les bases posées par les éducateurs français quelques années auparavant, qui se sont organisés en association nationale dès 1947 et qui ont d'emblée posé la nécessité d'œuvrer à une meilleure "compréhension internationale". L'association internationale en porte la trace, son intitulé déclinant le sigle français. Les statuts établis lors de la rencontre internationale de Fribourg en 1951 tirent profit de ceux de l'ANEJI, jusque dans la formulation des articles, même s'ils font constamment référence au "caractère international". Des nuances sont néanmoins repérables, à commencer par les adhérents (les associations nationales), mais aussi les moyens mis en œuvre pour parvenir à unir les éducateurs: stimulation d'associations nationales, organisation de congrès, échanges de documentation, collaboration avec d'autres organisations préoccupées de sauvegarde de l'enfance.[24] Enfin, la forte présence française se lit à travers sa place dans les instances, puisqu'Henri Joubrel occupe le poste de vice-président de 1951 à 1955, avant d'en devenir le président à cette date, fonction qu'il quitte en 1978, tandis que Jacques Guyomarc'h en devient

---

[20]Cette manne financière est liée aux crédits d'occupation. Une très grande autonomie est laissée aux acteurs sur le terrain, ce qui permet la réalisation d'expériences alors impossibles à mener en France. Emmanuelle Picard, "L'occupation française en Allemagne: un laboratoire d'expériences (1945–1963)," in *Cadres de jeunesse et d'éducation populaire (1918–1971)*, ed. Denise Barriolade, Valérie Brousselle, Jean-Paul Egret et Françoise Tétard (Paris: La Documentation française, 2010).

[21]Journaliste d'origine juive, proche des milieux chrétiens progressistes et résistant, il est arrêté et déporté à Dachau en 1944. A sa libération, il milite pour l'amitié franco-allemande et est chargé de réorganiser les mouvements de jeunesse et d'éducation populaire allemands dans la zone d'occupation française. Il participera à la création de l'OFAJ (Office franco-allemand de la jeunesse). Guy Saez, "Joseph Rovan," in *Dictionnaire biographique des militants XIXe–XXe siècle. De l'éducation populaire à l'action culturelle*, ed. Geneviève Poujol et Madeleine Romer (Paris: L'Harmattan, 1996), 336.

[22]Samuel Boussion, "Les premiers éducateurs spécialisés: l'empreinte des chefs (années 1940–1950)," in *Cadres de jeunesse,* ed. Barriolade et al., 156–63.

[23]Elles se tiennent à Hambourg en 1957.

[24]Statuts de l'AIEJI, 1951 (ANMT, fonds Jacques Guyomarc'h 2002040 / 633).

le secrétaire général, poste stratégique, qu'il cumule avec celui de secrétaire général de l'association française.

L'AIEJI est aussi redevable aux circulations régulières d'éducateurs, aux connexions et amitiés tissées dans ces occasions. La pratique des voyages d'étude prend de la vigueur parmi les jeunes professionnels de l'éducation spécialisée. Ainsi, la troisième semaine de septembre 1949, une trentaine de Français partent vers les Pays-Bas pour un séjour d'une dizaine de jours dans le but d'y visiter les institutions de protection de l'enfance et rencontrer leurs *alter-egos*. La délégation en revient conquise, notamment par la partition entre maisons "catholiques", "protestantes", "neutres" et "d'Etat", ou encore parce que certains établissements visités, mixtes, emploient de nombreuses éducatrices, dans une co-éducation qui se révèle alors très rare en France.[25] En mai de l'année suivante, trente cinq spécialistes hollandais rendent la pareille et effectuent leur itinéraire en rééducation, à travers une sélection d'établissements et services dûment choisis. Ces échanges sont l'occasion de créer des connexions durables et à leur manière témoignent de l'expansion de l'AIEJI. En 1951–1952, un échange entre Belges et Français est organisé, tandis que la même année un groupe de Français part en Italie, notamment visiter quelques unes des foisonnantes Républiques d'enfants fondées dans l'immédiat après-guerre.

Au noyau primitif s'ajoutent d'autres maillons, venus surtout des pays frontaliers, au rythme des constitutions d'associations nationales. Les congrès portent la trace de ce rayonnement et se déroulent longtemps dans un bassin restreint: Amersfoort (1952), Bruxelles (1954), Fontainebleau (1956), Lausanne (1958), Rome (1960), Fribourg (1963). Dans cette configuration, les Pays-Bas jouent un rôle essentiel. Amersfoort est une place forte, depuis que s'y est tenu le congrès de l'UIPE du 20 mars au 2 avril 1949, consacré à la sélection, la formation et le statut du personnel éducatif des maisons de rééducation. C'est là aussi que se situent les établissements de Zandbergen, conçus sous la forme de petits pavillons pour restituer une ambiance familiale et qui ont beaucoup impressionné les Français, à la recherche de références et de modèles.[26] Le siège social de l'AIEJI est fixé à Amersfoort puisque la présidence est presque naturellement confiée au directeur de Zandbergen, Daniël Quirijn Robert Mulock Houwer (1903–1985), dont le déjà long parcours, la position et la personnalité enjouée et atypique font alors l'unanimité.[27] Enfant placé dans une famille d'accueil à la mort de ses parents, après des études en agriculture coloniale il part un temps pour Sumatra. A son retour, il est engagé comme chef de groupe à Zandbergen, devient directeur-adjoint puis directeur de la maison d'observation d'Amsterdam entre 1929 et 1933, date à laquelle il prend la direction de Zandbergen. Il est arrêté en 1942 pour faits de résistance et déporté à Dachau. Revenu de camp, il reprend en 1946 la direction de Zandbergen puis du Bureau néerlandais de protection de l'enfance. Entre deux générations, homme d'une grande expérience de terrain, marqué par la guerre, Daniël Mulock Houwer

---

[25]Henri Joubrel, "Un voyage d'études aux Pays-Bas," *Rééducation* 18 (1949): 26.
[26]Ibid.
[27]Le personnage est d'une étonnante actualité, en témoignent les biographies, certes apologétiques: Rob Mulock Houwer, *Ik heb mijn lied gezongen. Het leven van Daniël Quirijn Mulock Houwer (1903–1985)* (Den Haag: Eigen beheer, 2010); Maurice Van Lieshout, *Rebel without a Cause: Daan Mulock Houwer (1903–1985), vernieuwer van de jeugdzorg* (Utrecht: Nederlands Jeugdinstitut, 2011). La totalité des sources biographiques étant en néerlandais, je remercie chaleureusement Christine Bakker d'en avoir traduit quelques extraits.

est ainsi l'élément fédérateur, sa personnalité conviviale, son "rire fameux",[28] sa fantaisie[29] ainsi que son polyglottisme[30] faisant le reste.

La quête d'une méthodologie transmissible par-delà les frontières

Une partie du travail de l'AIEJI est d'approcher un langage commun pour des éducateurs dont la situation et le rôle ne sont pas les mêmes selon les pays. Cela passe d'abord par un souci constant de la confrontation des expériences. Une forme de socialisation internationale s'élabore progressivement et les voyages d'étude, les rencontres internationales témoignent de ce souci de la découverte "d'ailleurs pédagogiques", de pratiques et d'acteurs qui sont autant de formes d'altérité. L'éveil à l'international des éducateurs français est flagrant, dont rend bien compte leur revue, *Liaisons*, à partir de 1951. Les voyages d'étude, les missions se multiplient, qui envoient ainsi, entre 1951 et 1964, un ou des éducateurs français aux Etats-Unis, en Finlande, en Suisse, en Norvège, en Pologne, en URSS, en Afrique occidentale, au Danemark, au Canada, liste sans doute non exhaustive car seulement indexée sur les rapports ou notes publiés. Ce changement de perspective glisse même jusqu'aux jeunes pris en charge dans des institutions, quand en juillet 1955 l'ABEJI convie à Liège vingt et un jeunes gens et jeunes filles de divers pays comptant une association nationale.[31]

L'AIEJI joue alors son rôle de plate-forme d'échanges. Ses archives témoignent d'une accumulation continue de documentation sur divers pays et autant de systèmes de protection de l'enfance, à travers brochures, dépliants, monographies et autres traces de la mise en scène de "façades institutionnelles". Ces strates successives sont amassées au fil des rencontres, des congrès, des échanges de correspondance et si chaque institution est une expérience singulière, elle prend du relief dans le cadre international, à l'heure d'échanger sur ses propres réalisations. Le cadre national reste pendant longtemps une référence dans une pratique ritualisée de la comparaison (des législations, des pratiques éducatives, des modes de prise en charge), qui s'exerce autour de la problématique retard/avance. Un exemple parmi d'autres: du côté français, on se félicite après une conférence du belge Paul Vandergheynst sur la semi-liberté en 1951, de l'étendue des réalisations des voisins, considérées comme avant-gardistes dans l'entre-deux-guerres, mais pour mieux souligner que si "ces trois jours sont bien courts pour porter un jugement objectif sur ce qui se fait en Belgique ... il semble toutefois que la France ait rattrapé le retard de trente ans qu'elle avait encore il y a peu de temps ...".[32]

Mais l'AIEJI veille aussi à la constante recherche d'un langage commun qui relèverait d'une forme d'acculturation. D'abord, comment appeler ce personnage

---

[28]Henri Joubrel, "La rencontre internationale de Bad-Dürckheim," *Rééducation* 23 (1950): 101.
[29]Capable de raconter des histoires aux éducateurs lors d'une veillée ou d'adapter lors du même spectacle un test psychologique.
[30]Il parle néerlandais, allemand, anglais et français.
[31]L'ABEJI est l'Association belge des éducateurs de jeunes inadaptés, créée en 1950. Programme des rencontres internationales de jeunes, juillet 1955 (CNAHES, Fonds Jacques Gauneau). Les jeunes sont venus d'Allemagne, France, Hollande, Iles britanniques, Italie, Suisse et Etats-Unis, à la condition qu'ils appartiennent à un centre d'éducation dont au moins un éducateur ou le directeur est membre de l'association nationale adhérente de l'AIEJI.
[32]"Un Marly belge," *Liaisons* 1 (1951): 13.

que l'on nomme déjà en France "éducateur spécialisé"? Il est "celui qui est chargé en dehors des heures de classe et d'atelier de la surveillance et de l'éducation des enfants et adolescents", définition qui tient jusqu'à la fin des années 1950. Cette définition finit néanmoins par devenir assez restrictive, par exemple pour des éducateurs canadiens qui forgent à cette période une rééducation en internat qui se veut "totale", "où les activités, qu'elles soient scolaires, manuelles, culturelles ou autres, demeurent partie intégrante de la rééducation".[33] Quoiqu'il en soit, l'AIEJI a fait sienne ces définitions, parfois malgré les nuances dans les fonctions, par exemple pour les anglo-saxons qui connaissent *housemasters* ou *houseparents*, *case-workers* ou *group-workers*. L'un des enjeux primordiaux est de distinguer éducateurs et enseignants, ce qui pousse à plusieurs reprises Henri Joubrel à faire admettre, non sans abnégation, le terme d'"éducateurs" (en français dans le texte) en langue anglaise, à la place de *teacher* ou surtout *educator*, qui renvoient au monde enseignant et correspondent peu à la conception européenne de l'éducation spécialisée.

Au début des années 1950, l'heure est aussi à la recherche d'une culture professionnelle sous la forme d'une "méthodologie applicable et fructueuse de la rééducation individualisée des jeunes au sein des groupes", comme y invite son président, Mulock Houwer.[34] La question, mise sur l'ouvrage dès le congrès d'Amersfoort en 1952 puis déclinée au congrès de Bruxelles en 1954, est portée par Philip Van Praag, psychologue, directeur de l'école de formation d'éducateurs de Middeloo, près d'Amersfoort. La méthodologie transmissible y est abordée du point de vue de la formation, dans l'idée de dépasser la conception classique d'une éducation issue de la personnalité et des dons naturels de l'éducateur, pour plutôt "conjuguer ... l'intuition et la technique, l'empirisme et l'apprentissage".[35] A l'issue d'un recueil des diverses expériences, une formation est modélisée: sélection en deux temps (examen psychologique et psychiatrique, puis "épreuve de vie"), formation de base en deux ans (un an de théorie en groupes d'internat avec l'action d'un "superviseur" à teinte psychanalytique et un an de stage sous contrôle d'un "maître de pratique"), avant spécialisation.[36] Ce type d'approche est alors relativement inédit en France, hormis dans quelques îlots de recherche, tel l'Institut pédotechnique de Toulouse.[37] L'idée d'une formation s'appuyant sur une solide armature théorique en même temps qu'une déconstruction de la relation éducative suscite des interrogations, comme l'exprime un directeur d'établissement d'Eure-et-Loir à propos d'une rencontre que l'on devine être celle de Fribourg en 1954, qui a porté sur la collaboration entre l'éducateur, le psychologue et le psychiatre:

> Ne veut-on pas exiger de l'éducateur, en plus du baccalauréat, des connaissances biologiques, physiologiques, psycho-psychana-psychiatriques, et j'en passe! Nos amis hollandais menèrent l'assaut contre la citadelle française de l'empirisme, de l'intuition, du

---

[32] "Un Marly belge," *Liaisons* 1 (1951): 13.
[33] Jeanine Guindon, "Le concept d'éducateur spécialisé," *Actes du congrès de l'AIEJI* (Rome: AIEJI, 1960), 42.
[34] Henri Joubrel, "Le premier congrès international d'éducateurs de jeune inadaptés," *Rééducation* 42/43 (1952): 76.
[35] Henri Joubrel, "Le deuxième congrès international des éducateurs de jeunes inadaptés," *Rééducation* 58/59 (1954): 48.
[36] Jacques Gauneau, "Deuxième congrès de l'Association internationale des éducateurs de jeunes inadaptés, Bruxelles, 12 au 16 juillet 1954," *Liaisons* 12 (1954): 9.
[37] Capul, *L'invention de l'enfance inadaptée*.

"je-ne-sais-quoi" qui constitue, d'après eux, l'élément de base de notre action, auquel doit se substituer une solide culture académique. Les Allemands opinèrent du bonnet, les Belges ne soufflèrent mot....[38]

Non sans méfiance envers des importations depuis les Etats-Unis, Henri Joubrel met une certaine application à tempérer les ardeurs des théoriciens qui se sont exprimés lors du congrès de 1954. Pour la première fois dans *Liaisons* il s'exprime en tant que vice-président de l'AIEJI et relaie un certain malaise:

> Ce n'est pas critiquer l'animateur infatigable et si dévoué de nos travaux, Van Praag, que de laisser entendre que ses conceptions ont reçu l'empreinte des applications américaines de la psychanalyse, dont il a une vive connaissance tant par ses lectures que par ses séjours aux Etats-Unis....
>
> Quelques congressistes ont réagi très franchement contre certaines propositions qui leur paraissent porter atteinte à leurs vues spirituelles. C'était leur droit et c'était leur devoir. Des explications plus détaillées les ont généralement convaincus. Puissent-ils toutefois conserver leurs positions, si après examen attentif ils croient devoir n'en pas changer, puissent-ils toujours ne mettre en œuvre que partiellement les moyens qui leur sont offerts, s'ils pensent après réflexion qu'elles contiennent une part d'erreur.[39]

Il n'empêche, l'AIEJI est alors le lieu par excellence des circulations dans le champ de l'éducation spécialisée, notamment des approches analytiques et des démarches psychopédagogiques qui en découlent, ce qu'Henri Joubrel, avec lucidité et tempérance, réussit à synthétiser dans ce qui s'avère une forme de programme:

> Dans la montée de cette jeune profession, les partisans de la supériorité de l'empirisme sur l'apprentissage (partisans représentés surtout par les "pionniers" qui prirent si courageusement en charge les jeunes désaxés par la guerre et ses lendemains) ont à prendre conscience des progrès relatifs, mais certains, réalisés par la psychologie de l'enfant, la psychiatrie, la sociologie, pendant ces dernières années. En présence désormais de spécialistes qui ont pénétré dans leur champ de travail, il leur faut aussi, sous peine de se laisser remplacer, faire figure de véritables spécialistes. Il faut qu'ils puissent légitimement n'éprouver aucun sentiment d'infériorité au sein de l'équipe médico-psycho-pédagogique.[40]

En 1952, Jean Ughetto, jeune éducateur qui a bénéficié d'une bourse d'un an aux Etats-Unis pour y étudier le travail social, expose devant le congrès réuni à Amersfoort sa découverte du *case-work* et du *group-work*.[41] Le premier, à dimension analytique, vise à aider le "client" à mieux comprendre sa situation, prendre conscience de ce qui fait obstacle et ainsi contribuer à mettre en œuvre toutes les ressources disponibles. Le second traite avec l'individu en groupe et envisage une meilleure adaptation sociale de l'individu par le moyen du groupe. Si elles rencontrent peu d'écho en France et si elles suscitent alors "des réserves de principe formulées par beaucoup contre toute effraction de la personnalité des jeunes",[42] ces techniques se trouvent connectées aux travaux de certains spécialistes de l'associa-

---

[38] Jean Ziolkowski, *Les enfants de sable* (Banville-sur-mer: L'Amitié par le livre, 1957), 130.
[39] Henri Joubrel, "L'Art, la Science, l'Amour," *Liaisons* 12 (1954): 3–4.
[40] Joubrel, "Le deuxième congrès international," 46.
[41] Jean Ughetto, "Applications du case work américain dans un foyer de semi-liberté française," Comptes rendus du congrès d'Amersfoort, 1952 (ANMT fonds Jacques Guyomarc'h 2002040 / 664).

tion néerlandaise. Les thèmes développés dans le cadre des travaux de l'AIEJI se situent dans la lignée de cette psychologie dynamique. La supervision des éducateurs par exemple, dans le cadre de l'internat mais surtout dans la formation, est amplement discutée. Pour certains elle peut mieux éclairer la relation éducative, "par sa connaissance des tensions de l'enfant, entre les enfants et les éducateurs, entre les enfants dans le groupe, par sa connaissance des problèmes posés par les parents des enfants".[43] Jusqu'au début des années 1960, le groupe, dans sa dynamique et ses possibilités éducatives, constitue aussi un sujet d'étude récurrent, dans un premier temps parce qu'il correspond au quotidien des éducateurs en internat, dans un second temps parce qu'il est aussi le mode de socialisation juvénile par excellence (les bandes). La dynamique des groupes et la sociométrie sont souvent à l'ordre du jour, sous l'impulsion néerlandaise surtout, parce que certains y sont déjà très réceptifs aux travaux de Kurt Lewin et Jakob L. Moreno, du congrès de 1954 aux rencontres entièrement axées sur la dynamique des groupes en 1962, en passant par le congrès de 1956 où Paul Drillich, ancien élève de Philip Van Praag et *groupworker* à Amsterdam y expose les ressorts de la dynamique des groupes.

D'étonnants et révélateurs décalages se produisent sous l'effet de ces travaux. D'un côté, les Néerlandais Philip Van Praag et Paul Drillich, reprochent à l'AIEJI, particulièrement à Henri Joubrel, de vouloir demeurer une plate-forme d'échanges quand eux voudraient avancer sur une recherche scientifique correspondant mieux à leurs compétences de techniciens.[44] Dans le même temps, des éducateurs français investissent au contraire l'AIEJI parce qu'elle est le lieu où se débattent les questions éducatives, où se confrontent et s'élaborent des savoirs théoriques et pratiques, ce que n'est pas suffisamment leur association nationale. L'association devient même pour eux un lieu de "distinction",[45] une ouverture face à un milieu français de la rééducation aux limites de l'"anti-intellectualisme".[46] Educateurs diplômés, ayant suivi des études supérieures, engagés dans des pratiques éducatives en lien avec la recherche, ils font figure d'avant-garde en France et trouvent dans l'AIEJI un prolongement de leur activité professionnelle. Comme une manière de contenter toutes les forces autant que de répondre à ses propres développements, l'AIEJI créé à la fin des années 1950 un Comité technique chargé notamment de l'organisation de ses grands événements où se retrouvent les premiers et les seconds.[47]

La progressive montée de l'expertise

L'AIEJI n'est pas née sur une terre vierge et sa construction doit se comprendre à l'aune de son rapport à d'autres groupes d'experts œuvrant dans le même champ. Dès que sa création est formellement envisagée, en 1949, que se préparent les statuts et se négocient les places dans les instances, le patronage de l'UNESCO, nouvel épicentre de l'internationalisation, est envisagé. En 1948, cette organisation a en effet déjà encouragé et promu la FICE, constituée au Village Pestalozzi de Trogen, en

---

[42]Joubrel, "Le premier congrès," 77.
[43]Comptes rendus du congrès d'Amersfoort, 15–19 septembre 1952 (ANMT fonds Jacques Guyomarc'h 2002040 / 664).
[44]Compte rendu du conseil d'administration de l'AIEJI, 16 avril 1957; lettre de Philip Van Praag à Henri Joubrel, 24 juillet 1957 (ANMT fonds Jacques Guyomarc'h 2002040 / 639).
[45]Entretien avec Jacques Gauneau, 13 mai 2001 (Samuel Boussion).
[46]Boussion, *Les éducateurs spécialisés*.
[47]Le Comité technique abrite ainsi des éducateurs férus d'innovation et de recherche: Maurice Capul, Serge Ginger, Gilles Gendreau, Paul Drillich, Jacques Selosse.

Suisse.[48] Pour ne pas être en reste et parce qu'il en est aussi un collaborateur occasionnel – il intervient lors de sa conférence de Charleroi en 1949 – Henri Joubrel mobilise alors son entregent. Soucieux d'obtenir sa recommandation, il commence par son ami Louis François (1904–2002), ancien professeur d'histoire-géographie, cadre des Eclaireurs de France comme lui, devenu inspecteur général de l'Education nationale mais surtout secrétaire général de la commission française de l'UNESCO. Henri Joubrel rencontre aussi le Dr Thérèse Brosse, chargée du programme de l'enfance victime de la guerre au département de l'éducation du secrétariat de l'UNESCO, qui a œuvré à la constitution de la FICE et qu'il a invitée en 1948 aux conférences de Méridien, qu'il organise à Paris dans le cadre du Scoutisme français, pour traiter de "La jeunesse inadaptée en Europe: le rôle de l'éducation dans la prévention et le traitement des attitudes anti-sociales". Dans le même temps, il est dirigé vers M. Hercik, chargé au sein du département des relations extérieures des liaisons avec les organisations non gouvernementales, tandis que simultanément il prend langue avec Maurice Milhaud, chef du département européen de la Division des activités sociales de l'ONU, dans le but de participer à une enquête sur la délinquance juvénile ouverte par la Division des activités sociales de l'organisation à cette période.

Henri Joubrel insiste sur la concordance avec les buts fixés par l'UNESCO dans son programme lancé pour l'année 1950: "venir en aide aux enfants déficients ou déplacés, notamment par suite de la guerre". Il fait valoir les connexions avec des personnalités œuvrant près de l'UNESCO et soucieuses du sort des enfants victimes de la guerre.[49] Il rappelle par exemple que lui et Daniël Mulock Houwer ont pensé demander l'éminent patronage d'Adolphe Ferrière, du BIE (Bureau international d'éducation) et du professeur Hanselmann,[50] tous deux investis dans les SEPEG en 1945.[51] De même, les connexions avec la FICE sont réelles, notamment par les contacts pris en Italie avec Giovanni Mastropaolo ainsi que d'autres personnalités à la tête de communautés d'enfants, comme le Dr Robert Préaut, directeur du Hameau-école de Longueil-Annel, en France, par ailleurs premier président de la FICE,[52] ou encore le père Daniel Goens, tous deux venus parler en 1950 à Paris de leur expérience au sein des communautés d'enfants.

Outre l'argumentaire obligé sur la nécessité d'aider une association qui, par son action technique, peut apparaître sur le plan international comme une contribution des plus utiles à la construction de la paix, Henri Joubrel met en avant le souci de doter les éducateurs d'une certaine autonomie et de constituer un champ d'expertise qui leur serait propre. Jusque là en effet, plusieurs organismes internationaux ont déjà tenus congrès et journées d'étude, où purent être largement abordées les ques-

---

[48]Martine Ruchat, "Images, signes et sens de la communauté d'enfants: le Village Pestalozzi de Trogen," symposium "Les communautés d'enfants victimes de la guerre. Transferts, diffusions, circulations de modèles XIXe–XXe siècle," Genève, ISCHE, 2012.

[49]Rapport pour l'UNESCO, 1949 (ANMT fonds Jacques Guyomarc'h, 2002040 / 772).

[50]Valérie Lussi, "La pédagogie curative: un champ spécifique," in *Emergence des sciences de l'éducation en Suisse à la croisée de traditions académiques contrastées (fin du 19e–première moitié du 20e siècle)*, ed. Rita Hofstetter et Bernard Schneuwly (Berne: Peter Lang, 2007), 265–89.

[51]Samuel Boussion, "Le *self-government* sous contrôle clinique ou quand les psys s'en mêlent (années 1940–1950)," symposium "Les communautés d'enfants victimes de la guerre. Transferts, diffusions, circulations de modèles XIXe–XXe siècle," Genève, ISCHE, 2012.

[52]Samuel Boussion, "Le Hameau-école de l'Ile-de-France (1945–1964): République d'enfants modèle ou expérience déviante?" symposium "Républiques, villages et communautés d'enfants: un idéal concerté de l'après Seconde Guerre mondiale," congrès de l'AREF, Genève, 2010.

tions relatives au sauvetage de l'enfance mais en général vues sous l'angle des moyens matériels à mettre en œuvre, de l'élaboration législative et administrative, de la prise en charge médico-psychologique, et de surcroît assurées bien souvent par les élites médico-judiciaires ou politico-administratives:

> Je pense qu'il est grand temps de donner à l'éducateur la place qu'il mérite dans l'équipe des spécialistes de la rééducation. Au cours de la semaine d'études que vient d'organiser l'ONU à Paris sur le problème de l'enfance délinquante il a été demandé des exposés à des psychiatres, des juges, des assistants sociales, des administrateurs de ministères et pas à un seul directeur d'institution. On oublie trop souvent ceux qui vivent continuellement avec les jeunes, courent les véritables risques et ont la vraie responsabilité de la rééducation.[53]

Malgré le déploiement de ces stratégies, l'UNESCO, dans un premier temps, n'accorde pas son aide. Thérèse Brosse, chargée du programme de l'enfance victime de la guerre à la section de l'éducation, fait savoir en 1950 qu'une organisation vraiment internationale ne pourrait être formée qu'à la suite d'une conférence internationale sur l'enfance inadaptée, à laquelle auraient participé les différentes sections nationales. Or, il n'existe à cette date qu'une section, en France, qui lui semble en outre être plus spécifiquement corporative que technique.[54]

Cet attelage manqué n'empêche pas l'AIEJI d'être finalement admise au bénéfice des arrangements consultatifs de l'UNESCO, lors de la dixième session de la conférence générale tenue du 4 novembre au 5 décembre 1958. L'obtention de ce statut[55] consacre l'activité de l'AIEJI sur plusieurs plans. D'abord, elle s'est étendue et a progressivement dépassé le cadre des délégations fondatrices (France, Allemagne, Belgique et Pays-Bas) pour compter trois sections de plus en 1956 (Canada, Royaume-Uni et Maroc nouvellement indépendant). En 1959, cinq autres associations se sont jointes (Autriche, Israël, Italie, une seconde association au Royaume-Uni, Suisse), portant le total à douze. En 1964, dix-sept associations nationales sont affiliées depuis les adhésions de l'Algérie, de la Colombie, de la Nouvelle-Zélande et de la Yougoslavie. Ensuite, parce qu'Henri Joubrel n'a jamais cessé son *lobbying*, particulièrement auprès du chef de section au département de l'Education, W. D. Wall, qu'il rencontre en 1954 et 1955[56] et qui clôture le congrès de Fontainebleau en 1956 par une conférence sur "La réadaptation sociale des jeunes par le milieu".[57] Signe des temps aussi, Henri Joubrel s'est aussi mué en expert international, prenant les allures d'un "expert des Nations-Unies", "reçu à la fois comme ambassadeur et comme le Sphinx",[58] comme en 1954 lorsqu'il est missionné par le gouvernement suisse pour établir un rapport sur certaines institutions du pays.[59]

---

[53] Henri Joubrel, lettre à Louis François, 15 décembre 1949 (ANMT fonds Jacques Guyomarc'h, 2002040 / 772).
[54] Secrétariat de Thérèse Brosse, lettre à Henri Joubrel, 1er mars 1950 (ANMT, fonds AIEJI 2002062 / 273).
[55] Statut consultatif catégorie B.
[56] Henri Joubrel, lettres à Jacques Guyomarc'h, 9 mai 1954; 23 juin 1955 (ANMT, fonds Jacques Guyomarc'h 2002040 / 773).
[57] W. D. Wall intervient aussi dans le cadre des conférences de Méridien en 1955, sur les services psychologiques à l'école en Europe, travail entamé depuis 1952 dans le cadre de l'Institut d'éducation de l'UNESCO à Hambourg.
[58] Henri Joubrel, lettre à Jacques Guyomarc'h, 12 octobre 1954 (ANMT fonds Jacques Guyomarc'h 2002040 / 773).
[59] Rapport sur son séjour en Suisse, octobre 1954 (ANMT fonds Jacques Guyomarc'h 2002040 / 694).

C'est à la fin des années 1950 que les liens avec l'UNESCO se resserrent, ce qui peut s'expliquer par la nouvelle orientation de l'organisation, à la fois vers la jeunesse socialement inadaptée des pays occidentaux et vers l'aide aux pays en voie de développement. Dans un premier temps, l'inadaptation sociale des jeunes devient une préoccupation prioritaire et rejoint les projets de l'ONU, qui réunit en 1960 à Londres un second congrès mondial sur la prévention du crime et le traitement des délinquants. Si ce problème est jugé grave c'est que depuis quelques années, dans les pays occidentaux, la jeunesse fait la une. Les colonnes des journaux s'ouvrent largement aux "méfaits" de ces bandes de *teddy boys* en Angleterre, de *raggare* en Suède, de *teppisti* en Italie, de *blousons noirs* en France.[60] Les pays découvrent leur jeunesse par son versant menaçant, dans des temporalités décalées mais couvrant les années 1957 à 1962, s'inquiétant des agissements de ces "rebelles sans cause".[61] Le nouveau directeur général de l'UNESCO depuis fin 1958, Vittorino Veronese, dans une forme de réponse immédiate, contribue alors à ce que son organisation aide l'AIEJI pour qu'elle effectue une étude comparative sur les méthodes utilisées dans une vingtaine d'établissements de rééducation et de consultations en France, aux Pays-Bas et en Suisse, coordonnée par Jacques Selosse et Paul Drillich.[62] Une autre enquête du même type est commandée en 1964 à l'AIEJI par l'UNESCO, sur les méthodes éducatives employées en Autriche, France et Grande-Bretagne, rapport qui fait la part belle à la notion émergente de prévention, en vue du troisième congrès de défense sociale organisé par les Nations-Unies en 1965.

Dans un second temps, sous l'impulsion de l'ONU, dans un contexte marqué par l'affirmation du Tiers-monde et la décolonisation, l'UNESCO s'oriente vers l'aide au développement, surtout à partir de 1960, promouvant d'une part les apports scientifiques et technologiques et d'autre part l'éducation, notamment la lutte contre l'analphabétisme.[63] Le sixième congrès de l'AIEJI qui se tient à Fribourg en 1963 enregistre ces mutations. Les dirigeants s'enorgueillissent de la participation de treize pays en voie de développement, pour la plupart en fait des anciennes colonies françaises. Celle-ci a été facilitée par les contacts antérieurs développés dans le cadre de l'UGEAMJI (Union générale des éducateurs africains et malgaches de jeunes inadaptés), créée en 1959 sous l'impulsion de l'ANEJI dans le but "de développer et de faire connaître les méthodes d'éducation appropriées à l'Afrique et à Madagascar". Lors du congrès de 1963, un groupe de travail sur la formation et le perfectionnement des éducateurs sociaux dans les pays en voie de développement est mis en place, dont on peut retenir qu'il contribue à forger la définition de l'"éducateur social", un "travailleur qui exerce sa profession auprès des enfants et des adolescents victimes de situations économiques, sanitaires et sociales dans les pays où les

---

[60] Françoise Tétard, "Le phénomène 'blouson noir' en France, fin des années 1950–début des années 1960," in *Révolte et société*, ed. Fabienne Gambrelle, Michel Trebitsch et. al. (Paris: Publications de la Sorbonne, 1989), 205–14.

[61] Allusion récurrente au film *Rebel Without a Cause*, sorti en 1955. Henri Joubrel, *Jeunesse en danger* (Paris: Fayard, 1960), 11.

[62] AIEJI, *Les méthodes de rééducation dans les internats pour jeunes socialement inadaptés: étude effectuée dans quelques établissements de France, Pays-Bas et Suisse* (Paris: éd. AIEJI, 1960).

[63] Chloé Maurel, *Histoire de l'UNESCO. Les trente premières années. 1945–1974* (Paris: L'Harmattan, 2010), 267–74.

conditions de transformation des normes socio-culturelles sont sources de tensions et de conflits".[64]

Conclusion

Seuls les premiers jalons d'une histoire de l'AIEJI ont été posés ici. Ils montrent néanmoins les mutations de ce nouvel acteur de la protection de l'enfance. D'une organisation fraternelle à ses débuts, tout à fait dans la lignée de l'esprit de réparation d'après-guerre, elle est devenue un lieu d'échanges sur la fonction d'éducateur spécialisé. Elle est aussi parvenue à s'insérer dans les nouveaux lieux de fabrication de l'international, l'UNESCO par exemple, réussissant à faire reconnaître l'existence et l'utilité sociale des éducateurs spécialisés, jusqu'à se déployer dans des pays où il n'en existe pas. Au début des années 1960, l'AIEJI est une organisation reconnue, désormais bien implantée, même si des zones résistent encore (Etats-Unis, bloc soviétique). En retour, elle a certainement contribué à des ouvertures professionnelles dans les différents pays, en France notamment, par exemple en réfléchissant sur la pertinence de l'internat, sur les apports des sciences humaines, sur les approches analytiques, etc. De nouvelles pratiques ont émergé, dans le domaine de la prise en charge comme dans celui de la formation, et l'AIEJI y a joué son rôle. Elle n'a sans doute pas été le seul vecteur de circulations dans le champ de l'éducation spécialisée, loin s'en faut, et a pu être subvertie; nombre de voyages à l'étranger se font hors de son cadre par exemple. Il n'empêche, sans doute aussi qu'en se rapprochant des institutions d'expertise s'est-elle éloignée de la pratique de terrain, en tous cas dans ses pays fondateurs, engendrant une sensation de vertige devant cette internationalisation à marche forcée.

---

[64]"Le 6ᵉ congrès de l'AIEJI et les pays en voie de développement," *Liaisons* 49 (1964): 5.

Index

American Foundation for Overseas Blind (AFOB) 191
American Foundation for the International School of Geneva 142
Angus, D.L.: progressive education 60–1, 64–5
Antipoff, H. 193–5, 197–8, 200, 209–10; background 201–2; coefficient social 204; *Ecole de perfectionnement des enseignants* at Belo Horizonte 203–5; relationship with Claparède 201–2; special education in Belo Horizonte 201–2, 205–7; teacher training 203–5
Armytage, W.H.G.: progressive education 62, 65
Association internationale des éducateurs de jeunes inadaptés (AIEJI) 227–8, 241; background 228–30; development of transnational methodologies 234–7; increasing expertise 237–41; links with UNESCO 239–40; post-war reconstruction 230–4

Bache, A.D. 113
Baden-Powell, R. 92–3; scout movement in France and, 93–4, 98–99; translation of texts 100–1
Bailyn, B.: progressive education 70–2, 73–4
Barnard, H.C.: common school movement 110, 112; English secondary education system 65; London normal school 112; progressive education 65; Prussian model and 113
Beecher, C. 111, 114
Belo Horizonte: Antipoff, 203–5; *école de perfectionnement des enseignants* at Belo Horizonte 203–5; homogenous and special education compared 205–9; key principles for special education 207; *laboratoire de psychologie de l'école de perfectionnement des enseignants* 203, 206; special education of those with learning difficulties 200–1, 205–7, 209–10
Bertier, G. 92; New Education 173; scout movement in France 93, 96–7, 101–2

Bigot, L.: *Educational Studies: the child* 215–17
Blanchard Jerrold, W.: potential of internationality 10–11
blind students in Taiwan 180, 182; American Foundation for Overseas Blind 191; amma massage therapy 186–90; Braille literacy 185–6; education 185–6, 190–1; integration 190–2; physical therapy education 190–1; UNICEF funding 191
Bourdieu, P. 136–7, 148
Bourgeois, L. 22–3
Bovet, P. 92–93, 95–6; background 93–4; *Institut Rousseau* 172, 177–8, 199, 202; New Education 172, 177–8, 199; special education for those with learning difficulties 200; translation of scouting texts 93, 98–9, 103–5
Brazil, *see* Belo Horizonte
Brosse, T. 238–9
Bureau international catholique de l'enfance (BICE) 228–9
Burke, E. 17–18
Butler, J. 6, 167

Campbell, W.: amma massage therapy and 188; closure of Training Blind Hall 186; education of blind students 182–3, 185–6, 189
Carnegie Corporation (USA) 121, 122; Institute of Education and 126–9; internationalisation of educational research 126–9, 130–3; support of education in British Dominions 126, 134
Cartel romand d'hygiène sociale et morale 176–8
child psychology, 105, 217; Bovet 98–9; New School 54–5; study of 47, 96, 158
children's rights 151–2, 161–2; Geneva Declaration of the League of Nations 150, 152–3, 156; impact of World Wars 152–3; international principles 154–7; internationalisation 149–51; non-governmental organisations and 154–5, 159–61; UNCRC 149; UNDRC 150, 152–3
Chinese Braille: development 181–5

INDEX

circulatory dynamics of educational policies 8–9

Claparède, E. 96, 193–5; Antipoff and 198–200, 201–5, 209; recapitulation theory 216; special education of those with learning difficulties 195–6, 200, 208

Clarke, F.: Adviser to Overseas Students 132–3; background 121–22; Carnegie Corporation 127–9; Institute of Education 121–2, 125; internationalisation of educational research 124–5, 130–3, 134; metropolitanism 125; purpose of university departments of education 124; promotion of international cooperation 127–9; world tour 130–2, 134

Cohen, S.: progressive education 70

collective actors: AIEJI 227–41; Carnegie Corporation 126–9; common school and 110–11; Institute of Education 126–9; International School of Geneva 140–8; missionary organisations 180–92; non-government organisations 24–5, 154–5, 159–61 227–41; role of women 6; scientific networks 167–8, 177; support of education in British Dominions 126, 134; universities 13–14, 25

Committee of Ten: education reform reports 59–61, 68

common school movement 107, 109–11; teacher training 111–12; *see also* normal school movement

comprehensive schools 38, 66–7; debate in Netherlands 75, 78–80, 90–1; didactical solutions to heterogeneous classes 83–5; evaluating education systems 81–3; foreign examples 86–90; reform of secondary education in Netherlands 75–8

computer-assisted instruction (CAI) 84

computer-managed instruction (CMI) 84

Congrès international de propaganda et d'hygiene sociale 1923 169, 170, 174, 176–7

Congrès international d'éducation mouvelle 1924 173

Congrès international eugéniste 1912 170

Congrès internationaux d'éducation morale 1908-1934 (CIEM) 169–70, 174, 176–7; sex education and 172

Congrès internationaux d'hygiene scolaire 1904, 1907 and 1910 169, 174, 176–7

construction of national self-images 14–16

Cousin, M.V.: normal school movement 112–13

Cowen R. 123

Cremin, L.A.: metropolitanism 125; progressive education 70, 71

Cunningham, H.: best interests of the child 152

Cunningham, P.: progressive education 62, 66

Dearden, R.F.: progressive education 62

Decroly, O. 45, 199, 217, 221

Descoeudres, A. 194–5; special education of those with learning difficulties 199–200, 203, 206–8, 209

Dewey, J.: progressive education 73, 201; Turkish education system 47

disabilities: educational integration of students with 190–2; special education for blind children 180–1; *see also* learning disabilities

Drillich, P. 237, 240

Dupuy, P. 142–3

Durkheim, E. 44, 136–7, 204

Dwight, H.E.: normal school movement 113

Ecole de perfectionnement des enseignants: Laboratoire de psychologie at Belo Horizonte 201, 203, 206

Ecole des Roches 92; New Education 96, 173; pre-military training and 101; scout movement and 93

Eclaireurs de France (EDF) 92–4; *Ecole des Roches* and 96–7; *Mission populaire évangélique* and, 97–8; nationalism 94–5; romanticism and 98; translation of texts 100–1; *see also* scout movement in France

education reform reports 58; England 61–3; progressive education and 59–63; USA 59–61

education scholarship 58, 59; England 69–70, 72–3; USA 69–72

éducation sexuelle, *see* sex education

educational knowledge 16–18, 19; *see also* Rousseau, J.-J.

Eight-Year Study (USA): progressive education 64–5

Emile (Rousseau) 16–18, 96; reinforcement of national feelings 17–18

England: education reform reports 61–3; education scholarship 69–70, 72–3; Institute of Education and Carnegie Corporation 126–9; Moral Instruction League 169; Plowden report 61–3; progressive education, 59, 61–3; progressive education practices 65–8

Erasmus: construction of national self-images 15

eugenics 169–70; sex education and 170–71

Fédération abolitionniste internationale (FAI): sex education 167–9, 173

Fédération internationale des communautés d'enfants (FICE) 228–9, 237–8

Ferrière, A. 46, 142, 238; New School 51, 142–3, 145, 172; sex education 172; Turkish education system, 47

France: education system in Vietnam 28–30; educational knowledge 16–18; national self-assertion in educational matters 16–18;

INDEX

neo-Malthusianism 175; sex education 175; Vietnam occupancy 27–8; *see also Association internationale des éducateurs de jeunes inadaptés (AIEJI); Ecole des Roches;* French education system in Vietnam; scout movement in France

French education system in Vietnam 27, 28–30; failure 38–40; internal criticisms 37–8; targeting of elites 28–30, 36–7; US criticisms 34–7

Gaither, M.: progressive education 70–1
Gallaudet, T.H. 22
Gallienne, G. 92; *Mission populaire évangélique* 96–8
Galton, F.: eugenics 169–70
Gelder, L. van 81
Geneva Declaration of the League of Nations 1924 150, 152–3, 156
globalisation 1–4, 23–4, 26; impact on educational policies 4–7, 125, 134
Goblot, E. 92–3; scout movement in France 103–5
Goodenow R. 123
Gordon, P.: progressive education 67–8

Harris W.T. 109
Harvard University: transformation of university education 117–18
Hascall, O. 35–6
Hazewindus, N. 84
Herbst, J.: progressive education 60, 64, 68, 108
Herder, J.G. 16–17, 18
histoire croisée, 181, 197; *see also* Belo Horizonte
Hofstetter, R.: educational research 123, 152; New Education and Ottoman Empire 42, 56; public schools 152; special education of those with learning difficulties 200
homogeneous classrooms 193–4; analysis of benefits of 196, 199–200; Antipoff and 205; benefits for those with special needs 199–200; *Laboratoire de psychologie de l'école de perfectionnement des enseignants* 201, 203, 206
Horebeek, G. van, 82
Human Rights Commission (HRC) 158

individual and collective actors 5–6; rise of institutional actors 6
Institute of Education (UK) 134; Carnegie Corporation and 126–9; Clarke and 121–2, 132, 134; establishment 125, 134; overseas work 130–3, 134; *see also* Clarke, F.
Institut Rousseau, see Rousseau Institute
International Association for Child Welfare (IACW) 154–5

International Association of Workers for Maladjusted Children, *see* Association internationale des éducateurs de jeunes inadaptés
International School of Geneva 136–8; educational techniques 147; examinations 147; international civil service and 138–40, 143; investment 141–2; language 147–8; originality 138; origins 139–40, 146–7; psychology of internationalism 143–8; social capital 142, 143; social significance 148; student profile 144–6, 147–8
International Union for Child Welfare (IUCW), 155, 157; family and, 157–8; non-discrimination principle 157–8; social security principle 157–8
internationalisation 1; beyond nationalism 23–5; development of 15–16; differentiation from other forms of crossing boundaries 11; interest in 2; mechanisms of 1; national agency, as 11; potential of internationality 10–11; relations between "national" and "international 11; relations between nations 11; research in education 121–34; supranationalism 20–3
Istanbul: New School (characteristics) 51–4; New School (establishment) 50–1; New School (practices) 54–6; New School 49–50; Sata Bey and 48–57

Jansz, D. 81
Jones, K.: progressive education 62–3, 67
Joubrel, H. 231, 232; psychopedagogical methodologies 236, 237, 238–9
Journoud, P. 30, 37

Kandel, I. 126–8, 134
Katz, M.: common school movement 110–11
Kemenade, J.A. van: *Contourennota* 78–80, 83–4; reform of Dutch education system 78–80, 83–7, 89–1
Keppel, F., 126–9, 134
Kliebard, H.M.: progressive education 60, 64, 108
Klinken, L. van: Calvinist teacher training 220–1
Kohm, L.M.: best interests of the child 151
Koning, P. de 84–5
Krug, E.A.: progressive education 59, 63

Laboratoire de psychologie de l'école de perfectionnement des enseignants 201, 203, 206
League of Nations 7; children's rights 150–1, 154; Geneva Declaration 150–1; International School in Geneva and 137, 138–40; *Organization of Intellectual Work* 22–3

INDEX

learning difficulties 193–4; Antipoff 205; Belo Horizonte 203–9; benefits of homogeneous classes 196, 199–200; development of special education 195–8, 200–3; homogeneous and special education compared 205–9; *Laboratoire de psychologie de l'école de perfectionnement des enseignants* 201, 203, 206; special education in Belo Horizonte 200–2, 205–7; special education in Geneva 198–200

Lévy-Bruhl, L. de 204

London Day Training College (LDTC) 125–6

Lowe, R.: progressive education 66, 67–8, 69, 73

Mann, H. 110, 113–14

Marx, K. 136

medieval universities 13–14

Mendousse, P. 92–3, 103–4

Middle Ages: conceptualisation of nations 14–15; national-international dichotomy 12–15

middle school concept (Netherlands) 75–7, 90–1; implementation 83–5; importance of 89–90; influence of foreign education systems 81–3, 86–9; political debate 78–80

Mills, C.: common school movement 110

Mirel, J.E.: progressive education 60–1, 64–5

missionary organisations 180–92

monitorial system of education 16, 18–20; national character and 19

Montessori method 45, 50, 54–6, 216, 221, 222

Moral Instruction League (UK) 169–70

mouvement scoute en France, see scout movement in France

national-international dichotomy 5, 25–6; beyond nationalism 23–5; early modern period 15–16; Middle Ages 12–15; stages of changing relationship 12; supranationalism 20–3

national self-assertion in educational matters 16; *Emile* and 16–17; France 16–18

Netherlands (cultural reform): Calvinist influence 215, 219–22; move from philosophy to psychology 213–15; teacher training (reform) 217–19; teacher training (textbooks) 215–25; textbooks (orthodox Calvinist teachers) 219–22; textbooks (public school teachers) 215–19; textbooks (Roman Catholic teachers) 222–5

Netherlands (educational reform of the comprehensive system) 75–8; comprehensive system 75–8; foreign examples 86–90; middle school concept 89–90; observing children 86–7; political debate 78–80; scholarly debate on foreign comprehensive schools 80–91; scrutiny 87–9

Naville, F. 194; special education of those with learning difficulties 199–200, 202

New Education movement 21, 23, 41–3; *Contourennota* 79; middle school concept and 87–9; Ottoman empire 46–7, 56–7; Sata Bey and 48–57; sex education and 172–3, 179

New School in Istanbul 49–50; characteristics 51–4; establishment 50–1; practices 54–6; *see also* Istanbul

non-governmental organisations: AIEJI 227–41; rights of the child 24–5, 154–5, 159–61; supranationalism 20, 23

normal school movement 107, 108–9, 111–19

nouvelle éducation, see New Education movement

Nunn, P. 125–8, 130, 132

Ottoman empire: attempt at Europeanisation 47, 49–50; educational institutions 43–7; New Education movement 46–7, 56–7; *see also* Istanbul; New Education movement; New School in Istanbul

Pedagogische Studiën: comprehensive education 80–1, 90–1; cross-national attraction and decision-making 77; foreign education systems 81–3

Pestalozzi, J.H. 112

Pestalozzi Societies 194, 208–9

Pierce, J.D.: normal school movement 115

Pike, E.N. 35

Plowden report (UK) 61–3, 68

Powell, A.G.: progressive education 60, 64

practices: *Baccalaureate* examination 35–6; common school movement 109–11; Franco-indigenous education system in Vietnam 28–30; middle schooling 75–91; monitorial system of education 18–20; move from philosophy to psychology 211–15; New Education 21, 23, 41–57, 79, 87–9, 172–3, 179; New School in Istanbul 41–57; normal school movement 111–19; progressive education 63–8; sex education 163–79; special needs education (blind students) 180–92; special needs education (students with learning difficulties) 193–211

private education: International School of Geneva 138–40

progressive education 58–9, 73–4; criticisms of 68–9; education reform reports 59–63; England 61–3; European influence 112–15; place in history of education 59–69; USA 59–61; Whig reformers 112–13

Prosser, C.: progressive education 64

Prussian model of teacher training 107, 108–9; influence on teacher training in USA 109, 112–16; modification 116–17; normal

INDEX

schools 112, 113–16; *see also* teacher training
psychology, *see* child psychology
psychology of education: *Institut Rousseau* 140; Institute of Education 124, 134; move from philosophy of education to psychology of education 211–15
psychology of internationalism 137, 143–8

Rajchman, L.W. 141
Ravitch, D.: progressive education 61
Reese, W.J.: progressive education 61, 65, 68
Reus, J. de 82–3, 84
Rezende, N. 195; special education of those with learning difficulties 206–7
Richardson, W.: progressive education 72–3
Rombouts, S.: teacher training textbooks 222–5
Rousseau, J-J.: Claparède and 96; educational knowledge 16–18, 19; *Emile* 16–18
Rousseau Institute 140; child psychology and 201–2; New Education 172; *pédagogie scoute* 98, 101 105–6; progressive education 140; sex education 176, 177–8; special education for those with learning difficulties 199–200, 206, 208, 209

Sati Bey, M. 41, 48–9; development of New School concept 49–50; establishment of New School in Istanbul 50–1; *see also* New School in Istanbul
Save the Children International Union (SCIU) 154–5, 156, 157
Schneuwly, B.: educational research 123; New Education movement 42–3, 56
scout movement in France: acceptance of Bovet texts 101–5; autonomy 94–5, 96–8; establishment 93; '*génie national*', 94–5; linguistic autonomy 94–8; pedagogical diversity 94–5; rejection of *Scouting for Boys* 94–5; Swiss influence 95, 98–101; translation of texts 98–101, 105–6; World Scout Organisation and 101
secondary schools 139, 147; analysis of US reforms 64; comprehensive system in the UK 66–7; reform in the Netherlands 75–8, 87–8
Selleck, R.J.W.: progressive education 62, 65–6
sex education: debate surrounding necessity 164–6; eugenic sex education 170–1, 175; *hygiène sexuelle* 173–4; moral arguments 167–8; 'moralists' and 'eugenicists' compared 171; New Education movement and 172–3, 179; origins 164; political interference 174; public health arguments for 166–7; Switzerland 173–9; transnational debate 166–9; *see also* Swiss sex education
Simon, B.: progressive education 66–7, 69
Simon, T. 193, 201; Binet-Simon laboratory of psychology 194, 202

Smillie, R. 153
social and moral hygiene: *Cartel romand d'hygiène sociale et morale* 176–8; *Congrès international de propaganda et d'hygiene sociale 1923* 169, 170, 174, 176–7; sex education and 173–4; *see also* sex education; Swiss sex education
social cohesion: normal school movement 111–12; promotion through education 118–19; schooling movement in USA 111–19
Soëtard, M. 112
special education (blind students) 180–1; educational integration of students 190–2; *see also* blind students in Taiwan
special education (students with learning difficulties) 195–8; *Institut Rousseau* 199–200, 206, 208, 209; key principles 207; *see also* Belo Horizonte; learning difficulties
special educators, *see Association internationale des éducateurs de jeunes inadaptés (AIEJI)*
Stowe C.: common school movement 110; normal school movement 113–14; Prussian model 113–14
supranational education 20–3
Sweetser, A.W. 141, 142, 144
Swiss sex education, 173–8; controversy 176–8; eugenic sex education 175, 176; *hygiène sexuelle* 173–4; political interference 174; *Société Vaudoise pour le relèvement de la moralité* 173; Vaud approach and Geneva approach compared, 176–9

Taiwan, *see* blind students in Taiwan
Taylor, J.O. 107–8
teacher training (Belo Horizonte) 203–5
teacher training (Netherlands): reform 217–19; textbooks (orthodox Calvinist teachers) 219–22; textbooks (public school teachers) 215–19; textbooks (Roman Catholic teachers) 222–5
teacher training (USA) 107–9; common school movement 109–11; influence of Prussian model of teacher training 109, 113–16; international influence 119; isolationism 107–8; modification of Prussian model 116–17; normal school movement 111–19; Protestantism, influence of 110–11; social cohesion and 111–19
Teichler, U. 123, 134
Ticknor, G. 117
Tocqueville, A. de 107–8
Training Blind Hall: Campbell 182–3; closure 186
transformation of university education 117–18
transnational treaties: Geneva Declaration of the League of Nations 150, 152–3, 156; UHRD 158–9; UNCRC 149, 153–4;

INDEX

UNDRC 150, 152–3, 157–9; UNESCO 153, 228; UNICEF 160, 191

Tromp, H. 76–7, 88

Turkey, see Istanbul

Tyack, D.: progressive education 63

Ughetto, J. 236–7

Union international de protections de l'enfance (UIPE) 228

United Nations Convention on the Rights of the Child 1989 (UNCRC) 149, 153–4; adoption 161; drafting 159

United Nations Declaration of the Rights of the Child 1959 (UNDRC) 150, 152–3; drafting 157–9; demise 159

United Nations Educational, Scientific and Cultural Organisation (UNESCO) 153; child protection role 228

United Nations International Children Emergency Fund (UNICEF) 160; Integrated Project for the Blind Students of Taiwan 191

Universal Human Rights Declaration (UHRD) 158–9

universities, 13–14, 25; Harvard University: transformation of university education 117–18; medieval universities 13–14; purpose of university departments of education 124

university education: transformation of 117–18

Urban, W.: progressive education 61, 65, 68

USA: education reform reports 59–61; European influence 112–15; French legacy in Vietnam and 33–37; occupancy of Vietnam 28; progressive education 59–69; teacher education 107–19; Vietnam education system and 30–2

Van Praag, P. 235–7

Velema, E. 81

Vietnam: Franco-indigenous education system 28–30; French occupancy 27–8; French targeting of elites 29–30, 36–7; imposed globalisation 27–40; language 38–9; US occupancy 28

Vitry, J. de: national stereotypes 13

Vos, J.F. 81

Vu Tam Ich 34

Wagoner, J.: progressive education 61, 65, 68

Waldheim, K. 159

Waterink, J.: Calvinist teacher training textbooks 220–1, 223

Weber, M. 136, 138, 148

Weibe, R.: common school movement 111

Werner, M.: *histoire croisée* 181

Wielemans, F.J.W. 82

Woodbridge, W.C.: normal school movement 113

Zimmermann, B.: *histoire croisée* 181

For Product Safety Concerns and Information please contact our EU
representative GPSR@taylorandfrancis.com
Taylor & Francis Verlag GmbH, Kaufingerstraße 24, 80331 München, Germany

www.ingramcontent.com/pod-product-compliance
Lightning Source LLC
Chambersburg PA
CBHW080935300426
44115CB00017B/2833